VOLUME 6

ICARUS

BATMAN – DETECTIVE COMICS

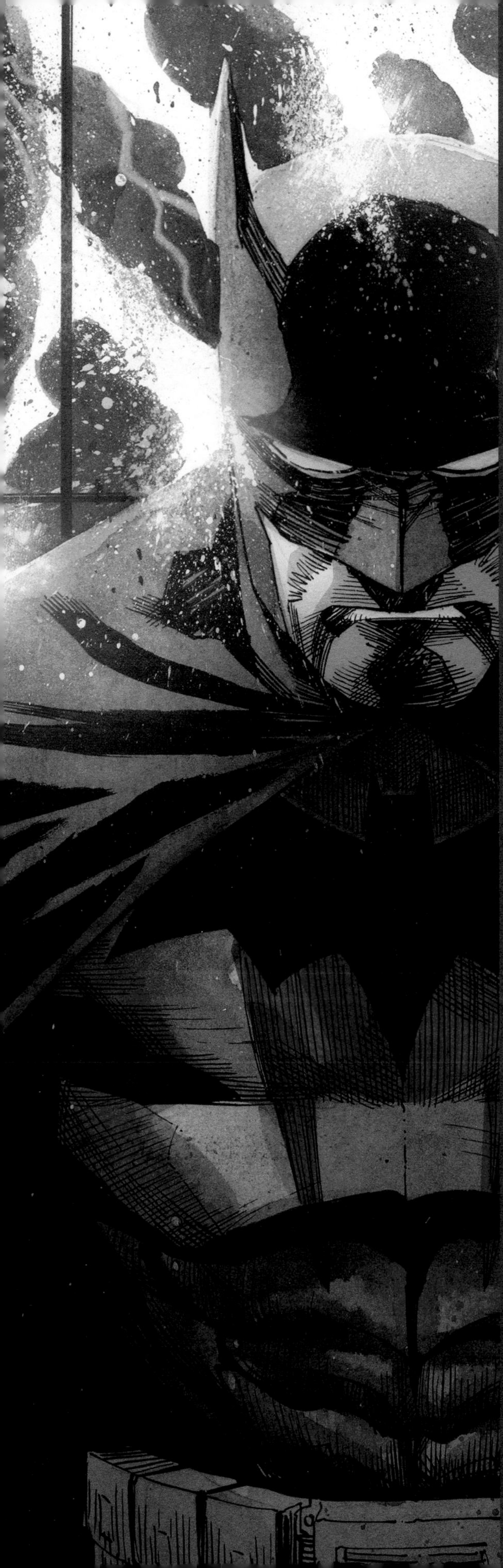

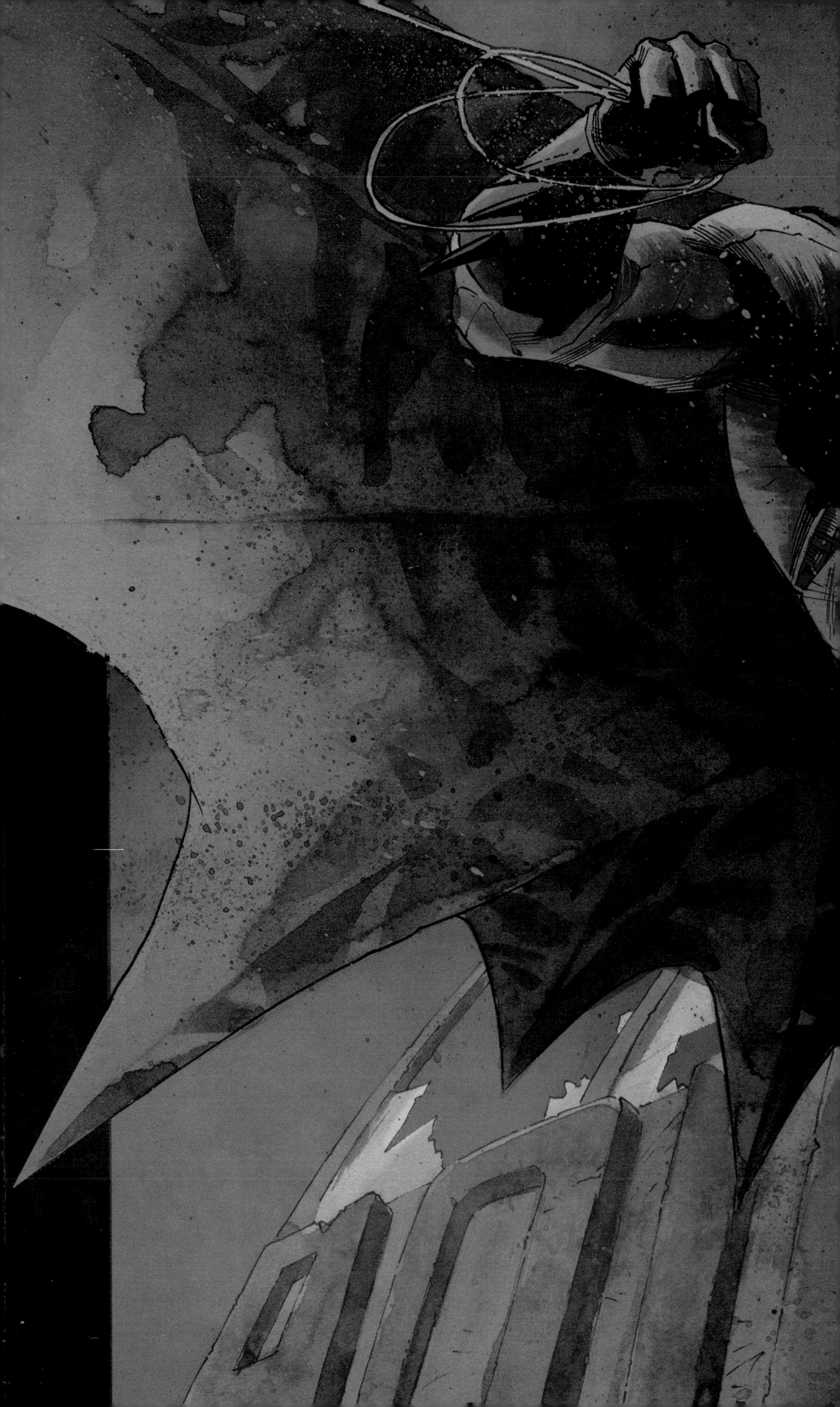

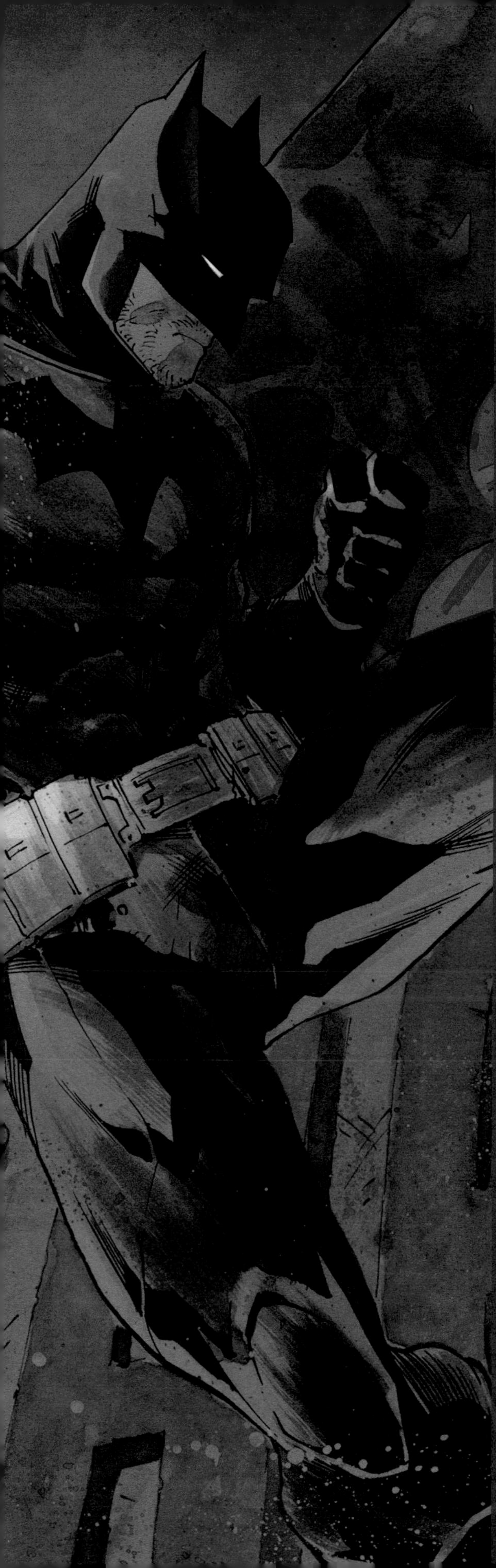

BATMAN – DETECTIVE COMICS

VOLUME 6

ICARUS

WRITTEN BY
FRANCIS MANAPUL
BRIAN BUCCELLATO

ART BY
FRANCIS MANAPUL
WERTHER DELL'EDERA
JORGE FORNÉS
SCOTT HEPBURN

COLOR BY
BRIAN BUCCELLATO
JOHN KALISZ
LEE LOUGHRIDGE
JON PROCTOR

LETTERS BY
JARED K. FLETCHER
STEVE WANDS
TAYLOR ESPOSITO
DEZI SIENTY
CARLOS M. MANGUAL

COLLECTION COVER ART BY
FRANCIS MANAPUL

BATMAN CREATED BY
BOB KANE

MARK DOYLE and RACHEL GLUCKSTERN Editors – Original Series
DARREN SHAN Associate Editor – Original Series
MATT HUMPHREYS Assistant Editor – Original Series
PETER HAMBOUSSI Editor
ROBBIN BROSTERMAN Design Director – Books
DAMIAN RYLAND Publication Design

BOB HARRAS Senior VP – Editor-in-Chief, DC Comics

DIANE NELSON President
DAN DIDIO and JIM LEE Co-Publishers
GEOFF JOHNS Chief Creative Officer
AMIT DESAI Senior VP – Marketing & Franchise Management
AMY GENKINS Senior VP – Business & Legal Affairs
NAIRI GARDINER Senior VP – Finance
JEFF BOISON VP – Publishing Planning
MARK CHIARELLO VP – Art Direction & Design
JOHN CUNNINGHAM VP – Marketing
TERRI CUNNINGHAM VP – Editorial Administration
LARRY GANEM VP – Talent Relations & Services
ALISON GILL Senior VP – Manufacturing & Operations
HANK KANALZ Senior VP – Vertigo & Integrated Publishing
JAY KOGAN VP – Business & Legal Affairs, Publishing
JACK MAHAN VP – Business Affairs, Talent
NICK NAPOLITANO VP – Manufacturing Administration
SUE POHJA VP – Book Sales
FRED RUIZ VP – Manufacturing Operations
COURTNEY SIMMONS Senior VP – Publicity
BOB WAYNE Senior VP – Sales

BATMAN – DETECTIVE COMICS VOLUME 6: ICARUS

DC Comics, 4000 Warner Blvd., Burbank, CA 91522
A Warner Bros. Entertainment Company
Printed by RR Donnelley, Salem, VA, USA. 4/17/15.
ISBN: 978-1-4012-5442-1
First Printing.

Library of Congress Cataloging-in-Publication Data

Manapul, Francis.
Batman/Detective Comics. Volume 6, Icarus / Francis Manapul, Brian Buccellato ; illustrated by Francis Manapul.
pages cm. — (The New 52!)
ISBN 978-1-4012-5442-1 (hardback)
1. Graphic novels. I. Buccellato, Brian. II. Manapul, Francis. III. Title. IV. Title: Icarus.
PN6728.B36M25 2015
741.5'973—dc23
2015000604

SUSTAINABLE
FORESTRY
INITIATIVE

Certified Chain of Custody
20% Certified Forest Content,
80% Certified Sourcing
www.sfiprogram.org
SFI-01042
APPLIES TO TEXT STOCK ONLY

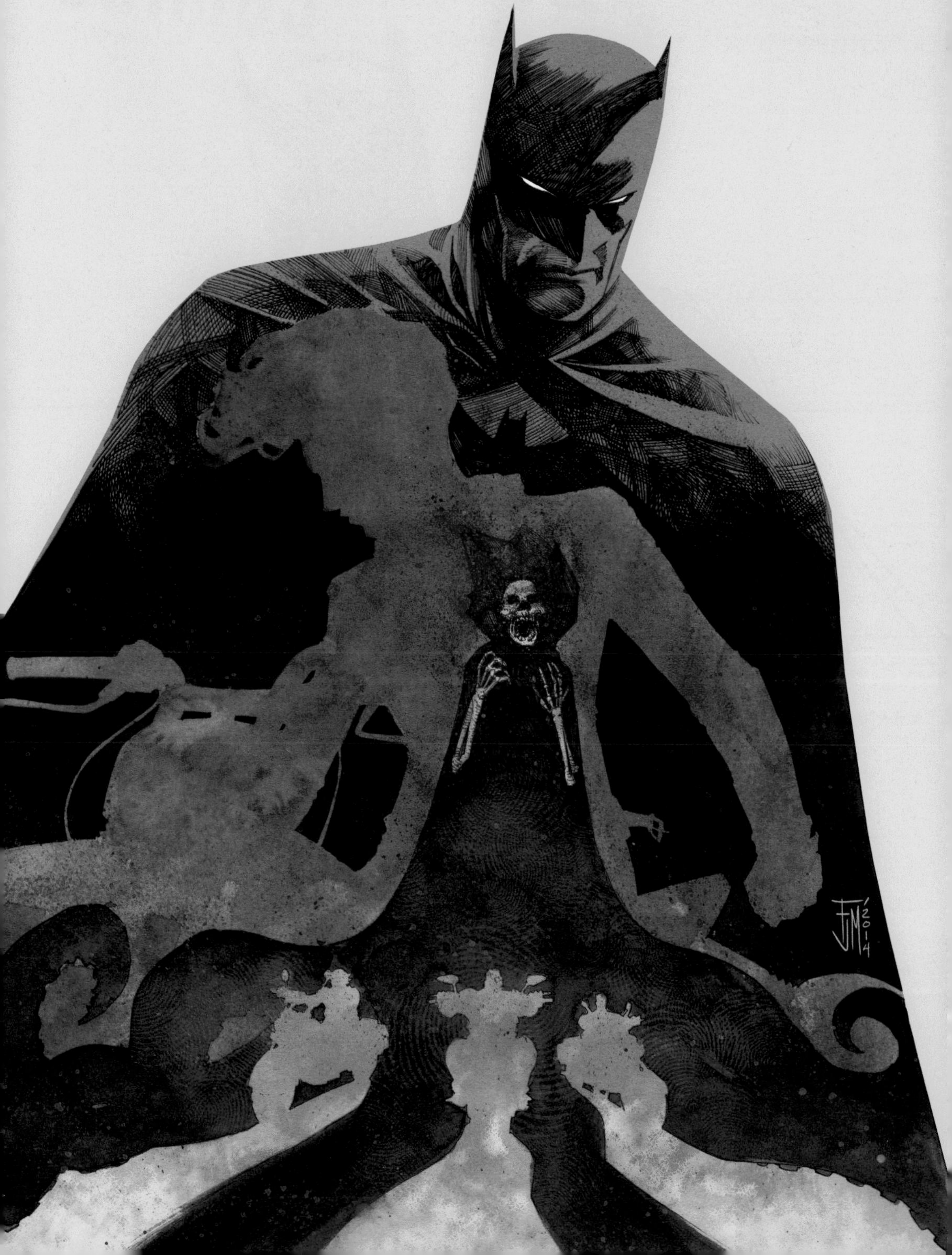

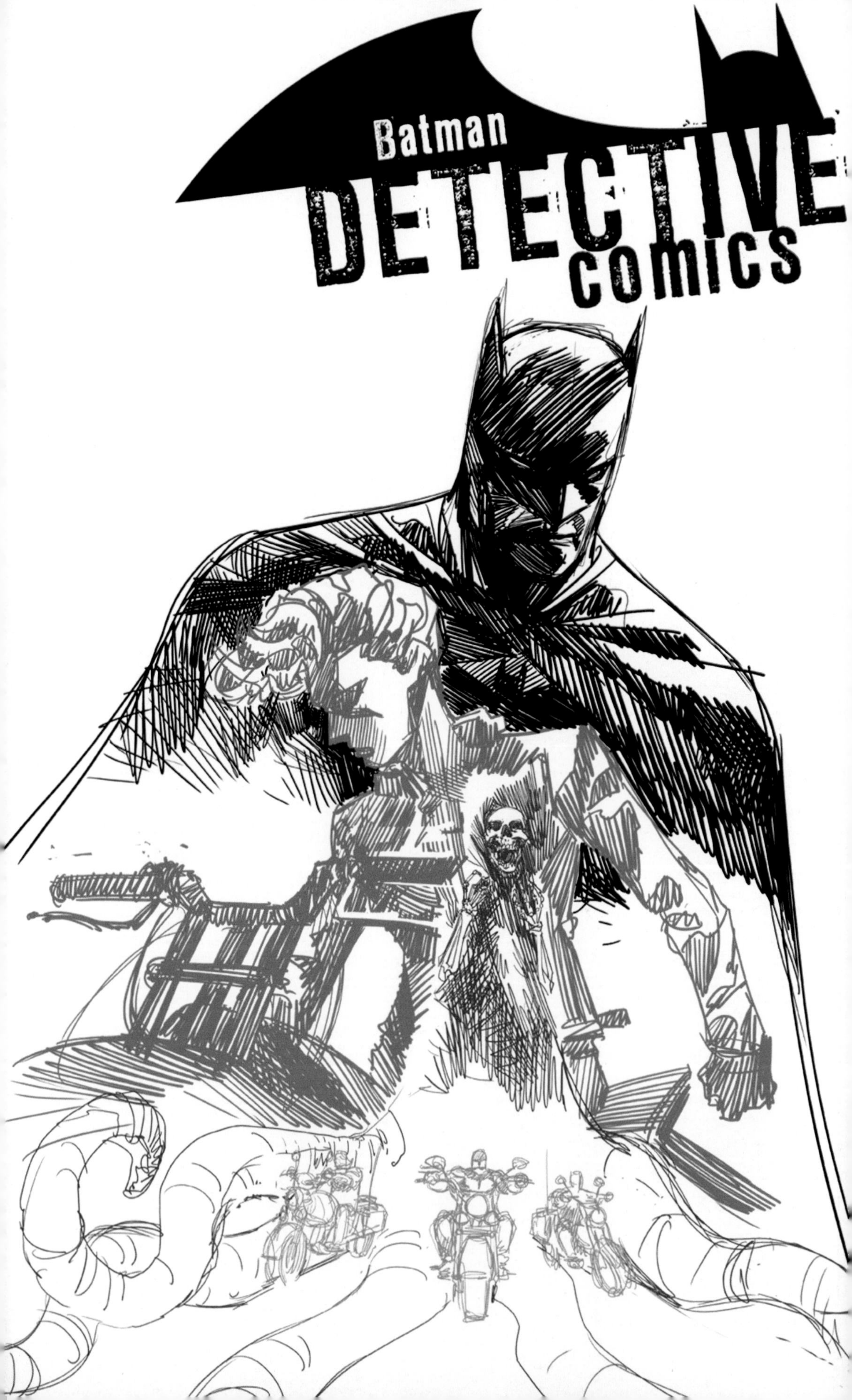
Batman
DETECTIVE
COMICS

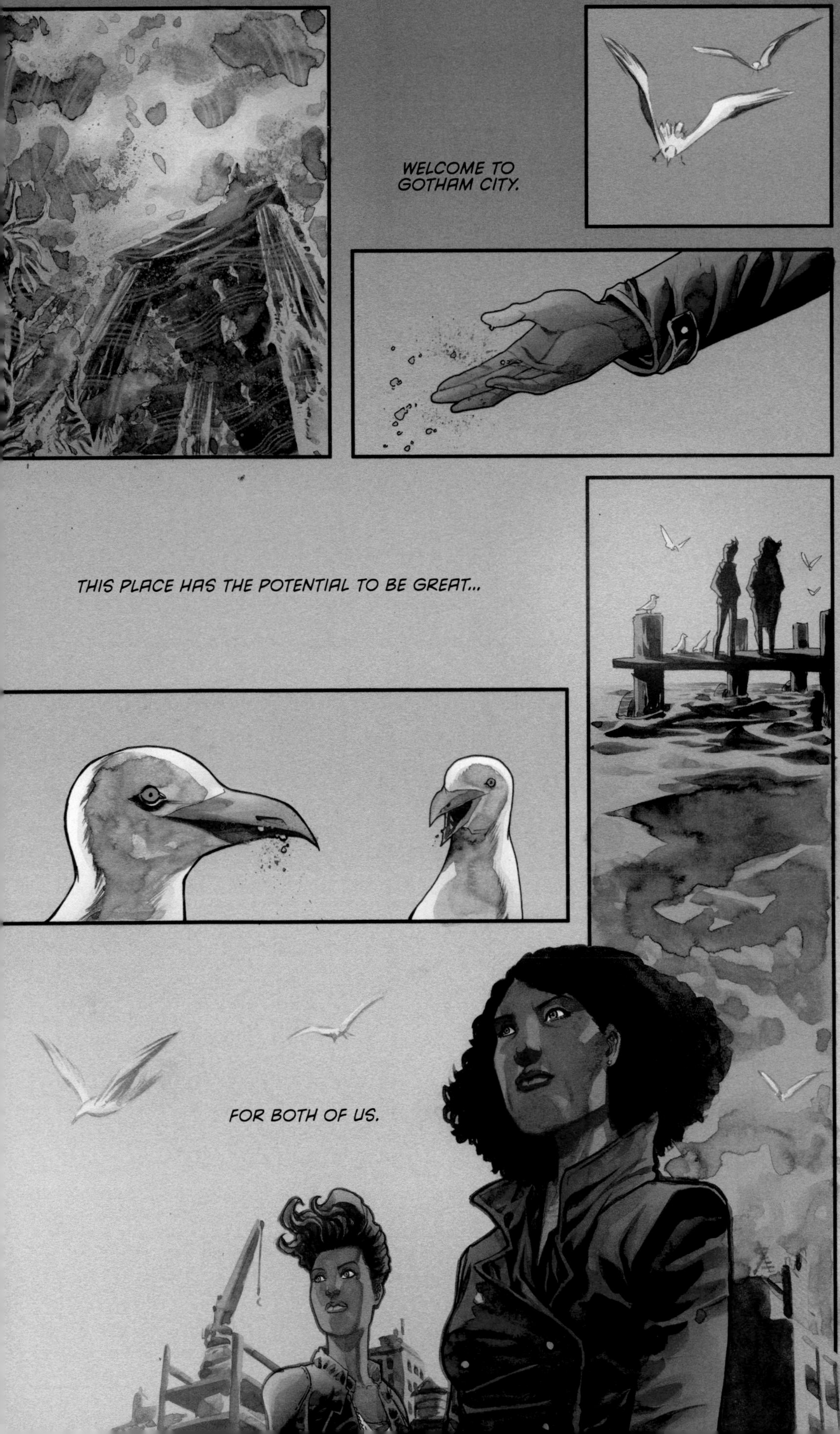
WELCOME TO GOTHAM CITY.
THIS PLACE HAS THE POTENTIAL TO BE GREAT...
FOR BOTH OF US.

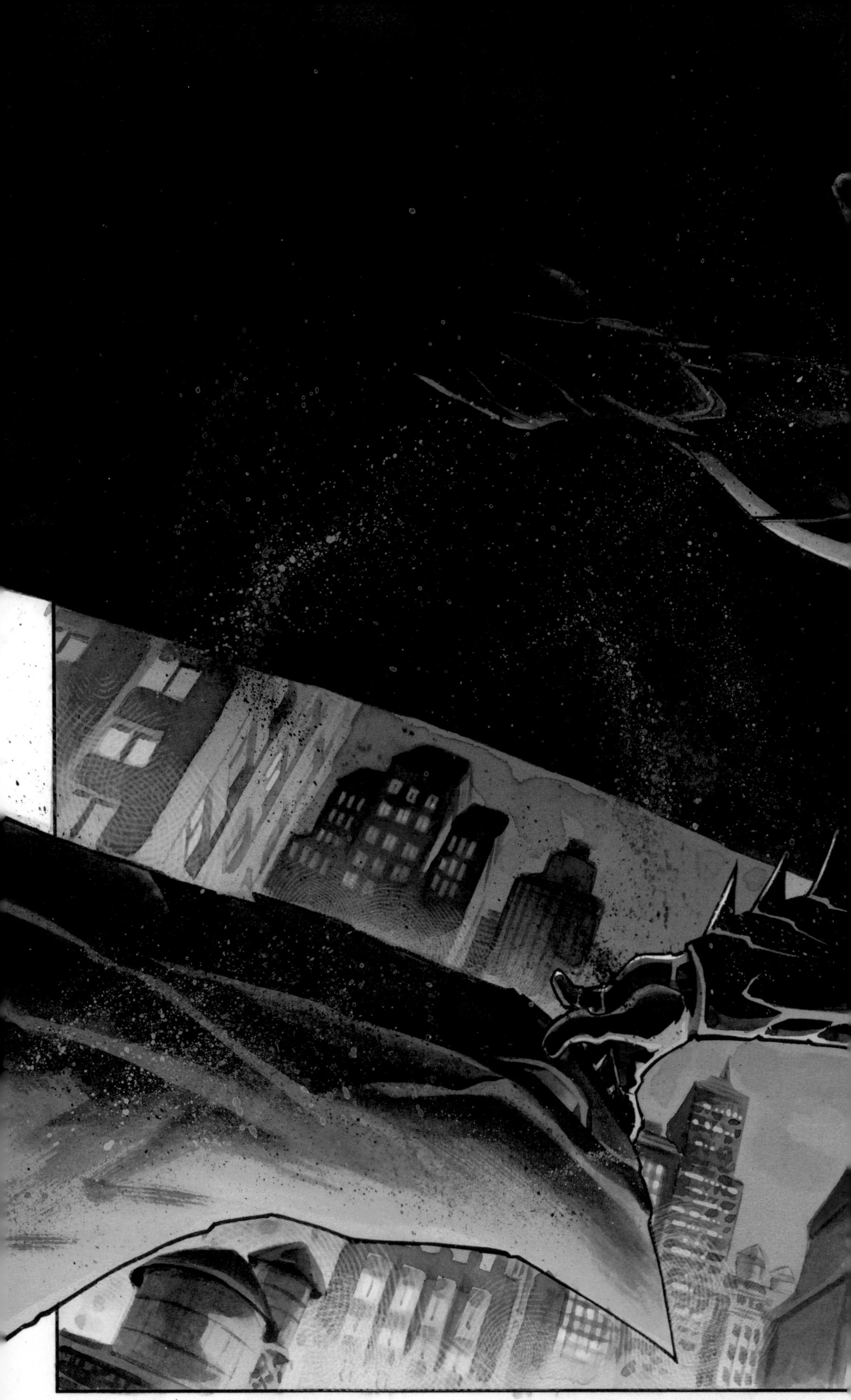

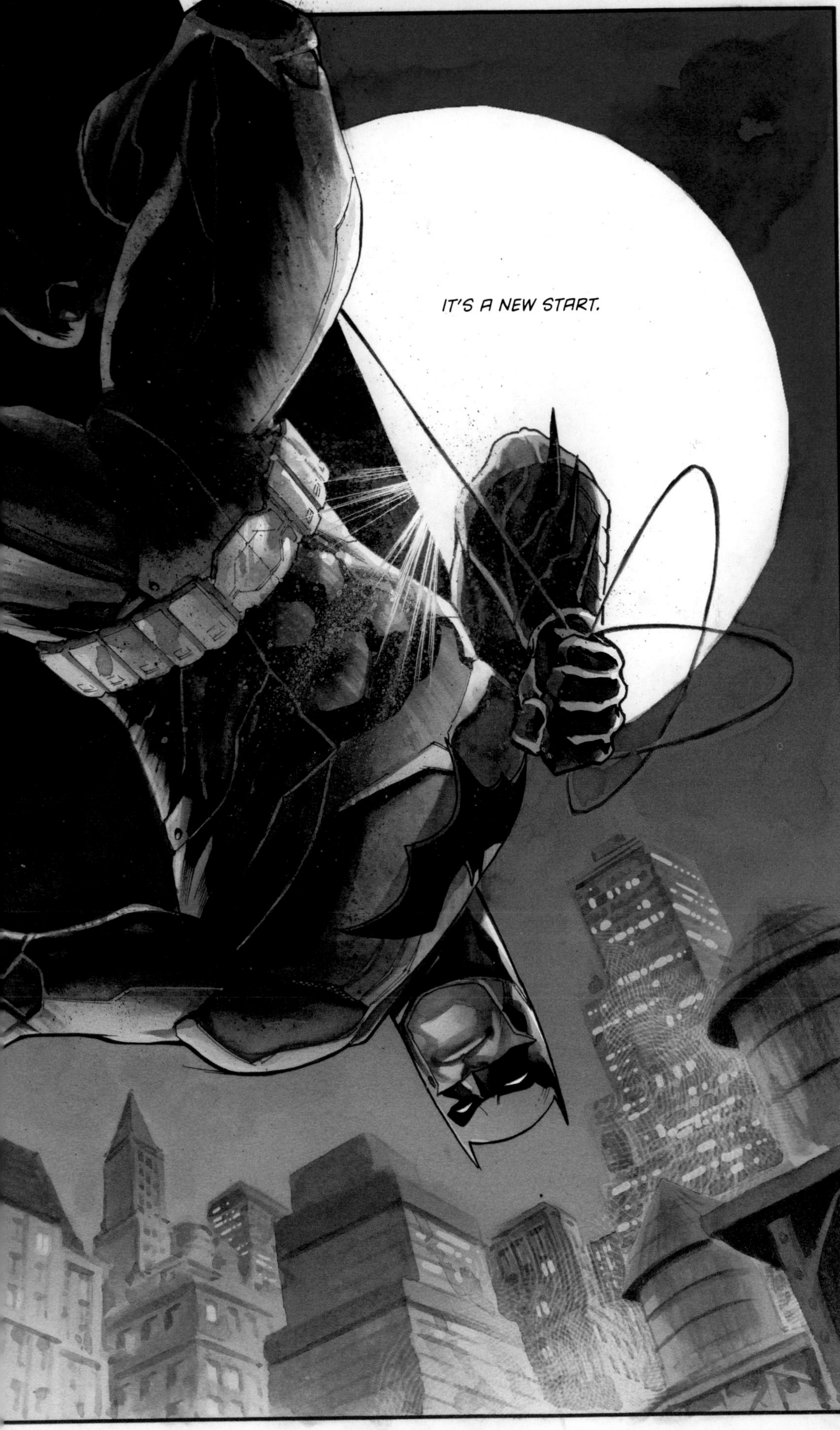
IT'S A NEW START.

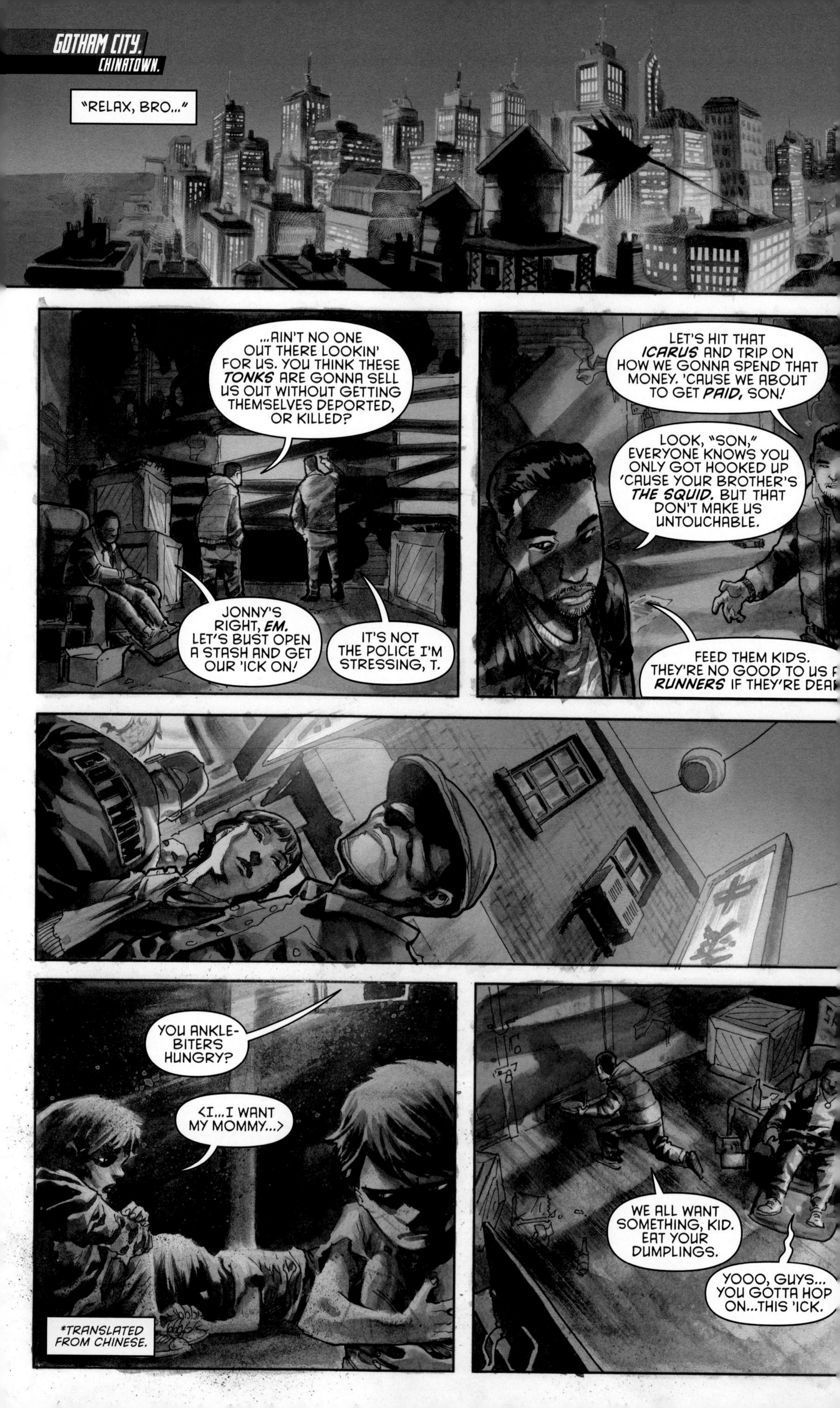
GOTHAM CITY.
CHINATOWN.
"RELAX, BRO..."
...AIN'T NO ONE OUT THERE LOOKIN' FOR US. YOU THINK THESE TONKS ARE GONNA SELL US OUT WITHOUT GETTING THEMSELVES DEPORTED, OR KILLED?
JONNY'S RIGHT, EM. LET'S BUST OPEN A STASH AND GET OUR 'ICK ON!
IT'S NOT THE POLICE I'M STRESSING, T.
LET'S HIT THAT ICARUS AND TRIP ON HOW WE GONNA SPEND THAT MONEY. 'CAUSE WE ABOUT TO GET PAID, SON!
LOOK, "SON," EVERYONE KNOWS YOU ONLY GOT HOOKED UP 'CAUSE YOUR BROTHER'S THE SQUID. BUT THAT DON'T MAKE US UNTOUCHABLE.
FEED THEM KIDS. THEY'RE NO GOOD TO US
RUNNERS IF THEY'RE DEA
GOTHAM
YOU ANKLE-BITERS HUNGRY?
<I...I WANT MY MOMMY...>
*TRANSLATED FROM CHINESE.
WE ALL WANT SOMETHING, KID. EAT YOUR DUMPLINGS.
YOOO, GUYS... YOU GOTTA HOP ON...THIS 'ICK.

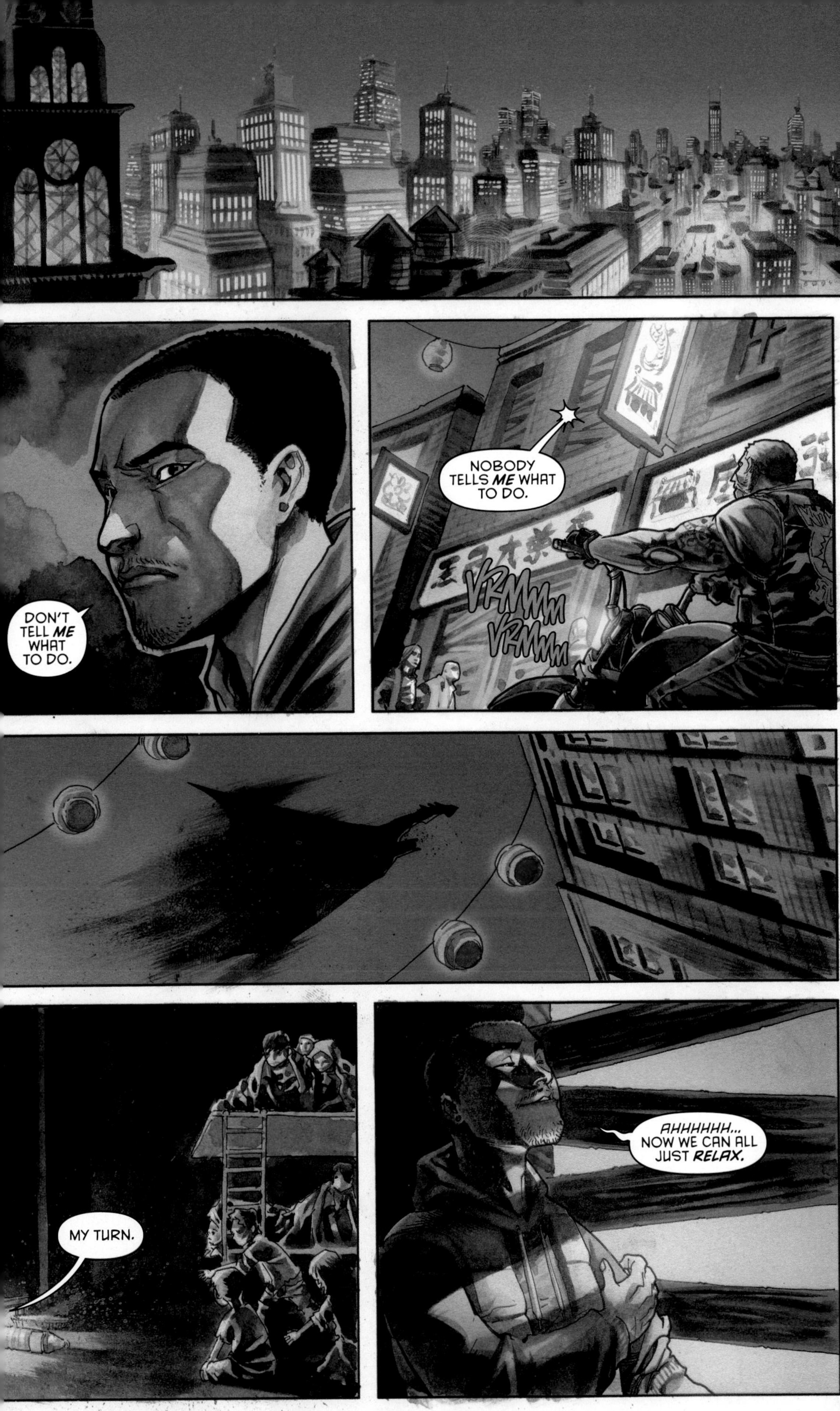
DON'T TELL ME WHAT TO DO.
NOBODY TELLS ME WHAT TO DO.
VRMMMM VRMMMM
MY TURN.
AHHHHHH... NOW WE CAN ALL JUST RELAX.

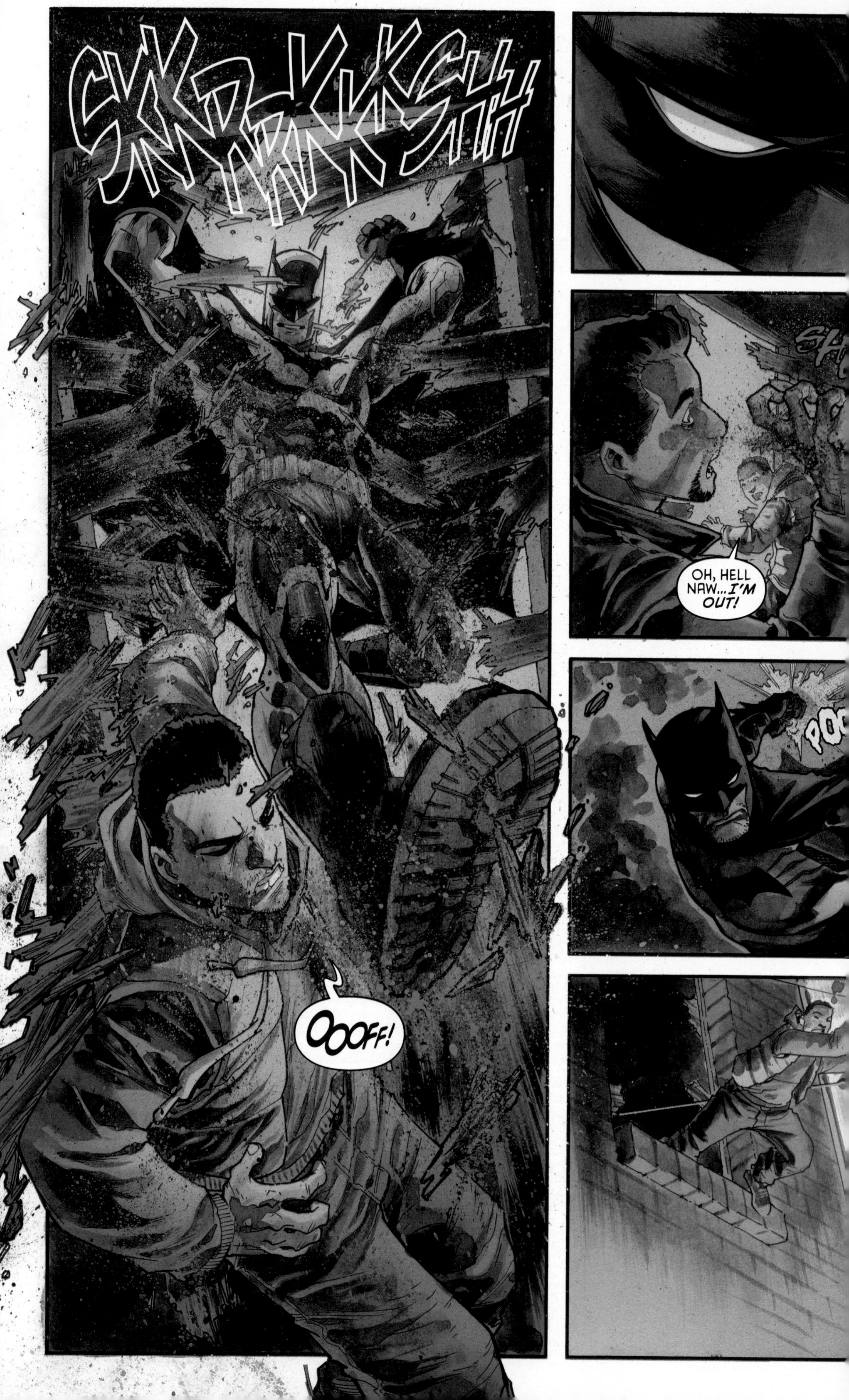
OH, HELL NAW... *I'M OUT!*
OOOFF!

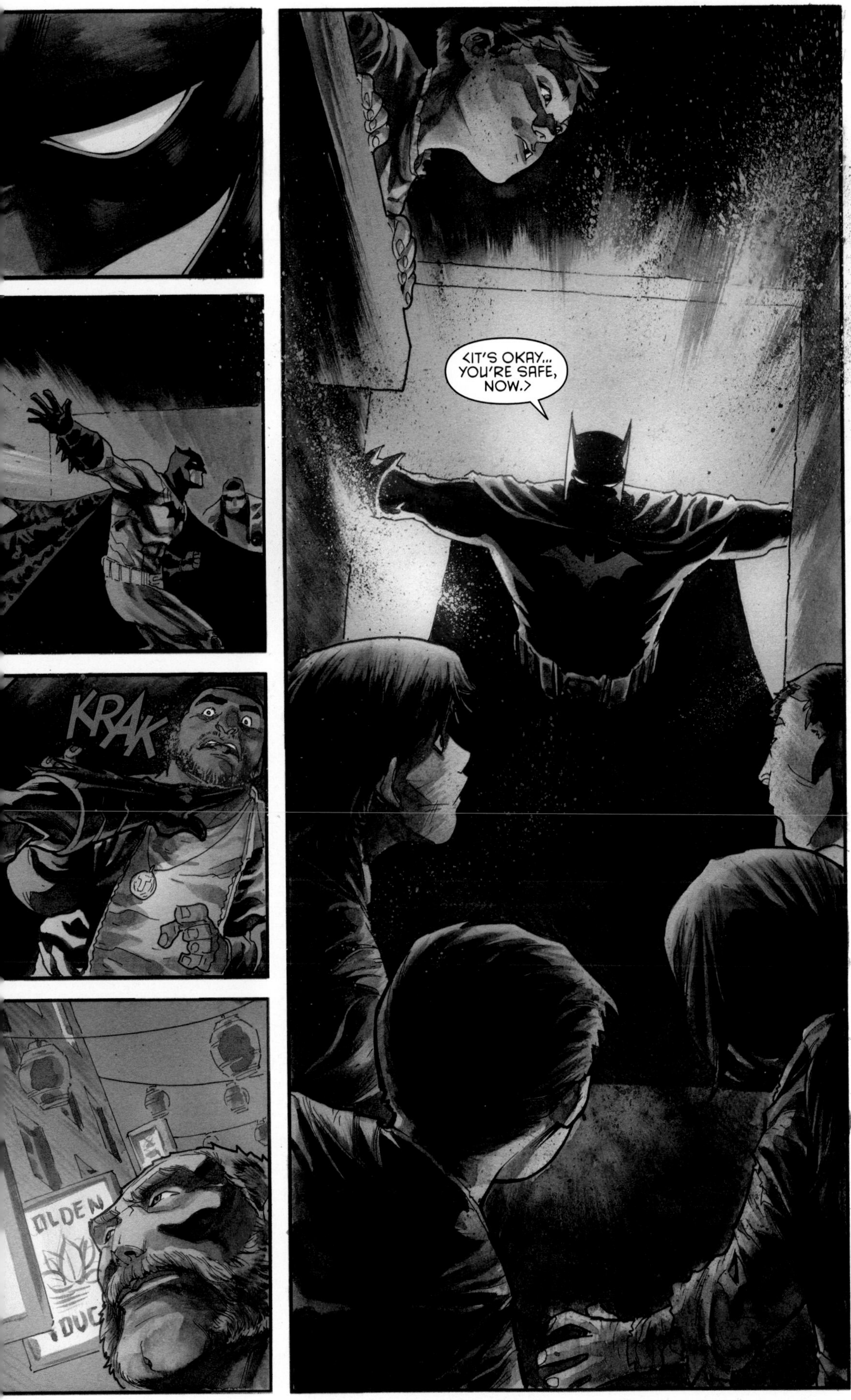
KRAK
<IT'S OKAY... YOU'RE SAFE, NOW.>

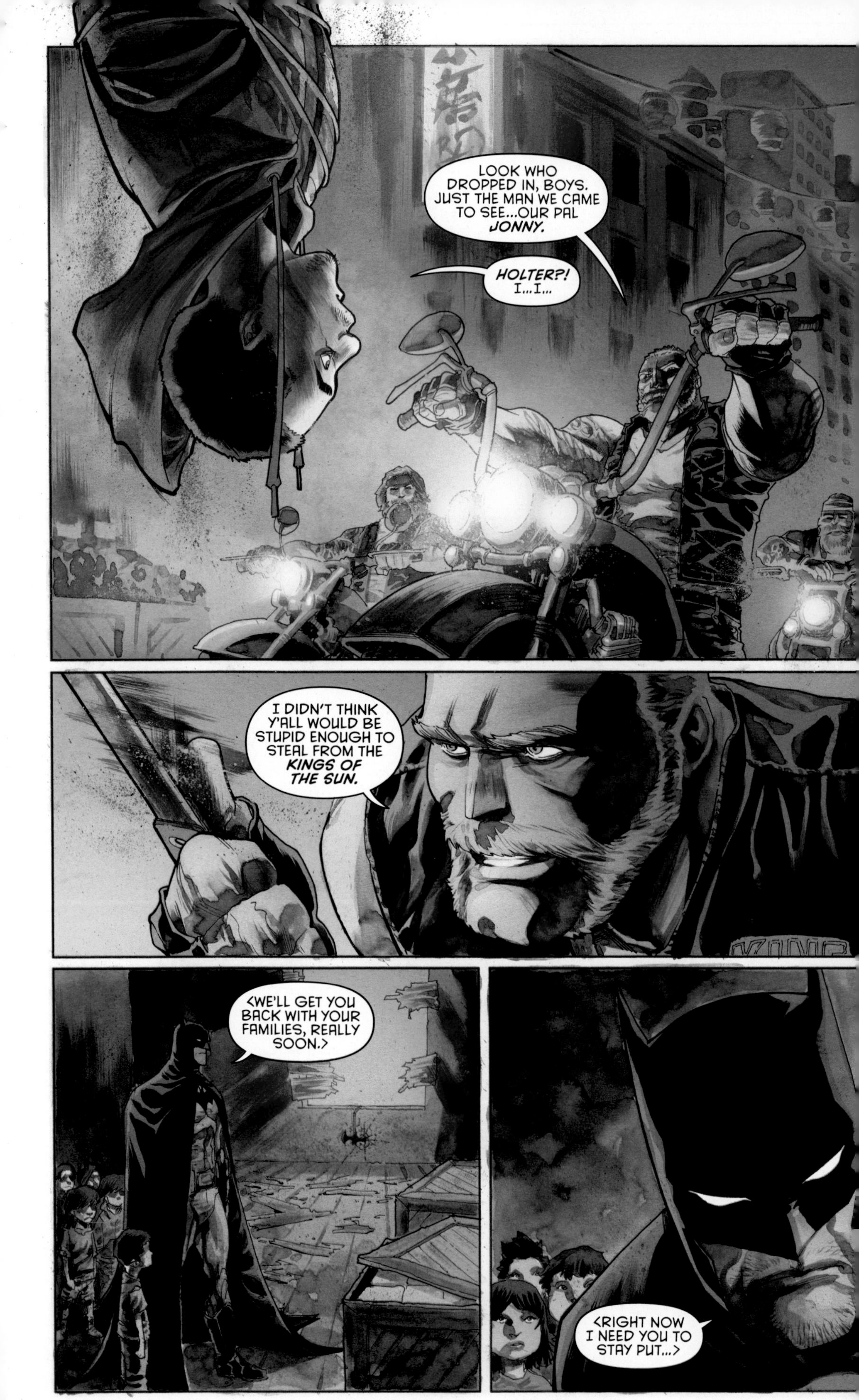
LOOK WHO DROPPED IN, BOYS. JUST THE MAN WE CAME TO SEE...OUR PAL *JONNY.*
HOLTER?! I...I...
I DIDN'T THINK Y'ALL WOULD BE STUPID ENOUGH TO STEAL FROM THE *KINGS OF THE SUN.*
<WE'LL GET YOU BACK WITH YOUR FAMILIES, REALLY SOON.>
<RIGHT NOW I NEED YOU TO STAY PUT...>

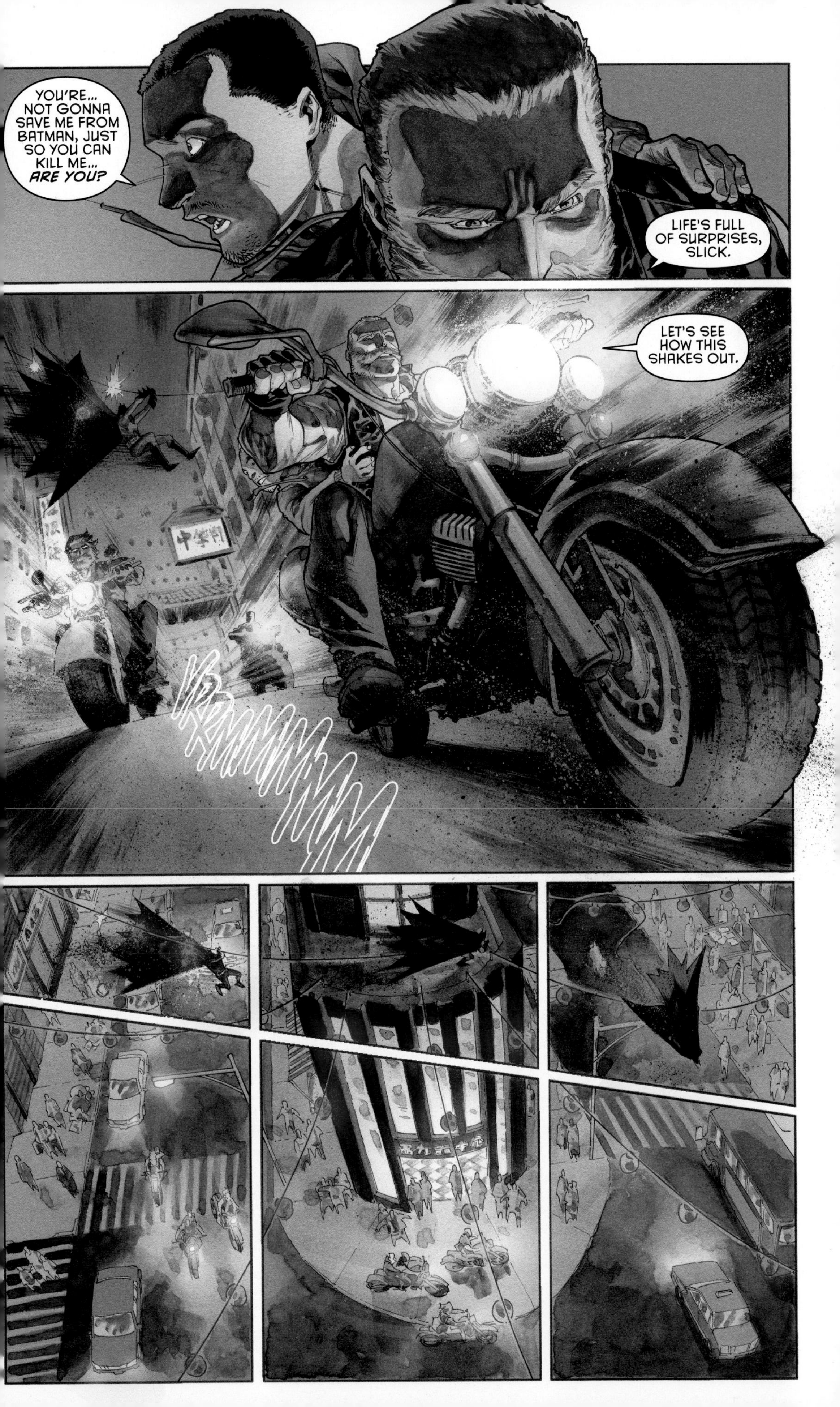
YOU'RE... NOT GONNA SAVE ME FROM BATMAN, JUST SO YOU CAN KILL ME... *ARE YOU?*
LIFE'S FULL OF SURPRISES, SLICK.
LET'S SEE HOW THIS SHAKES OUT.
中华门

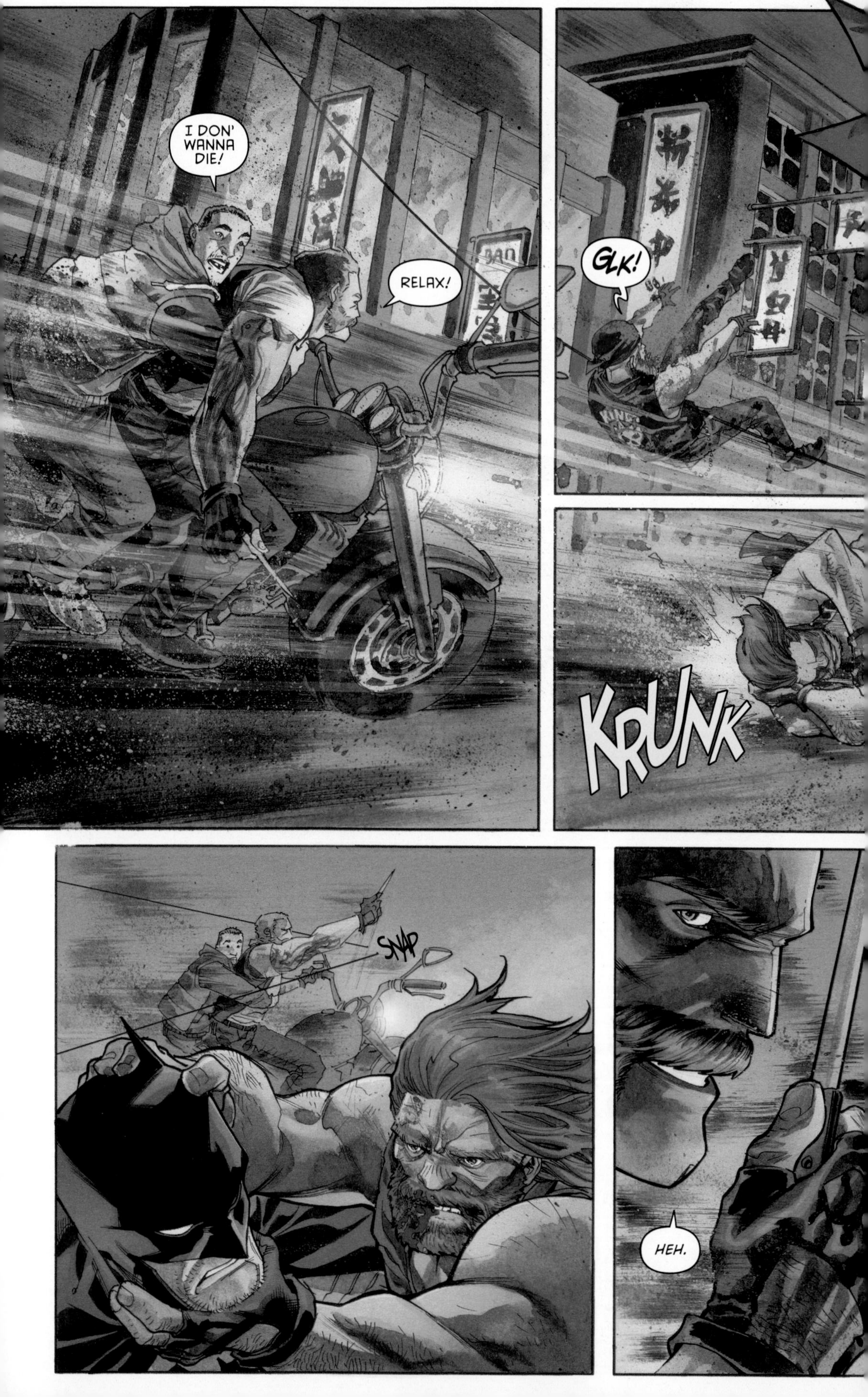
I DON' WANNA DIE!
RELAX!
GLK!
KRUNK
SNAP
HEH.

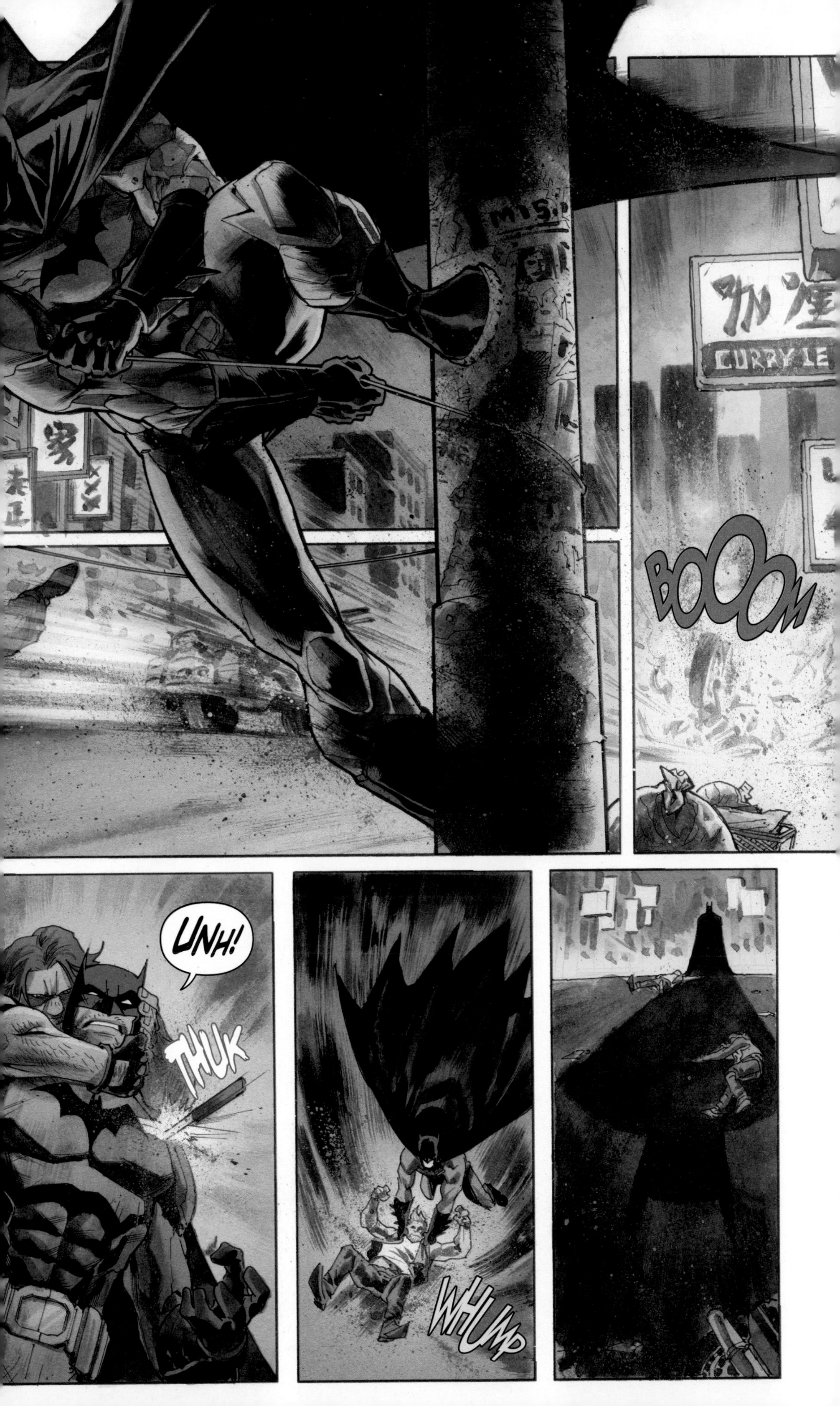
CURRY LE
BOOOM
UNH!
THUK
WHUMP

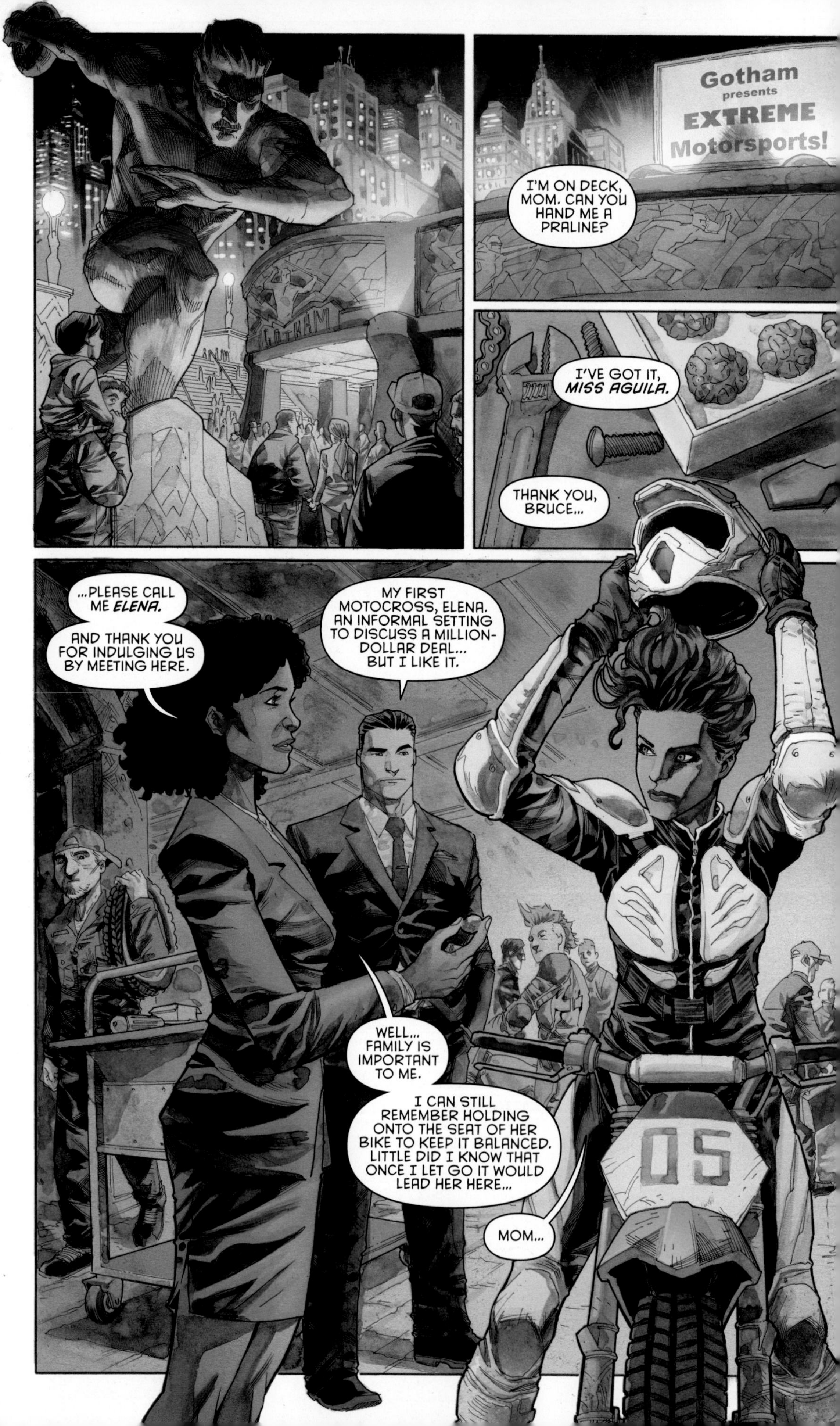
Gotham presents EXTREME Motorsports!
GOTHAM
I'M ON DECK, MOM. CAN YOU HAND ME A PRALINE?
I'VE GOT IT, *MISS AGUILA.*
THANK YOU, BRUCE...
...PLEASE CALL ME *ELENA.*
AND THANK YOU FOR INDULGING US BY MEETING HERE.
MY FIRST MOTOCROSS, ELENA. AN INFORMAL SETTING TO DISCUSS A MILLION-DOLLAR DEAL... BUT I LIKE IT.
WELL... FAMILY IS IMPORTANT TO ME.
I CAN STILL REMEMBER HOLDING ONTO THE SEAT OF HER BIKE TO KEEP IT BALANCED. LITTLE DID I KNOW THAT ONCE I LET GO IT WOULD LEAD HER HERE...
MOM...
05

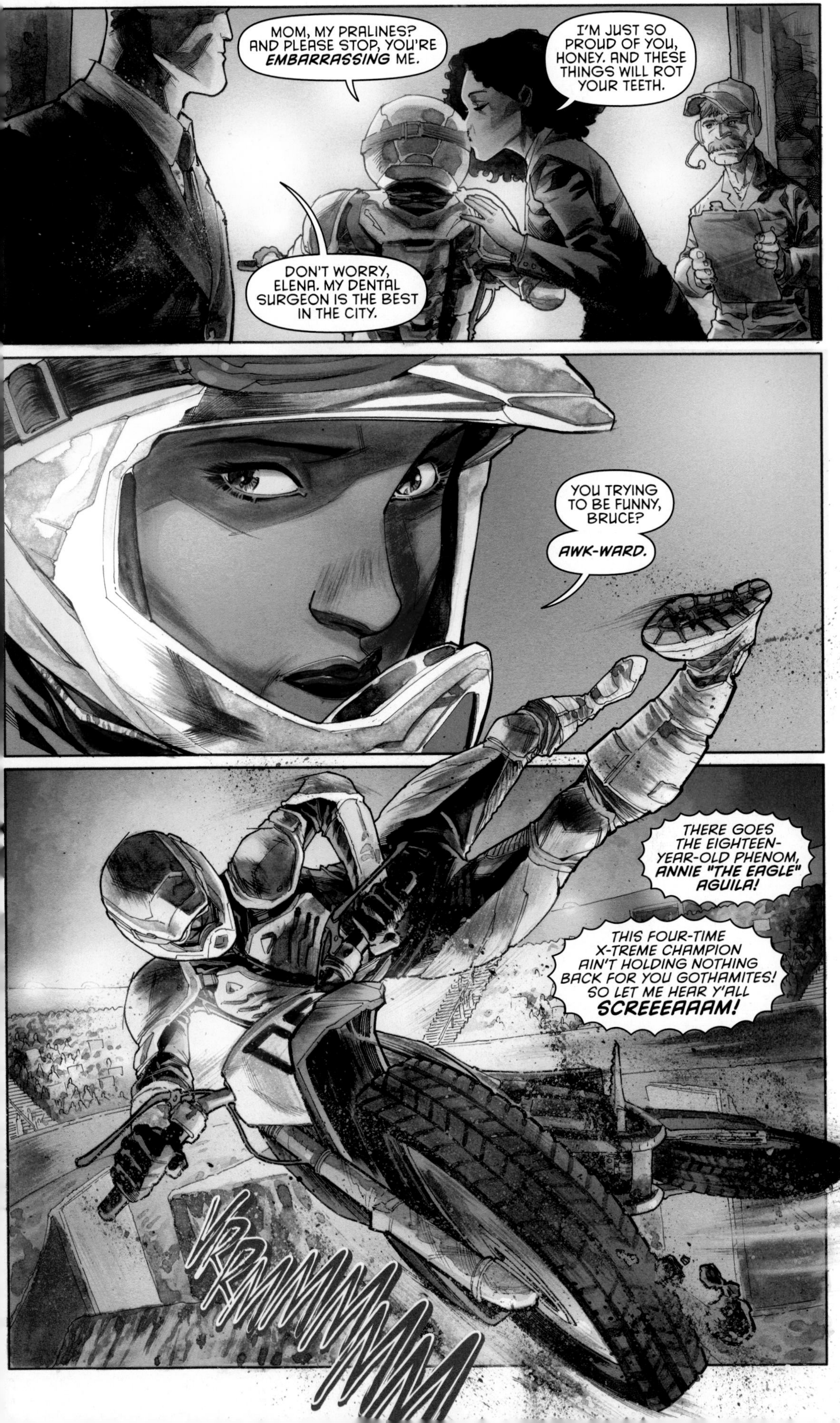
MOM, MY PRALINES? AND PLEASE STOP, YOU'RE *EMBARRASSING* ME.
I'M JUST SO PROUD OF YOU, HONEY. AND THESE THINGS WILL ROT YOUR TEETH.
DON'T WORRY, ELENA. MY DENTAL SURGEON IS THE BEST IN THE CITY.
YOU TRYING TO BE FUNNY, BRUCE?
AWK-WARD.
THERE GOES THE EIGHTEEN-YEAR-OLD PHENOM, *ANNIE "THE EAGLE" AGUILA!*
THIS FOUR-TIME X-TREME CHAMPION AIN'T HOLDING NOTHING BACK FOR YOU GOTHAMITES! SO LET ME HEAR Y'ALL **SCREEEAAAM!**

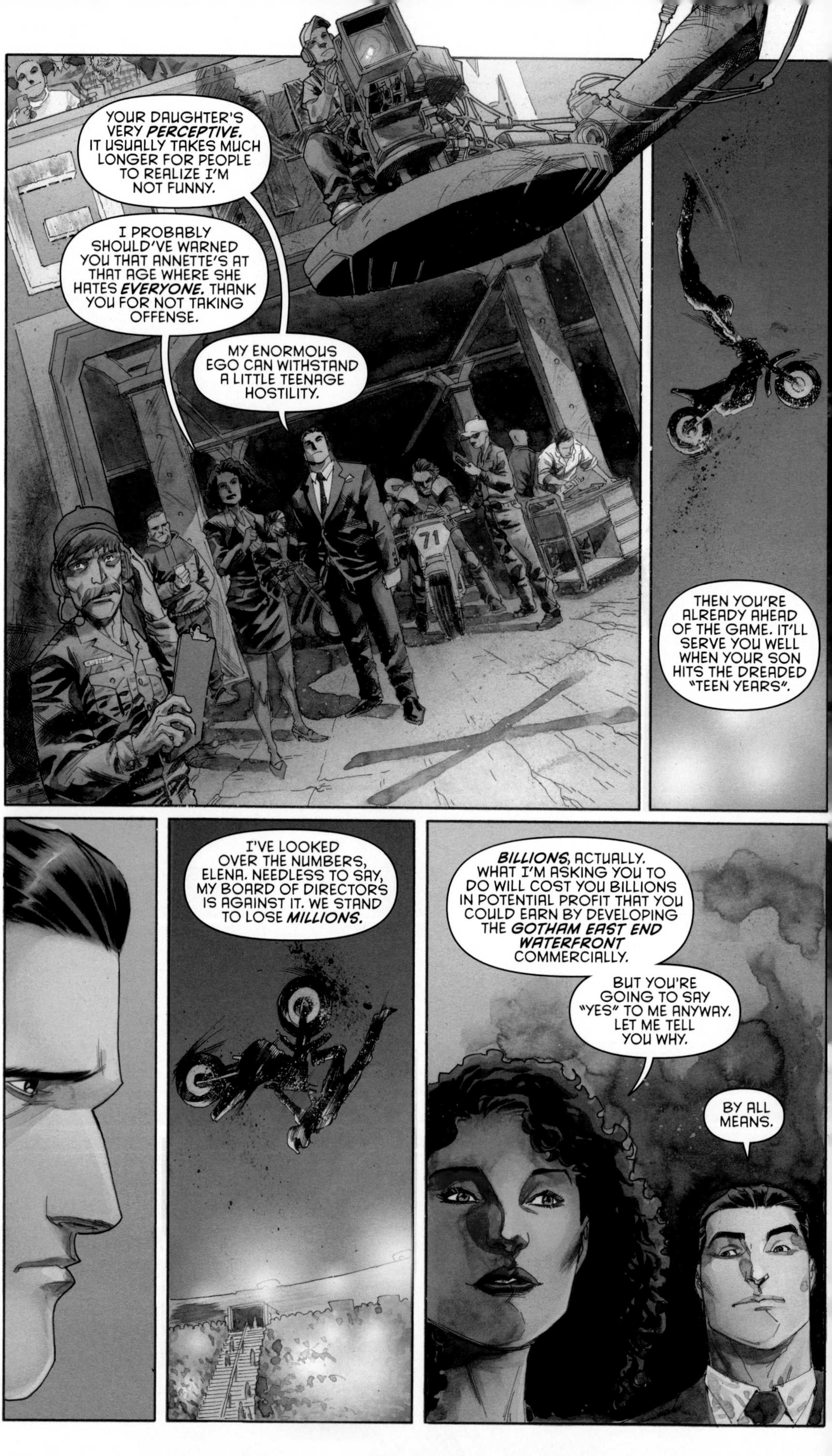
YOUR DAUGHTER'S VERY *PERCEPTIVE.* IT USUALLY TAKES MUCH LONGER FOR PEOPLE TO REALIZE I'M NOT FUNNY.
I PROBABLY SHOULD'VE WARNED YOU THAT ANNETTE'S AT THAT AGE WHERE SHE HATES *EVERYONE.* THANK YOU FOR NOT TAKING OFFENSE.
MY ENORMOUS EGO CAN WITHSTAND A LITTLE TEENAGE HOSTILITY.
71
THEN YOU'RE ALREADY AHEAD OF THE GAME. IT'LL SERVE YOU WELL WHEN YOUR SON HITS THE DREADED "TEEN YEARS".
I'VE LOOKED OVER THE NUMBERS, ELENA. NEEDLESS TO SAY, MY BOARD OF DIRECTORS IS AGAINST IT. WE STAND TO LOSE *MILLIONS.*
BILLIONS, ACTUALLY. WHAT I'M ASKING YOU TO DO WILL COST YOU BILLIONS IN POTENTIAL PROFIT THAT YOU COULD EARN BY DEVELOPING THE *GOTHAM EAST END WATERFRONT* COMMERCIALLY.
BUT YOU'RE GOING TO SAY "YES" TO ME ANYWAY. LET ME TELL YOU WHY.
BY ALL MEANS.

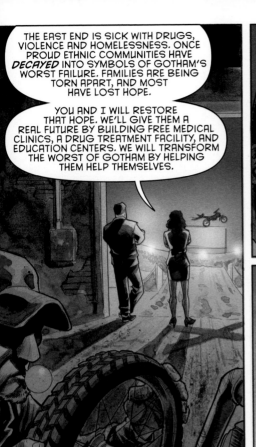

THE EAST END IS SICK WITH DRUGS, VIOLENCE AND HOMELESSNESS. ONCE PROUD ETHNIC COMMUNITIES HAVE *DECAYED* INTO SYMBOLS OF GOTHAM'S WORST FAILURE. FAMILIES ARE BEING TORN APART, AND MOST HAVE LOST HOPE.

YOU AND I WILL RESTORE THAT HOPE. WE'LL GIVE THEM A REAL FUTURE BY BUILDING FREE MEDICAL CLINICS, A DRUG TREATMENT FACILITY, AND EDUCATION CENTERS. WE WILL TRANSFORM THE WORST OF GOTHAM BY HELPING THEM HELP THEMSELVES.

I RESPECT YOUR SINCERITY, ELENA. YOU PROJECT AN INTEGRITY AND EMPATHY THAT'S USUALLY IN SHORT SUPPLY IN BUSINESS RELATIONSHIPS.

BUT I HAVE TO ASK, YOU'RE NOT FROM HERE... SO *WHY?*

SIX YEARS AGO, I SAW A YOUNG MAN STAND IN FRONT OF CAMERAS AND TELL THE WORLD WHAT GOTHAM CITY MEANT TO HIM. HE SPOKE OF A PLACE THAT'S *TRANS-FORMATIVE...*

A PLACE WHERE YOU CAN BECOME SOMETHING MORE THAN YOU ARE. WHERE HARD WORK AND CONVICTION ENABLES FOLKS TO PULL THEMSELVES UP FROM THE DEPTHS OF DESPAIR.

TODAY HE'S TRANSFORMED INTO A GROWN MAN. A *HANDSOME* MAN, EVEN. AND A PARENT...BACK THEN, YOU GAVE ME THE COURAGE TO *START OVER.* TOGETHER WE'LL DO THE SAME FOR EVERYONE.

AND YOU WOULDN'T HAVE TRUDGED THROUGH THIS DIRT WITH EXPENSIVE SHOES LIKE THOSE IF YOUR ANSWER WASN'T A *YES.*

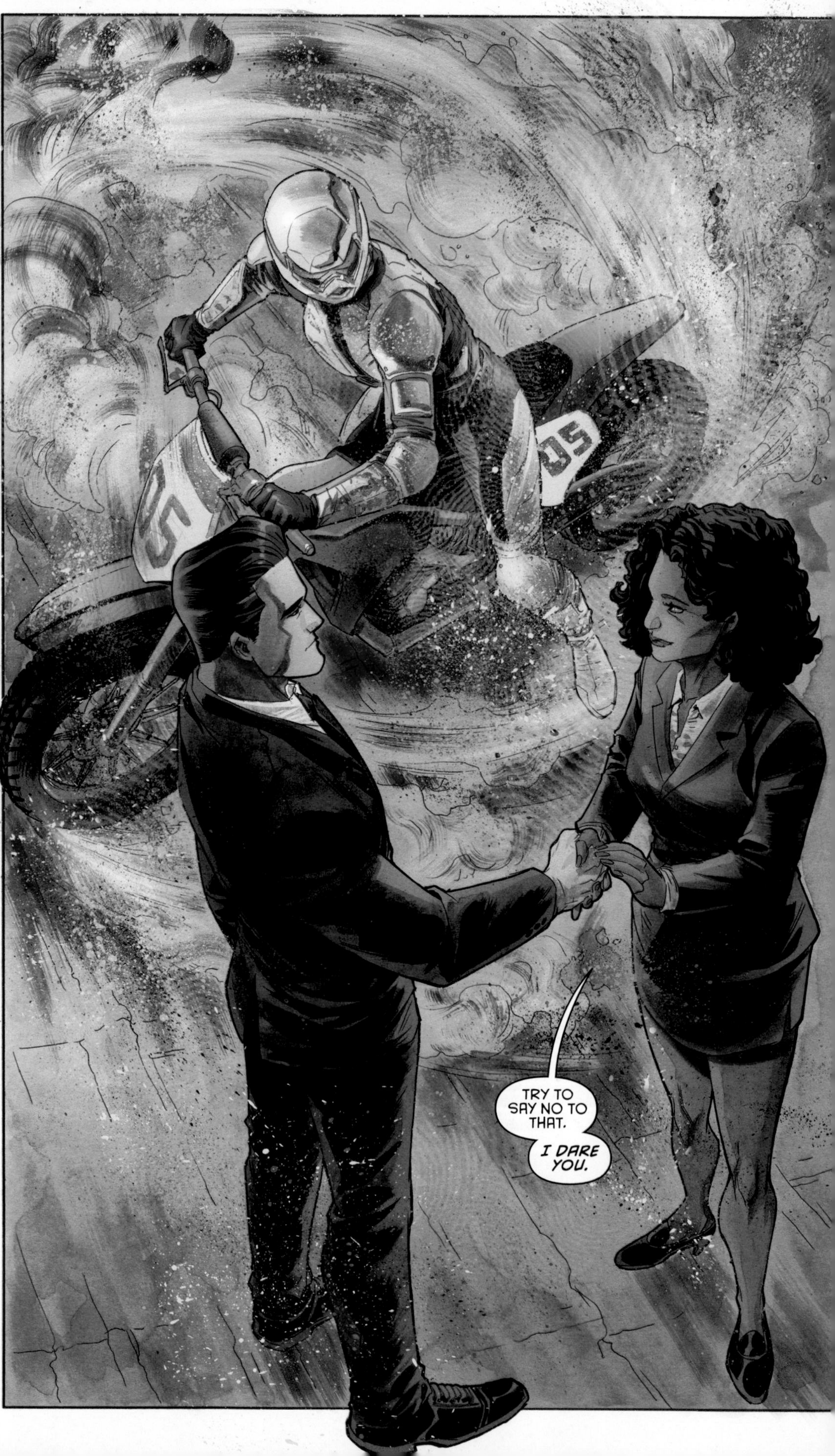
TRY TO SAY NO TO THAT.
I DARE YOU.

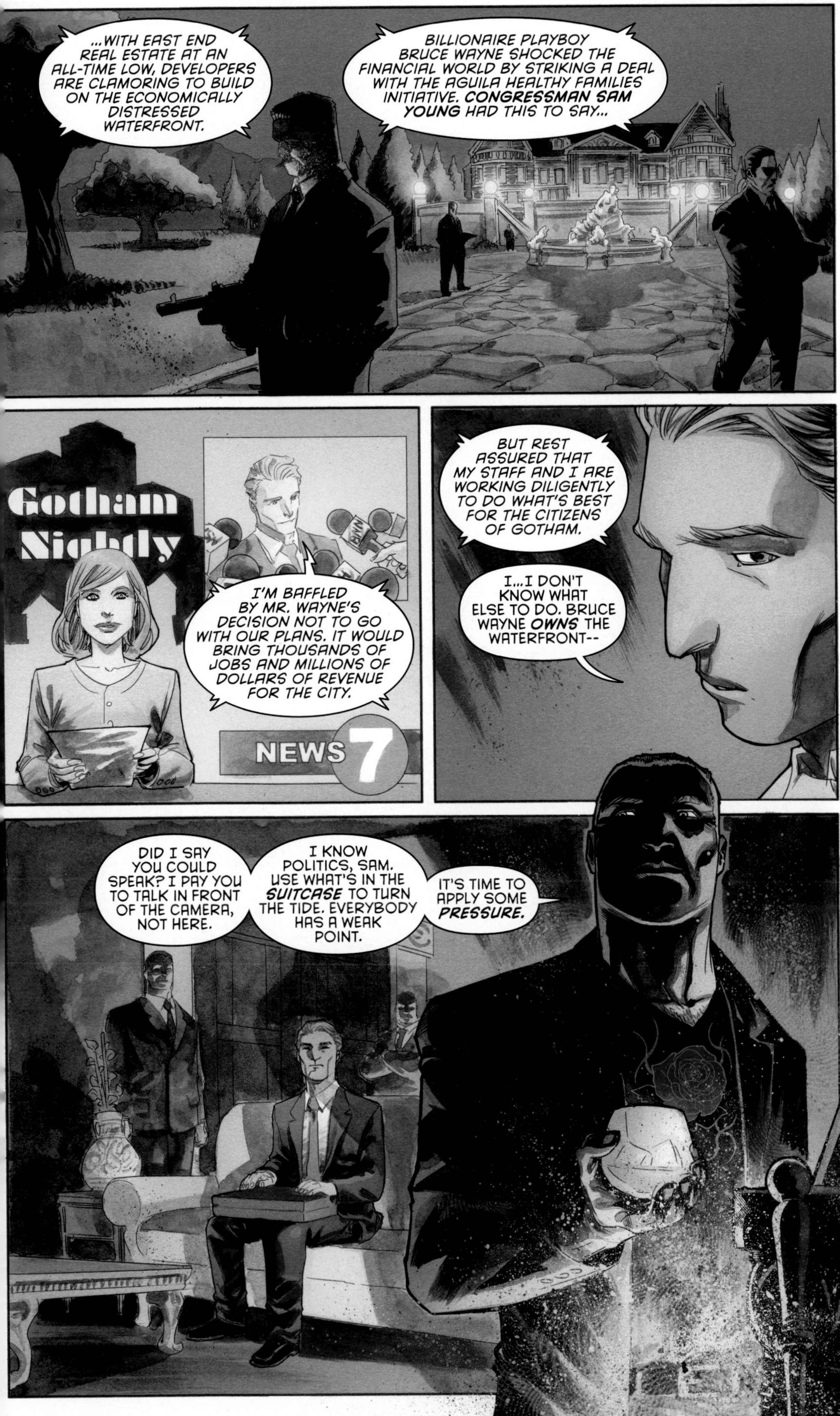
...WITH EAST END REAL ESTATE AT AN ALL-TIME LOW, DEVELOPERS ARE CLAMORING TO BUILD ON THE ECONOMICALLY DISTRESSED WATERFRONT.
BILLIONAIRE PLAYBOY BRUCE WAYNE SHOCKED THE FINANCIAL WORLD BY STRIKING A DEAL WITH THE AGUILA HEALTHY FAMILIES INITIATIVE. CONGRESSMAN SAM YOUNG HAD THIS TO SAY...
Gotham Nightly
I'M BAFFLED BY MR. WAYNE'S DECISION NOT TO GO WITH OUR PLANS. IT WOULD BRING THOUSANDS OF JOBS AND MILLIONS OF DOLLARS OF REVENUE FOR THE CITY.
NEWS 7
BUT REST ASSURED THAT MY STAFF AND I ARE WORKING DILIGENTLY TO DO WHAT'S BEST FOR THE CITIZENS OF GOTHAM.
I...I DON'T KNOW WHAT ELSE TO DO. BRUCE WAYNE OWNS THE WATERFRONT--
DID I SAY YOU COULD SPEAK? I PAY YOU TO TALK IN FRONT OF THE CAMERA, NOT HERE.
I KNOW POLITICS, SAM. USE WHAT'S IN THE SUITCASE TO TURN THE TIDE. EVERYBODY HAS A WEAK POINT.
IT'S TIME TO APPLY SOME PRESSURE.

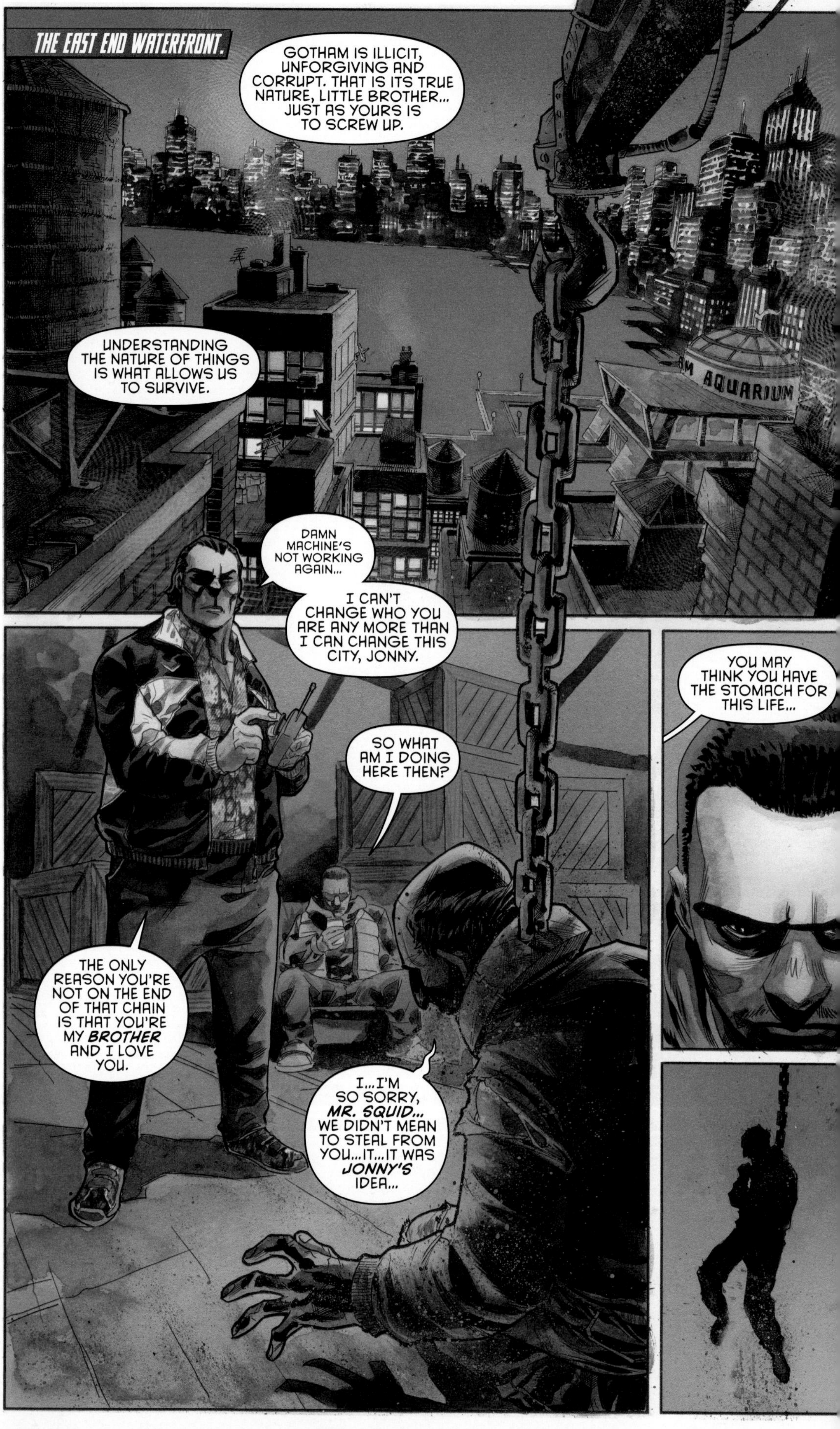

THE EAST END WATERFRONT.
GOTHAM IS ILLICIT, UNFORGIVING AND CORRUPT. THAT IS ITS TRUE NATURE, LITTLE BROTHER... JUST AS YOURS IS TO SCREW UP.
UNDERSTANDING THE NATURE OF THINGS IS WHAT ALLOWS US TO SURVIVE.
AQUARIUM
DAMN MACHINE'S NOT WORKING AGAIN...
I CAN'T CHANGE WHO YOU ARE ANY MORE THAN I CAN CHANGE THIS CITY, JONNY.
SO WHAT AM I DOING HERE THEN?
THE ONLY REASON YOU'RE NOT ON THE END OF THAT CHAIN IS THAT YOU'RE MY BROTHER AND I LOVE YOU.
I...I'M SO SORRY, MR. SQUID... WE DIDN'T MEAN TO STEAL FROM YOU...IT...IT WAS JONNY'S IDEA...
YOU MAY THINK YOU HAVE THE STOMACH FOR THIS LIFE...

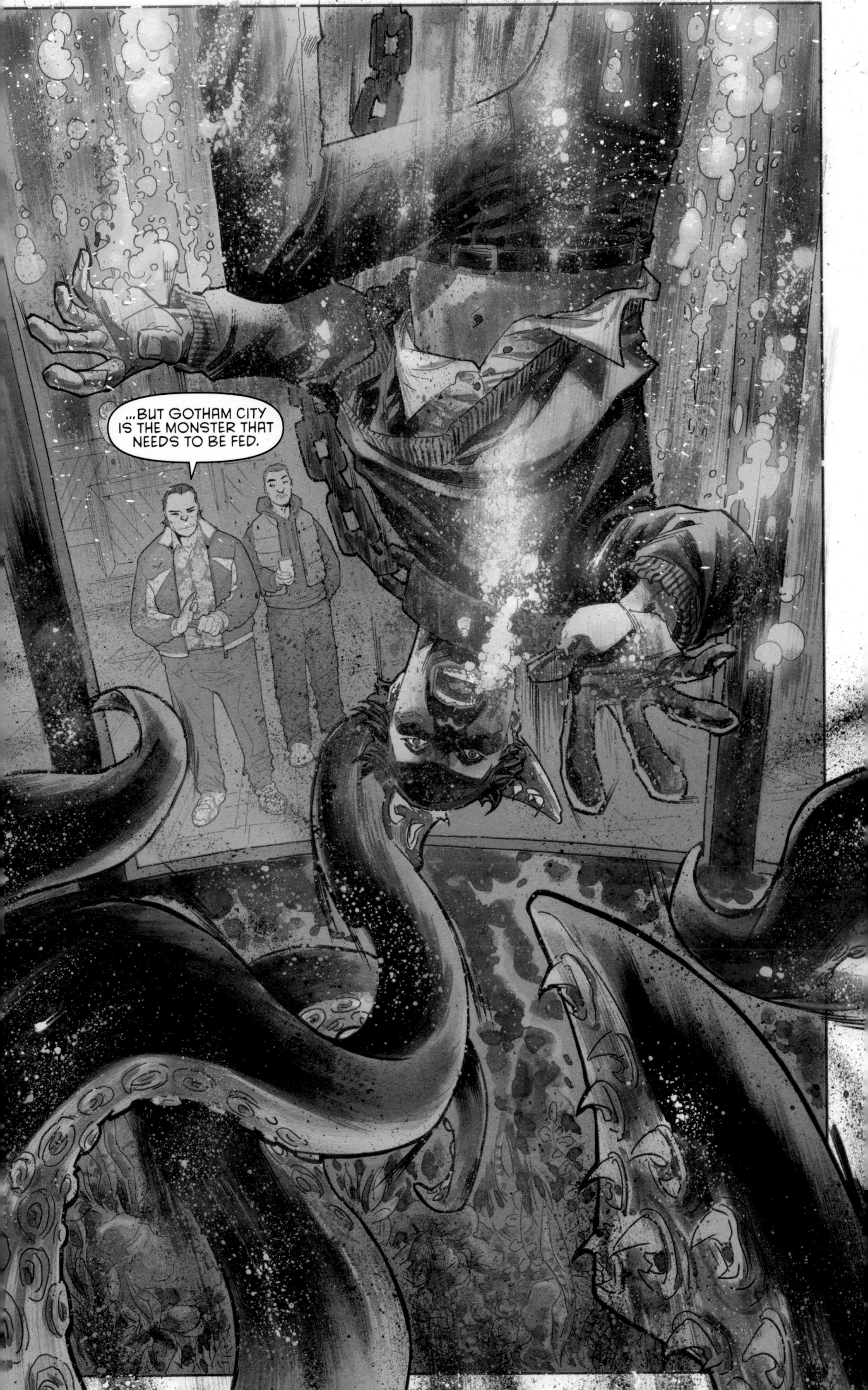
...BUT GOTHAM CITY IS THE MONSTER THAT NEEDS TO BE FED.

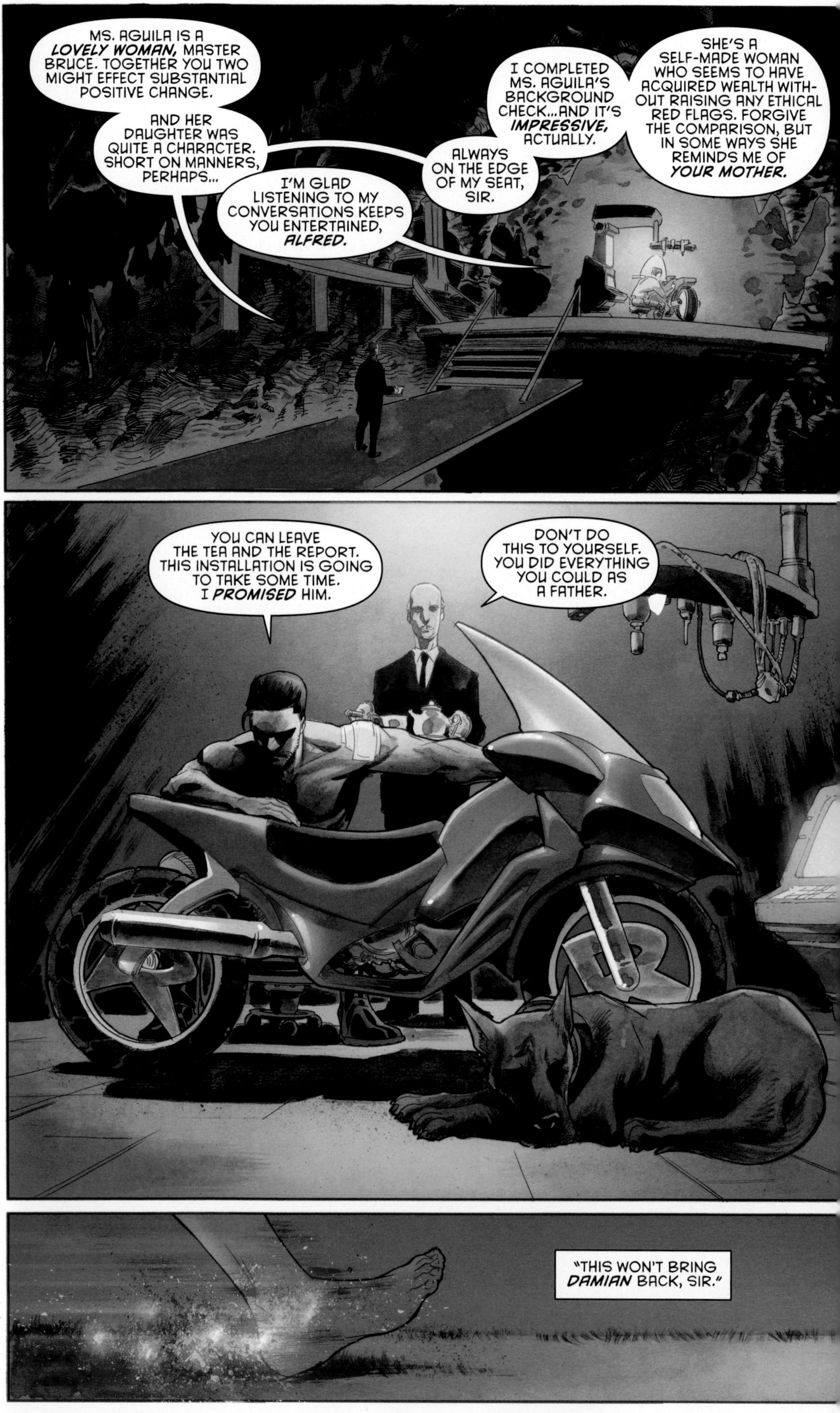
MS. AGUILA IS A LOVELY WOMAN, MASTER BRUCE. TOGETHER YOU TWO MIGHT EFFECT SUBSTANTIAL POSITIVE CHANGE.
AND HER DAUGHTER WAS QUITE A CHARACTER. SHORT ON MANNERS, PERHAPS...
I'M GLAD LISTENING TO MY CONVERSATIONS KEEPS YOU ENTERTAINED, ALFRED.
ALWAYS ON THE EDGE OF MY SEAT, SIR.
I COMPLETED MS. AGUILA'S BACKGROUND CHECK...AND IT'S IMPRESSIVE, ACTUALLY.
SHE'S A SELF-MADE WOMAN WHO SEEMS TO HAVE ACQUIRED WEALTH WITH-OUT RAISING ANY ETHICAL RED FLAGS. FORGIVE THE COMPARISON, BUT IN SOME WAYS SHE REMINDS ME OF YOUR MOTHER.
YOU CAN LEAVE THE TEA AND THE REPORT. THIS INSTALLATION IS GOING TO TAKE SOME TIME. I PROMISED HIM.
DON'T DO THIS TO YOURSELF. YOU DID EVERYTHING YOU COULD AS A FATHER.
"THIS WON'T BRING DAMIAN BACK, SIR."

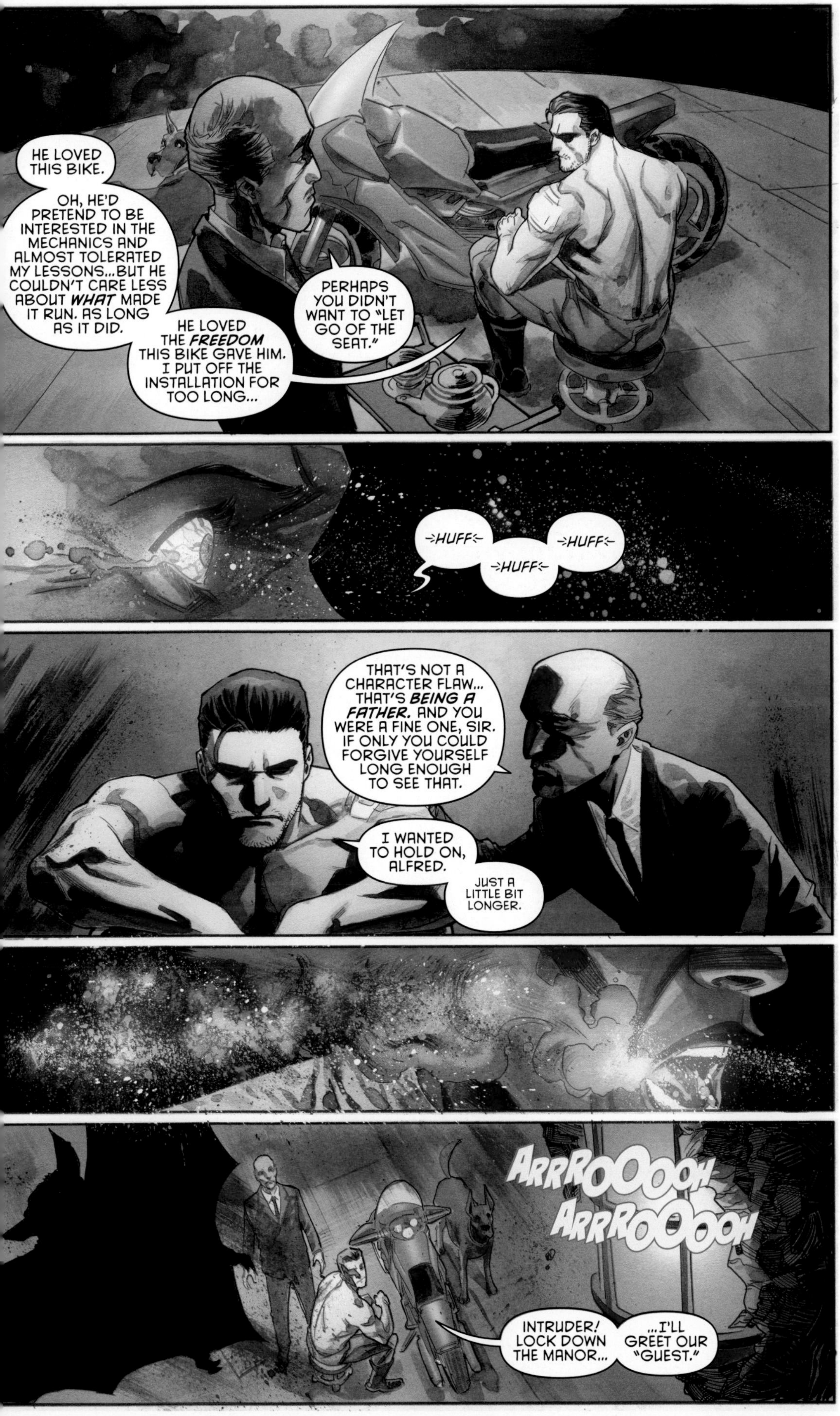
HE LOVED THIS BIKE.
OH, HE'D PRETEND TO BE INTERESTED IN THE MECHANICS AND ALMOST TOLERATED MY LESSONS...BUT HE COULDN'T CARE LESS ABOUT WHAT MADE IT RUN. AS LONG AS IT DID.
HE LOVED THE FREEDOM THIS BIKE GAVE HIM. I PUT OFF THE INSTALLATION FOR TOO LONG...
PERHAPS YOU DIDN'T WANT TO "LET GO OF THE SEAT."
HUFF
HUFF
HUFF
THAT'S NOT A CHARACTER FLAW... THAT'S BEING A FATHER. AND YOU WERE A FINE ONE, SIR. IF ONLY YOU COULD FORGIVE YOURSELF LONG ENOUGH TO SEE THAT.
I WANTED TO HOLD ON, ALFRED.
JUST A LITTLE BIT LONGER.
ARRROOOOOH
ARRROOOOOH
INTRUDER! LOCK DOWN THE MANOR...
...I'LL GREET OUR "GUEST."

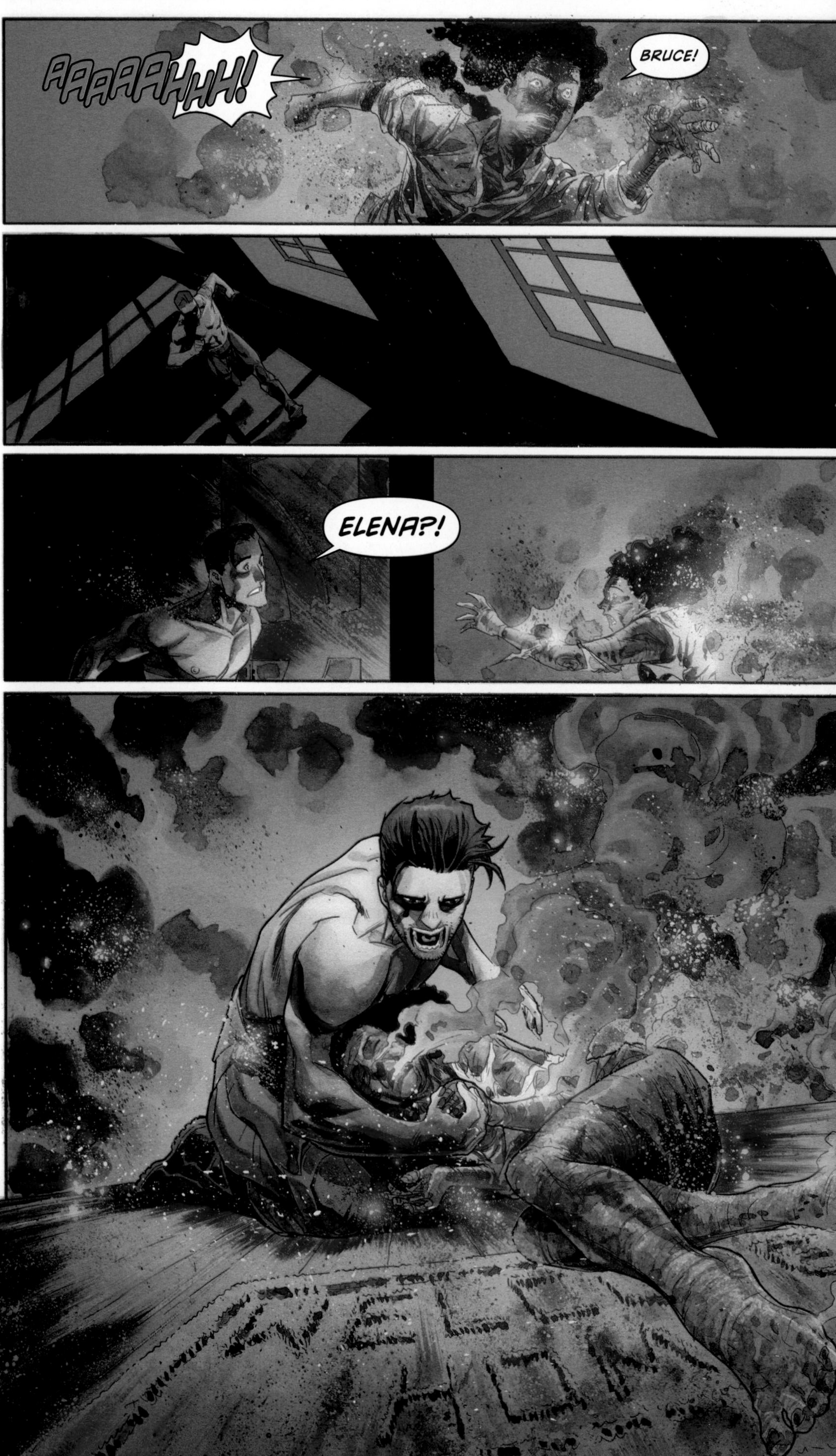
AAAAAAHHH!
BRUCE!
ELENA?!

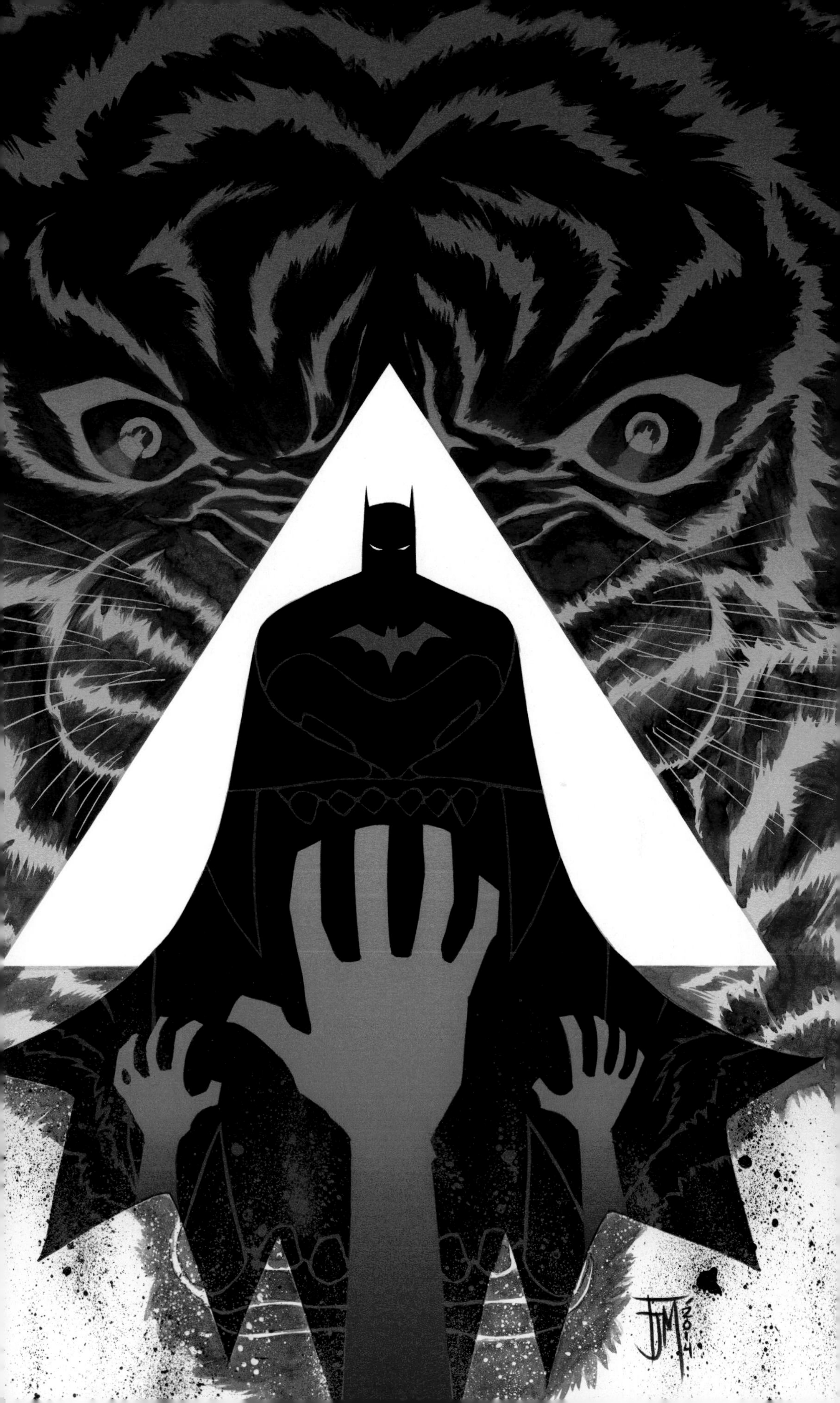

A

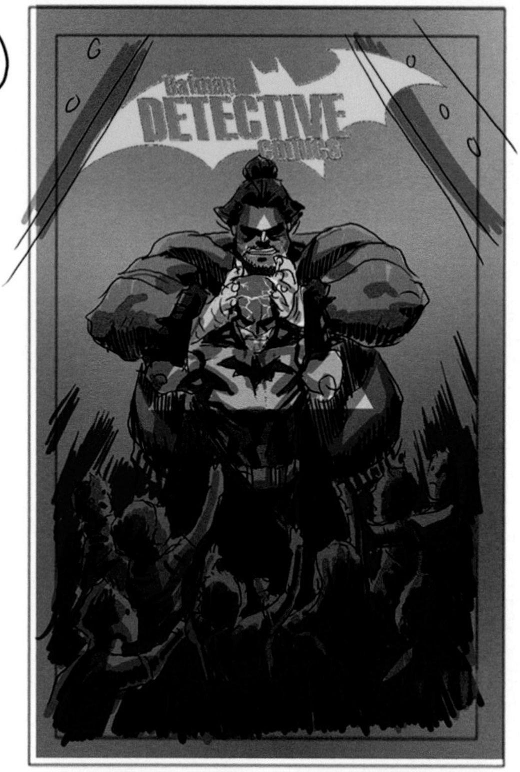
Batman
DETECTIVE
comics

B

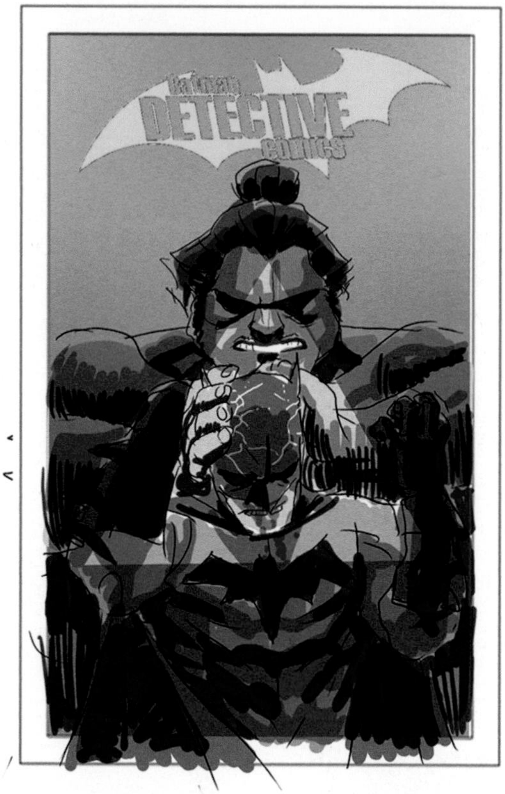
Batman
DETECTIVE
comics

C

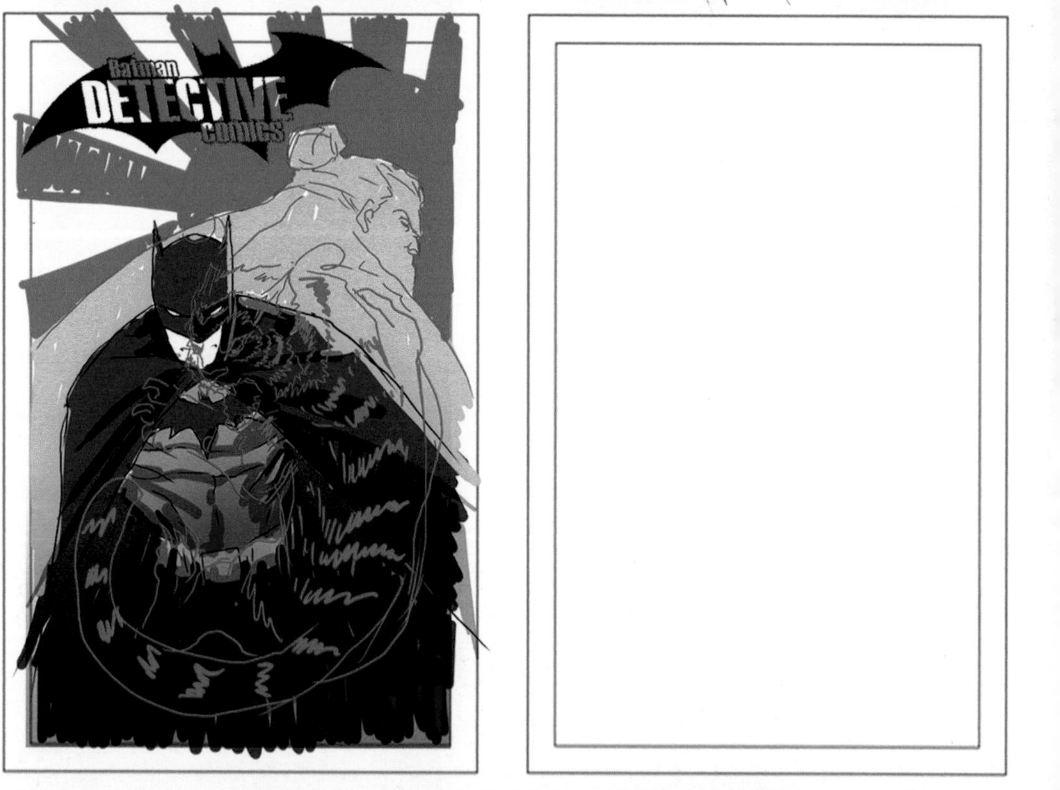
Batman
DETECTIVE
comics

"Six years ago, during the great storm, my partner and I were investigating a drug called *Icarus*.

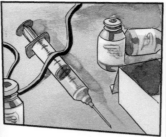

"We were able to put the drug out of circulation at the cost of my partner's life. Gotham's been clean of it ever since.

"So imagine my surprise to see it resurface on *your* doorsteps..."

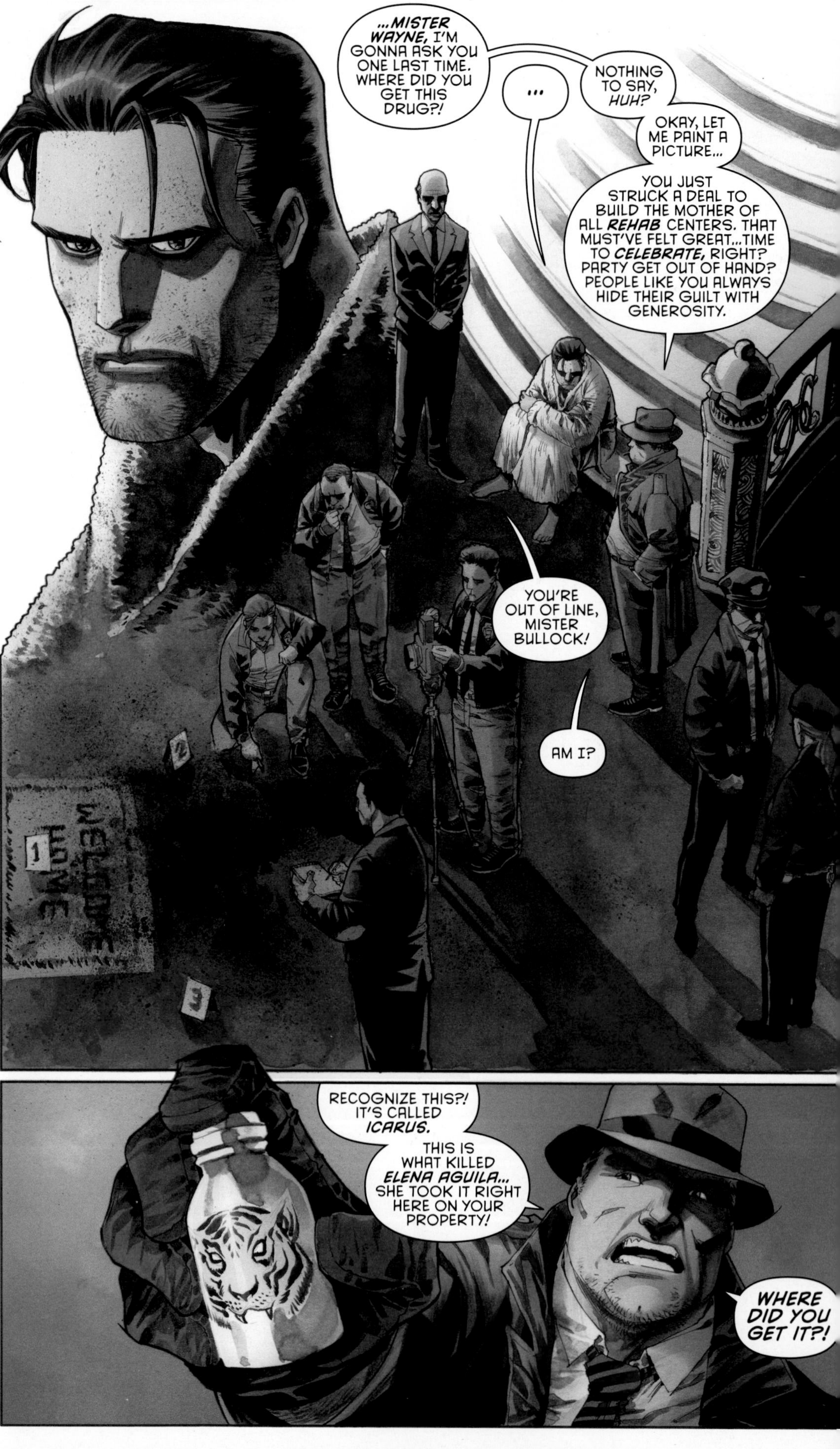
...MISTER WAYNE, I'M GONNA ASK YOU ONE LAST TIME. WHERE DID YOU GET THIS DRUG?!
...
NOTHING TO SAY, HUH?
OKAY, LET ME PAINT A PICTURE...
YOU JUST STRUCK A DEAL TO BUILD THE MOTHER OF ALL REHAB CENTERS. THAT MUST'VE FELT GREAT...TIME TO CELEBRATE, RIGHT? PARTY GET OUT OF HAND? PEOPLE LIKE YOU ALWAYS HIDE THEIR GUILT WITH GENEROSITY.
YOU'RE OUT OF LINE, MISTER BULLOCK!
AM I?
WELCOME HOME
RECOGNIZE THIS?! IT'S CALLED ICARUS.
THIS IS WHAT KILLED ELENA AGUILA... SHE TOOK IT RIGHT HERE ON YOUR PROPERTY!
WHERE DID YOU GET IT?!

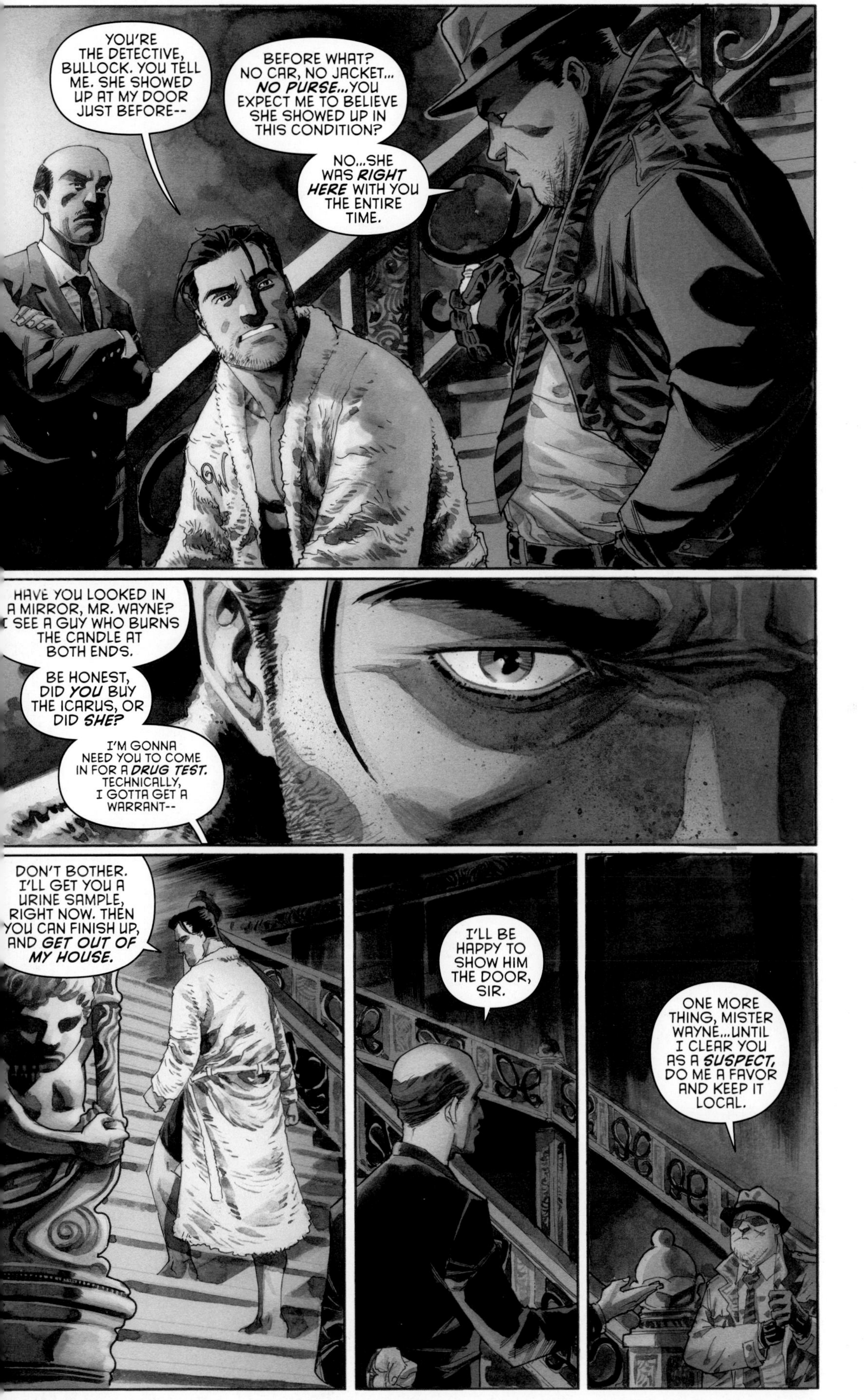
YOU'RE THE DETECTIVE, BULLOCK. YOU TELL ME. SHE SHOWED UP AT MY DOOR JUST BEFORE--
BEFORE WHAT? NO CAR, NO JACKET... *NO PURSE...*YOU EXPECT ME TO BELIEVE SHE SHOWED UP IN THIS CONDITION?
NO...SHE WAS *RIGHT HERE* WITH YOU THE ENTIRE TIME.
HAVE YOU LOOKED IN A MIRROR, MR. WAYNE? I SEE A GUY WHO BURNS THE CANDLE AT BOTH ENDS.
BE HONEST, DID *YOU* BUY THE ICARUS, OR DID *SHE?*
I'M GONNA NEED YOU TO COME IN FOR A *DRUG TEST.* TECHNICALLY, I GOTTA GET A WARRANT--
DON'T BOTHER. I'LL GET YOU A URINE SAMPLE, RIGHT NOW. THEN YOU CAN FINISH UP, AND *GET OUT OF MY HOUSE.*
I'LL BE HAPPY TO SHOW HIM THE DOOR, SIR.
ONE MORE THING, MISTER WAYNE...UNTIL I CLEAR YOU AS A *SUSPECT,* DO ME A FAVOR AND KEEP IT LOCAL.

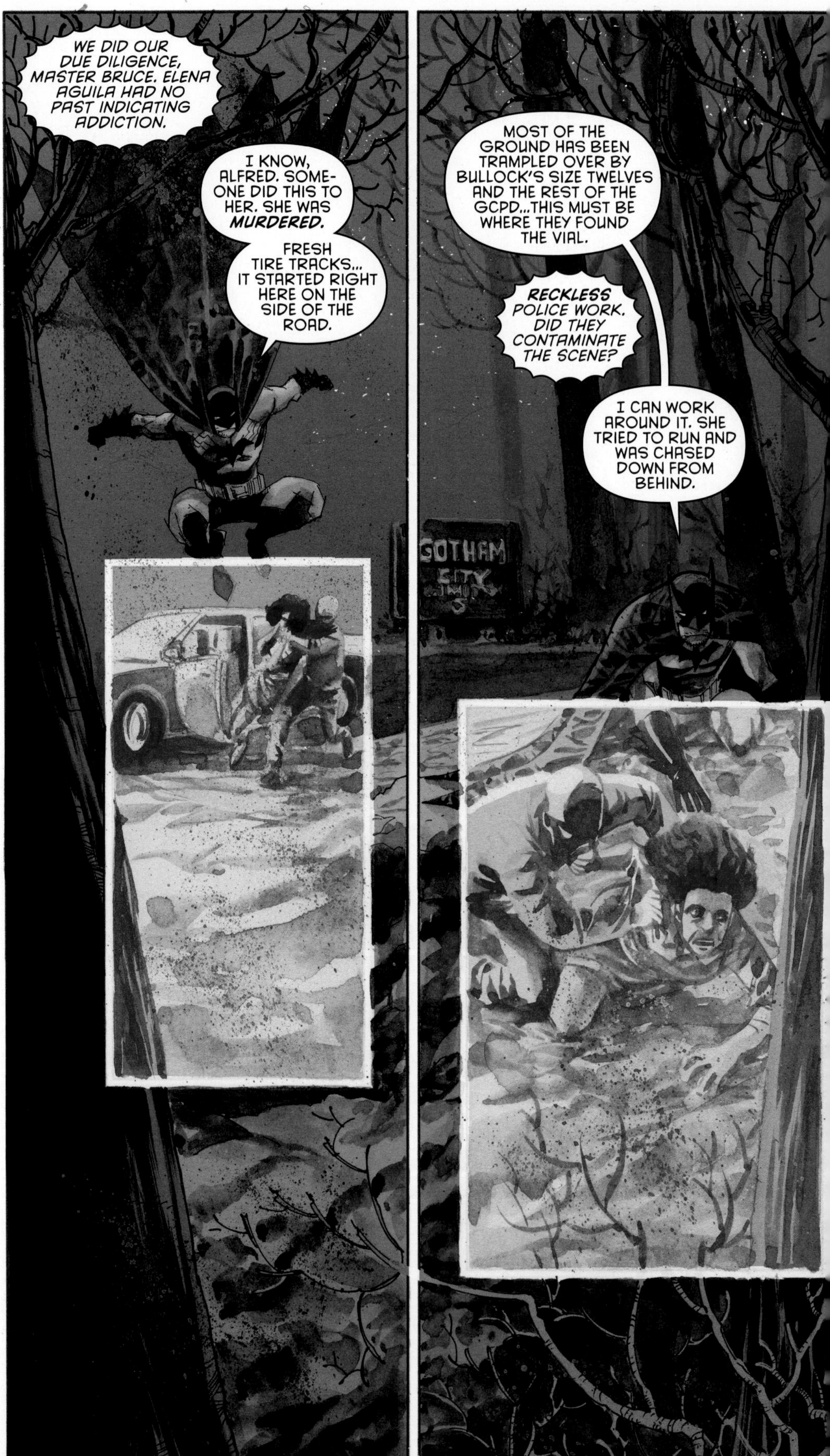
WE DID OUR DUE DILIGENCE, MASTER BRUCE. ELENA AGUILA HAD NO PAST INDICATING ADDICTION.
I KNOW, ALFRED. SOME-ONE DID THIS TO HER. SHE WAS ***MURDERED.***
FRESH TIRE TRACKS... IT STARTED RIGHT HERE ON THE SIDE OF THE ROAD.
MOST OF THE GROUND HAS BEEN TRAMPLED OVER BY BULLOCK'S SIZE TWELVES AND THE REST OF THE GCPD...THIS MUST BE WHERE THEY FOUND THE VIAL.
RECKLESS POLICE WORK. DID THEY CONTAMINATE THE SCENE?
I CAN WORK AROUND IT. SHE TRIED TO RUN AND WAS CHASED DOWN FROM BEHIND.
GOTHAM

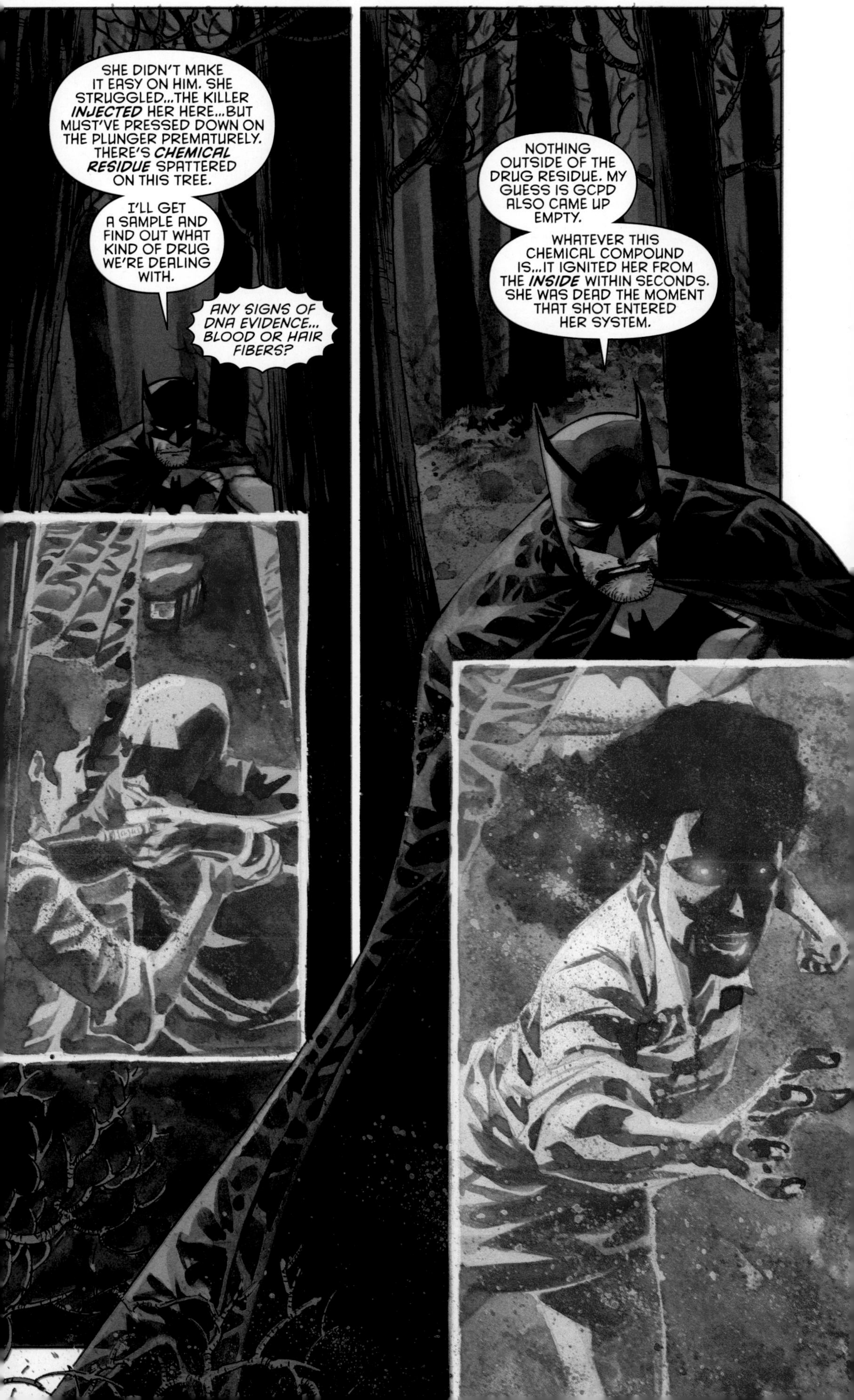
SHE DIDN'T MAKE IT EASY ON HIM. SHE STRUGGLED...THE KILLER INJECTED HER HERE...BUT MUST'VE PRESSED DOWN ON THE PLUNGER PREMATURELY. THERE'S CHEMICAL RESIDUE SPATTERED ON THIS TREE.
I'LL GET A SAMPLE AND FIND OUT WHAT KIND OF DRUG WE'RE DEALING WITH.
ANY SIGNS OF DNA EVIDENCE... BLOOD OR HAIR FIBERS?
NOTHING OUTSIDE OF THE DRUG RESIDUE. MY GUESS IS GCPD ALSO CAME UP EMPTY.
WHATEVER THIS CHEMICAL COMPOUND IS...IT IGNITED HER FROM THE INSIDE WITHIN SECONDS. SHE WAS DEAD THE MOMENT THAT SHOT ENTERED HER SYSTEM.

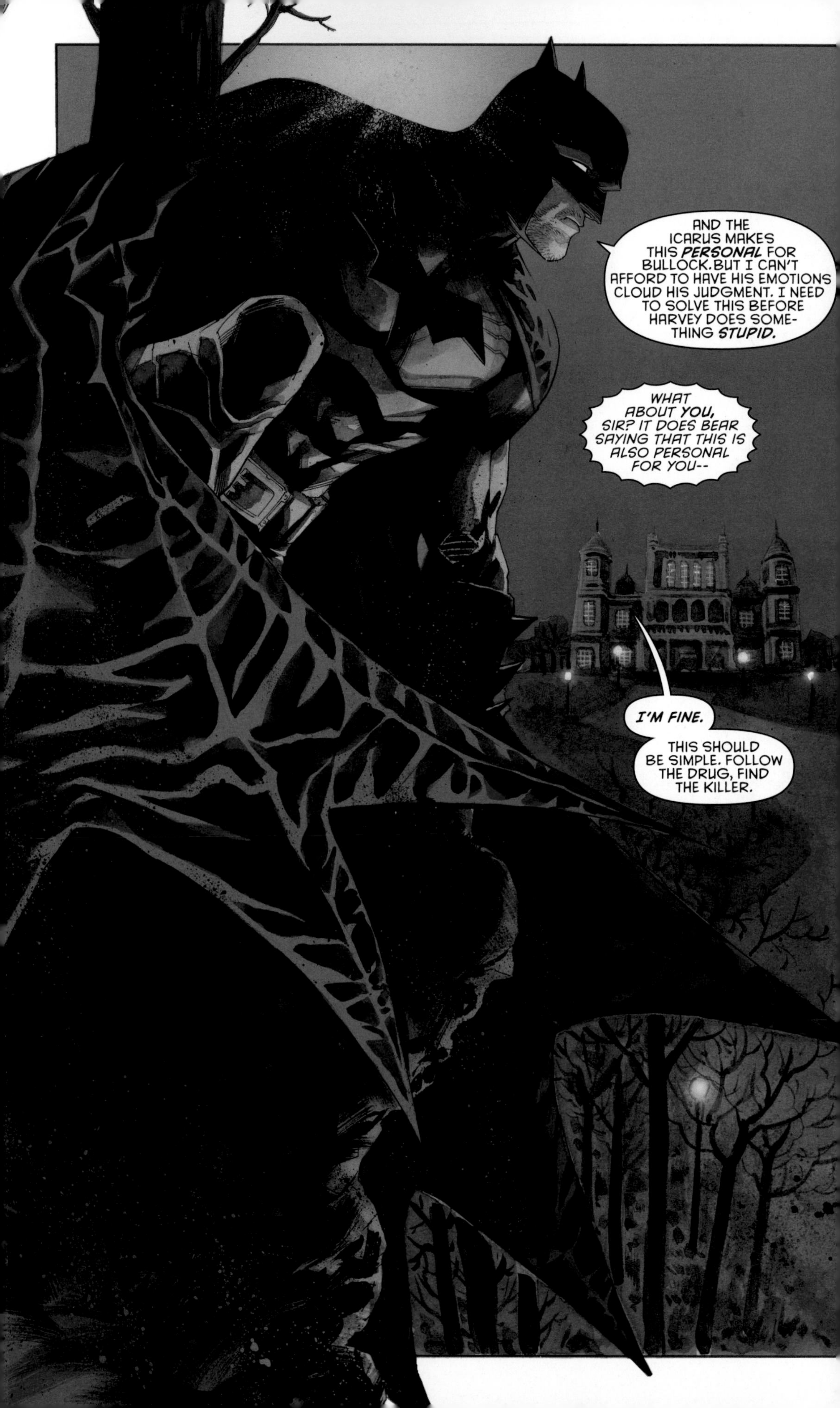
AND THE ICARUS MAKES THIS PERSONAL FOR BULLOCK. BUT I CAN'T AFFORD TO HAVE HIS EMOTIONS CLOUD HIS JUDGMENT. I NEED TO SOLVE THIS BEFORE HARVEY DOES SOME-THING STUPID.
WHAT ABOUT YOU, SIR? IT DOES BEAR SAYING THAT THIS IS ALSO PERSONAL FOR YOU--
I'M FINE.
THIS SHOULD BE SIMPLE. FOLLOW THE DRUG, FIND THE KILLER.

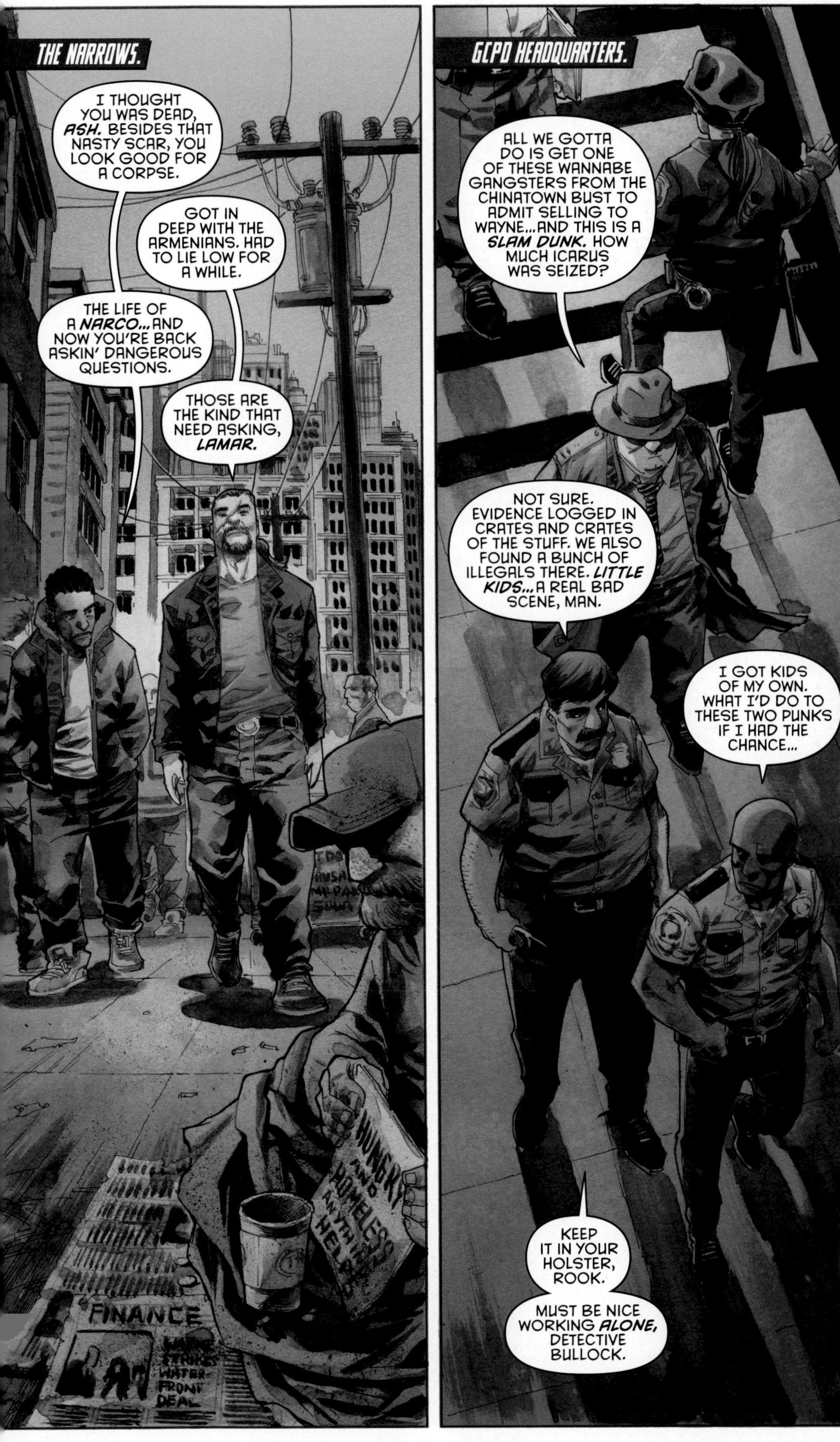
THE NARROWS.
I THOUGHT YOU WAS DEAD, ASH. BESIDES THAT NASTY SCAR, YOU LOOK GOOD FOR A CORPSE.
GOT IN DEEP WITH THE ARMENIANS. HAD TO LIE LOW FOR A WHILE.
THE LIFE OF A NARCO... AND NOW YOU'RE BACK ASKIN' DANGEROUS QUESTIONS.
THOSE ARE THE KIND THAT NEED ASKING, LAMAR.
HUNGRY AND HOMELESS
FINANCE
GCPD HEADQUARTERS.
ALL WE GOTTA DO IS GET ONE OF THESE WANNABE GANGSTERS FROM THE CHINATOWN BUST TO ADMIT SELLING TO WAYNE... AND THIS IS A SLAM DUNK. HOW MUCH ICARUS WAS SEIZED?
NOT SURE. EVIDENCE LOGGED IN CRATES AND CRATES OF THE STUFF. WE ALSO FOUND A BUNCH OF ILLEGALS THERE. LITTLE KIDS... A REAL BAD SCENE, MAN.
I GOT KIDS OF MY OWN. WHAT I'D DO TO THESE TWO PUNKS IF I HAD THE CHANCE...
KEEP IT IN YOUR HOLSTER, ROOK.
MUST BE NICE WORKING ALONE, DETECTIVE BULLOCK.

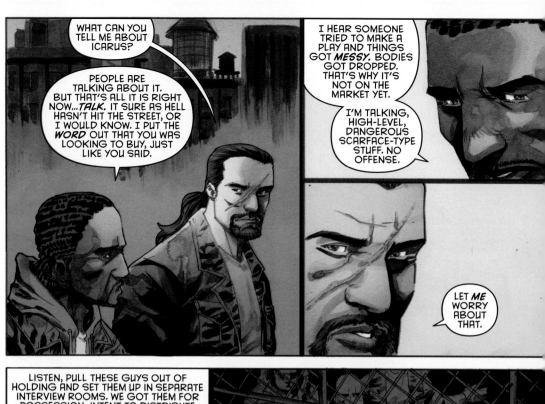

WHAT CAN YOU TELL ME ABOUT ICARUS?

PEOPLE ARE TALKING ABOUT IT. BUT THAT'S ALL IT IS RIGHT NOW...*TALK.* IT SURE AS HELL HASN'T HIT THE STREET, OR I WOULD KNOW. I PUT THE *WORD* OUT THAT YOU WAS LOOKING TO BUY, JUST LIKE YOU SAID.

I HEAR SOMEONE TRIED TO MAKE A PLAY AND THINGS GOT *MESSY.* BODIES GOT DROPPED. THAT'S WHY IT'S NOT ON THE MARKET YET.

I'M TALKING, HIGH-LEVEL, DANGEROUS SCARFACE-TYPE STUFF. NO OFFENSE.

LET *ME* WORRY ABOUT THAT.

LISTEN, PULL THESE GUYS OUT OF HOLDING AND SET THEM UP IN SEPARATE INTERVIEW ROOMS. WE GOT THEM FOR POSSESSION, INTENT TO DISTRIBUTE AND KIDNAPPING. I'LL TURN THESE TWO ON EACH OTHER FASTER THAN A COUPLE'A--

--WILD DOGS?!

EVERYONE STEP BACK! HANDS WHERE I CAN SEE THEM! NOW!

AW, JEEZ... DON'T TELL ME...

I'M SORRY, BULLOCK. *THAT'S THEM.*

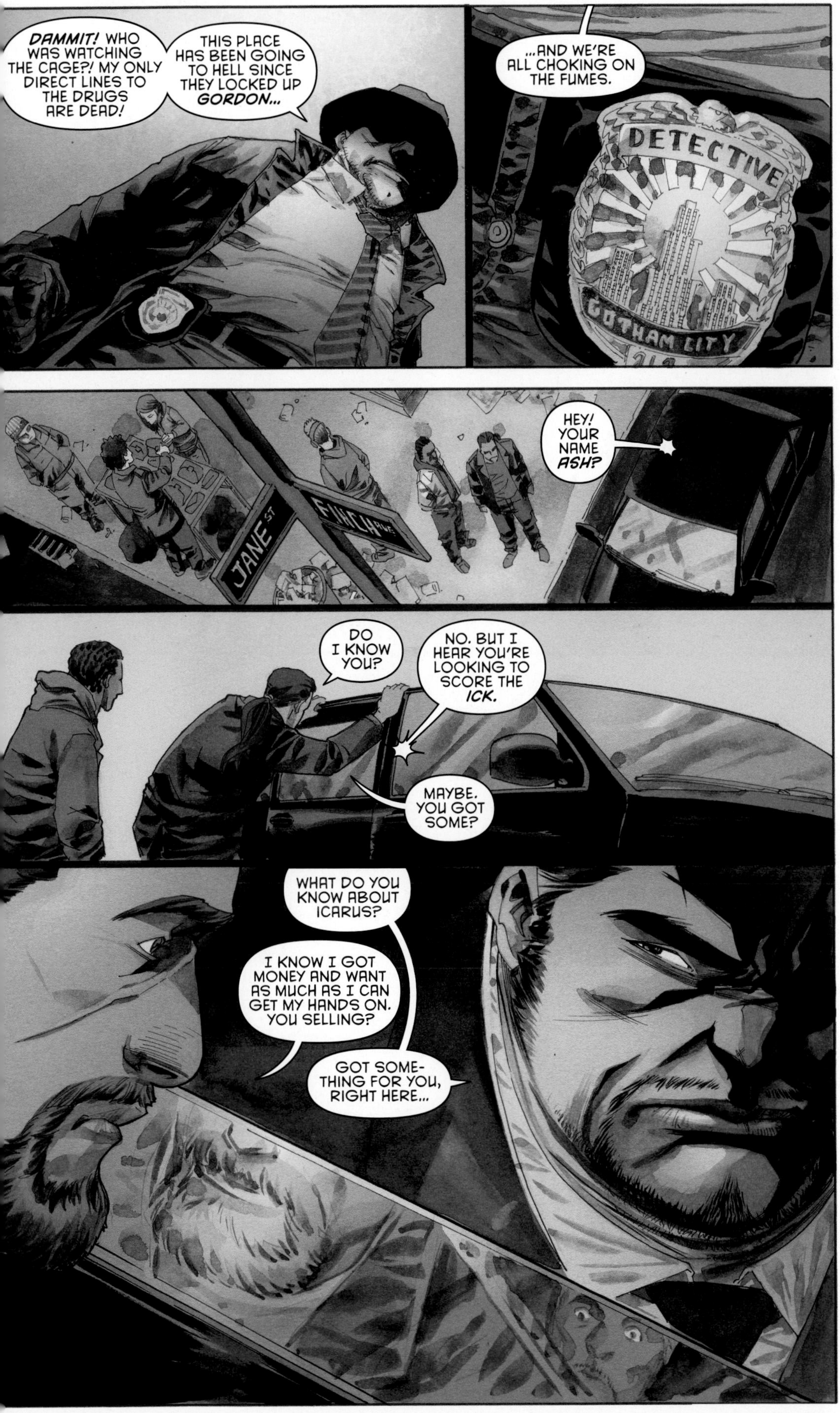
DAMMIT! WHO WAS WATCHING THE CAGE?! MY ONLY DIRECT LINES TO THE DRUGS ARE DEAD!
THIS PLACE HAS BEEN GOING TO HELL SINCE THEY LOCKED UP GORDON...
...AND WE'RE ALL CHOKING ON THE FUMES.
DETECTIVE
GOTHAM CITY
JANE ST
FINCH AVE
HEY! YOUR NAME ASH?
DO I KNOW YOU?
NO. BUT I HEAR YOU'RE LOOKING TO SCORE THE ICK.
MAYBE. YOU GOT SOME?
WHAT DO YOU KNOW ABOUT ICARUS?
I KNOW I GOT MONEY AND WANT AS MUCH AS I CAN GET MY HANDS ON. YOU SELLING?
GOT SOMETHING FOR YOU, RIGHT HERE...

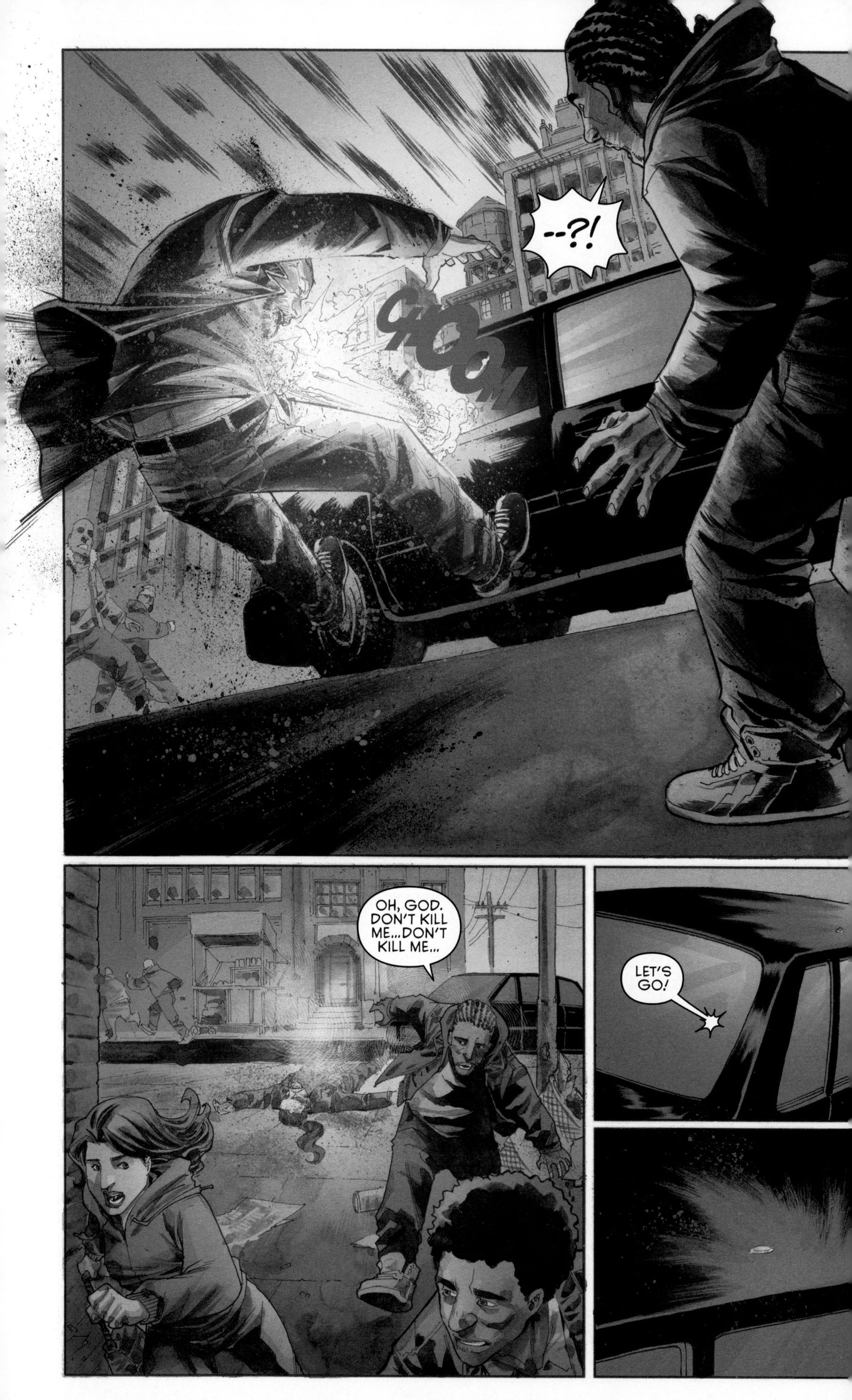
--?!
CHOOM
OH, GOD. DON'T KILL ME...DON'T KILL ME...
LET'S GO!

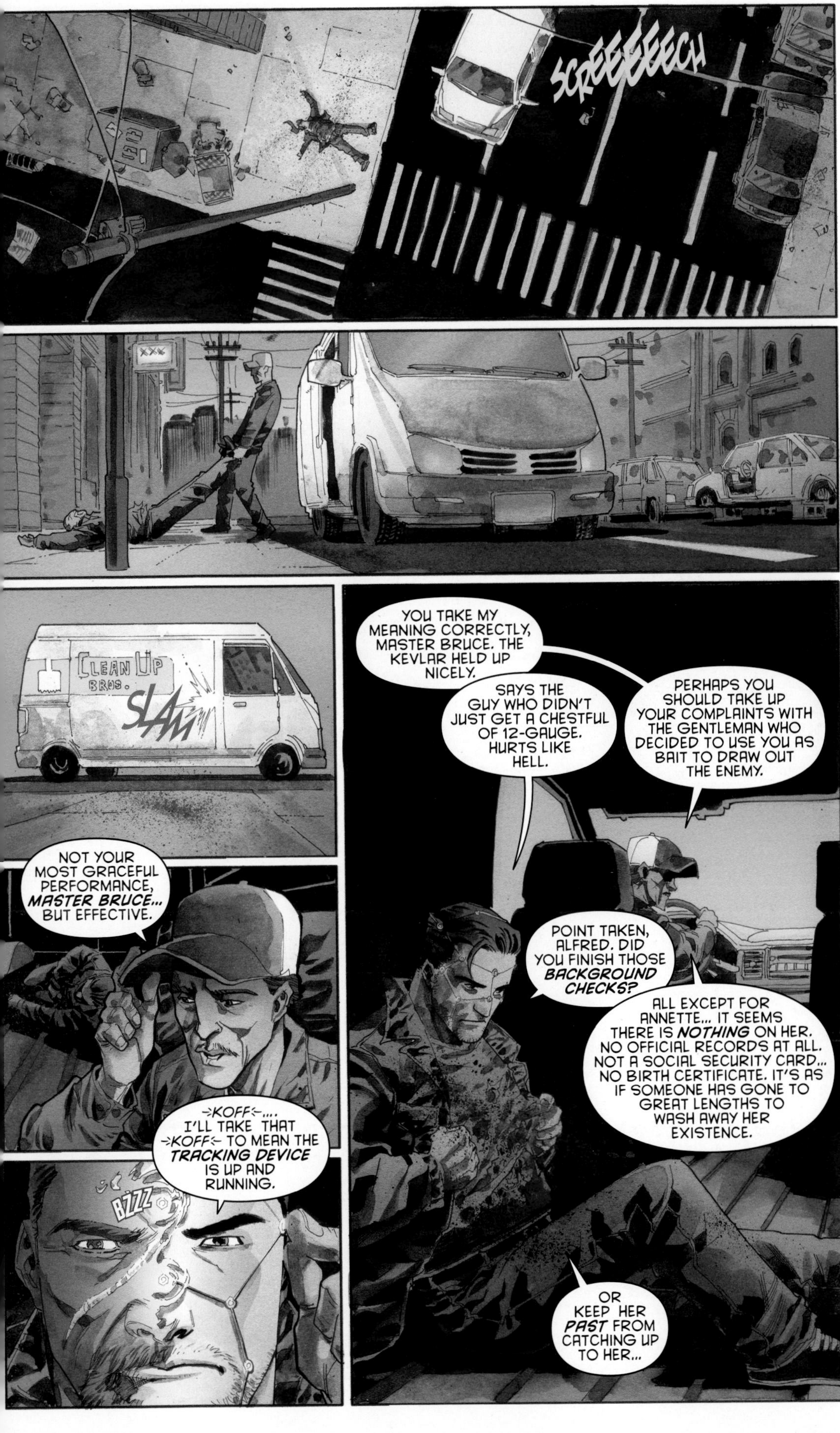
SCREEEEECH
CLEAN UP BROS.
SLAM
NOT YOUR MOST GRACEFUL PERFORMANCE, *MASTER BRUCE...* BUT EFFECTIVE.
BZZZ
-KOFF-.... I'LL TAKE THAT -KOFF- TO MEAN THE *TRACKING DEVICE* IS UP AND RUNNING.
YOU TAKE MY MEANING CORRECTLY, MASTER BRUCE. THE KEVLAR HELD UP NICELY.
SAYS THE GUY WHO DIDN'T JUST GET A CHESTFUL OF 12-GAUGE. HURTS LIKE HELL.
PERHAPS YOU SHOULD TAKE UP YOUR COMPLAINTS WITH THE GENTLEMAN WHO DECIDED TO USE YOU AS BAIT TO DRAW OUT THE ENEMY.
POINT TAKEN, ALFRED. DID YOU FINISH THOSE *BACKGROUND CHECKS?*
ALL EXCEPT FOR ANNETTE... IT SEEMS THERE IS *NOTHING* ON HER. NO OFFICIAL RECORDS AT ALL. NOT A SOCIAL SECURITY CARD... NO BIRTH CERTIFICATE. IT'S AS IF SOMEONE HAS GONE TO GREAT LENGTHS TO WASH AWAY HER EXISTENCE.
OR KEEP HER *PAST* FROM CATCHING UP TO HER...

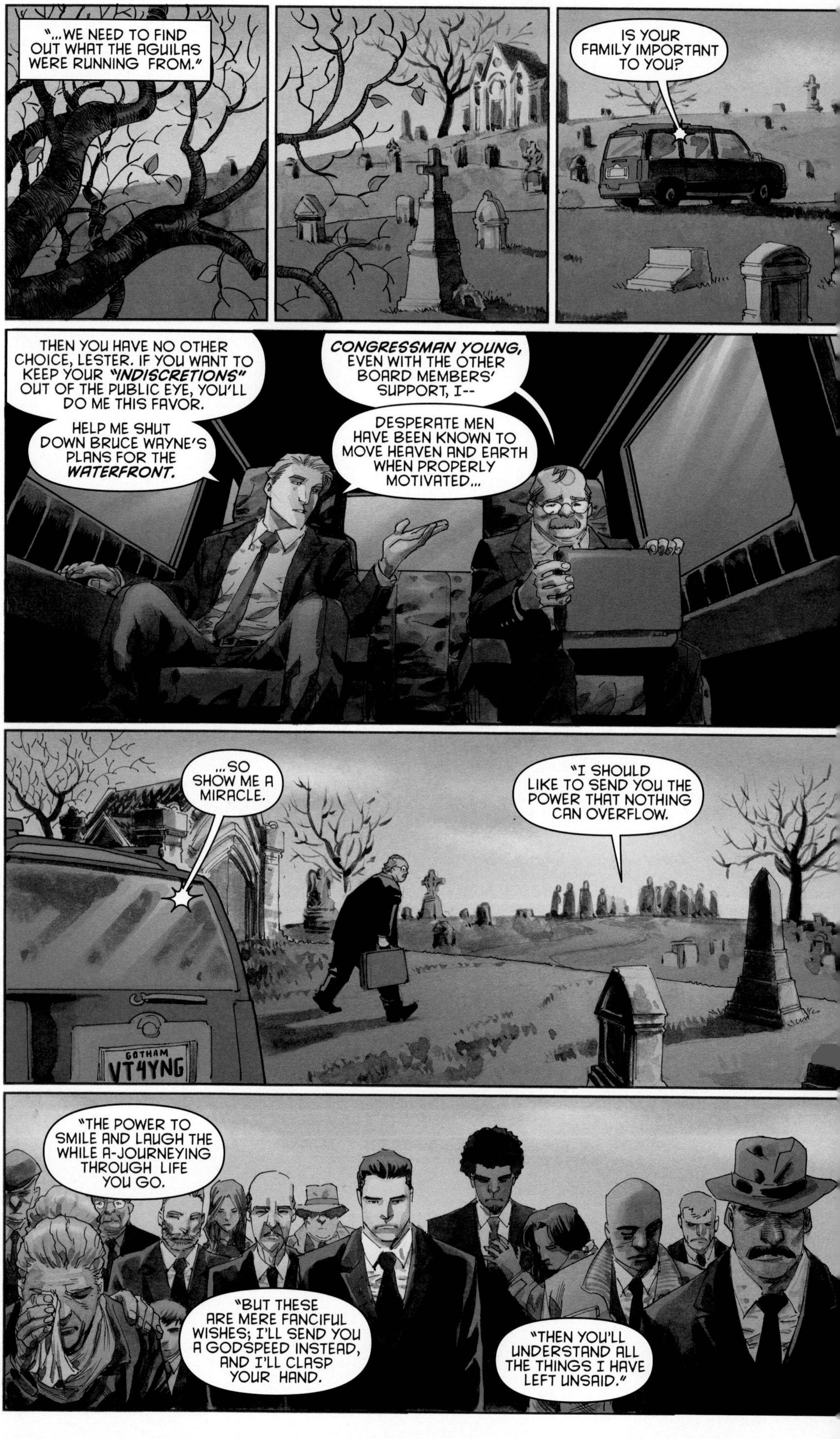
"...WE NEED TO FIND OUT WHAT THE AGUILAS WERE RUNNING FROM."
IS YOUR FAMILY IMPORTANT TO YOU?
THEN YOU HAVE NO OTHER CHOICE, LESTER. IF YOU WANT TO KEEP YOUR "INDISCRETIONS" OUT OF THE PUBLIC EYE, YOU'LL DO ME THIS FAVOR.
HELP ME SHUT DOWN BRUCE WAYNE'S PLANS FOR THE WATERFRONT.
CONGRESSMAN YOUNG, EVEN WITH THE OTHER BOARD MEMBERS' SUPPORT, I--
DESPERATE MEN HAVE BEEN KNOWN TO MOVE HEAVEN AND EARTH WHEN PROPERLY MOTIVATED...
...SO SHOW ME A MIRACLE.
"I SHOULD LIKE TO SEND YOU THE POWER THAT NOTHING CAN OVERFLOW.
GOTHAM
VT4YNG
"THE POWER TO SMILE AND LAUGH THE WHILE A-JOURNEYING THROUGH LIFE YOU GO.
"BUT THESE ARE MERE FANCIFUL WISHES; I'LL SEND YOU A GODSPEED INSTEAD, AND I'LL CLASP YOUR HAND.
"THEN YOU'LL UNDERSTAND ALL THE THINGS I HAVE LEFT UNSAID."

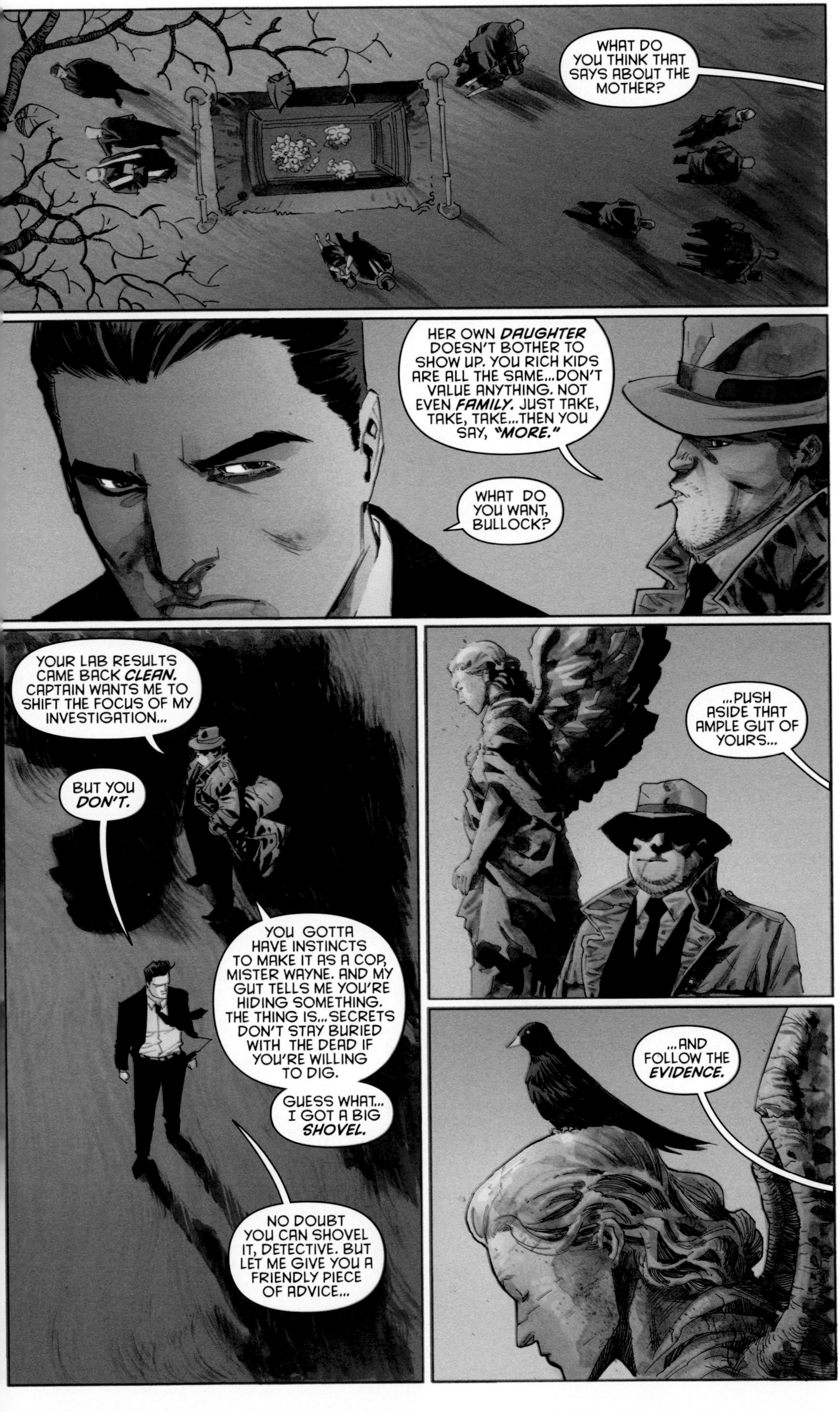
WHAT DO YOU THINK THAT SAYS ABOUT THE MOTHER?
HER OWN DAUGHTER DOESN'T BOTHER TO SHOW UP. YOU RICH KIDS ARE ALL THE SAME...DON'T VALUE ANYTHING. NOT EVEN FAMILY. JUST TAKE, TAKE, TAKE...THEN YOU SAY, "MORE."
WHAT DO YOU WANT, BULLOCK?
YOUR LAB RESULTS CAME BACK CLEAN. CAPTAIN WANTS ME TO SHIFT THE FOCUS OF MY INVESTIGATION...
BUT YOU DON'T.
YOU GOTTA HAVE INSTINCTS TO MAKE IT AS A COP, MISTER WAYNE. AND MY GUT TELLS ME YOU'RE HIDING SOMETHING. THE THING IS...SECRETS DON'T STAY BURIED WITH THE DEAD IF YOU'RE WILLING TO DIG.
GUESS WHAT... I GOT A BIG SHOVEL.
NO DOUBT YOU CAN SHOVEL IT, DETECTIVE. BUT LET ME GIVE YOU A FRIENDLY PIECE OF ADVICE...
...PUSH ASIDE THAT AMPLE GUT OF YOURS...
...AND FOLLOW THE EVIDENCE.

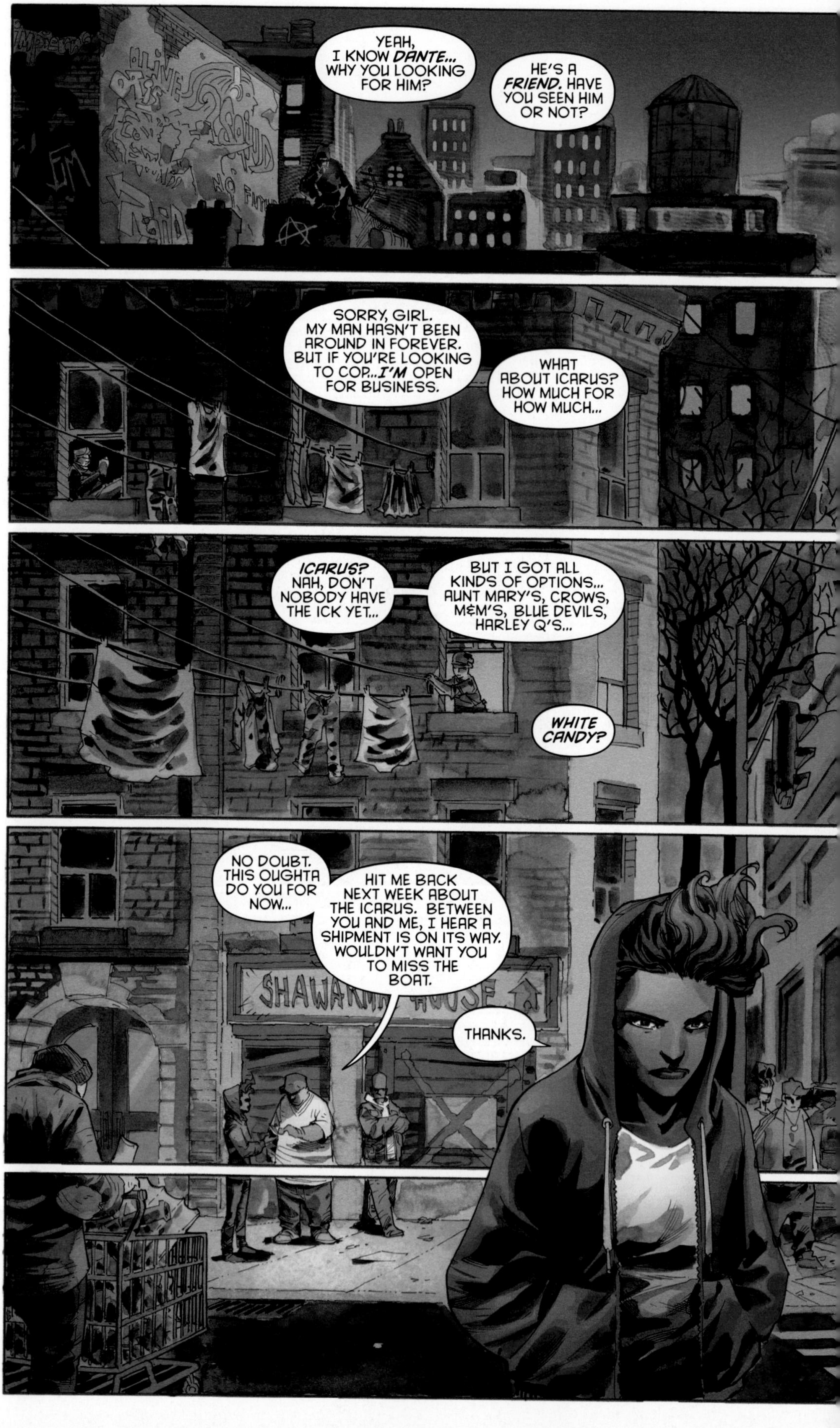
YEAH, I KNOW DANTE... WHY YOU LOOKING FOR HIM?
HE'S A FRIEND. HAVE YOU SEEN HIM OR NOT?
SORRY, GIRL. MY MAN HASN'T BEEN AROUND IN FOREVER. BUT IF YOU'RE LOOKING TO COP...I'M OPEN FOR BUSINESS.
WHAT ABOUT ICARUS? HOW MUCH FOR HOW MUCH...
ICARUS? NAH, DON'T NOBODY HAVE THE ICK YET...
BUT I GOT ALL KINDS OF OPTIONS... AUNT MARY'S, CROWS, M&M'S, BLUE DEVILS, HARLEY Q'S...
WHITE CANDY?
NO DOUBT. THIS OUGHTA DO YOU FOR NOW...
HIT ME BACK NEXT WEEK ABOUT THE ICARUS. BETWEEN YOU AND ME, I HEAR A SHIPMENT IS ON ITS WAY. WOULDN'T WANT YOU TO MISS THE BOAT.
THANKS.
SHAWARMA HOUSE

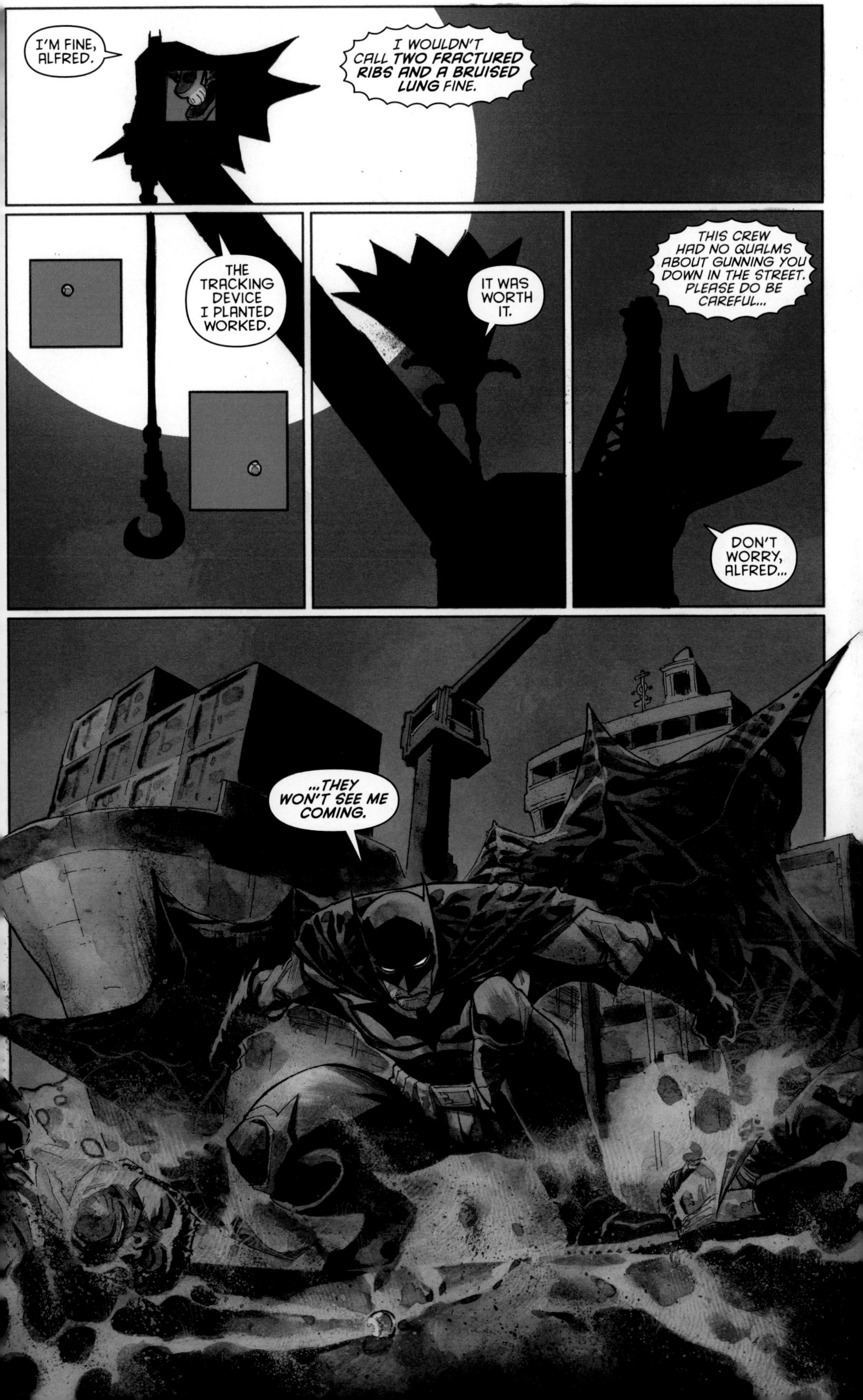
I'M FINE, ALFRED.
I WOULDN'T CALL TWO FRACTURED RIBS AND A BRUISED LUNG FINE.
THE TRACKING DEVICE I PLANTED WORKED.
IT WAS WORTH IT.
THIS CREW HAD NO QUALMS ABOUT GUNNING YOU DOWN IN THE STREET. PLEASE DO BE CAREFUL...
DON'T WORRY, ALFRED...
...THEY WON'T SEE ME COMING.

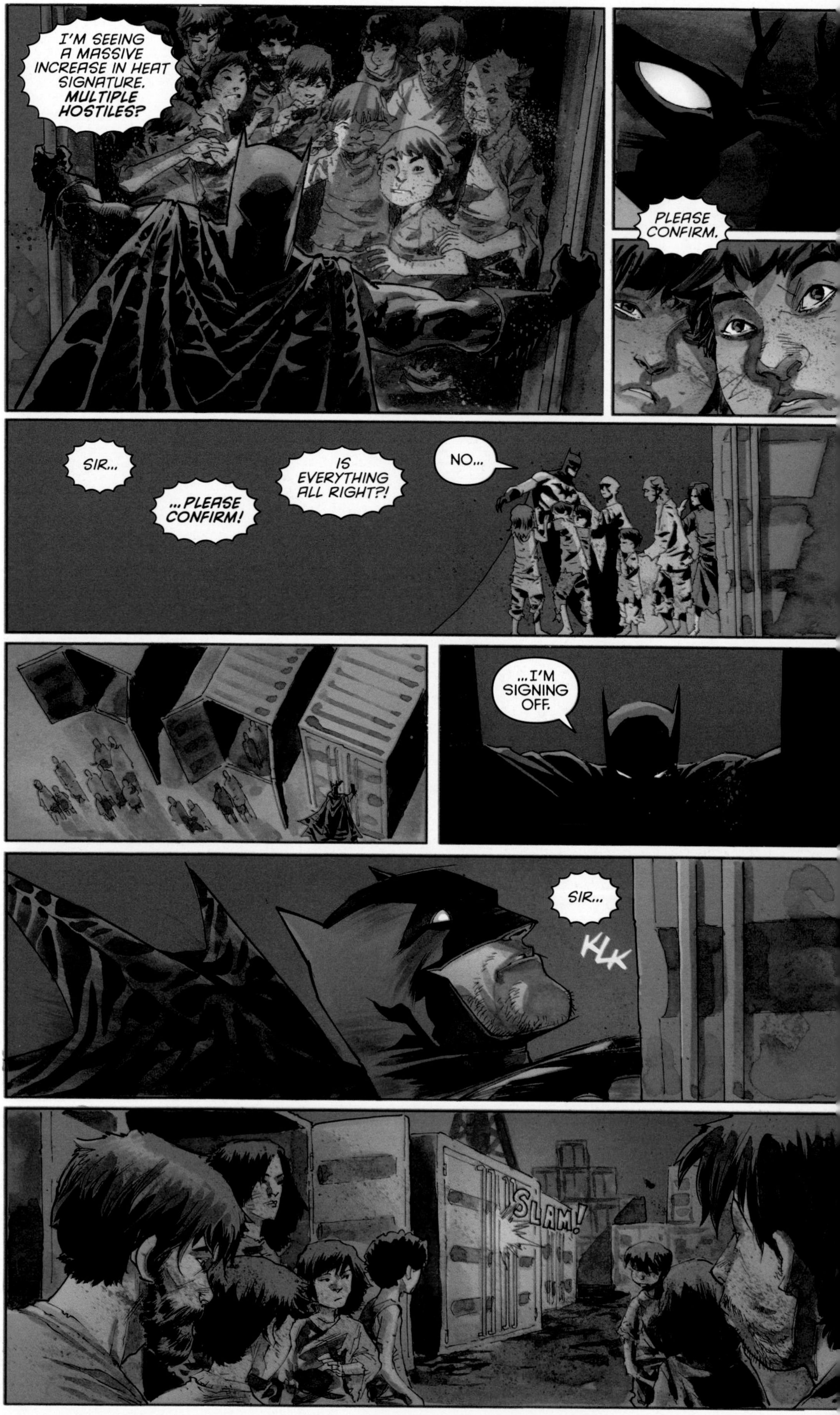
I'M SEEING A MASSIVE INCREASE IN HEAT SIGNATURE. MULTIPLE HOSTILES?
PLEASE CONFIRM.
SIR...
...PLEASE CONFIRM!
IS EVERYTHING ALL RIGHT?!
NO...
...I'M SIGNING OFF.
SIR...
KLK
SLAM!

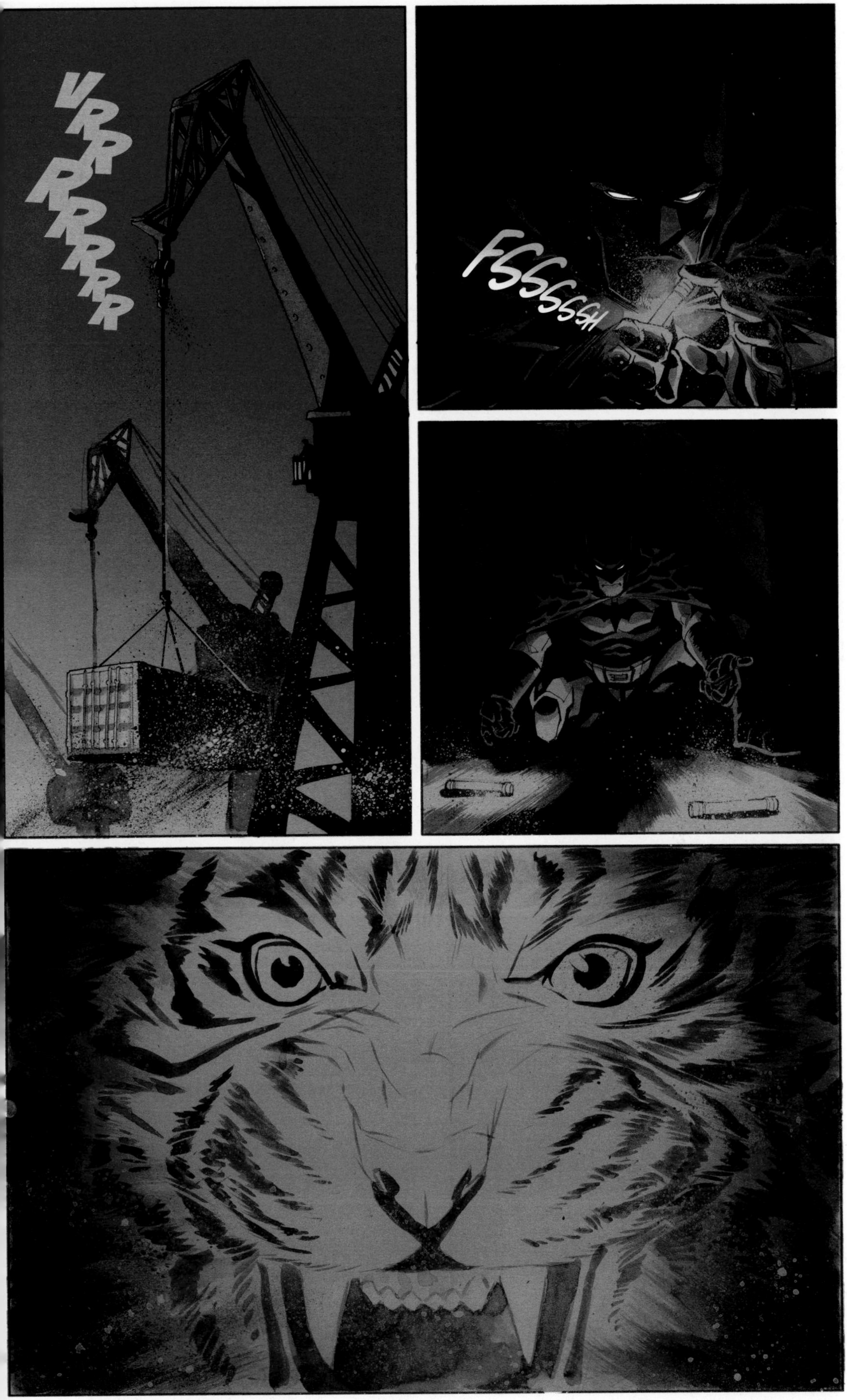
VRRRRRRR
FSSSSSSH

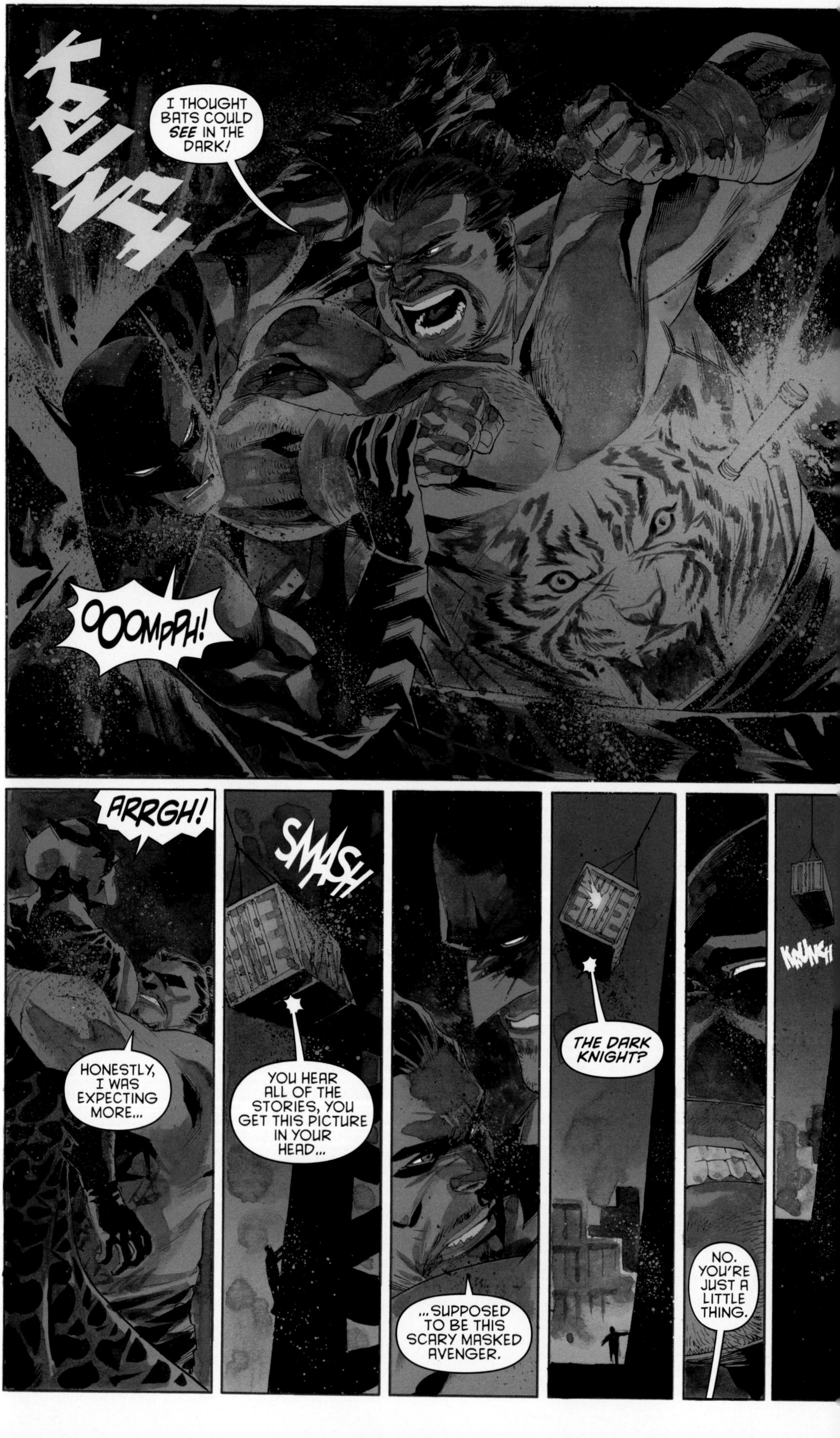
KRUNCH
I THOUGHT BATS COULD SEE IN THE DARK!
OOOMPPH!
ARRGH!
HONESTLY, I WAS EXPECTING MORE...
SMASH
YOU HEAR ALL OF THE STORIES, YOU GET THIS PICTURE IN YOUR HEAD...
...SUPPOSED TO BE THIS SCARY MASKED AVENGER.
THE DARK KNIGHT?
KRUNCH
NO. YOU'RE JUST A LITTLE THING.

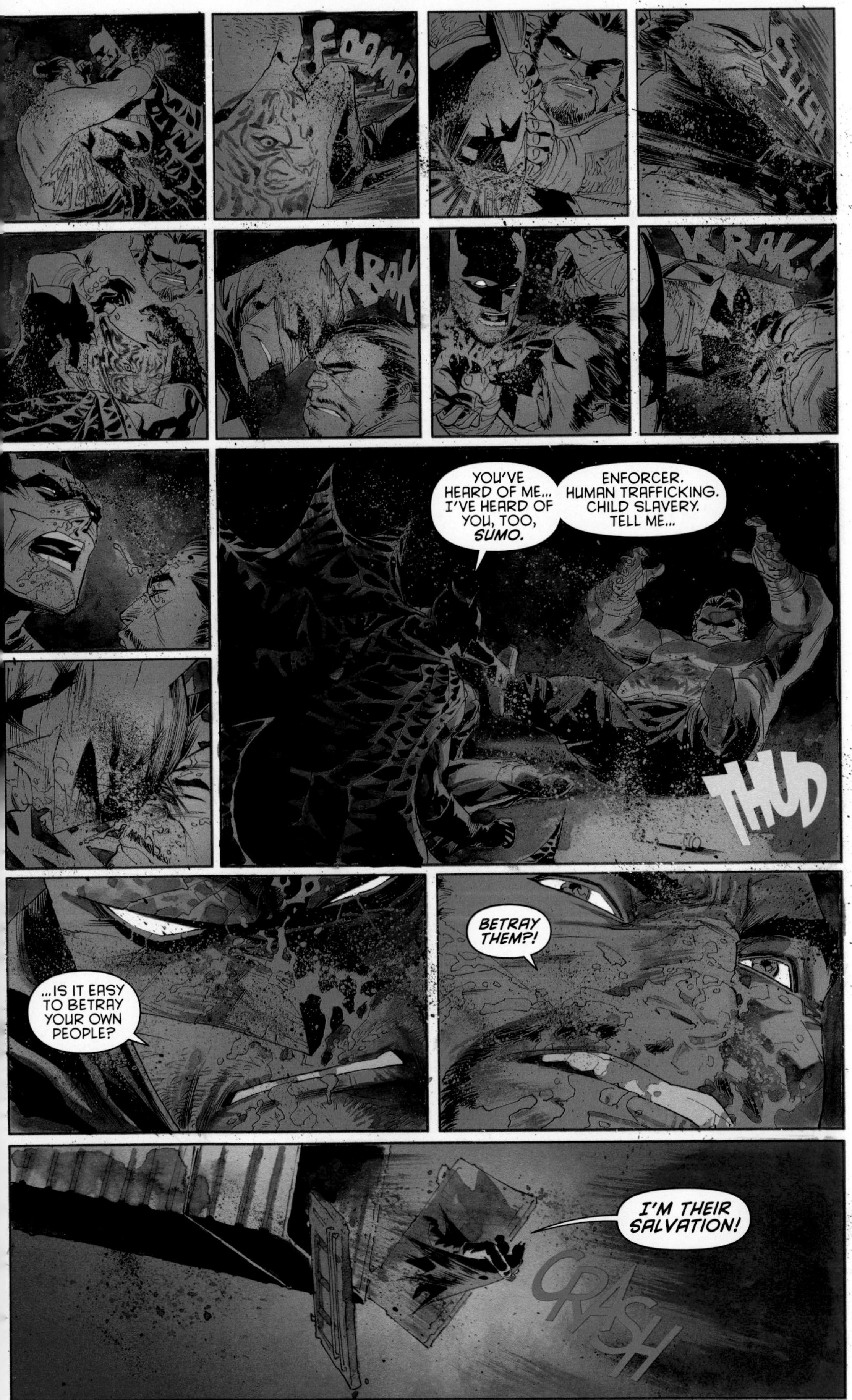
FOOMP
KRAK
KRAK!
YOU'VE HEARD OF ME... I'VE HEARD OF YOU, TOO, SUMO.
ENFORCER. HUMAN TRAFFICKING. CHILD SLAVERY. TELL ME...
THUD
...IS IT EASY TO BETRAY YOUR OWN PEOPLE?
BETRAY THEM?!
I'M THEIR SALVATION!
CRASH

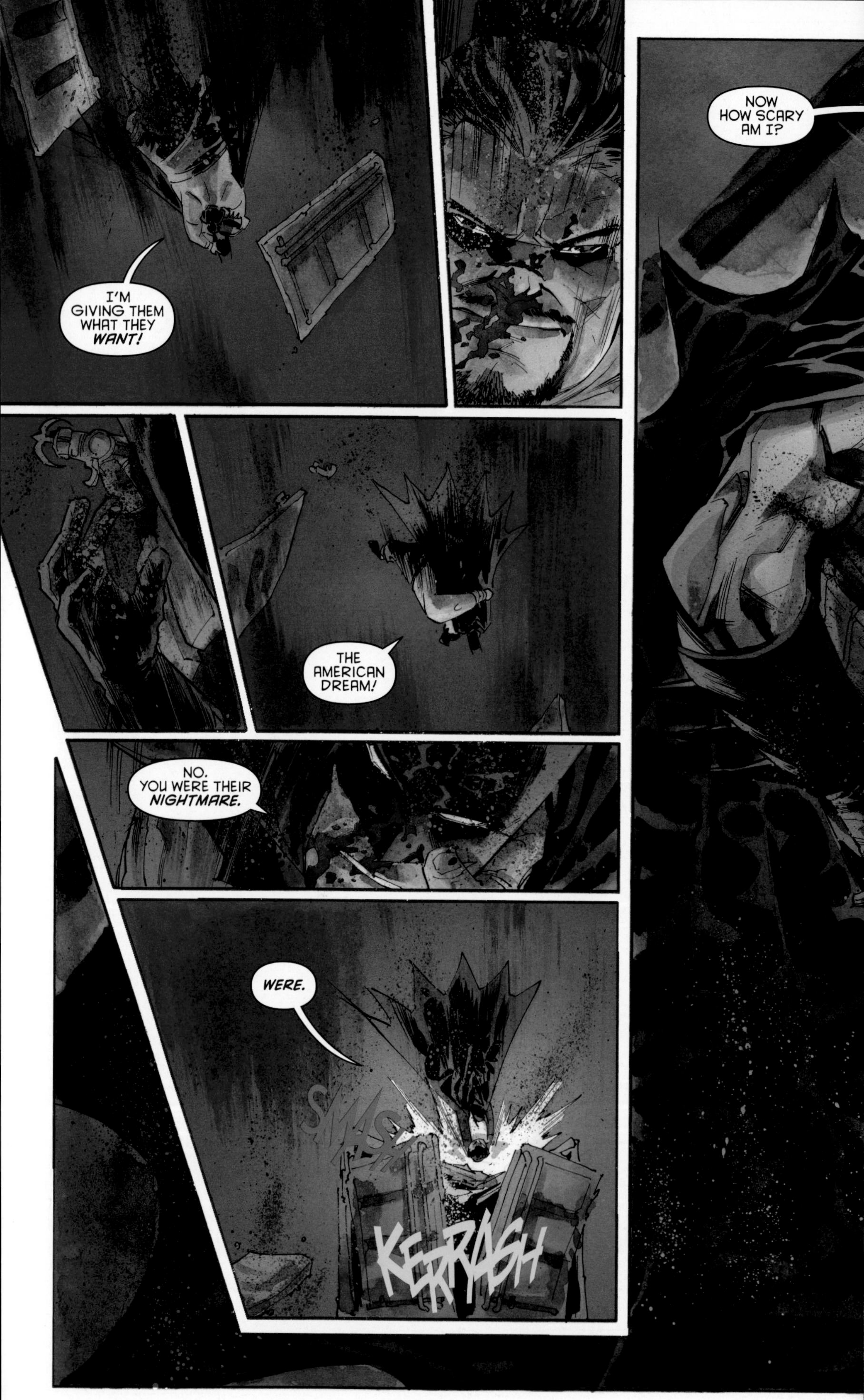
I'M GIVING THEM WHAT THEY *WANT!*
NOW HOW SCARY AM I?
THE AMERICAN DREAM!
NO. YOU WERE THEIR *NIGHTMARE.*
WERE.
SMASH
KERRASH

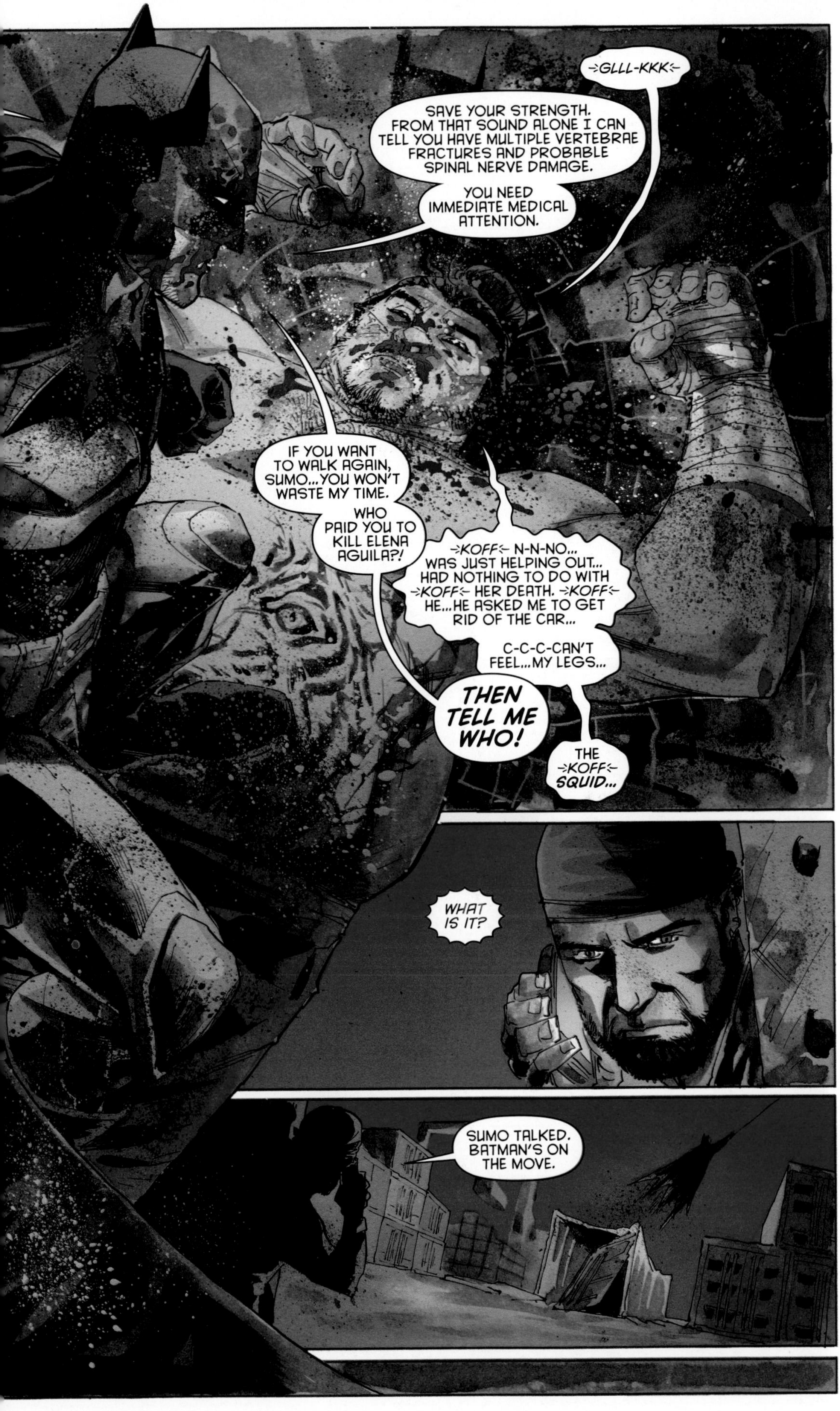

-GLLL-KKK-
SAVE YOUR STRENGTH. FROM THAT SOUND ALONE I CAN TELL YOU HAVE MULTIPLE VERTEBRAE FRACTURES AND PROBABLE SPINAL NERVE DAMAGE.
YOU NEED IMMEDIATE MEDICAL ATTENTION.
IF YOU WANT TO WALK AGAIN, SUMO...YOU WON'T WASTE MY TIME.
WHO PAID YOU TO KILL ELENA AGUILA?!
-KOFF- N-N-NO... WAS JUST HELPING OUT... HAD NOTHING TO DO WITH -KOFF- HER DEATH. -KOFF- HE...HE ASKED ME TO GET RID OF THE CAR...
C-C-C-CAN'T FEEL...MY LEGS...
THEN TELL ME WHO!
THE -KOFF- SQUID...
WHAT IS IT?
SUMO TALKED. BATMAN'S ON THE MOVE.

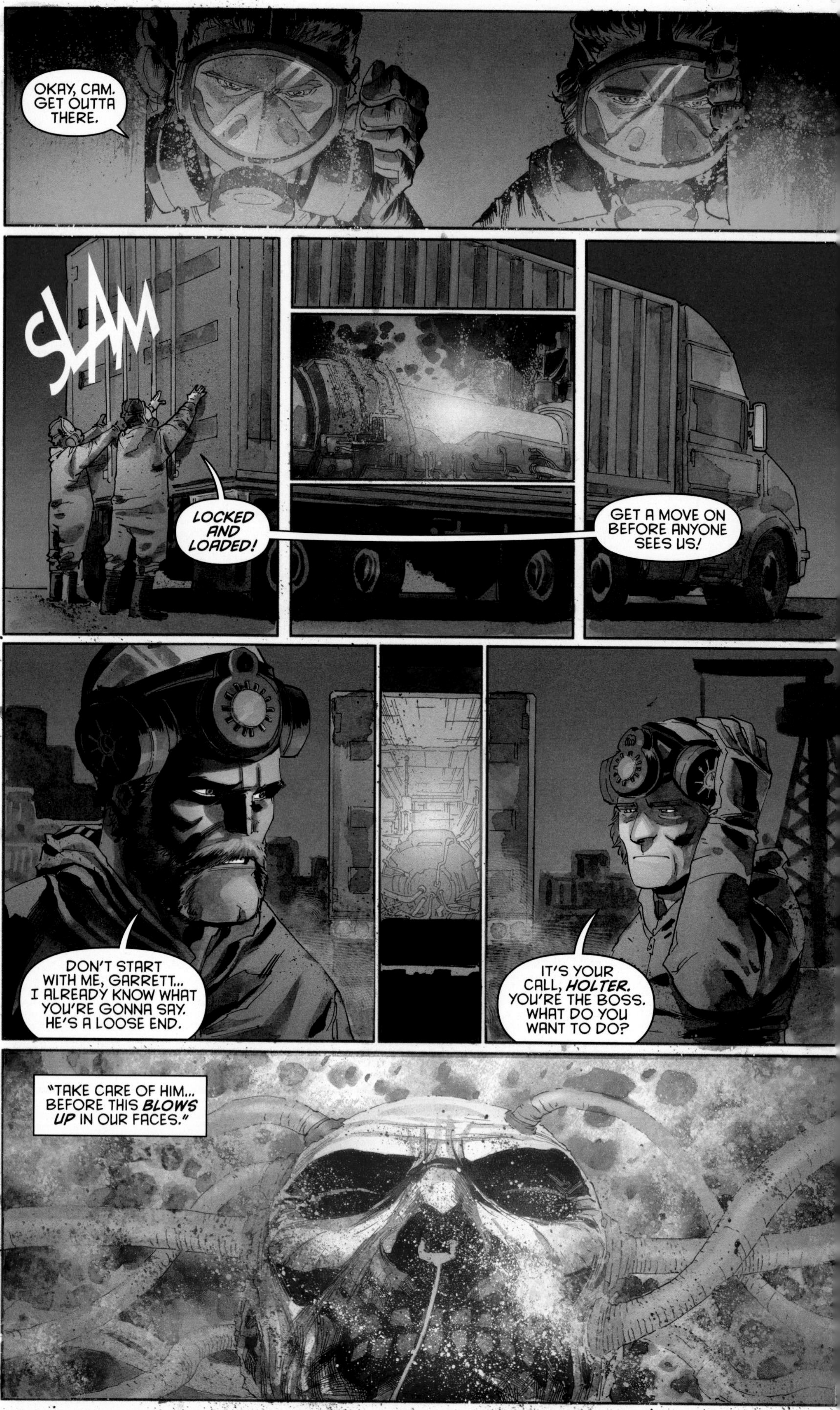
OKAY, CAM. GET OUTTA THERE.
SLAM
LOCKED AND LOADED!
GET A MOVE ON BEFORE ANYONE SEES US!
DON'T START WITH ME, GARRETT... I ALREADY KNOW WHAT YOU'RE GONNA SAY. HE'S A LOOSE END.
IT'S YOUR CALL, HOLTER. YOU'RE THE BOSS. WHAT DO YOU WANT TO DO?
"TAKE CARE OF HIM... BEFORE THIS BLOWS UP IN OUR FACES."

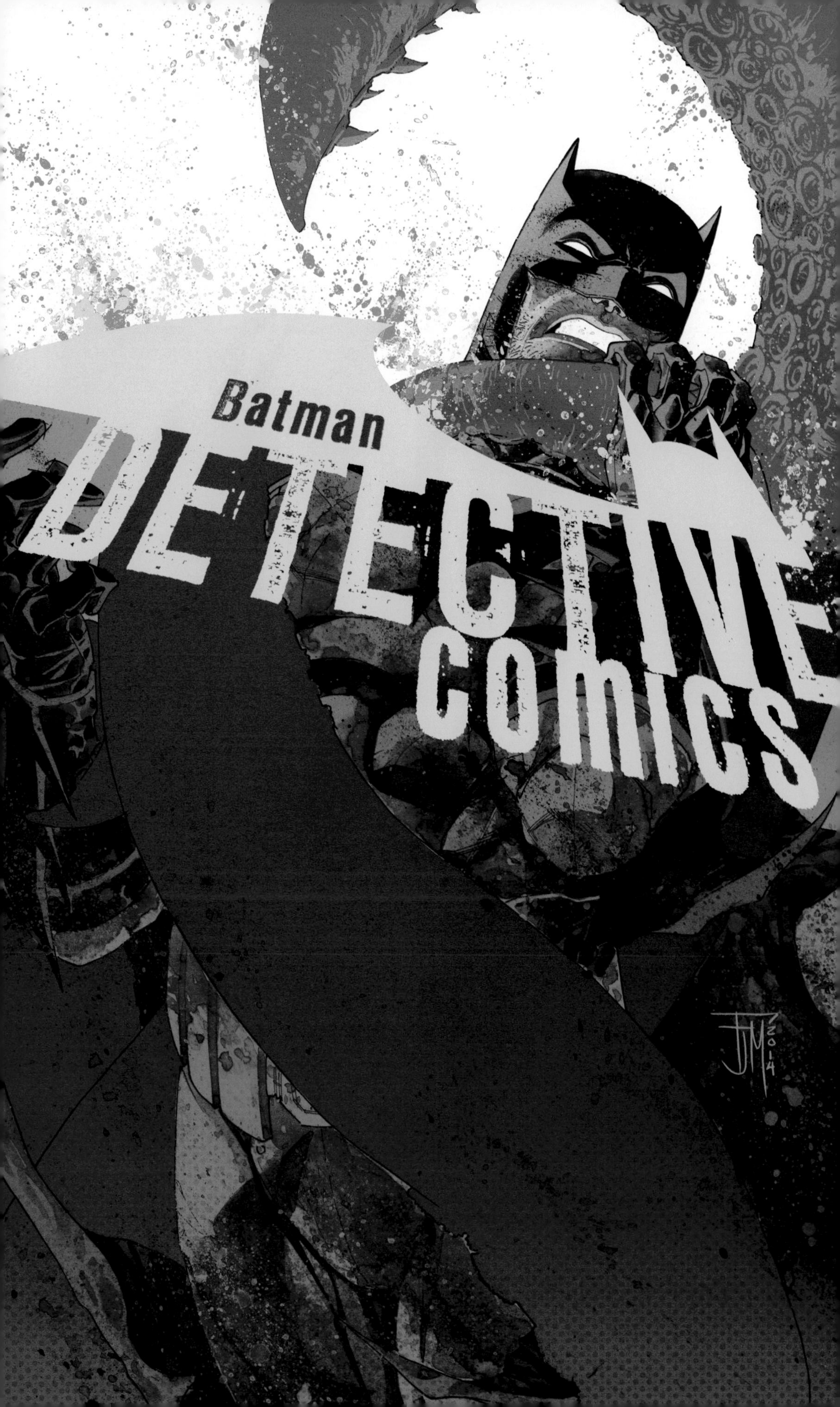
Batman
DETECTIVE
COMICS
FJM
2014

A

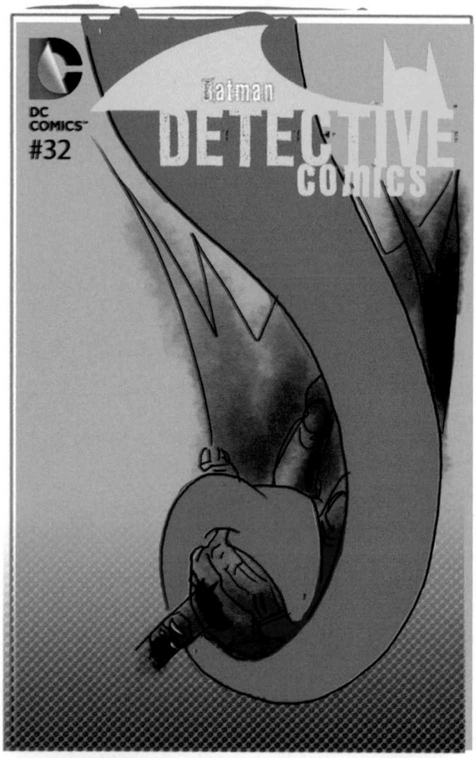
DC
COMICS™
#32
Batman
DETECTIVE
comics

B

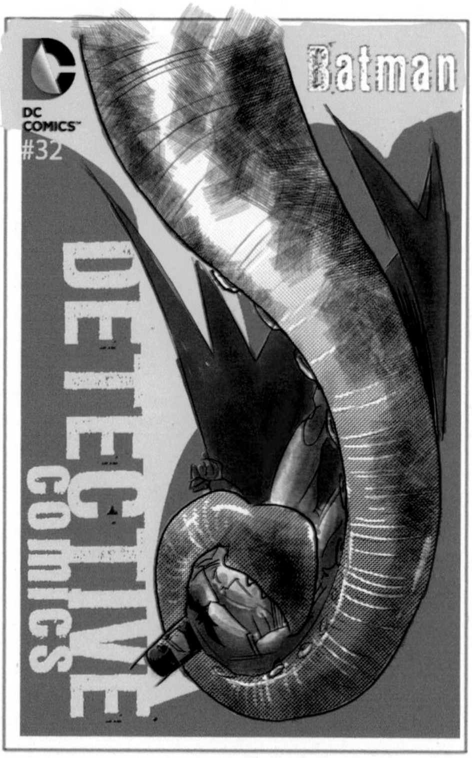
DC
COMICS™
#32
Batman
DETECTIVE
comics

C

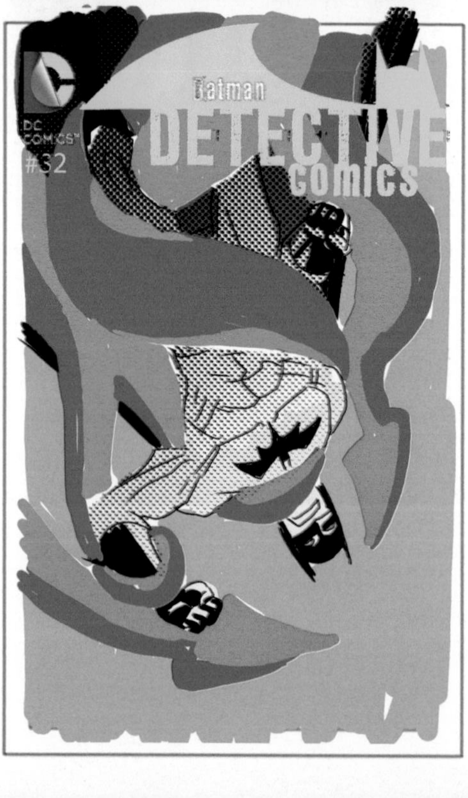
DC
COMICS™
#32
Batman
DETECTIVE
comics

D

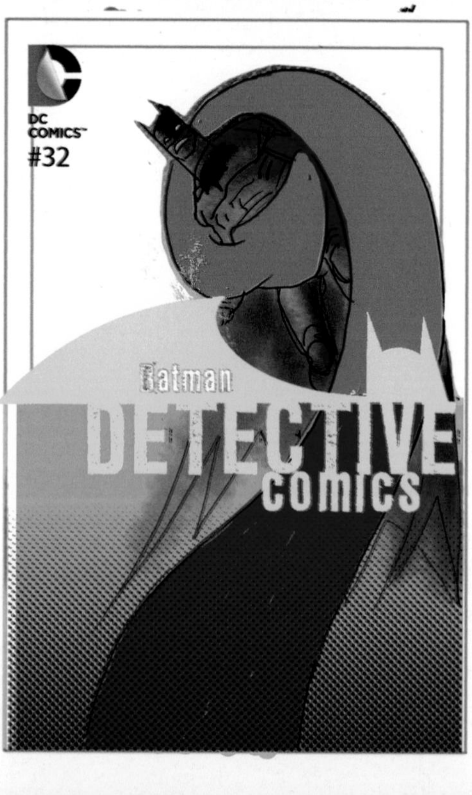
DC
COMICS™
#32
Batman
DETECTIVE
comics

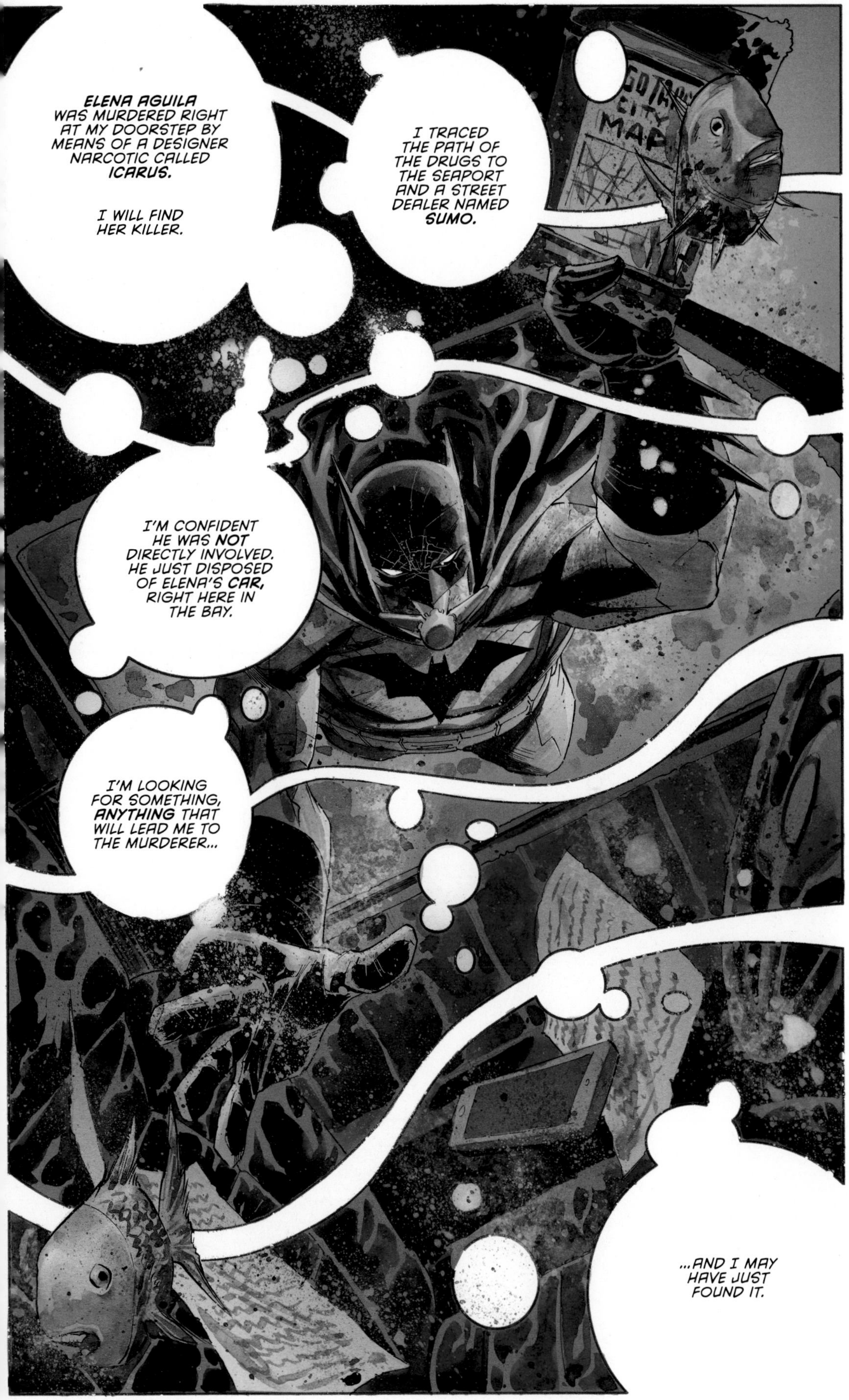
ELENA AGUILA WAS MURDERED RIGHT AT MY DOORSTEP BY MEANS OF A DESIGNER NARCOTIC CALLED ICARUS.
I WILL FIND HER KILLER.
I TRACED THE PATH OF THE DRUGS TO THE SEAPORT AND A STREET DEALER NAMED SUMO.
GOTHAM CITY MAP
I'M CONFIDENT HE WAS NOT DIRECTLY INVOLVED. HE JUST DISPOSED OF ELENA'S CAR, RIGHT HERE IN THE BAY.
I'M LOOKING FOR SOMETHING, ANYTHING THAT WILL LEAD ME TO THE MURDERER...
...AND I MAY HAVE JUST FOUND IT.

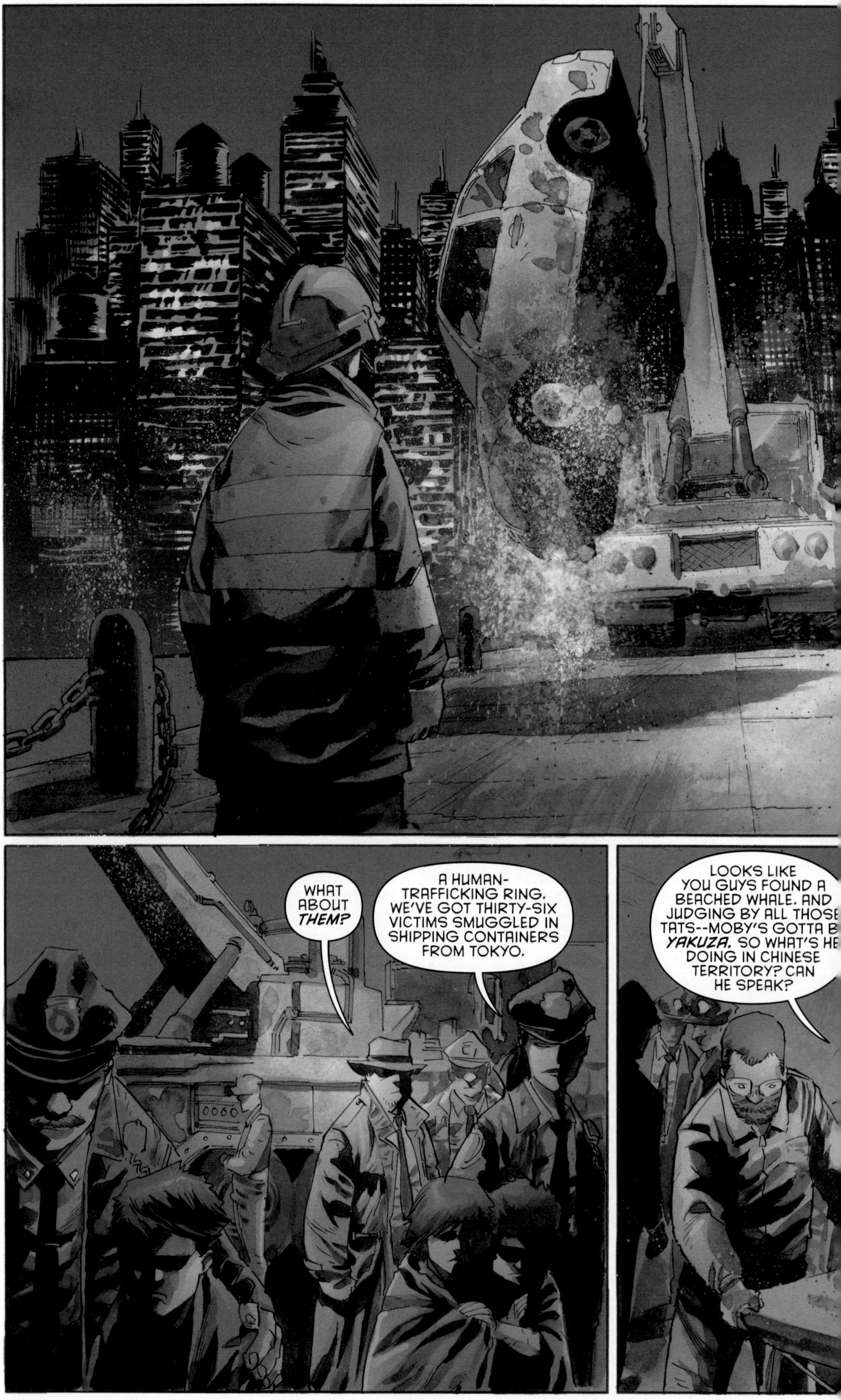

WHAT ABOUT *THEM?*
A HUMAN-TRAFFICKING RING. WE'VE GOT THIRTY-SIX VICTIMS SMUGGLED IN SHIPPING CONTAINERS FROM TOKYO.
LOOKS LIKE YOU GUYS FOUND A BEACHED WHALE. AND JUDGING BY ALL THOSE TATS--MOBY'S GOTTA B *YAKUZA.* SO WHAT'S HE DOING IN CHINESE TERRITORY? CAN HE SPEAK?

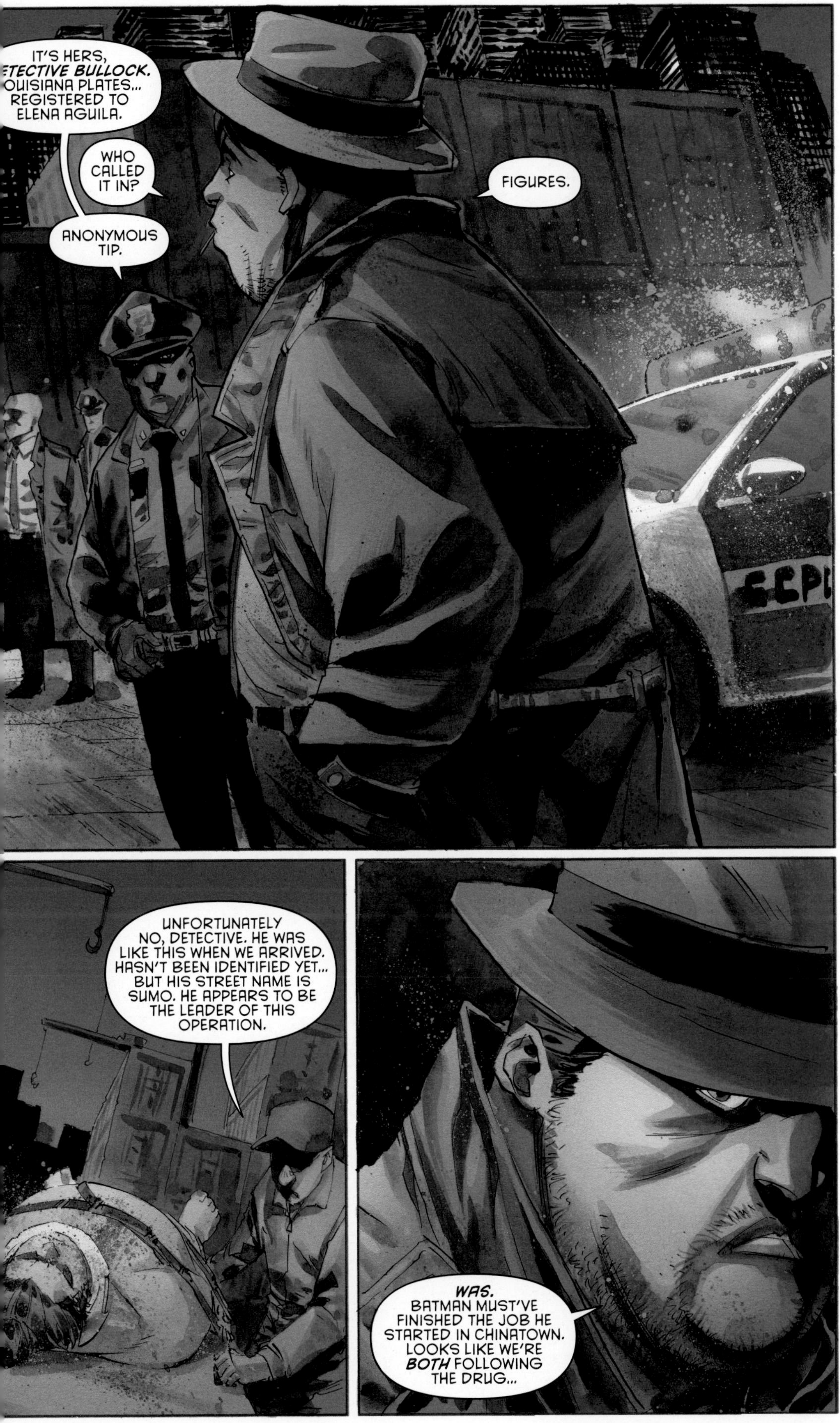
IT'S HERS, ETECTIVE BULLOCK. OUISIANA PLATES... REGISTERED TO ELENA AGUILA.
WHO CALLED IT IN?
ANONYMOUS TIP.
FIGURES.
UNFORTUNATELY NO, DETECTIVE. HE WAS LIKE THIS WHEN WE ARRIVED. HASN'T BEEN IDENTIFIED YET... BUT HIS STREET NAME IS SUMO. HE APPEARS TO BE THE LEADER OF THIS OPERATION.
WAS. BATMAN MUST'VE FINISHED THE JOB HE STARTED IN CHINATOWN. LOOKS LIKE WE'RE BOTH FOLLOWING THE DRUG...

DAMMIT. HE'S ONE STEP AHEAD OF ME.

SIR?

DON'T CALL ME "SIR." I LOOK LIKE YOUR *FATHER* OR SOMETHING?

NO, S-- DETECTIVE.

JUST SHUT IT, WILLYA?! POINT IS, BATMAN'S *ALREADY* BEEN HERE...

THERE ARE HAND MARKS ON THE WINDOW AND DOOR...AND HE MUST'VE GRABBED HOLD OF THE VISOR. SEE HOW IT'S WARPED?

MAYBE *HE* CALLED IN THE TIP.

YOU FIGURE THAT OUT ALL BY YOURSELF, PAL?

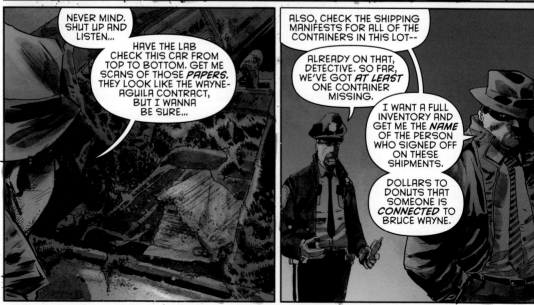

NEVER MIND. SHUT UP AND LISTEN...

HAVE THE LAB CHECK THIS CAR FROM TOP TO BOTTOM. GET ME SCANS OF THOSE *PAPERS*. THEY LOOK LIKE THE WAYNE-AGUILA CONTRACT, BUT I WANNA BE SURE...

ALSO, CHECK THE SHIPPING MANIFESTS FOR ALL OF THE CONTAINERS IN THIS LOT--

ALREADY ON THAT, DETECTIVE. SO FAR, WE'VE GOT *AT LEAST* ONE CONTAINER MISSING.

I WANT A FULL INVENTORY AND GET ME THE *NAME* OF THE PERSON WHO SIGNED OFF ON THESE SHIPMENTS.

DOLLARS TO DONUTS THAT SOMEONE IS *CONNECTED* TO BRUCE WAYNE.

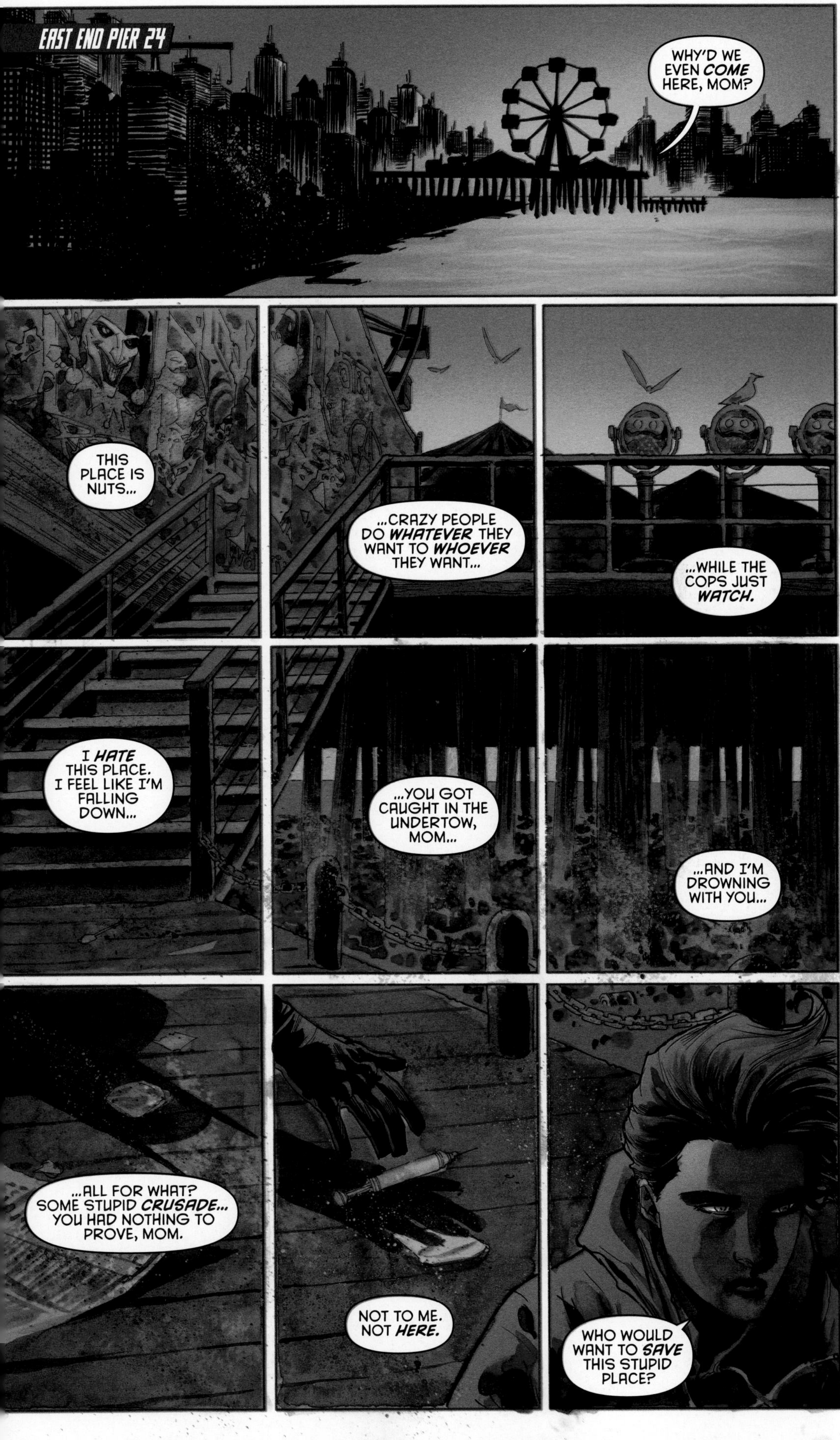
EAST END PIER 24
WHY'D WE EVEN COME HERE, MOM?
THIS PLACE IS NUTS...
...CRAZY PEOPLE DO WHATEVER THEY WANT TO WHOEVER THEY WANT...
...WHILE THE COPS JUST WATCH.
I HATE THIS PLACE. I FEEL LIKE I'M FALLING DOWN...
...YOU GOT CAUGHT IN THE UNDERTOW, MOM...
...AND I'M DROWNING WITH YOU...
...ALL FOR WHAT? SOME STUPID CRUSADE... YOU HAD NOTHING TO PROVE, MOM.
NOT TO ME. NOT HERE.
WHO WOULD WANT TO SAVE THIS STUPID PLACE?

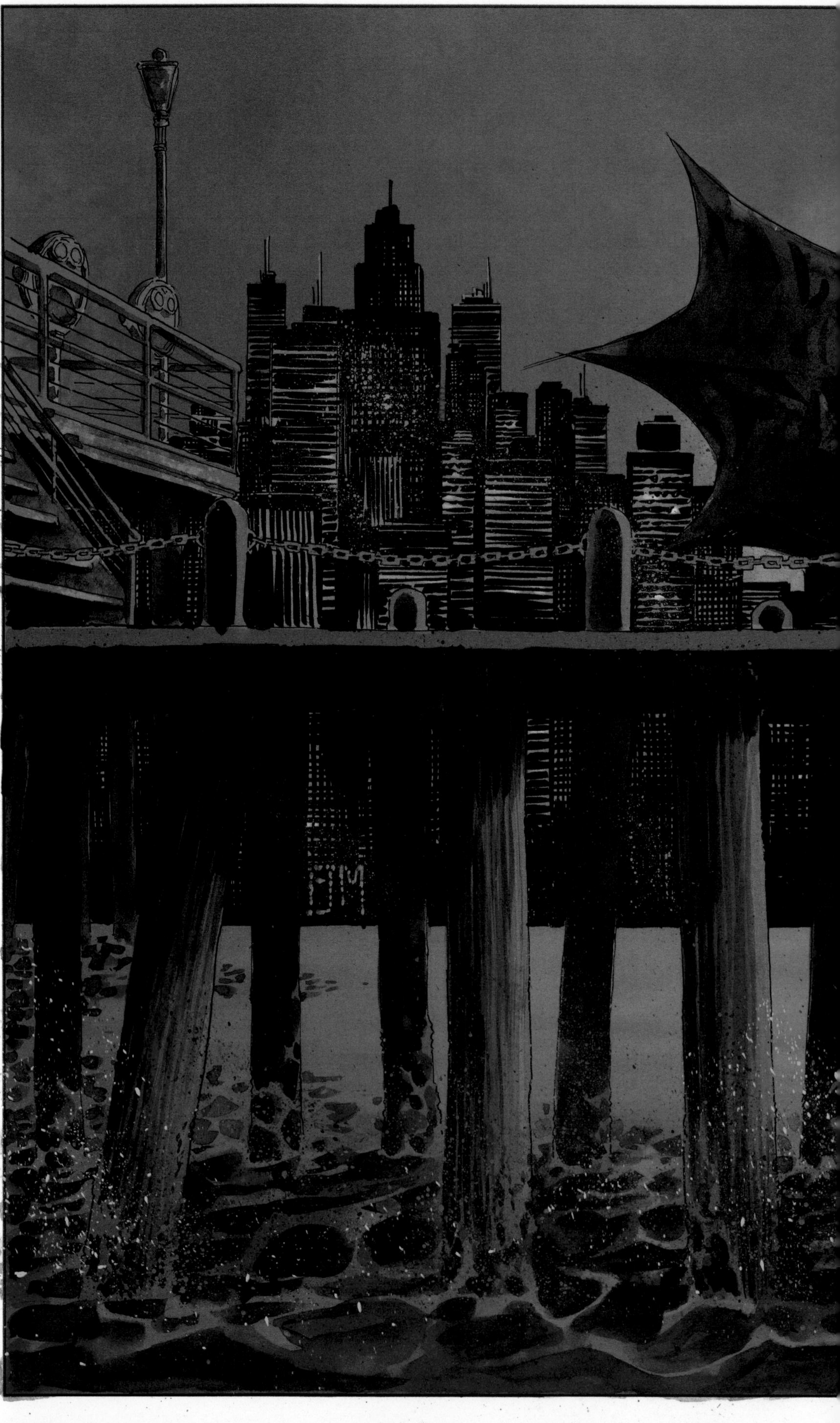

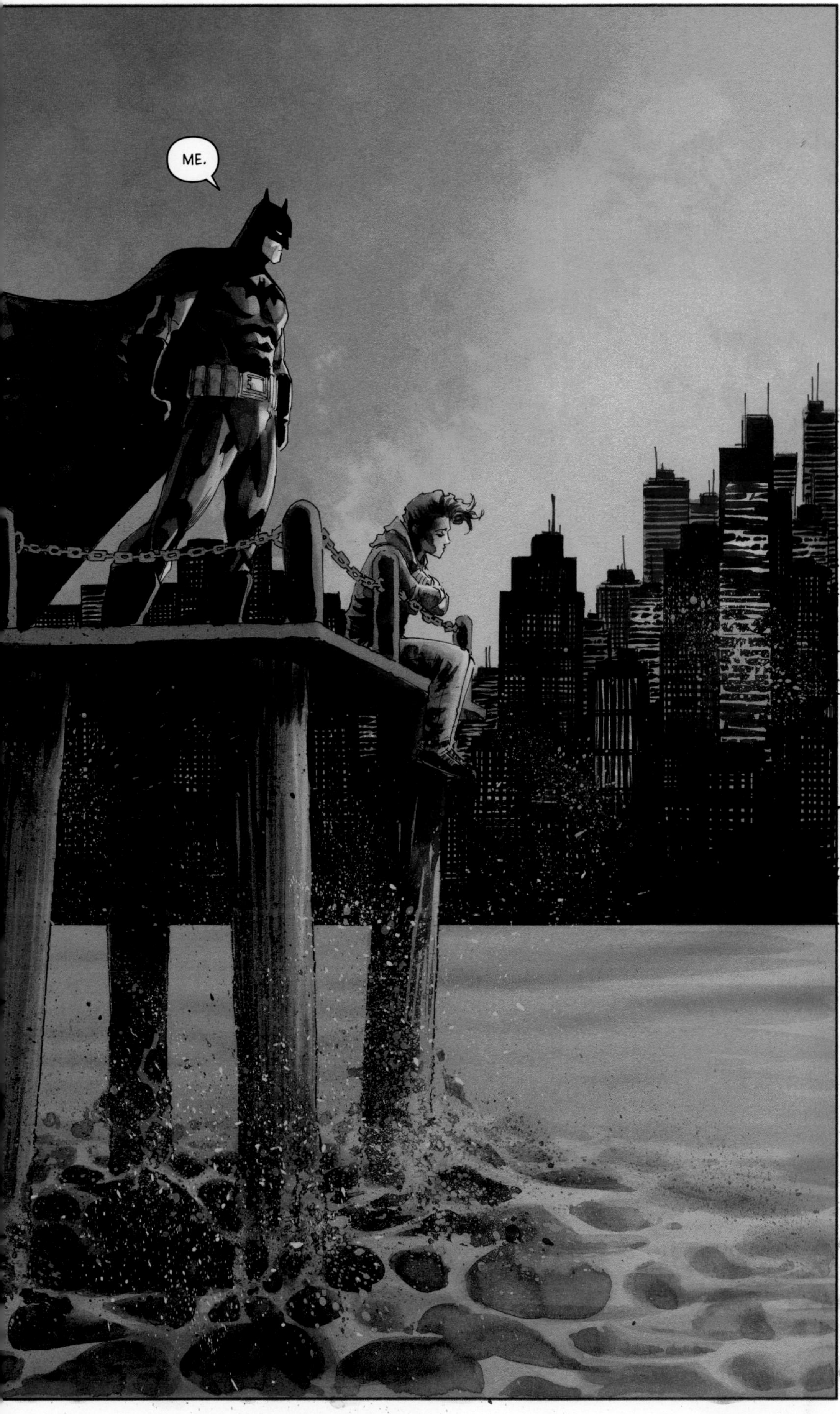
ME.

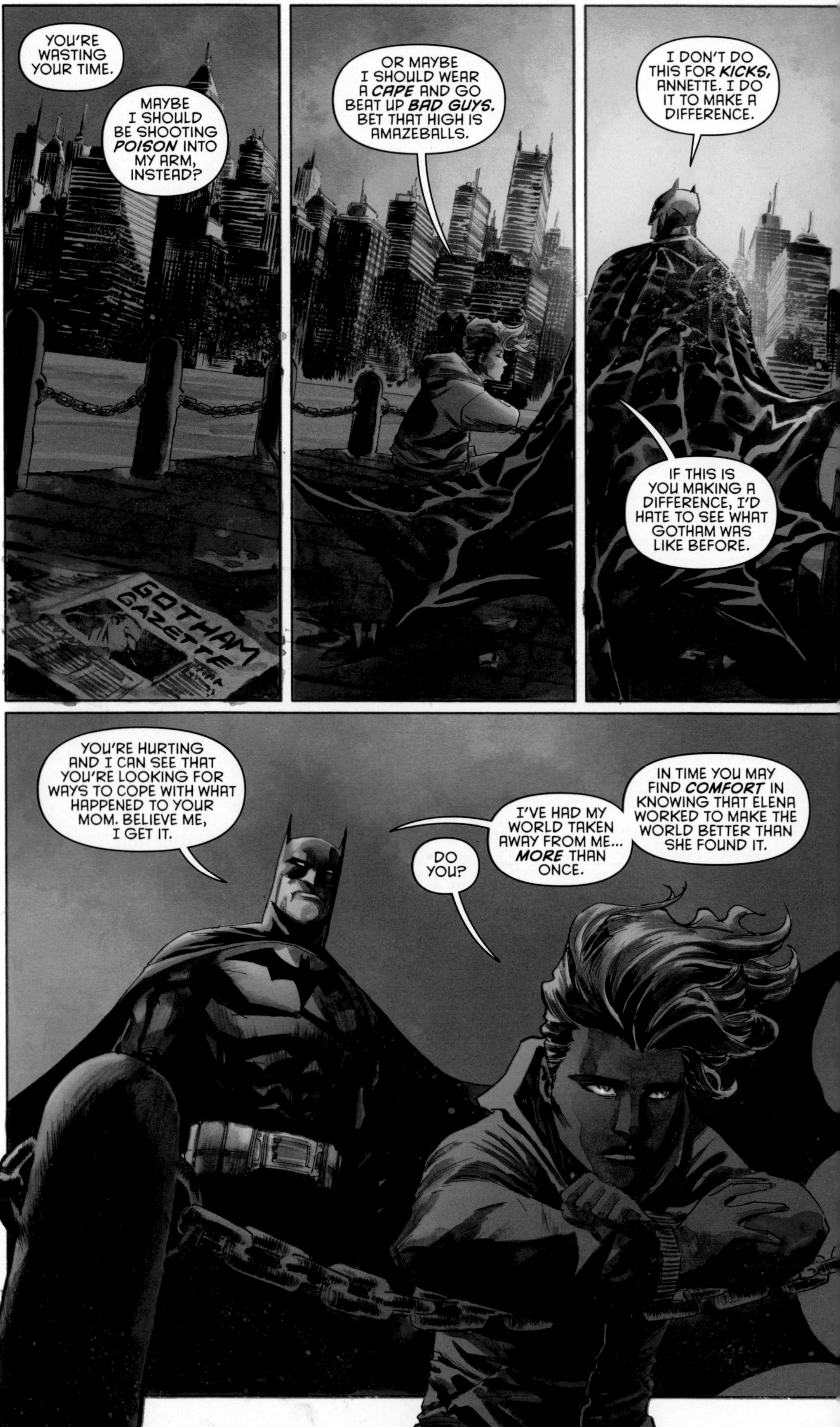

YOU'RE WASTING YOUR TIME.
MAYBE I SHOULD BE SHOOTING *POISON* INTO MY ARM, INSTEAD?
GOTHAM GAZETTE
OR MAYBE I SHOULD WEAR A *CAPE* AND GO BEAT UP *BAD GUYS.* BET THAT HIGH IS AMAZEBALLS.
I DON'T DO THIS FOR *KICKS,* ANNETTE. I DO IT TO MAKE A DIFFERENCE.
IF THIS IS YOU MAKING A DIFFERENCE, I'D HATE TO SEE WHAT GOTHAM WAS LIKE BEFORE.
YOU'RE HURTING AND I CAN SEE THAT YOU'RE LOOKING FOR WAYS TO COPE WITH WHAT HAPPENED TO YOUR MOM. BELIEVE ME, I GET IT.
DO YOU?
I'VE HAD MY WORLD TAKEN AWAY FROM ME... *MORE* THAN ONCE.
IN TIME YOU MAY FIND *COMFORT* IN KNOWING THAT ELENA WORKED TO MAKE THE WORLD BETTER THAN SHE FOUND IT.

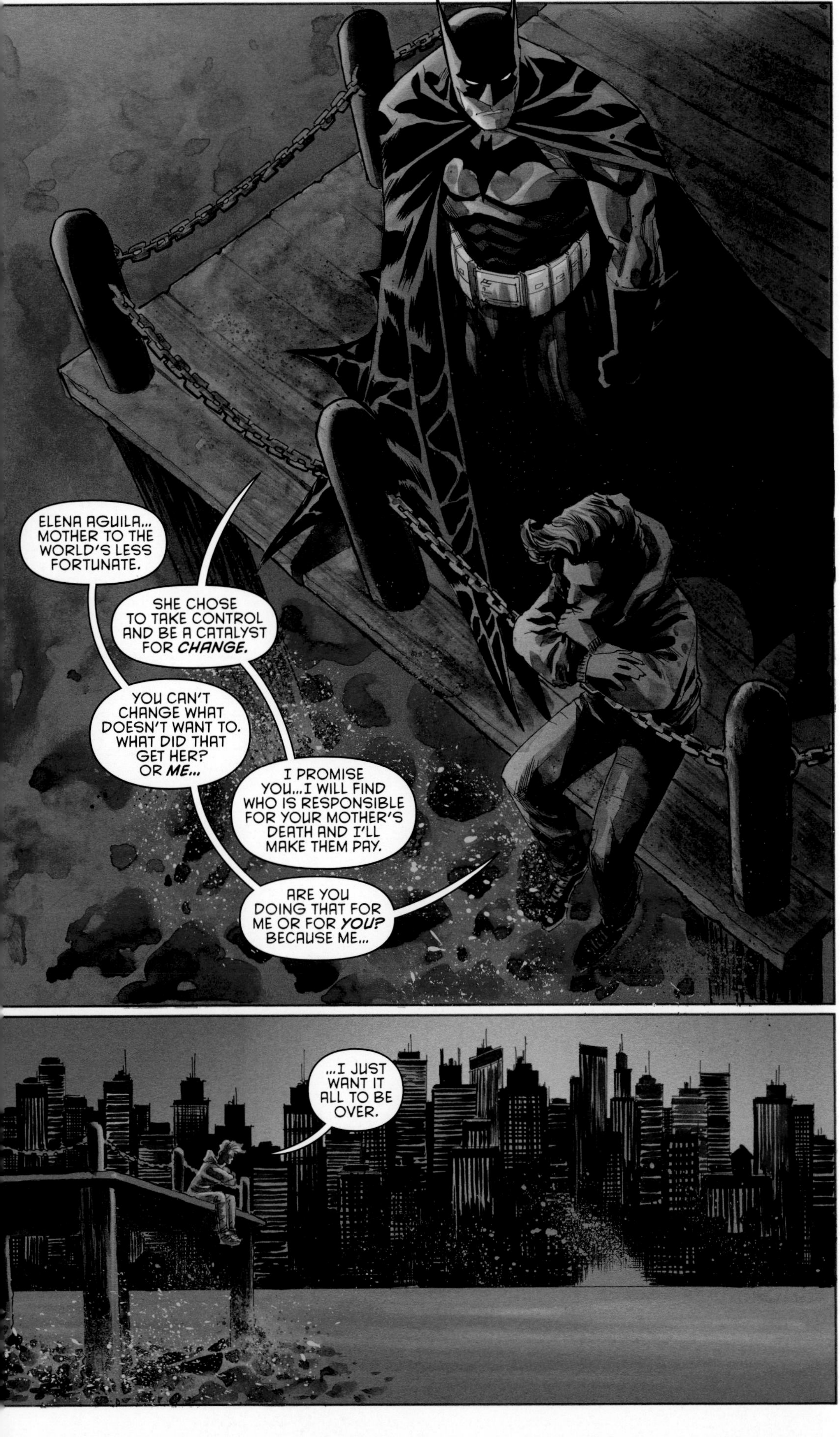
ELENA AGUILA... MOTHER TO THE WORLD'S LESS FORTUNATE.
SHE CHOSE TO TAKE CONTROL AND BE A CATALYST FOR *CHANGE.*
YOU CAN'T CHANGE WHAT DOESN'T WANT TO. WHAT DID THAT GET HER? OR *ME...*
I PROMISE YOU...I WILL FIND WHO IS RESPONSIBLE FOR YOUR MOTHER'S DEATH AND I'LL MAKE THEM PAY.
ARE YOU DOING THAT FOR ME OR FOR *YOU?* BECAUSE ME...
...I JUST WANT IT ALL TO BE OVER.

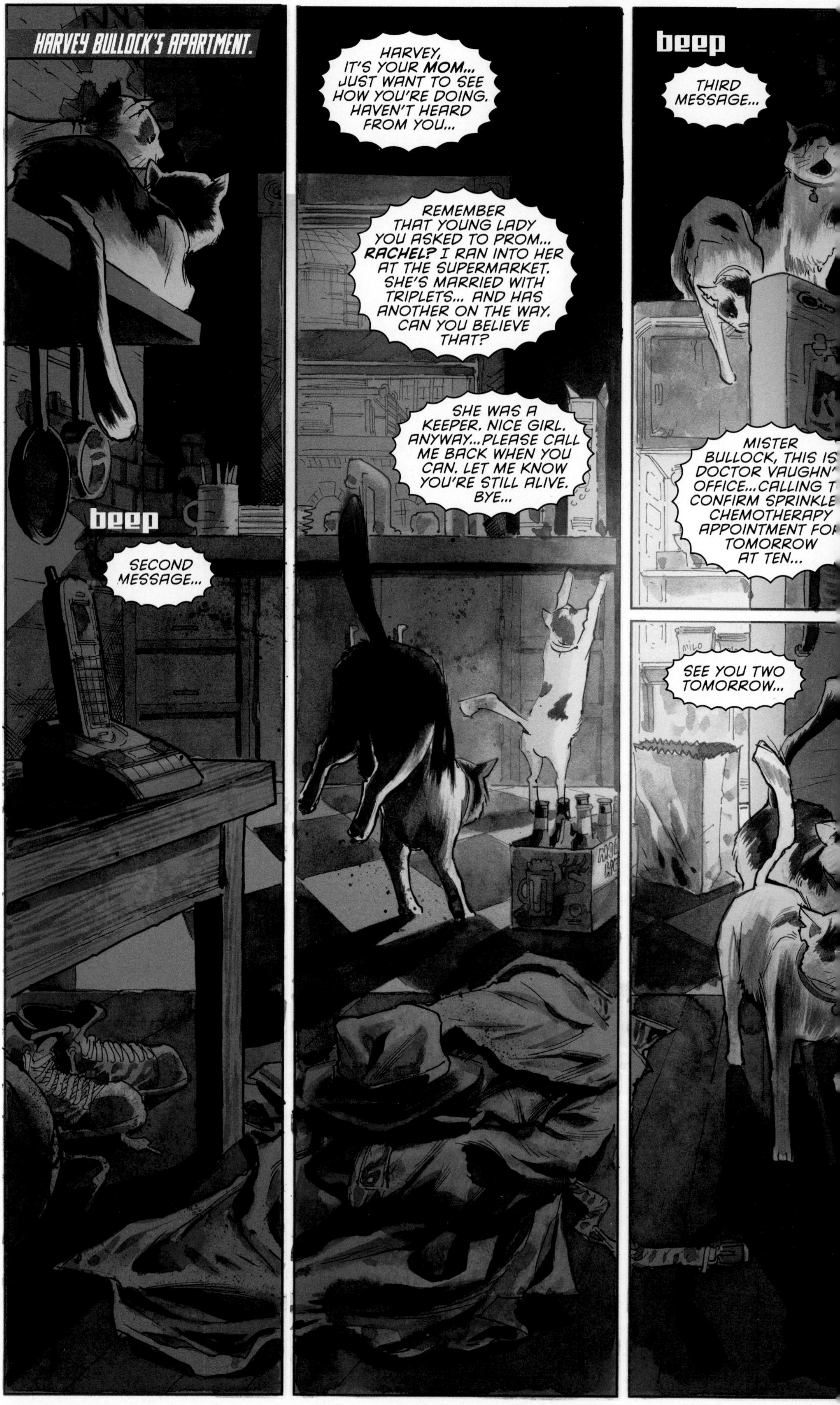
HARVEY BULLOCK'S APARTMENT.
beep
SECOND MESSAGE...
HARVEY, IT'S YOUR MOM... JUST WANT TO SEE HOW YOU'RE DOING. HAVEN'T HEARD FROM YOU...
REMEMBER THAT YOUNG LADY YOU ASKED TO PROM... RACHEL? I RAN INTO HER AT THE SUPERMARKET. SHE'S MARRIED WITH TRIPLETS... AND HAS ANOTHER ON THE WAY. CAN YOU BELIEVE THAT?
SHE WAS A KEEPER. NICE GIRL. ANYWAY...PLEASE CALL ME BACK WHEN YOU CAN. LET ME KNOW YOU'RE STILL ALIVE. BYE...
beep
THIRD MESSAGE...
MISTER BULLOCK, THIS IS DOCTOR VAUGHN' OFFICE...CALLING T CONFIRM SPRINKLE CHEMOTHERAPY APPOINTMENT FO TOMORROW AT TEN...
SEE YOU TWO TOMORROW...

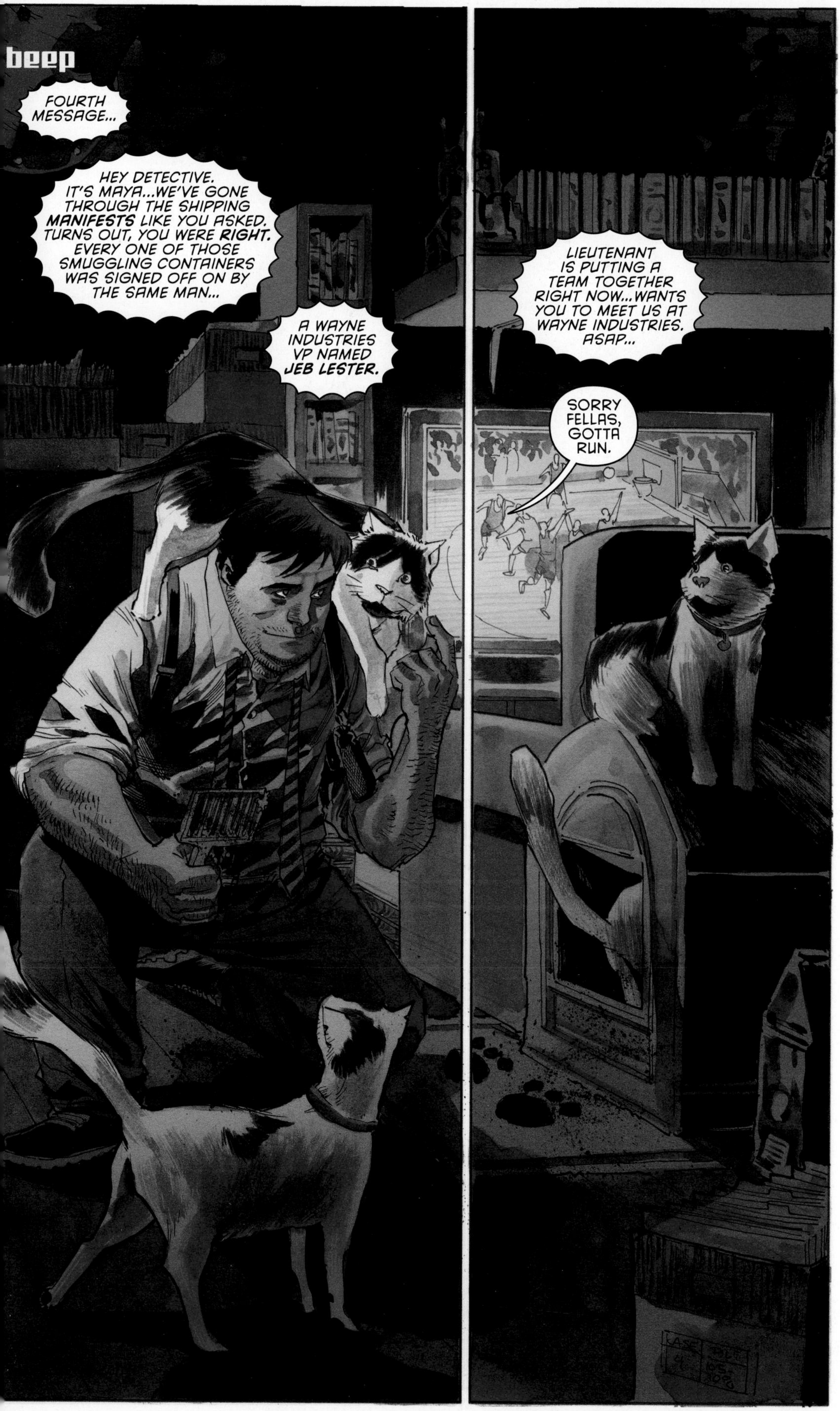
beep
FOURTH MESSAGE...
HEY DETECTIVE. IT'S MAYA...WE'VE GONE THROUGH THE SHIPPING **MANIFESTS** LIKE YOU ASKED. TURNS OUT, YOU WERE **RIGHT.** EVERY ONE OF THOSE SMUGGLING CONTAINERS WAS SIGNED OFF ON BY THE SAME MAN...
A WAYNE INDUSTRIES VP NAMED **JEB LESTER.**
LIEUTENANT IS PUTTING A TEAM TOGETHER RIGHT NOW...WANTS YOU TO MEET US AT WAYNE INDUSTRIES. ASAP...
SORRY FELLAS, GOTTA RUN.

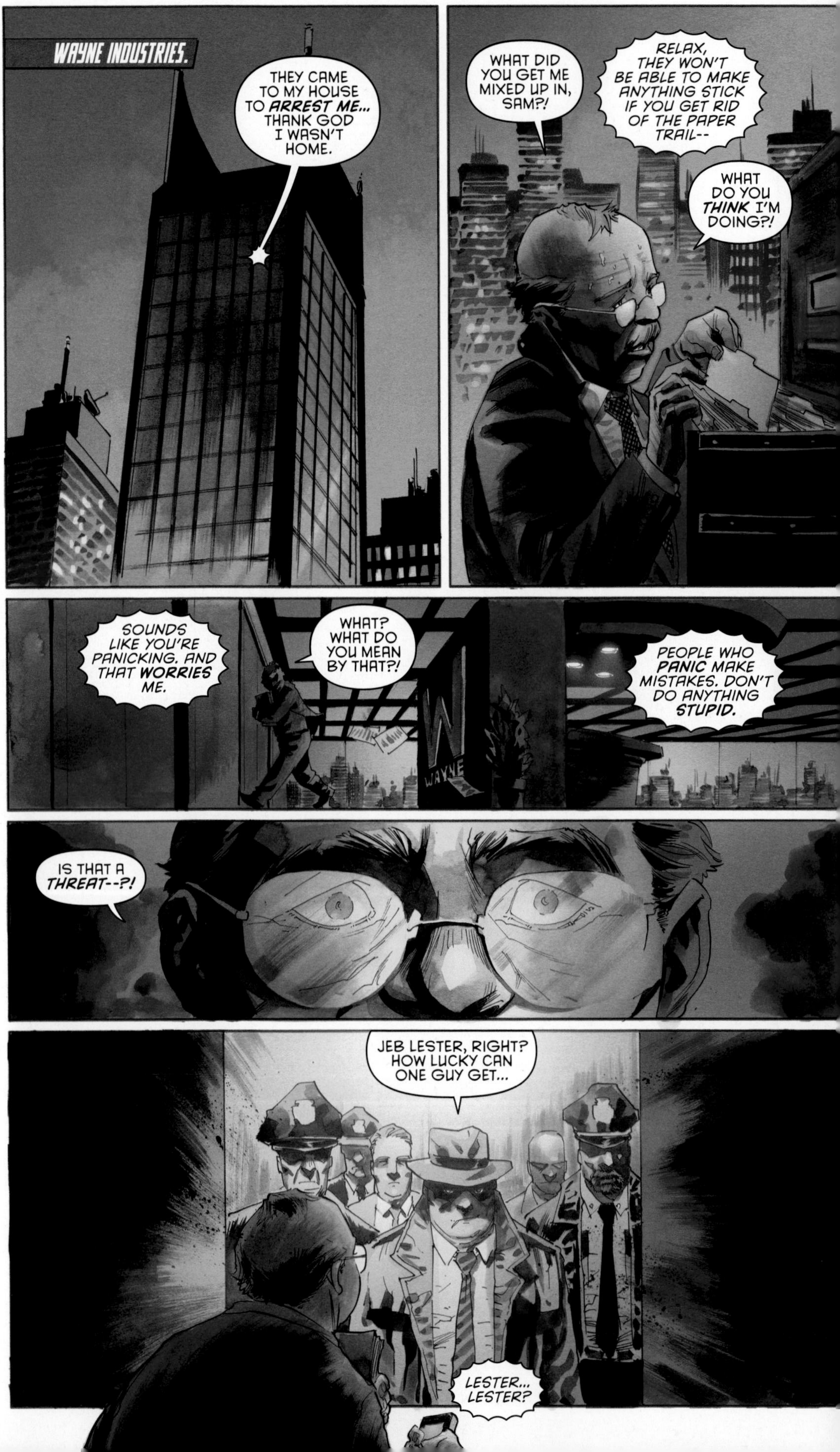

WAYNE INDUSTRIES.
THEY CAME TO MY HOUSE TO ARREST ME... THANK GOD I WASN'T HOME.
WHAT DID YOU GET ME MIXED UP IN, SAM?!
RELAX, THEY WON'T BE ABLE TO MAKE ANYTHING STICK IF YOU GET RID OF THE PAPER TRAIL--
WHAT DO YOU THINK I'M DOING?!
SOUNDS LIKE YOU'RE PANICKING. AND THAT WORRIES ME.
WHAT? WHAT DO YOU MEAN BY THAT?!
PEOPLE WHO PANIC MAKE MISTAKES. DON'T DO ANYTHING STUPID.
WAYNE
IS THAT A THREAT--?!
JEB LESTER, RIGHT? HOW LUCKY CAN ONE GUY GET...
LESTER... LESTER?

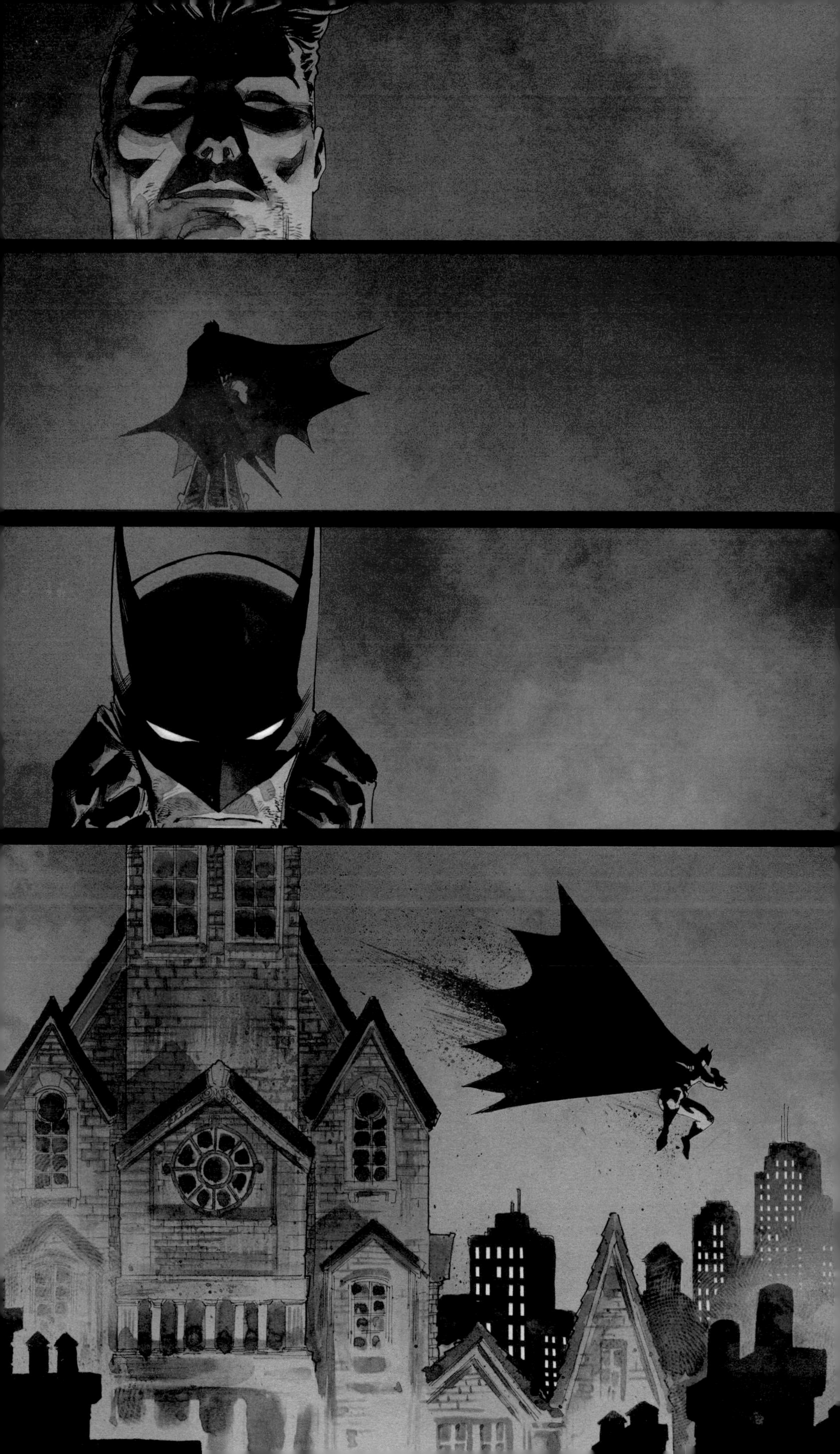

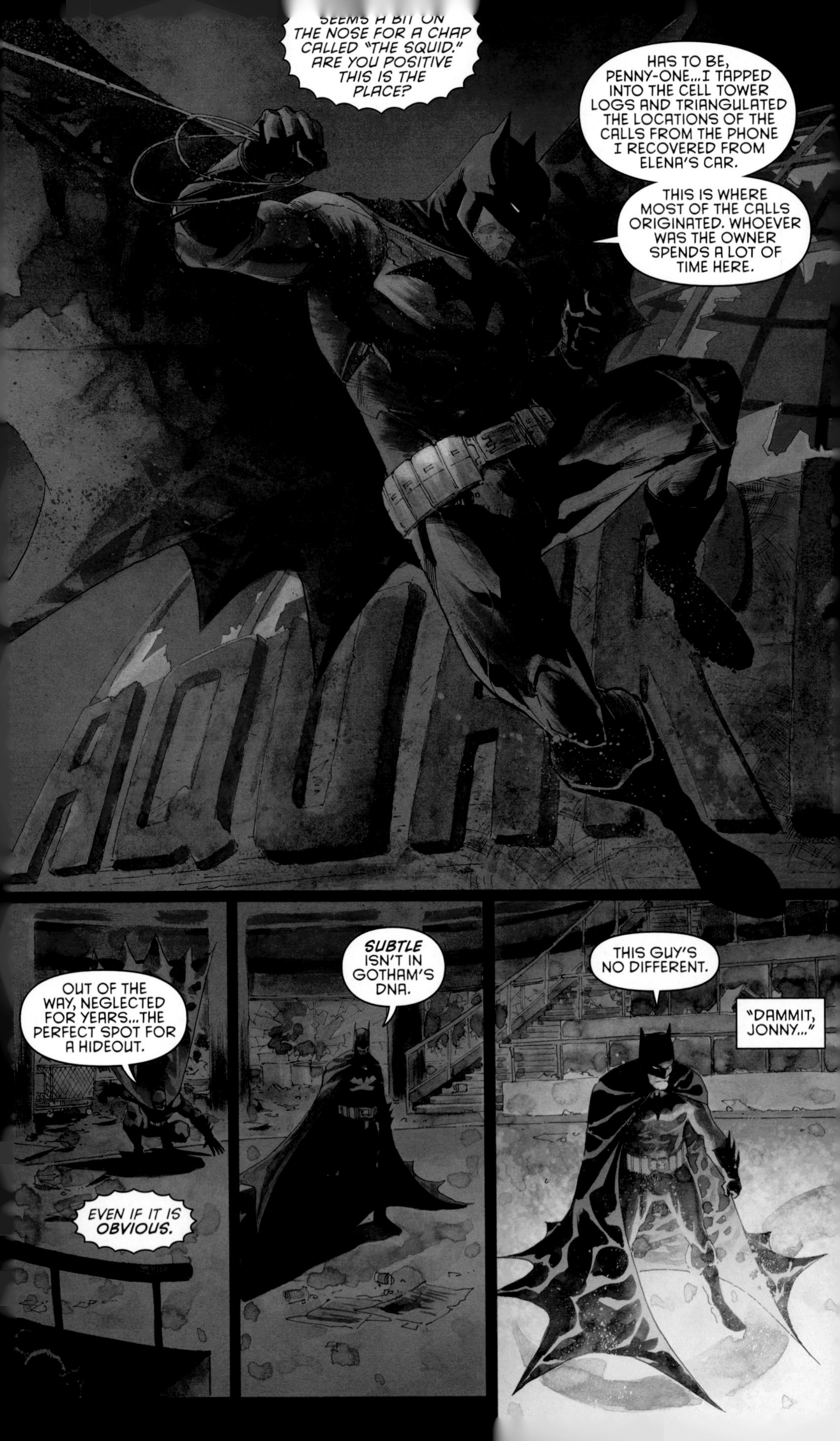
SEEMS A BIT ON THE NOSE FOR A CHAP CALLED "THE SQUID." ARE YOU POSITIVE THIS IS THE PLACE?
HAS TO BE, PENNY-ONE...I TAPPED INTO THE CELL TOWER LOGS AND TRIANGULATED THE LOCATIONS OF THE CALLS FROM THE PHONE I RECOVERED FROM ELENA'S CAR.
THIS IS WHERE MOST OF THE CALLS ORIGINATED. WHOEVER WAS THE OWNER SPENDS A LOT OF TIME HERE.
OUT OF THE WAY, NEGLECTED FOR YEARS...THE PERFECT SPOT FOR A HIDEOUT.
EVEN IF IT IS *OBVIOUS.*
SUBTLE ISN'T IN GOTHAM'S DNA.
THIS GUY'S NO DIFFERENT.
"DAMMIT, JONNY..."

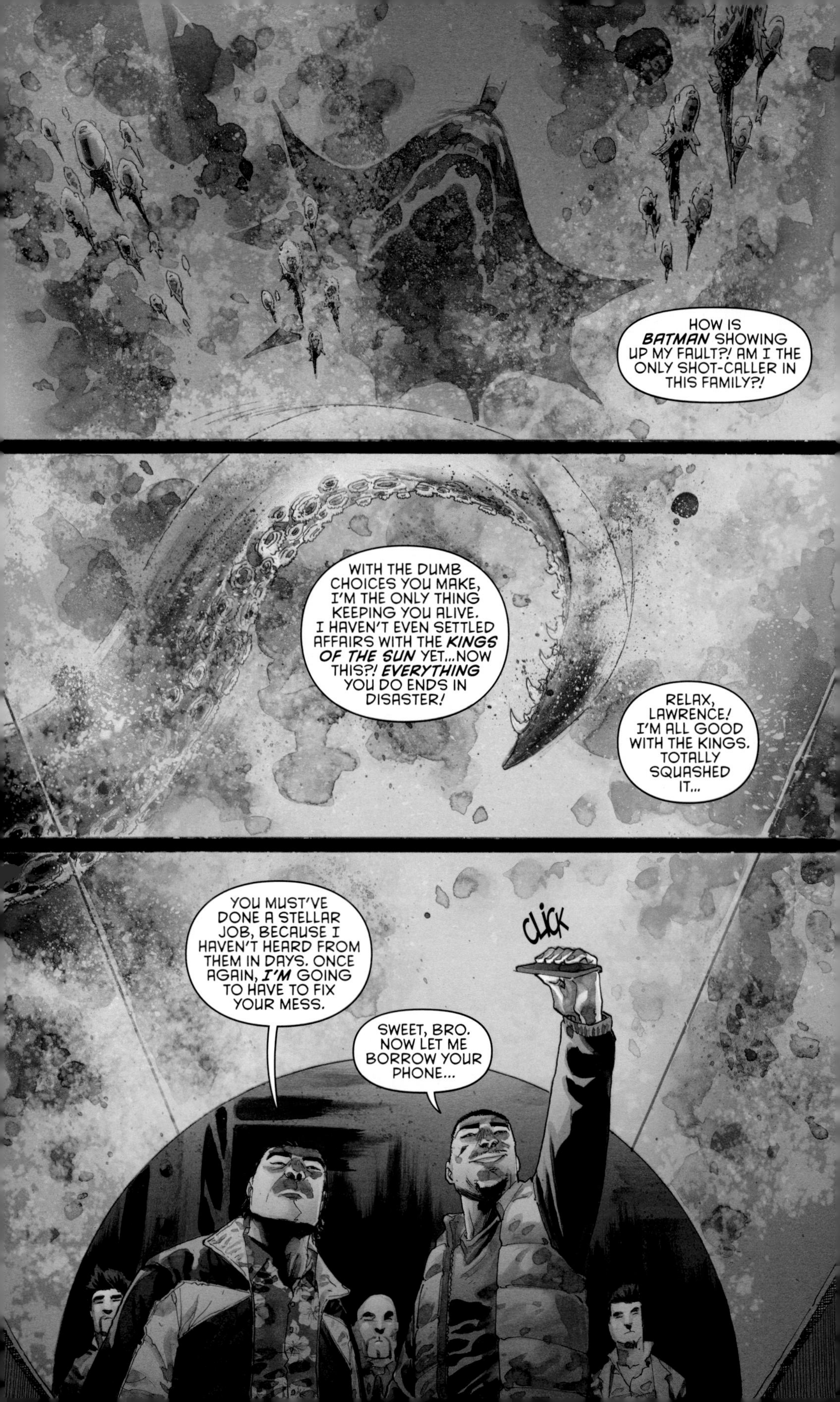
HOW IS BATMAN SHOWING UP MY FAULT?! AM I THE ONLY SHOT-CALLER IN THIS FAMILY?!
WITH THE DUMB CHOICES YOU MAKE, I'M THE ONLY THING KEEPING YOU ALIVE. I HAVEN'T EVEN SETTLED AFFAIRS WITH THE KINGS OF THE SUN YET...NOW THIS?! EVERYTHING YOU DO ENDS IN DISASTER!
RELAX, LAWRENCE! I'M ALL GOOD WITH THE KINGS. TOTALLY SQUASHED IT...
YOU MUST'VE DONE A STELLAR JOB, BECAUSE I HAVEN'T HEARD FROM THEM IN DAYS. ONCE AGAIN, I'M GOING TO HAVE TO FIX YOUR MESS.
CLICK
SWEET, BRO. NOW LET ME BORROW YOUR PHONE...

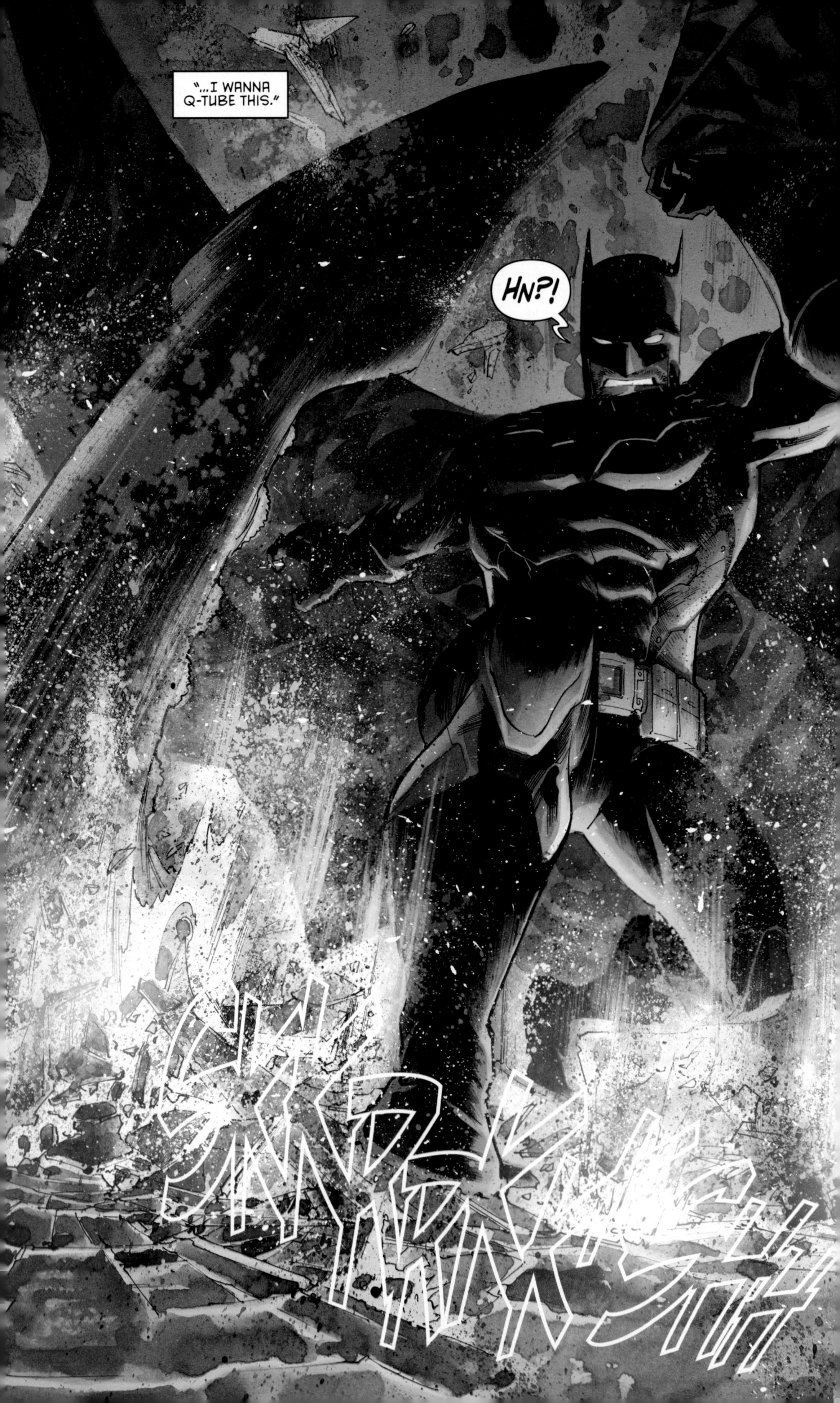
"...I WANNA Q-TUBE THIS."
HN?!
SKRUNNCH

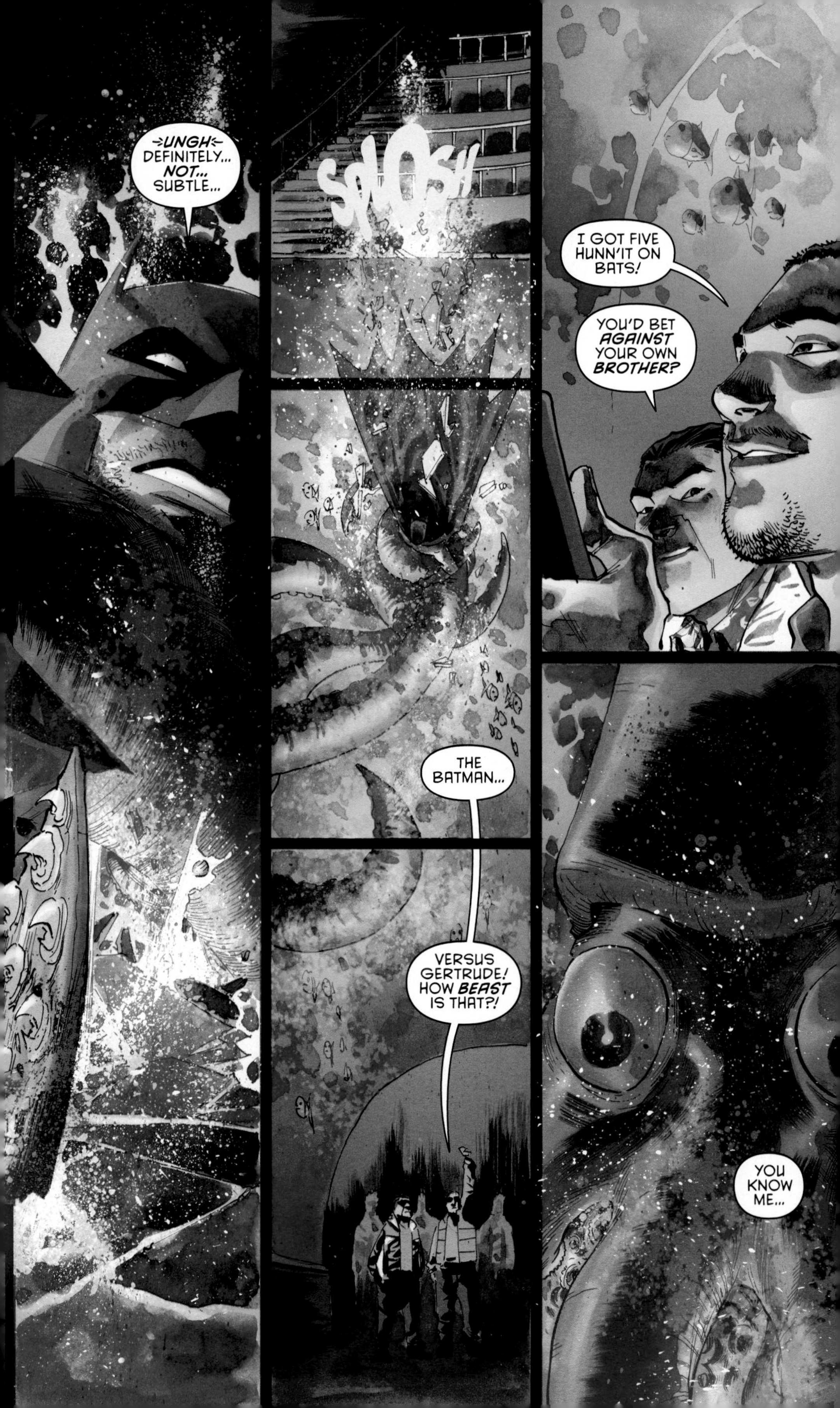
UNGH DEFINITELY... NOT... SUBTLE...
SPLOSH
THE BATMAN...
VERSUS GERTRUDE! HOW BEAST IS THAT?!
I GOT FIVE HUNN'IT ON BATS!
YOU'D BET AGAINST YOUR OWN BROTHER?
YOU KNOW ME...

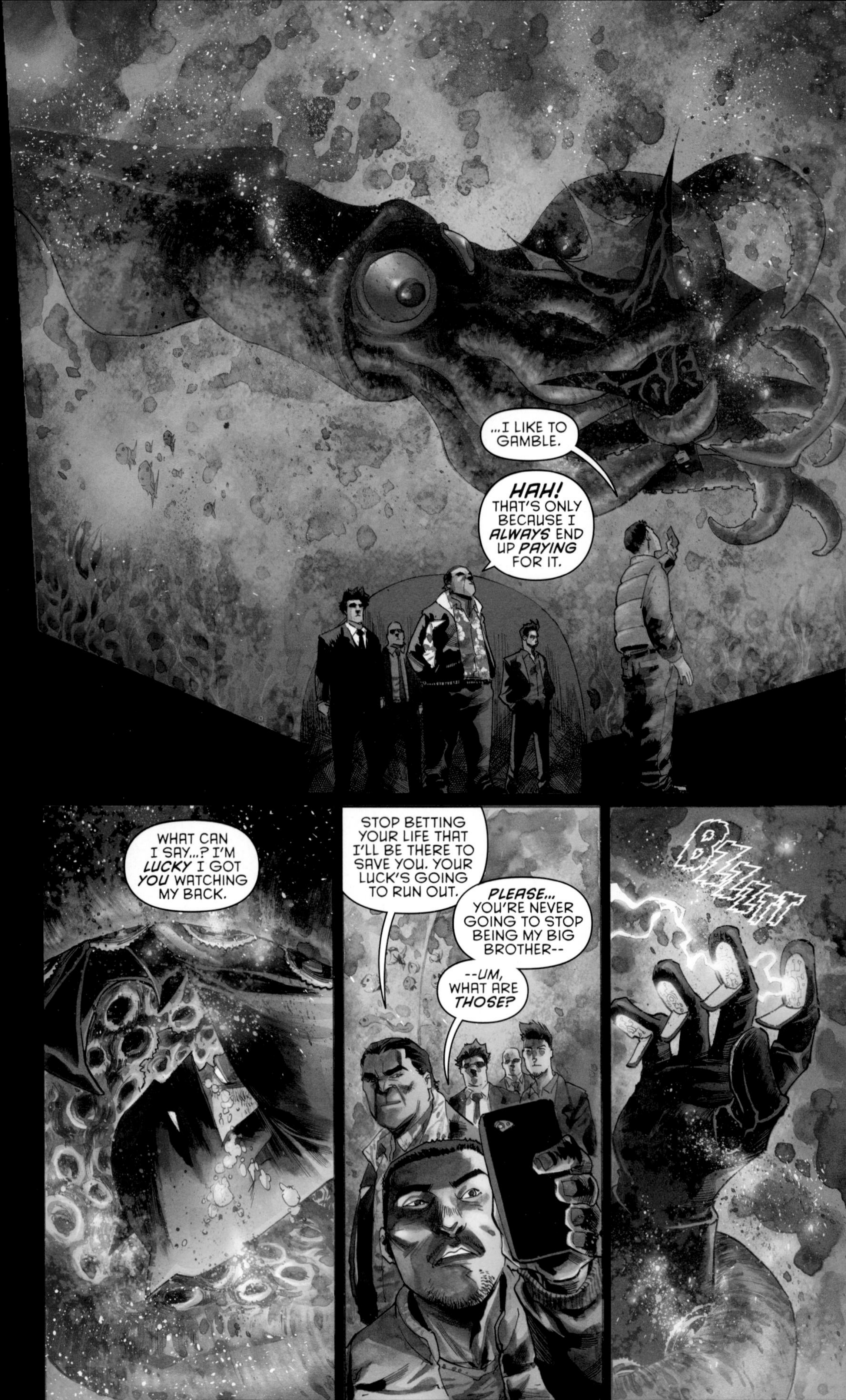
...I LIKE TO GAMBLE.
HAH! THAT'S ONLY BECAUSE I ALWAYS END UP PAYING FOR IT.
WHAT CAN I SAY...? I'M LUCKY I GOT YOU WATCHING MY BACK.
STOP BETTING YOUR LIFE THAT I'LL BE THERE TO SAVE YOU. YOUR LUCK'S GOING TO RUN OUT.
PLEASE... YOU'RE NEVER GOING TO STOP BEING MY BIG BROTHER--
--UM, WHAT ARE THOSE?
BZZZT

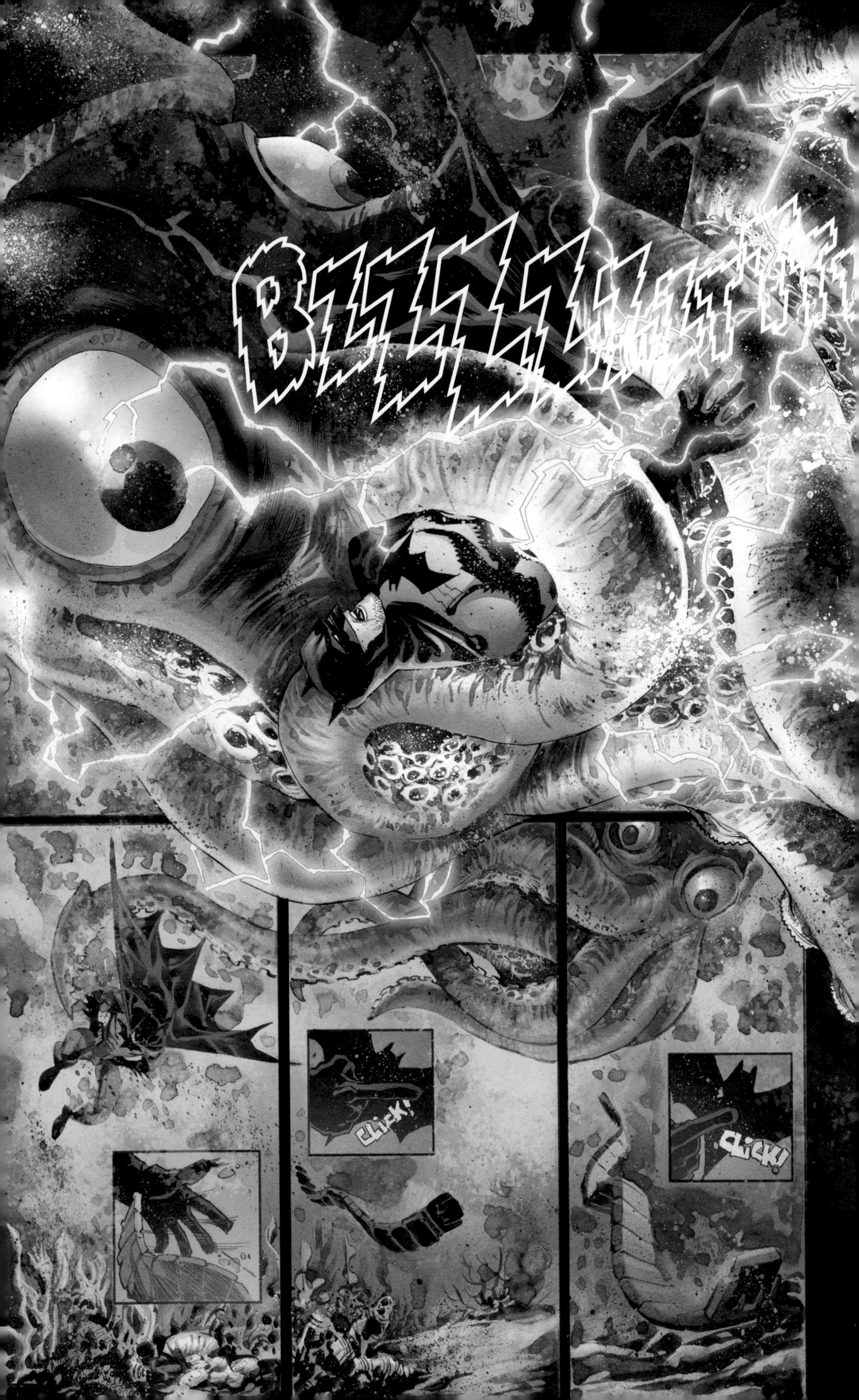
CLICK!
CLICK!

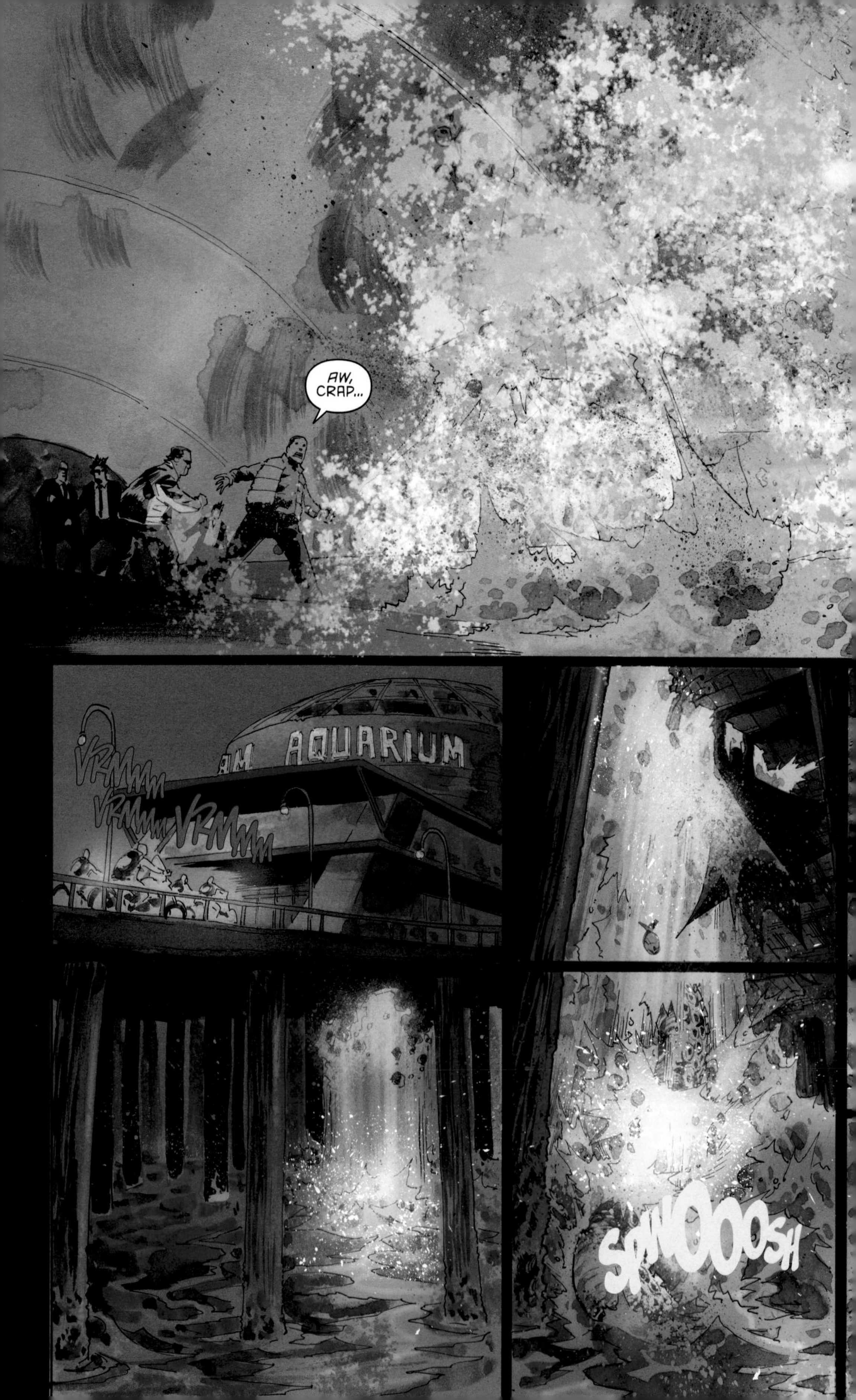
AW, CRAP...
AQUARIUM
VRMMM
VRMMM
VRMMM
SPLOOOSH

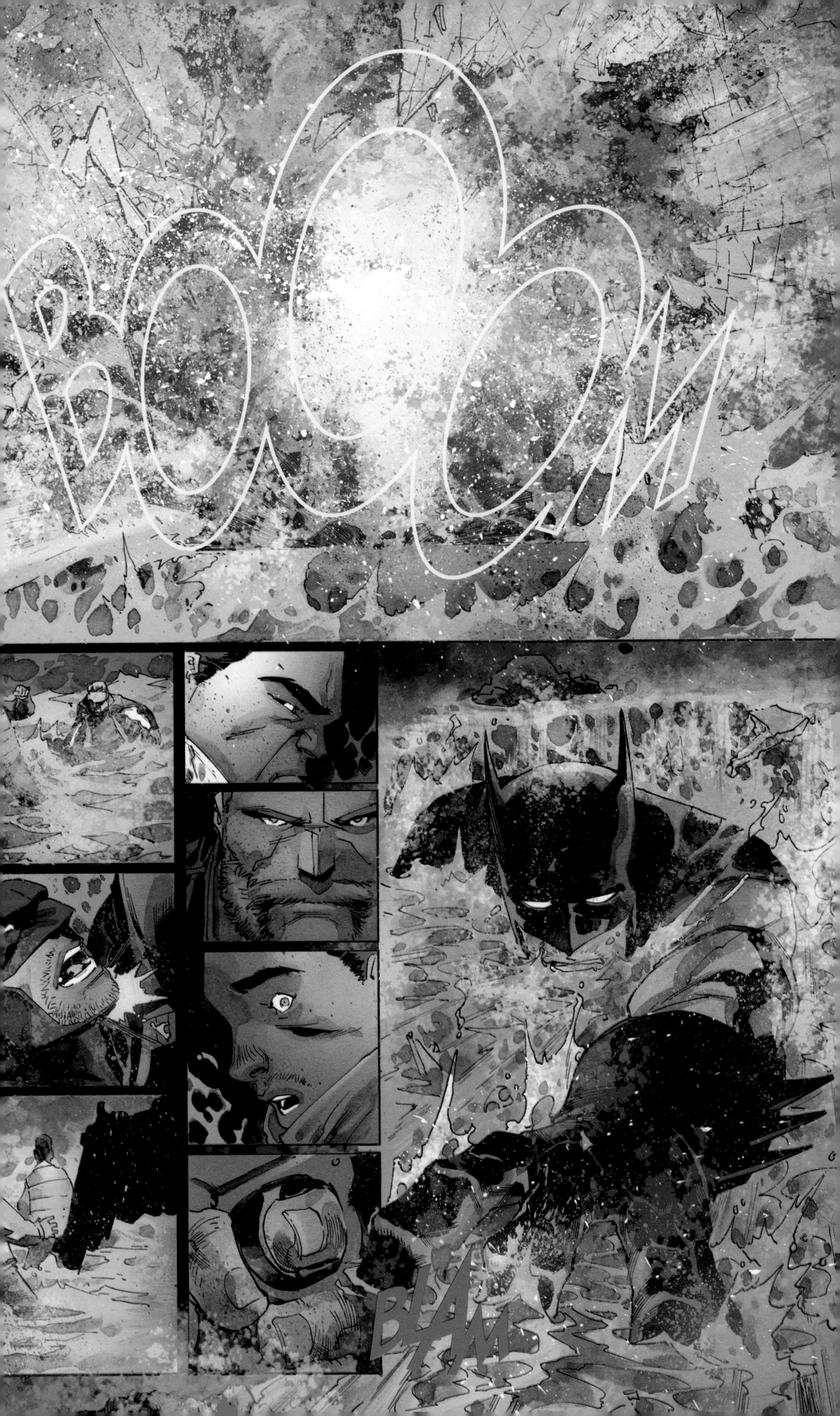
BOOOM
BLAM

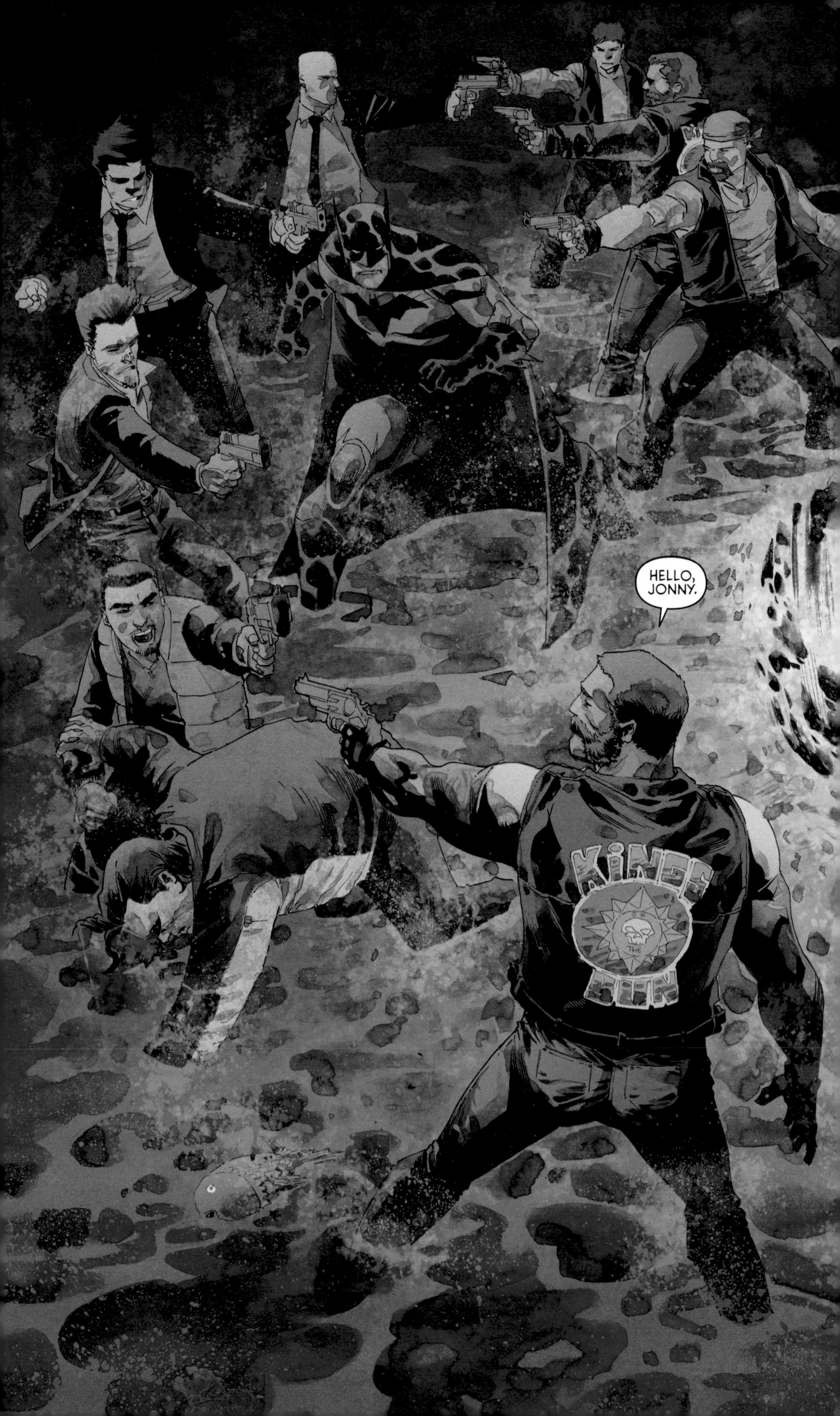
HELLO, JONNY.

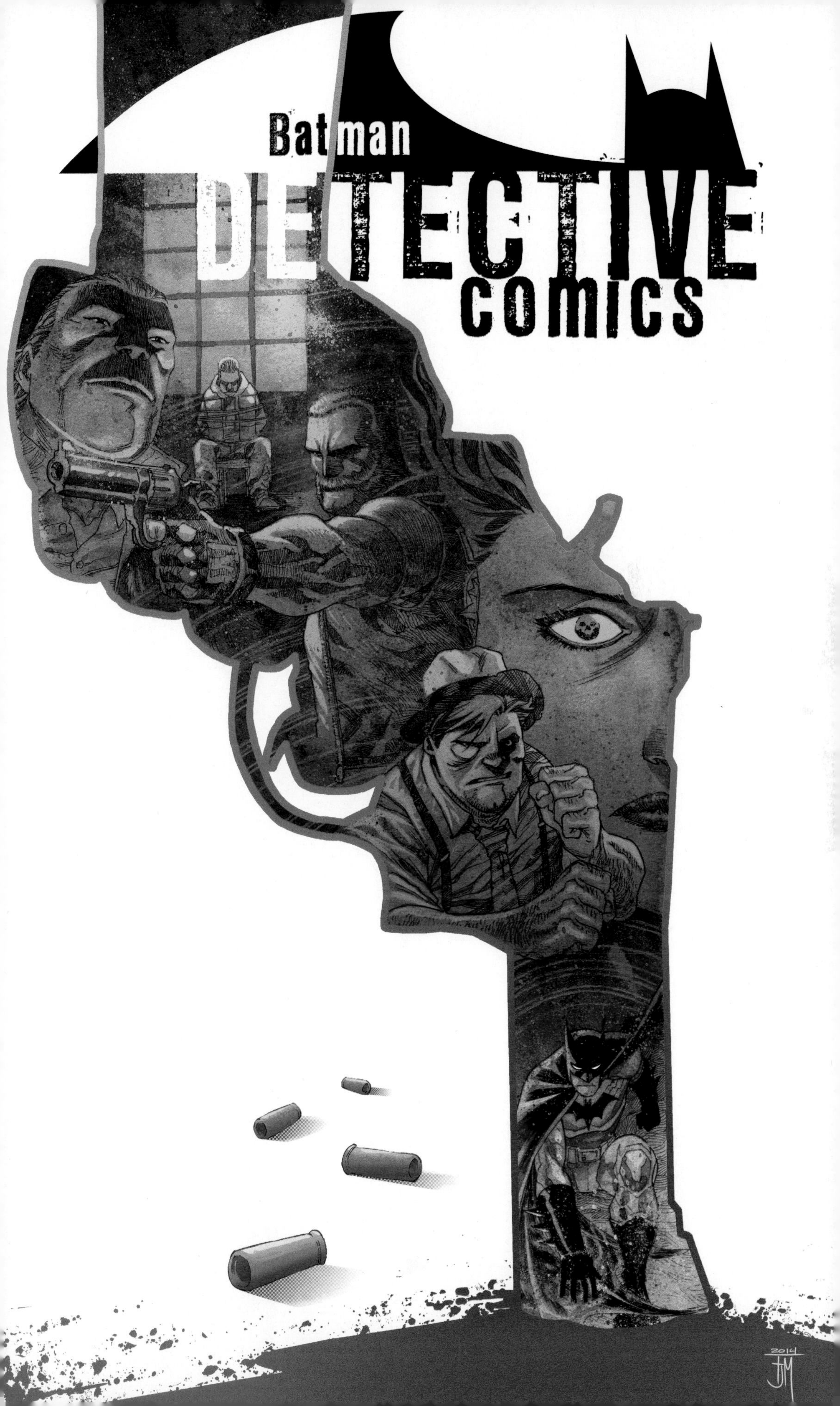

Batman
DETECTIVE
comics
2014

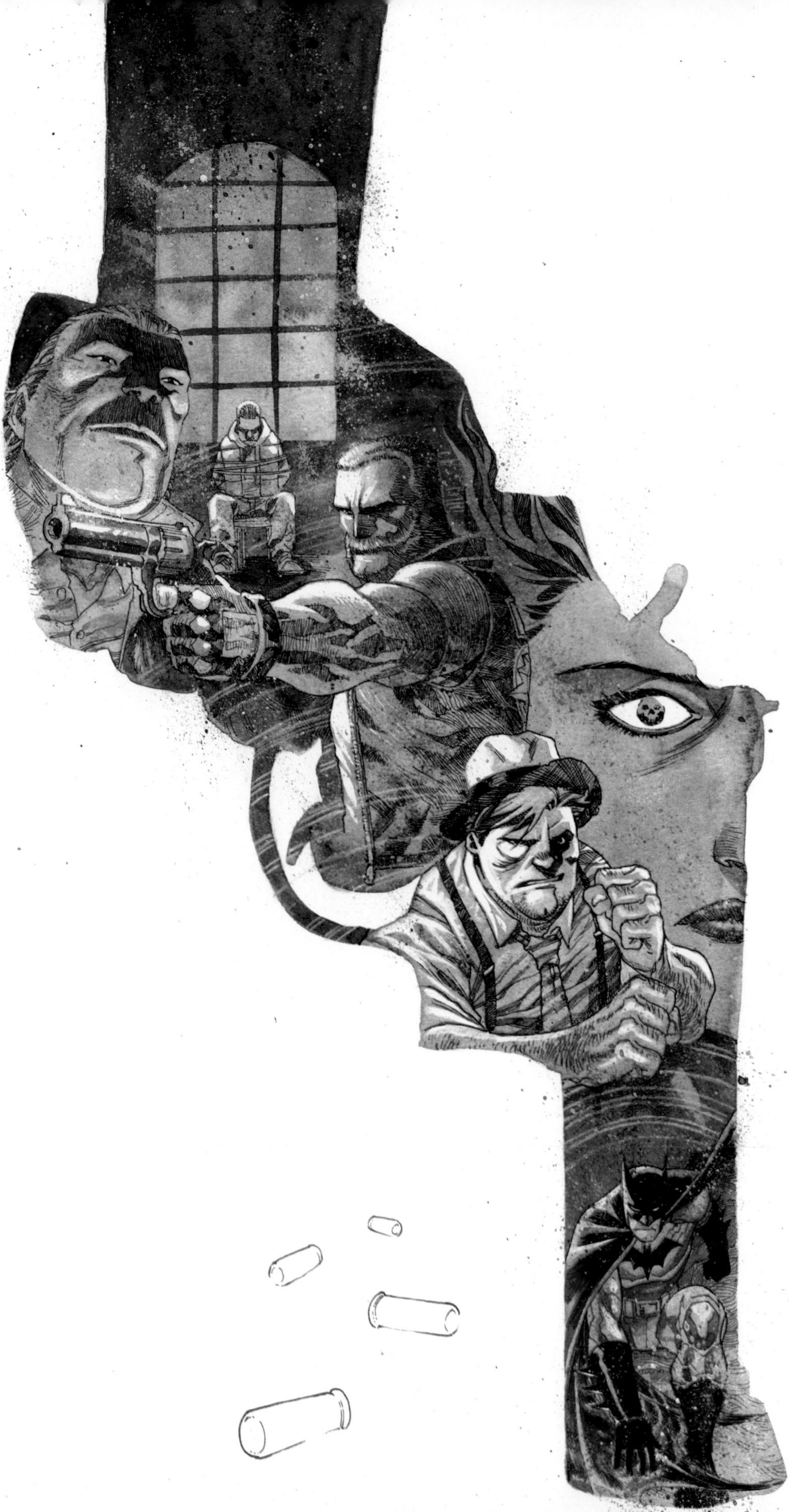

YOU--YOU SHOT MY *BROTHER...* MY FREAKIN' BROTHER! WE HAD A *DEAL,* HOLTER! I TOOK CARE OF YOUR PROBLEMS, AND YOU WERE SUPPOSED TO TAKE CARE OF ME!

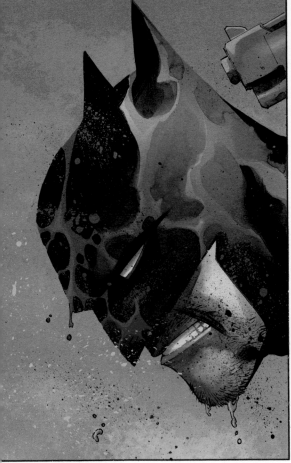

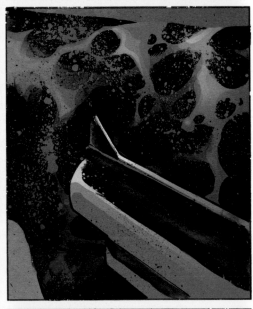

I'M SO SORRY, LAWRENCE. YOU ALWAYS HAD MY BACK...NOW I'M GONNA GET YOURS. STAY WITH ME, BRO...LONG ENOUGH TO WATCH ME *KILL* THIS BASTARD FOR YOU!

I'LL KILL THEM ALL!

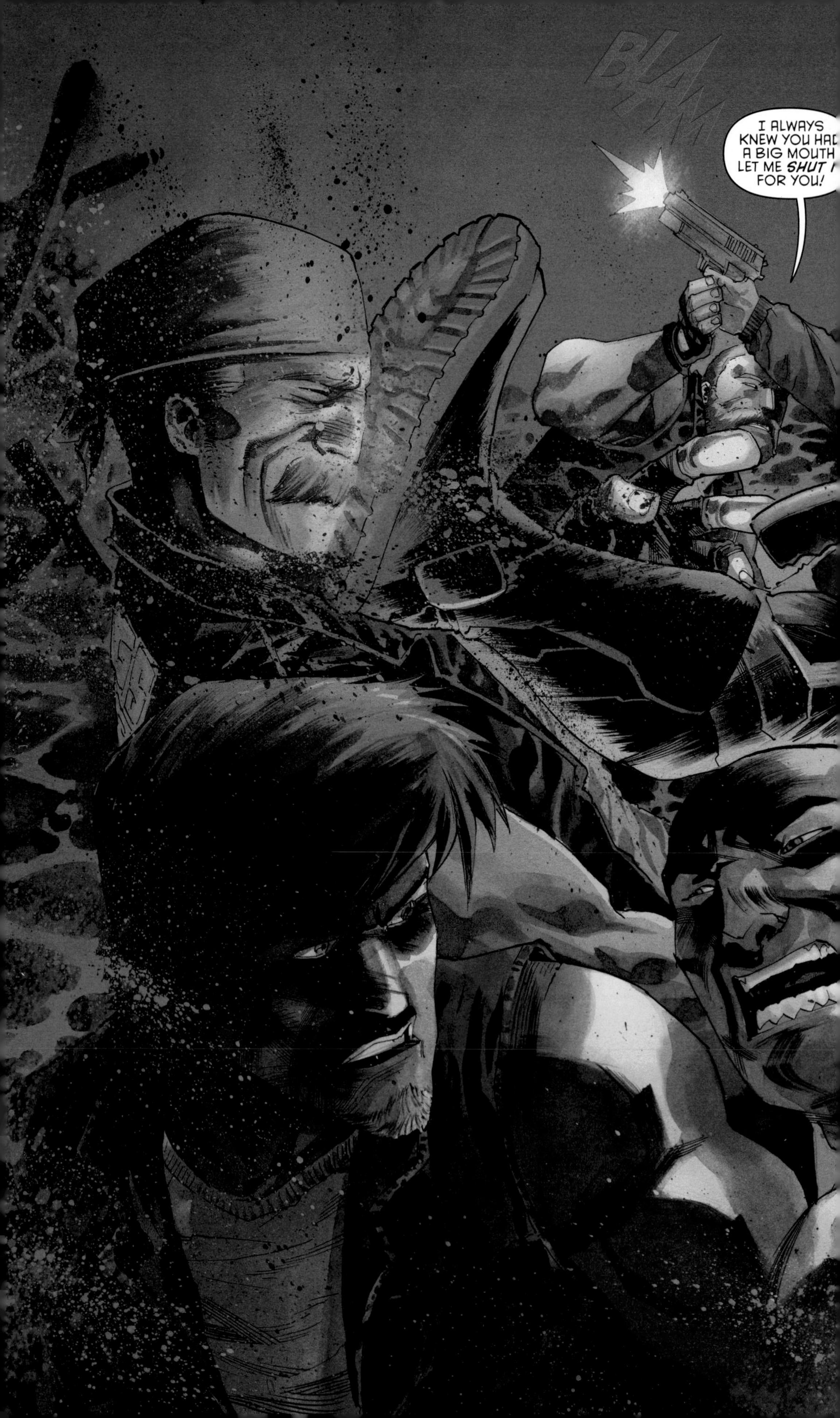
I ALWAYS KNEW YOU HAD A BIG MOUTH LET ME SHUT FOR YOU!

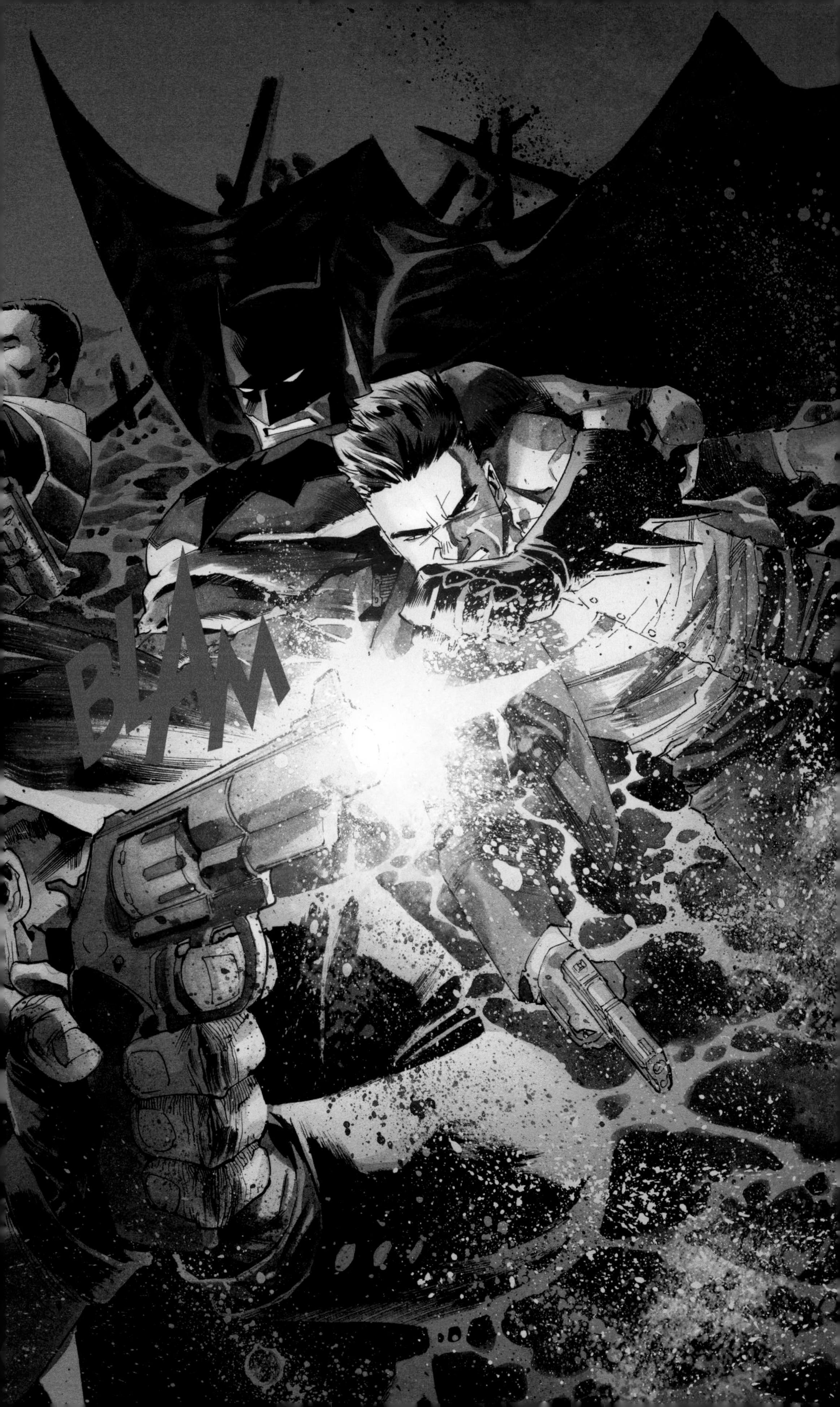
BLAM

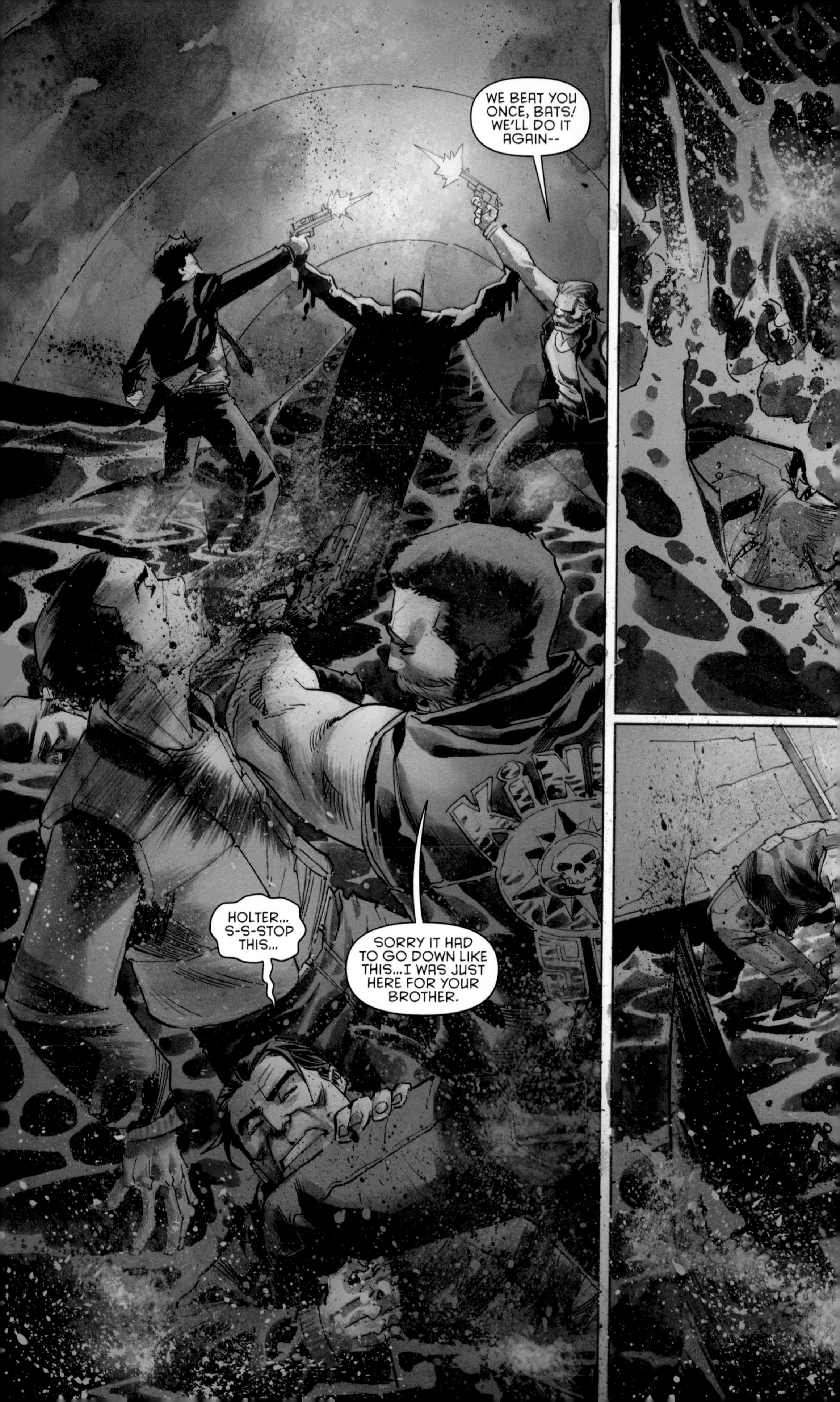
WE BEAT YOU ONCE, BATS! WE'LL DO IT AGAIN--
HOLTER... S-S-STOP THIS...
SORRY IT HAD TO GO DOWN LIKE THIS...I WAS JUST HERE FOR YOUR BROTHER.

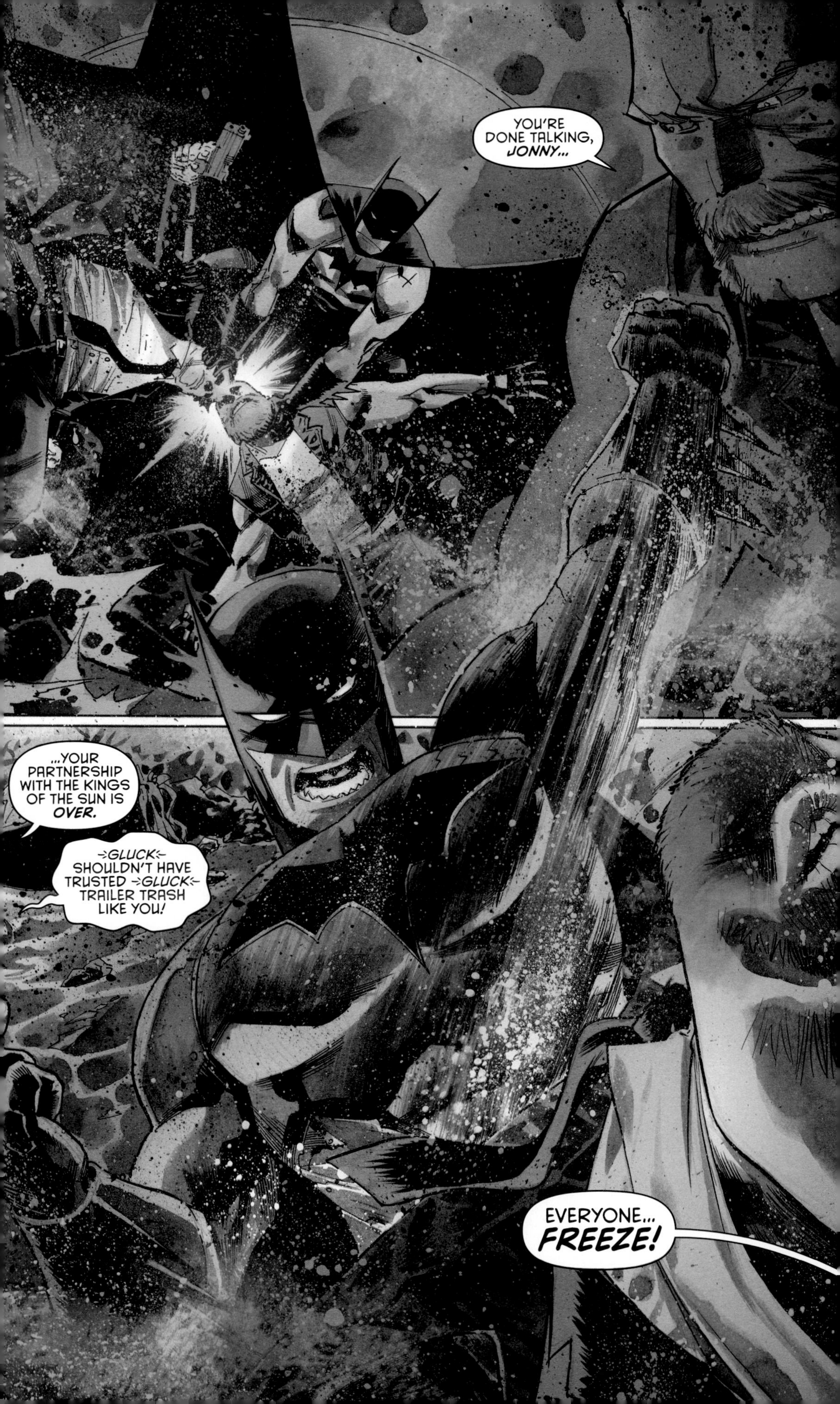
YOU'RE DONE TALKING, JONNY...
...YOUR PARTNERSHIP WITH THE KINGS OF THE SUN IS OVER.
-GLUCK- SHOULDN'T HAVE TRUSTED -GLUCK- TRAILER TRASH LIKE YOU!
EVERYONE... FREEZE!

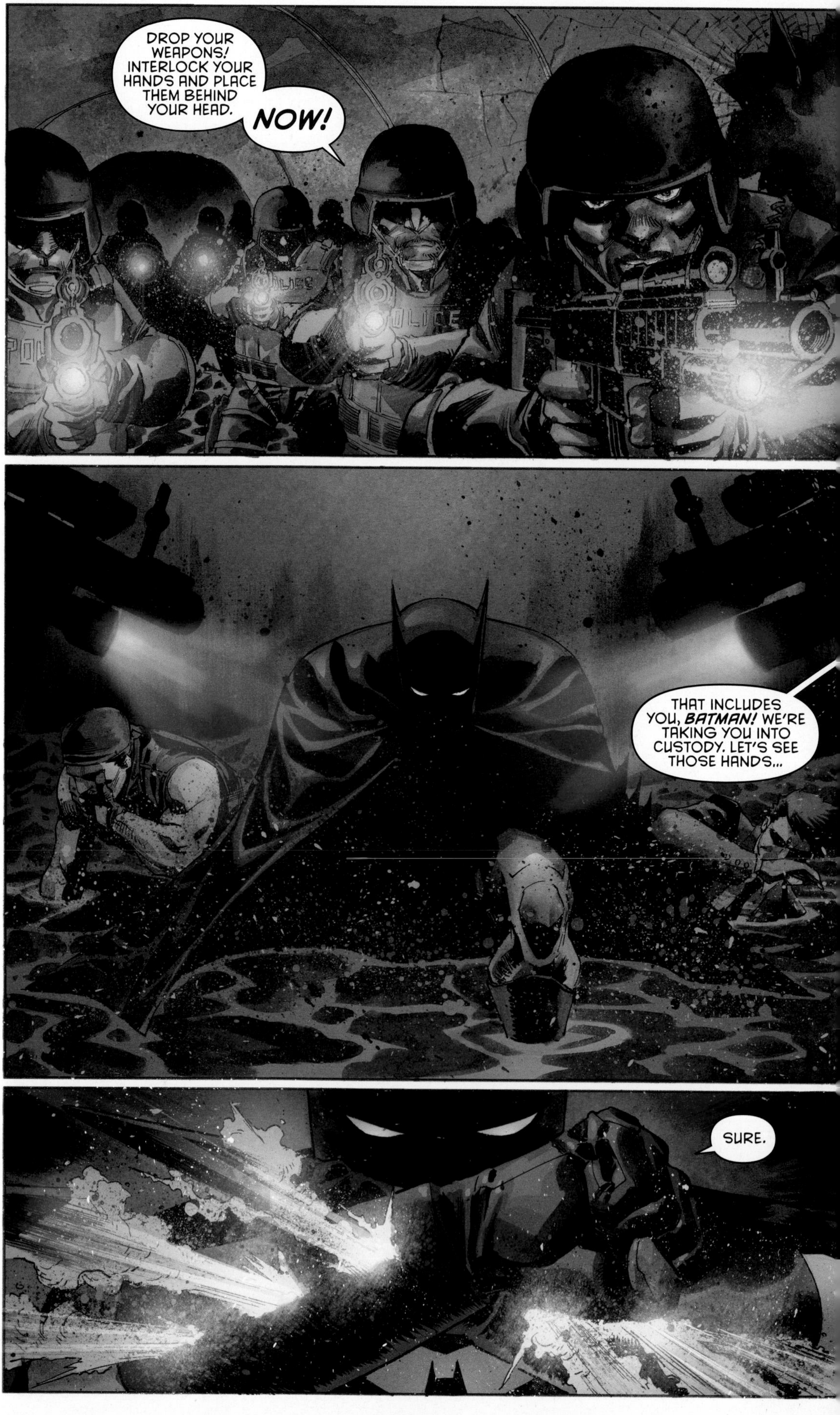

DROP YOUR WEAPONS! INTERLOCK YOUR HANDS AND PLACE THEM BEHIND YOUR HEAD.
NOW!
THAT INCLUDES YOU, BATMAN! WE'RE TAKING YOU INTO CUSTODY. LET'S SEE THOSE HANDS...
SURE.

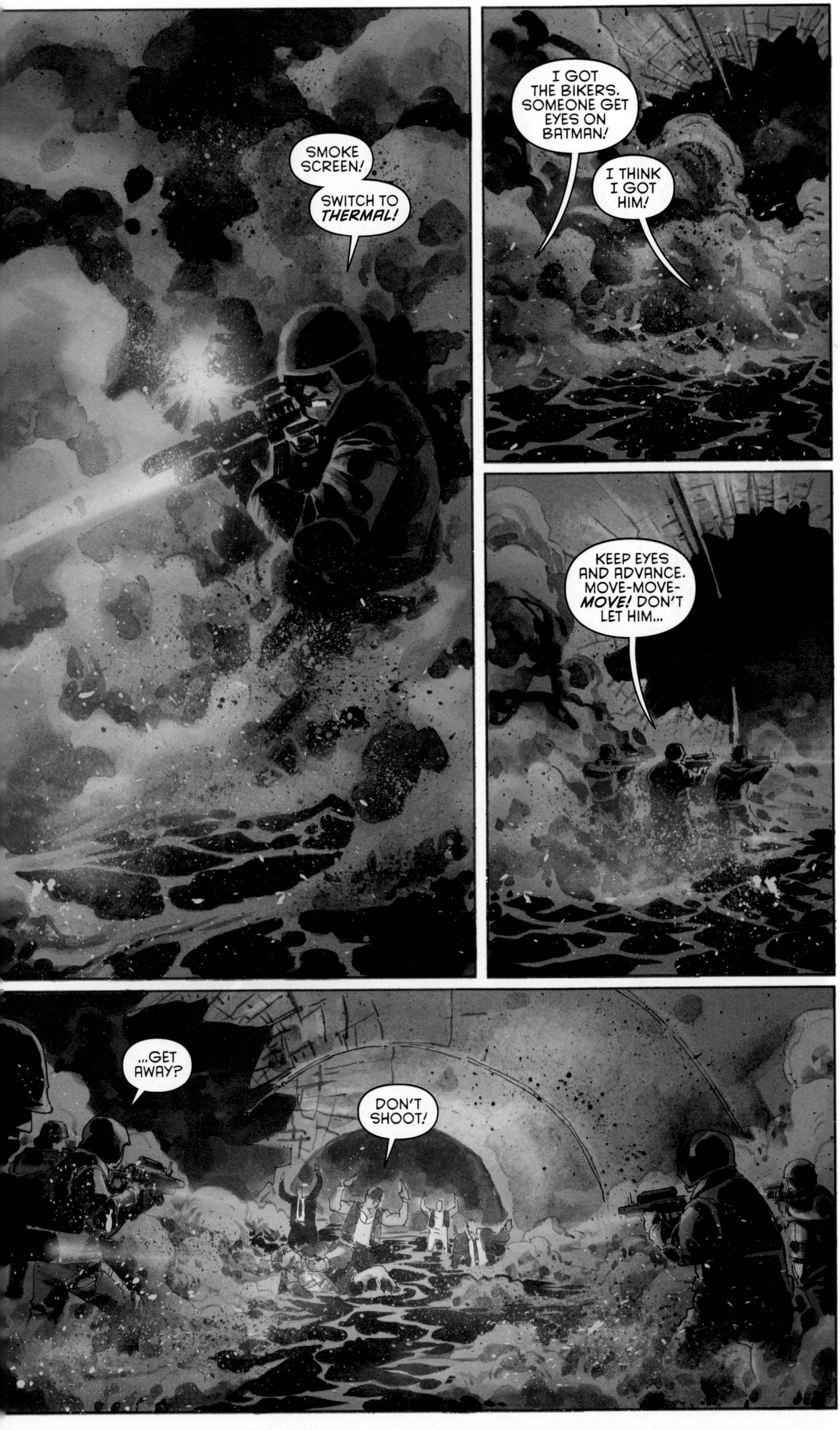
SMOKE SCREEN!
SWITCH TO THERMAL!
I GOT THE BIKERS. SOMEONE GET EYES ON BATMAN!
I THINK I GOT HIM!
KEEP EYES AND ADVANCE. MOVE-MOVE-MOVE! DON'T LET HIM...
...GET AWAY?
DON'T SHOOT!

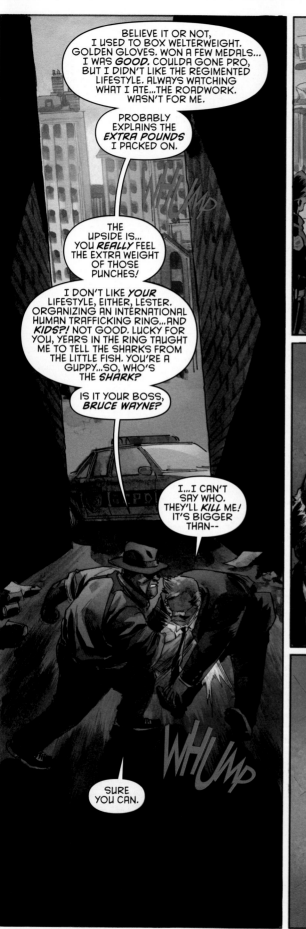

BELIEVE IT OR NOT, I USED TO BOX WELTERWEIGHT. GOLDEN GLOVES. WON A FEW MEDALS... I WAS *GOOD.* COULDA GONE PRO, BUT I DIDN'T LIKE THE REGIMENTED LIFESTYLE. ALWAYS WATCHING WHAT I ATE...THE ROADWORK. WASN'T FOR ME.

PROBABLY EXPLAINS THE *EXTRA POUNDS* I PACKED ON.

THE UPSIDE IS... YOU *REALLY* FEEL THE EXTRA WEIGHT OF THOSE PUNCHES!

I DON'T LIKE *YOUR* LIFESTYLE, EITHER, LESTER. ORGANIZING AN INTERNATIONAL HUMAN TRAFFICKING RING...AND *KIDS?!* NOT GOOD. LUCKY FOR YOU, YEARS IN THE RING TAUGHT ME TO TELL THE SHARKS FROM THE LITTLE FISH. YOU'RE A GUPPY...SO, WHO'S THE *SHARK?*

IS IT YOUR BOSS, *BRUCE WAYNE?*

I...I CAN'T SAY WHO. THEY'LL *KILL* ME! IT'S BIGGER THAN--

WHUMP

SURE YOU CAN.

→KOFF← IT'S NOT WAYNE. →KOFF← HE'S GOT NOTHING TO DO WITH IT.

I NEED A NAME.

CONGRESSMAN SAM YOUNG.

YOU MADE A *SMART* CHOICE.

YOU'LL BE SAFE IN HERE.

I WON'T BE SAFE *ANYWHERE.*

HEY, BULLOCK... I THINK I GOT A LEAD ON THAT MISSING CARGO YOU'RE LOOKING FOR. GOT A SECOND?

FOR YOU, *DETECTIVE YIP...* I GOT A LIFETIME. AFTER YOU.

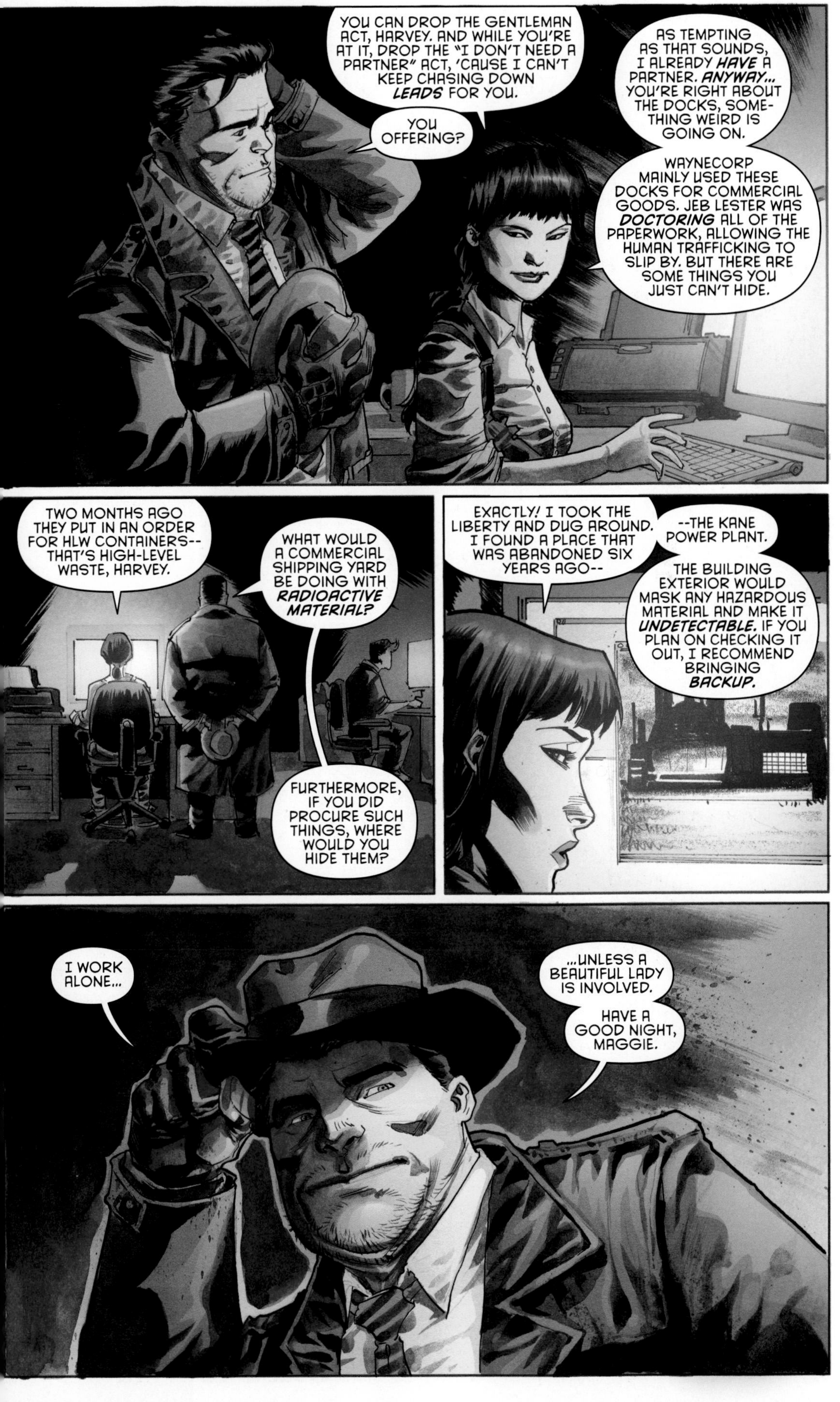
YOU CAN DROP THE GENTLEMAN ACT, HARVEY. AND WHILE YOU'RE AT IT, DROP THE "I DON'T NEED A PARTNER" ACT, 'CAUSE I CAN'T KEEP CHASING DOWN LEADS FOR YOU.
YOU OFFERING?
AS TEMPTING AS THAT SOUNDS, I ALREADY HAVE A PARTNER. ANYWAY... YOU'RE RIGHT ABOUT THE DOCKS, SOMETHING WEIRD IS GOING ON.
WAYNECORP MAINLY USED THESE DOCKS FOR COMMERCIAL GOODS. JEB LESTER WAS DOCTORING ALL OF THE PAPERWORK, ALLOWING THE HUMAN TRAFFICKING TO SLIP BY. BUT THERE ARE SOME THINGS YOU JUST CAN'T HIDE.
TWO MONTHS AGO THEY PUT IN AN ORDER FOR HLW CONTAINERS-- THAT'S HIGH-LEVEL WASTE, HARVEY.
WHAT WOULD A COMMERCIAL SHIPPING YARD BE DOING WITH RADIOACTIVE MATERIAL?
FURTHERMORE, IF YOU DID PROCURE SUCH THINGS, WHERE WOULD YOU HIDE THEM?
EXACTLY! I TOOK THE LIBERTY AND DUG AROUND. I FOUND A PLACE THAT WAS ABANDONED SIX YEARS AGO--
--THE KANE POWER PLANT.
THE BUILDING EXTERIOR WOULD MASK ANY HAZARDOUS MATERIAL AND MAKE IT UNDETECTABLE. IF YOU PLAN ON CHECKING IT OUT, I RECOMMEND BRINGING BACKUP.
I WORK ALONE...
...UNLESS A BEAUTIFUL LADY IS INVOLVED.
HAVE A GOOD NIGHT, MAGGIE.

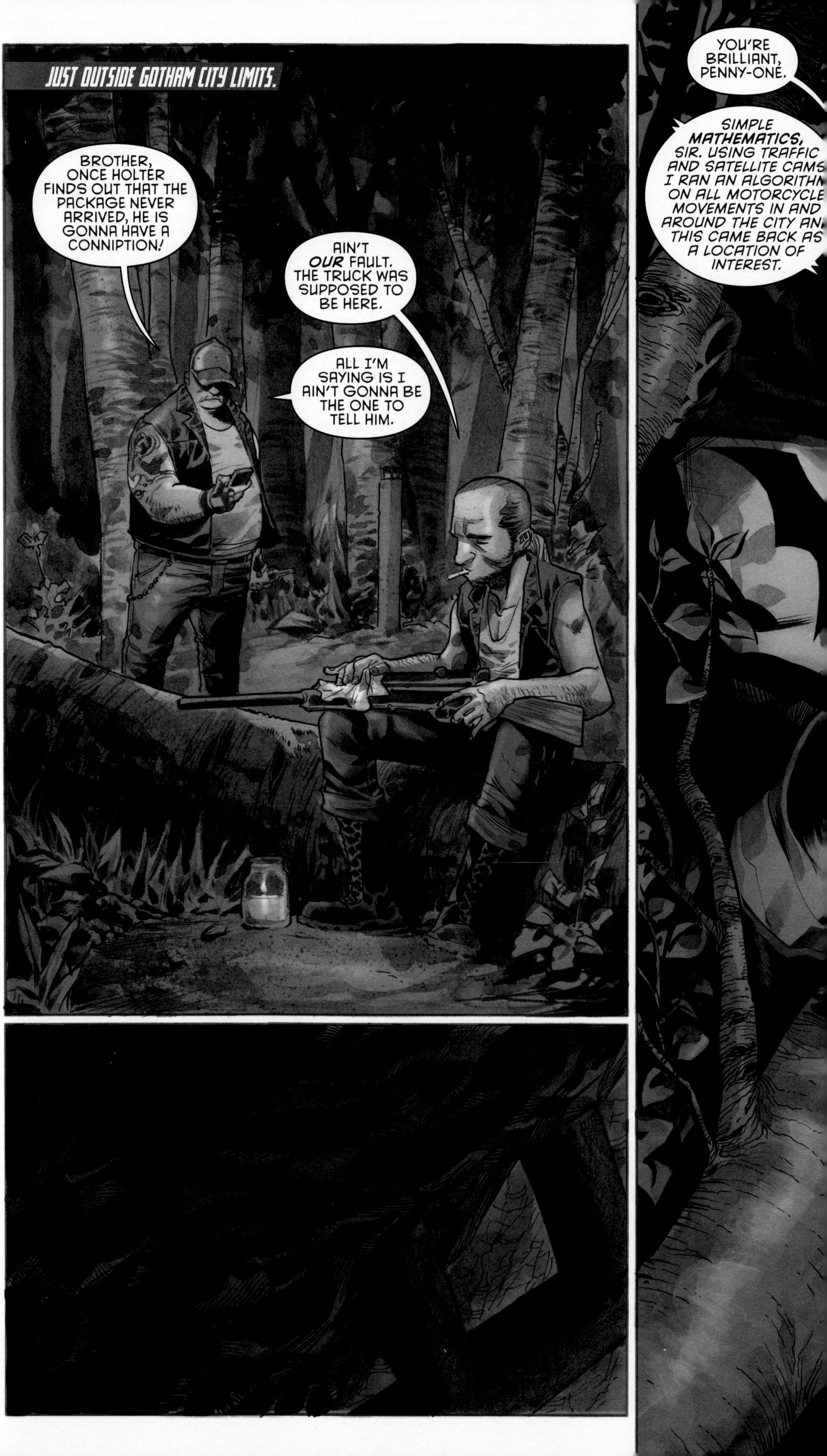
JUST OUTSIDE GOTHAM CITY LIMITS.
BROTHER, ONCE HOLTER FINDS OUT THAT THE PACKAGE NEVER ARRIVED, HE IS GONNA HAVE A CONNIPTION!
AIN'T OUR FAULT. THE TRUCK WAS SUPPOSED TO BE HERE.
ALL I'M SAYING IS I AIN'T GONNA BE THE ONE TO TELL HIM.
YOU'RE BRILLIANT, PENNY-ONE.
SIMPLE MATHEMATICS, SIR. USING TRAFFIC AND SATELLITE CAMS I RAN AN ALGORITHM ON ALL MOTORCYCLE MOVEMENTS IN AND AROUND THE CITY AND THIS CAME BACK AS A LOCATION OF INTEREST.

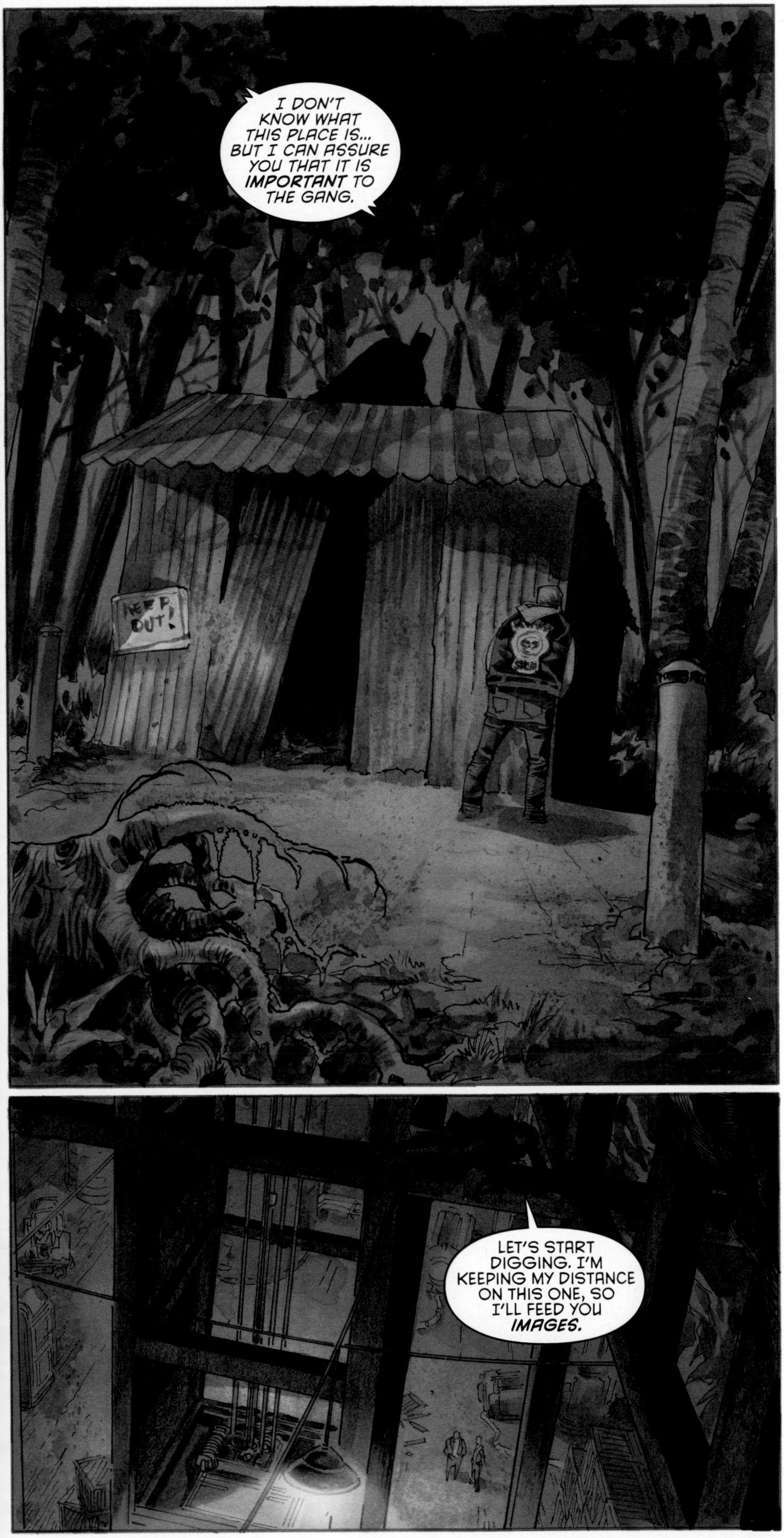
I DON'T KNOW WHAT THIS PLACE IS... BUT I CAN ASSURE YOU THAT IT IS IMPORTANT TO THE GANG.
KEEP OUT!
LET'S START DIGGING. I'M KEEPING MY DISTANCE ON THIS ONE, SO I'LL FEED YOU IMAGES.

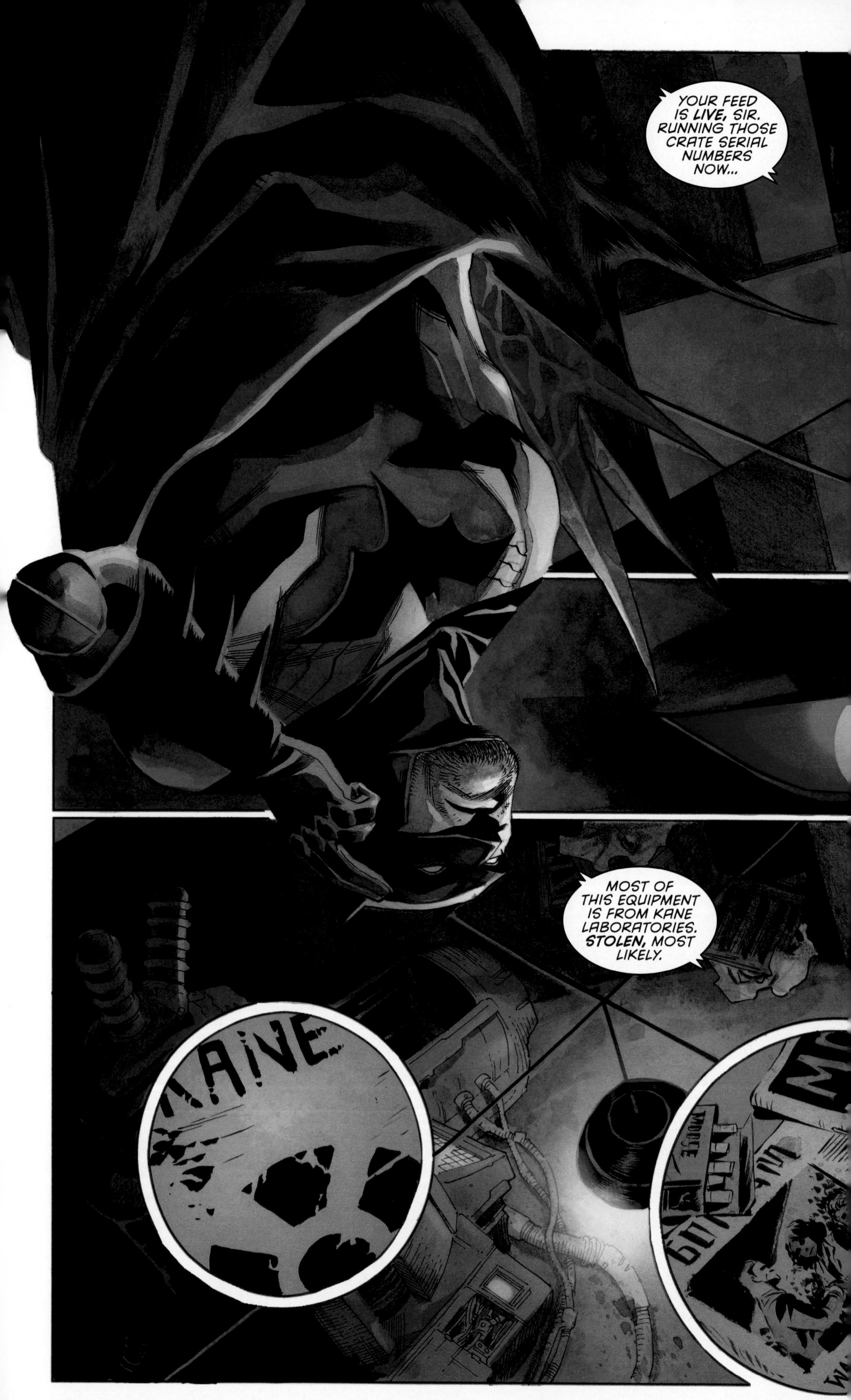
YOUR FEED IS LIVE, SIR. RUNNING THOSE CRATE SERIAL NUMBERS NOW...
MOST OF THIS EQUIPMENT IS FROM KANE LABORATORIES. STOLEN, MOST LIKELY.

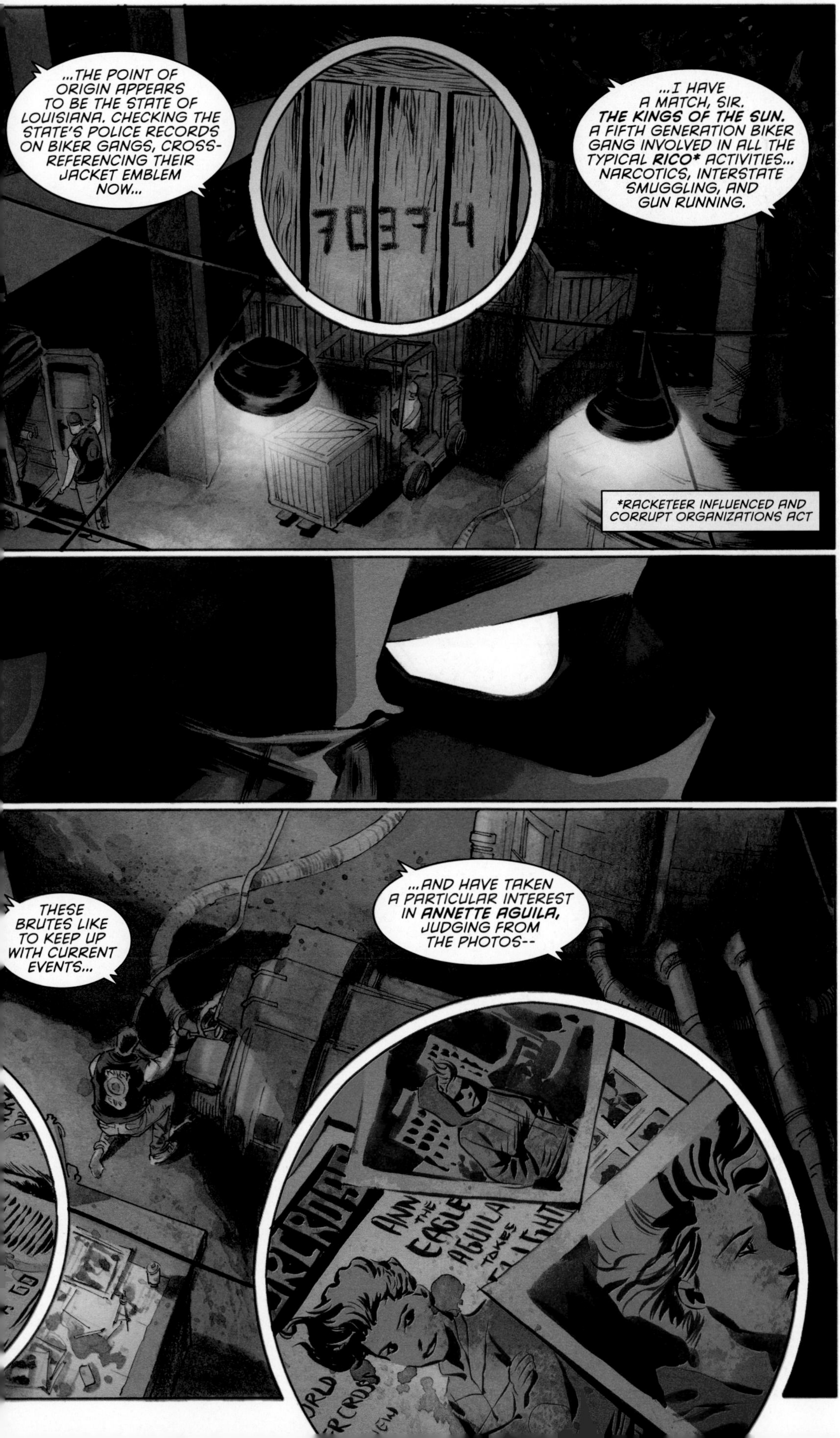
...THE POINT OF ORIGIN APPEARS TO BE THE STATE OF LOUISIANA. CHECKING THE STATE'S POLICE RECORDS ON BIKER GANGS, CROSS-REFERENCING THEIR JACKET EMBLEM NOW...
70374
...I HAVE A MATCH, SIR. **THE KINGS OF THE SUN.** A FIFTH GENERATION BIKER GANG INVOLVED IN ALL THE TYPICAL **RICO*** ACTIVITIES... NARCOTICS, INTERSTATE SMUGGLING, AND GUN RUNNING.
*RACKETEER INFLUENCED AND CORRUPT ORGANIZATIONS ACT
THESE BRUTES LIKE TO KEEP UP WITH CURRENT EVENTS...
...AND HAVE TAKEN A PARTICULAR INTEREST IN **ANNETTE AGUILA,** JUDGING FROM THE PHOTOS--
ANN THE EAGLE AGUILA TAKES

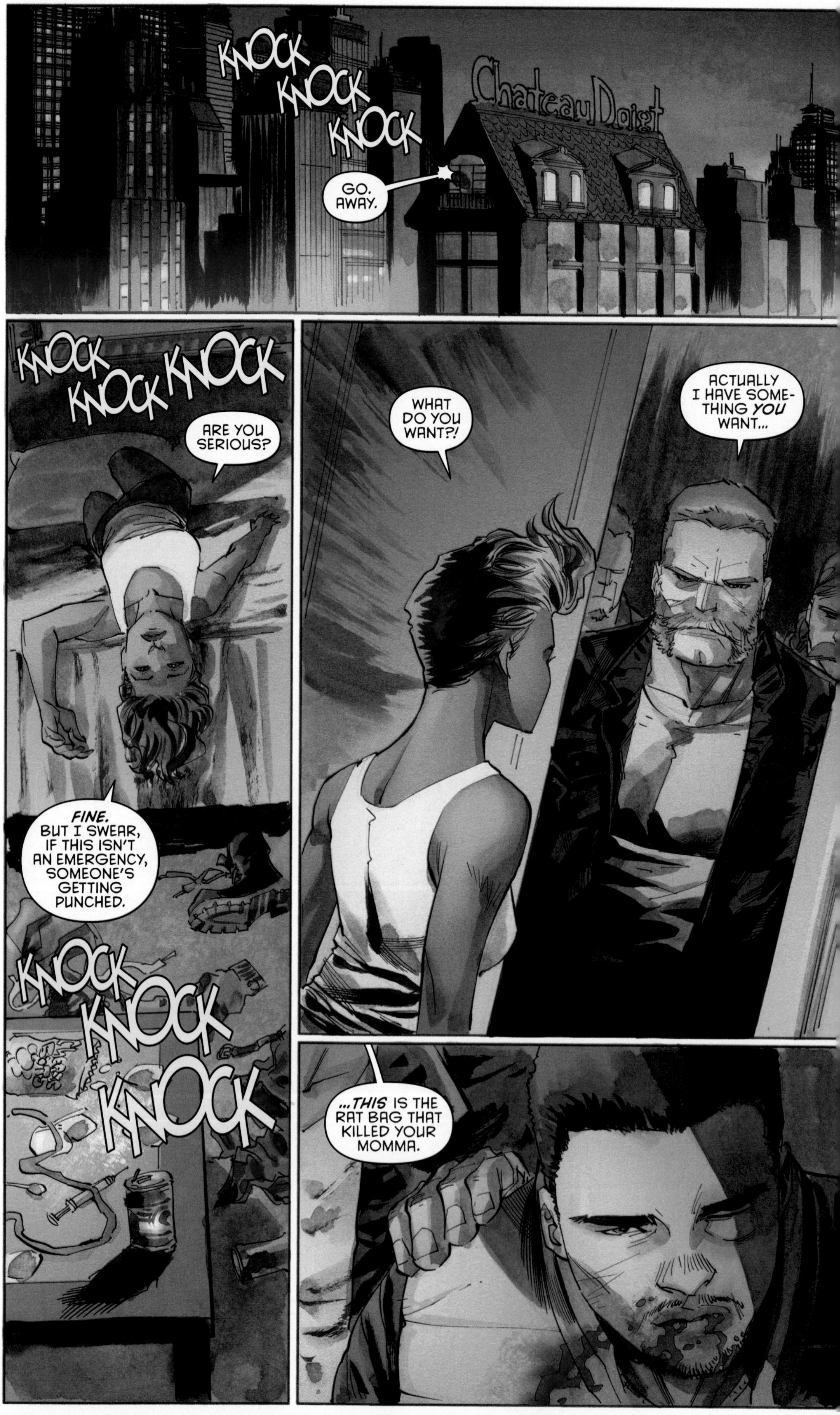

Chateau Doigt
KNOCK KNOCK KNOCK
GO. AWAY.
KNOCK KNOCK KNOCK
ARE YOU SERIOUS?
FINE. BUT I SWEAR, IF THIS ISN'T AN EMERGENCY, SOMEONE'S GETTING PUNCHED.
KNOCK KNOCK KNOCK
WHAT DO YOU WANT?!
ACTUALLY I HAVE SOME-THING YOU WANT...
...THIS IS THE RAT BAG THAT KILLED YOUR MOMMA.

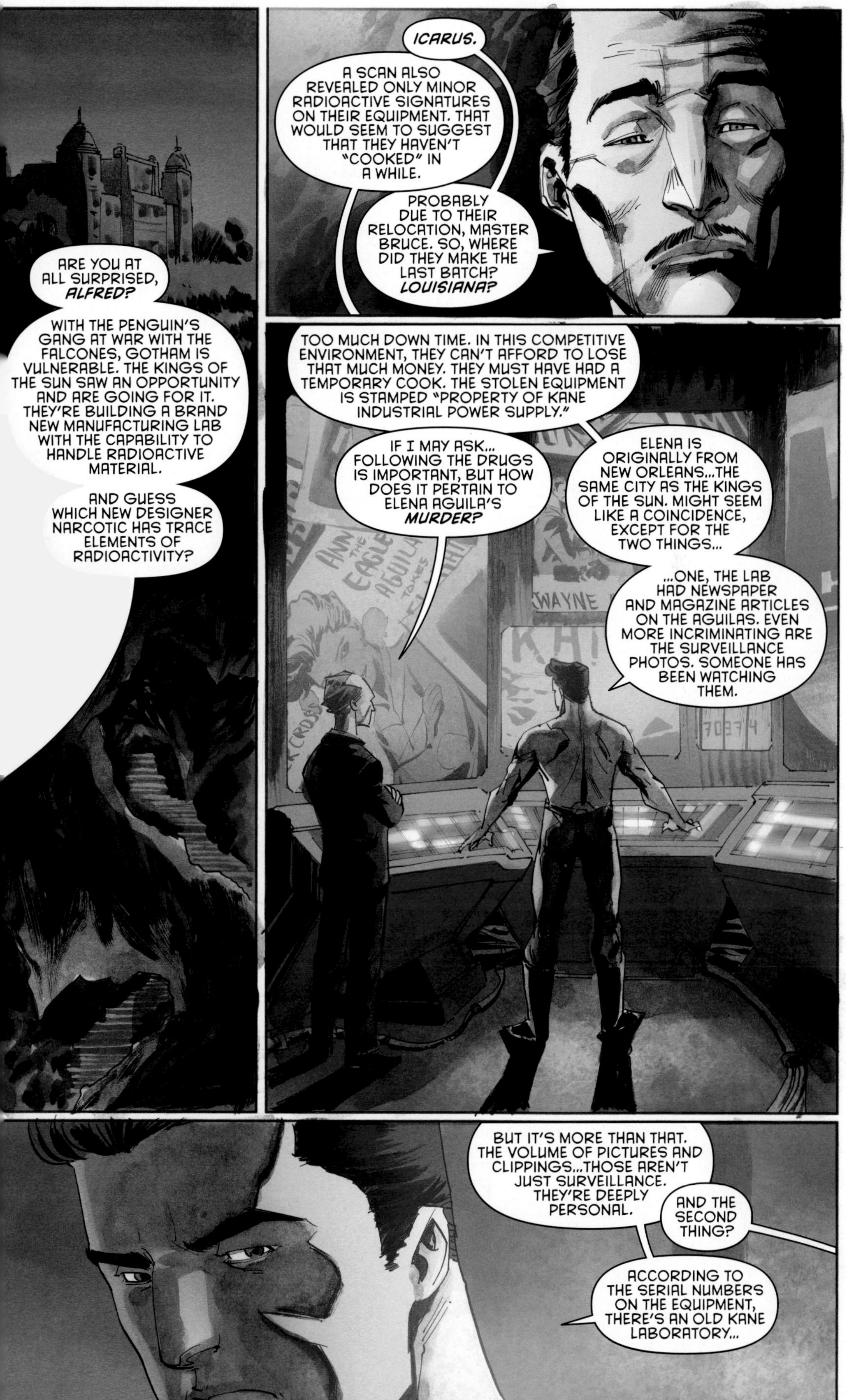
ARE YOU AT ALL SURPRISED, ALFRED?
WITH THE PENGUIN'S GANG AT WAR WITH THE FALCONES, GOTHAM IS VULNERABLE. THE KINGS OF THE SUN SAW AN OPPORTUNITY AND ARE GOING FOR IT. THEY'RE BUILDING A BRAND NEW MANUFACTURING LAB WITH THE CAPABILITY TO HANDLE RADIOACTIVE MATERIAL.
AND GUESS WHICH NEW DESIGNER NARCOTIC HAS TRACE ELEMENTS OF RADIOACTIVITY?
ICARUS.
A SCAN ALSO REVEALED ONLY MINOR RADIOACTIVE SIGNATURES ON THEIR EQUIPMENT. THAT WOULD SEEM TO SUGGEST THAT THEY HAVEN'T "COOKED" IN A WHILE.
PROBABLY DUE TO THEIR RELOCATION, MASTER BRUCE. SO, WHERE DID THEY MAKE THE LAST BATCH? LOUISIANA?
TOO MUCH DOWN TIME. IN THIS COMPETITIVE ENVIRONMENT, THEY CAN'T AFFORD TO LOSE THAT MUCH MONEY. THEY MUST HAVE HAD A TEMPORARY COOK. THE STOLEN EQUIPMENT IS STAMPED "PROPERTY OF KANE INDUSTRIAL POWER SUPPLY."
IF I MAY ASK... FOLLOWING THE DRUGS IS IMPORTANT, BUT HOW DOES IT PERTAIN TO ELENA AGUILA'S MURDER?
ELENA IS ORIGINALLY FROM NEW ORLEANS...THE SAME CITY AS THE KINGS OF THE SUN. MIGHT SEEM LIKE A COINCIDENCE, EXCEPT FOR THE TWO THINGS...
...ONE, THE LAB HAD NEWSPAPER AND MAGAZINE ARTICLES ON THE AGUILAS. EVEN MORE INCRIMINATING ARE THE SURVEILLANCE PHOTOS. SOMEONE HAS BEEN WATCHING THEM.
BUT IT'S MORE THAN THAT. THE VOLUME OF PICTURES AND CLIPPINGS...THOSE AREN'T JUST SURVEILLANCE. THEY'RE DEEPLY PERSONAL.
AND THE SECOND THING?
ACCORDING TO THE SERIAL NUMBERS ON THE EQUIPMENT, THERE'S AN OLD KANE LABORATORY...

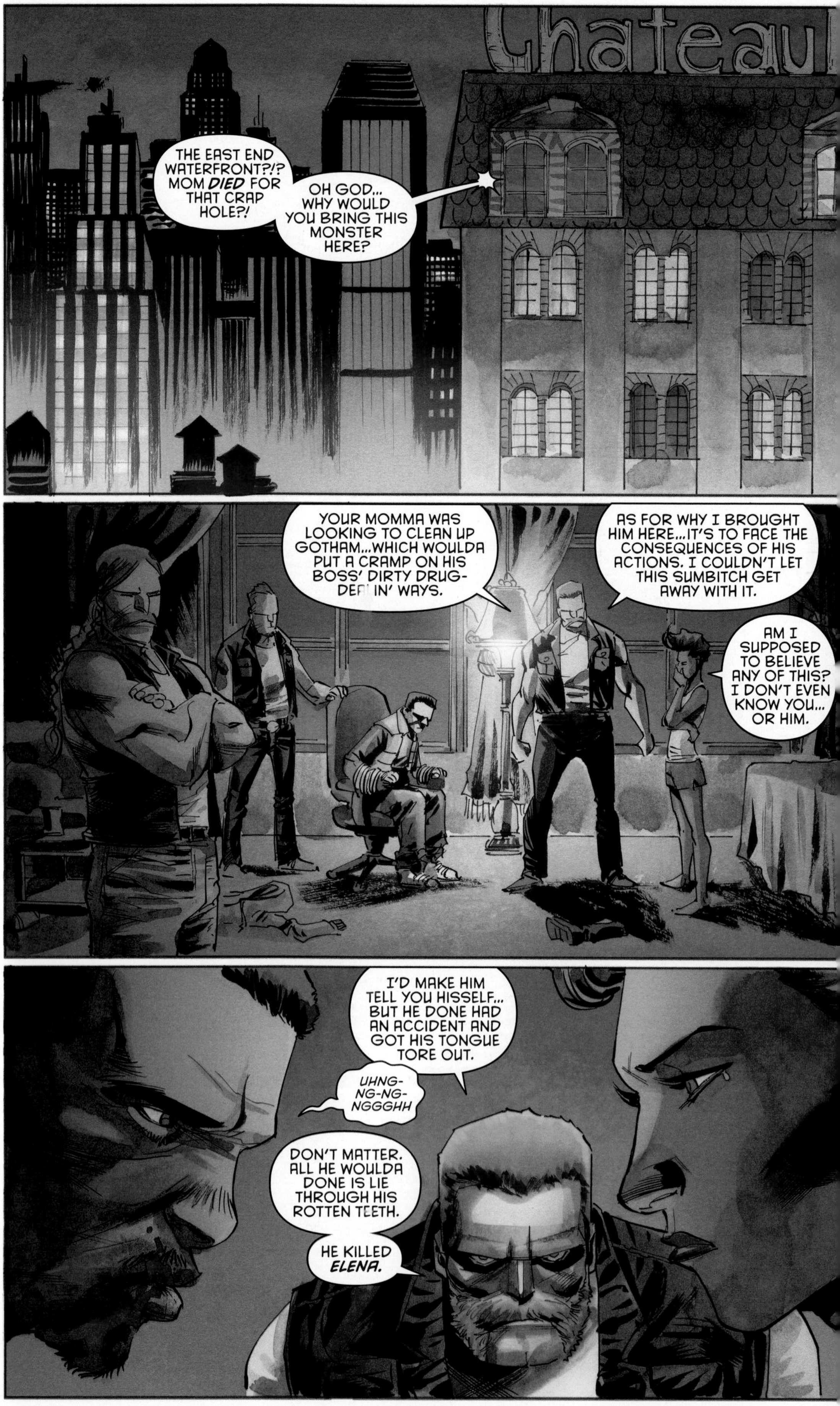
THE EAST END WATERFRONT?!? MOM DIED FOR THAT CRAP HOLE?!
OH GOD... WHY WOULD YOU BRING THIS MONSTER HERE?
Chateau
YOUR MOMMA WAS LOOKING TO CLEAN UP GOTHAM...WHICH WOULDA PUT A CRAMP ON HIS BOSS' DIRTY DRUG-DEALIN' WAYS.
AS FOR WHY I BROUGHT HIM HERE...IT'S TO FACE THE CONSEQUENCES OF HIS ACTIONS. I COULDN'T LET THIS SUMBITCH GET AWAY WITH IT.
AM I SUPPOSED TO BELIEVE ANY OF THIS? I DON'T EVEN KNOW YOU... OR HIM.
I'D MAKE HIM TELL YOU HISSELF... BUT HE DONE HAD AN ACCIDENT AND GOT HIS TONGUE TORE OUT.
UHNG-NG-NG-NGGGHH
DON'T MATTER. ALL HE WOULDA DONE IS LIE THROUGH HIS ROTTEN TEETH.
HE KILLED ELENA.

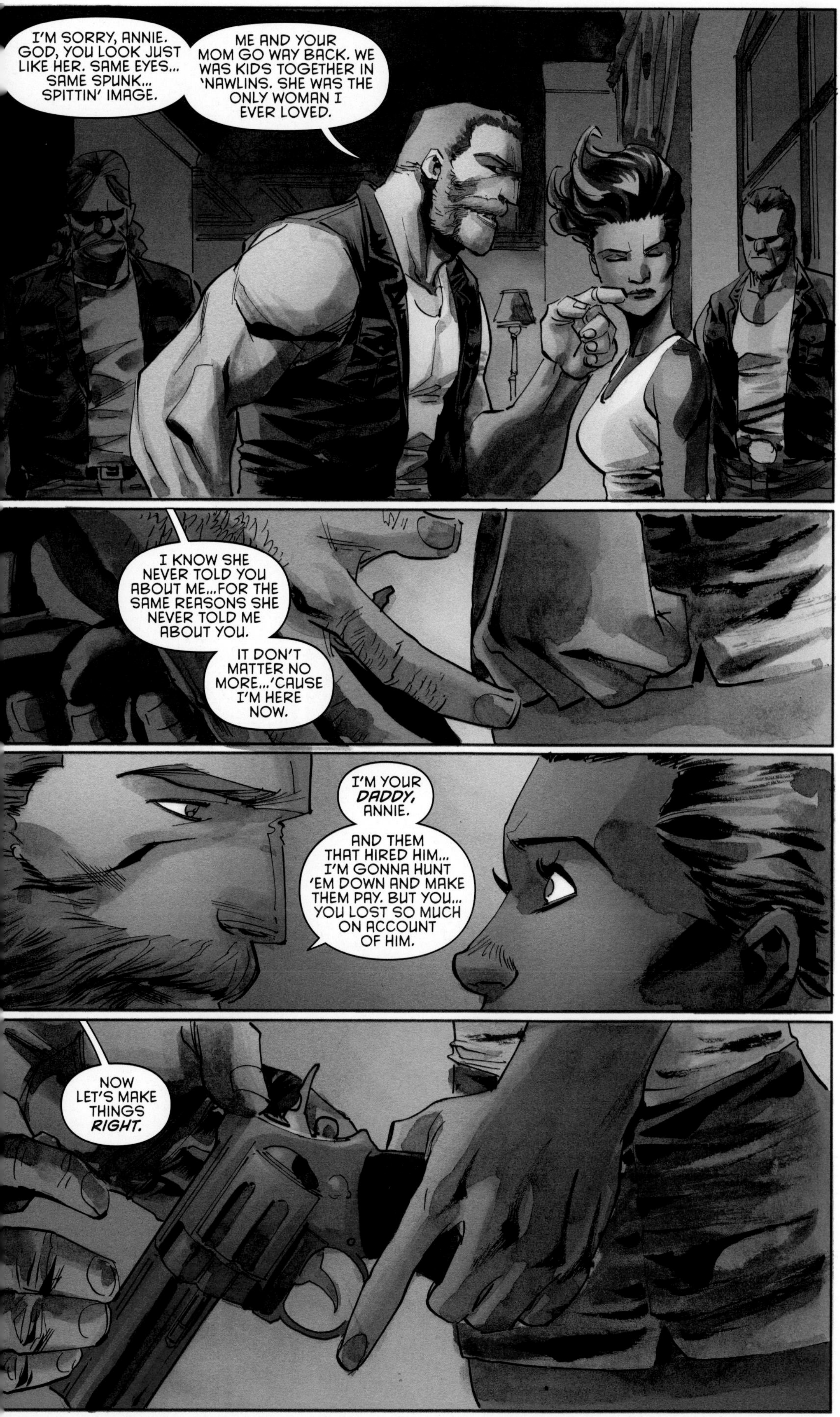
I'M SORRY, ANNIE. GOD, YOU LOOK JUST LIKE HER. SAME EYES... SAME SPUNK... SPITTIN' IMAGE.
ME AND YOUR MOM GO WAY BACK. WE WAS KIDS TOGETHER IN 'NAWLINS. SHE WAS THE ONLY WOMAN I EVER LOVED.
I KNOW SHE NEVER TOLD YOU ABOUT ME...FOR THE SAME REASONS SHE NEVER TOLD ME ABOUT YOU.
IT DON'T MATTER NO MORE...'CAUSE I'M HERE NOW.
I'M YOUR *DADDY,* ANNIE.
AND THEM THAT HIRED HIM... I'M GONNA HUNT 'EM DOWN AND MAKE THEM PAY. BUT YOU... YOU LOST SO MUCH ON ACCOUNT OF HIM.
NOW LET'S MAKE THINGS *RIGHT.*

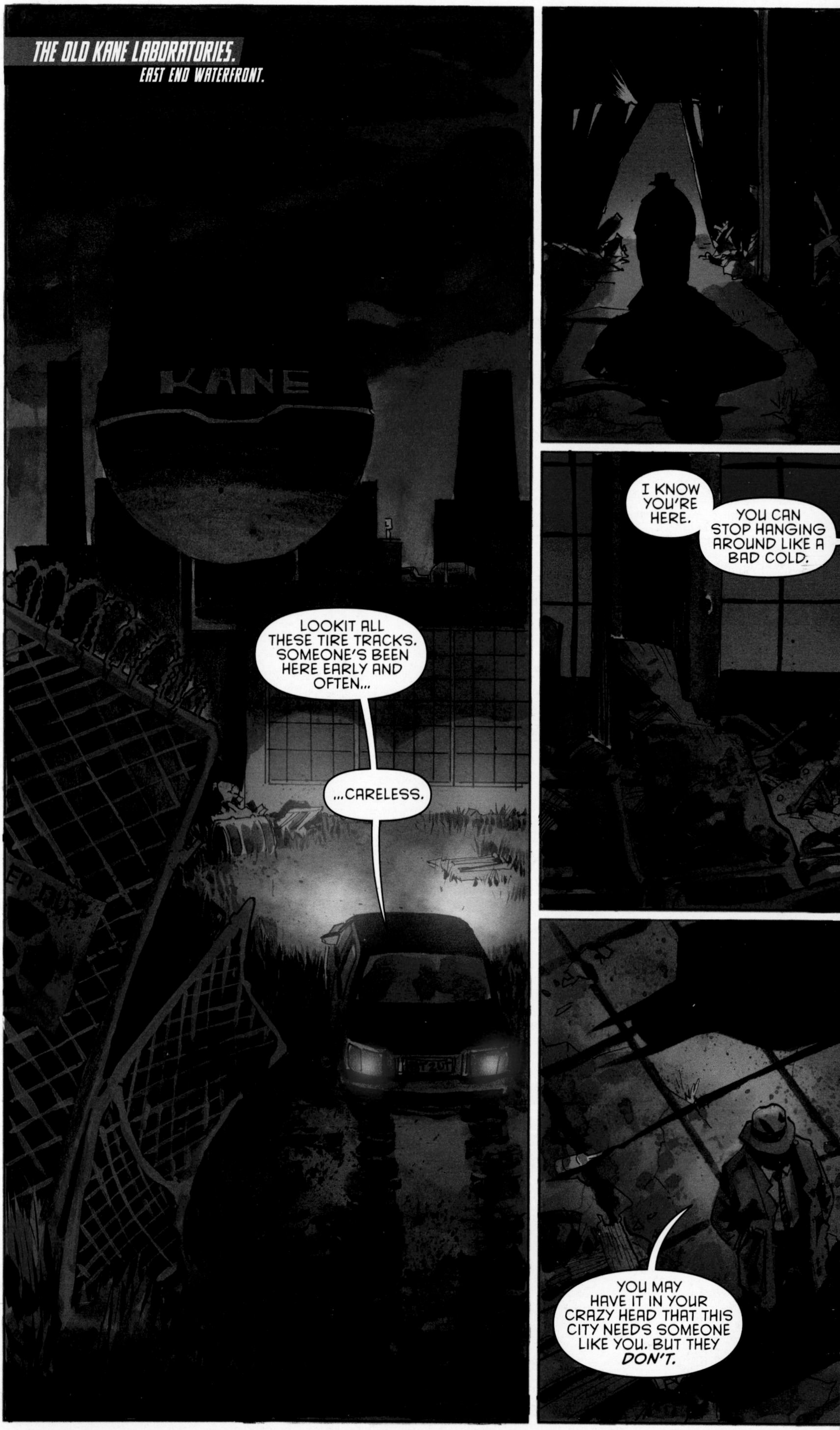
THE OLD KANE LABORATORIES.
EAST END WATERFRONT.
KANE
LOOKIT ALL THESE TIRE TRACKS. SOMEONE'S BEEN HERE EARLY AND OFTEN...
...CARELESS.
I KNOW YOU'RE HERE.
YOU CAN STOP HANGING AROUND LIKE A BAD COLD.
YOU MAY HAVE IT IN YOUR CRAZY HEAD THAT THIS CITY NEEDS SOMEONE LIKE YOU. BUT THEY *DON'T.*

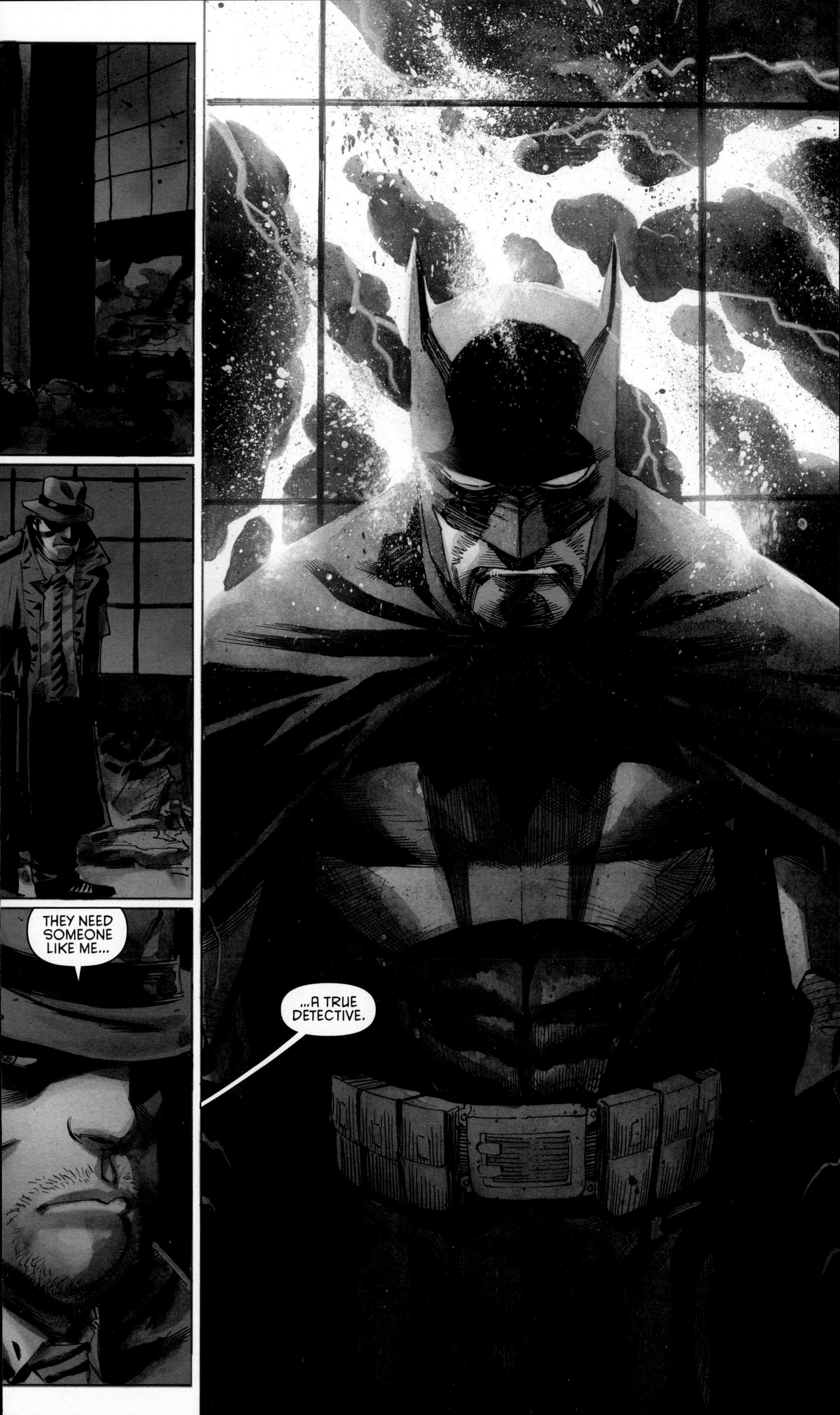
THEY NEED SOMEONE LIKE ME...
...A TRUE DETECTIVE.

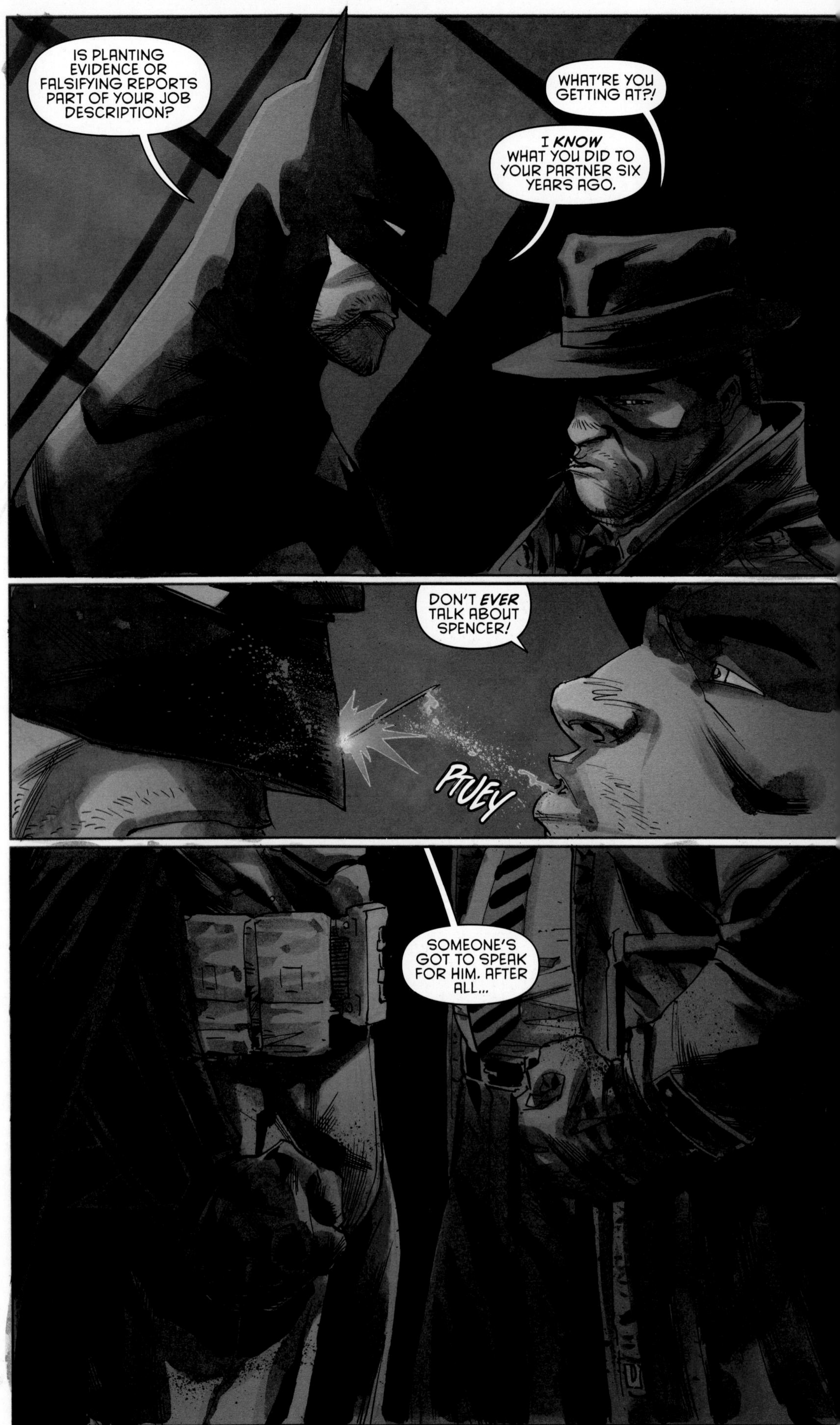
IS PLANTING EVIDENCE OR FALSIFYING REPORTS PART OF YOUR JOB DESCRIPTION?
WHAT'RE YOU GETTING AT?!
I *KNOW* WHAT YOU DID TO YOUR PARTNER SIX YEARS AGO.
DON'T *EVER* TALK ABOUT SPENCER!
PTUEY
SOMEONE'S GOT TO SPEAK FOR HIM. AFTER ALL...

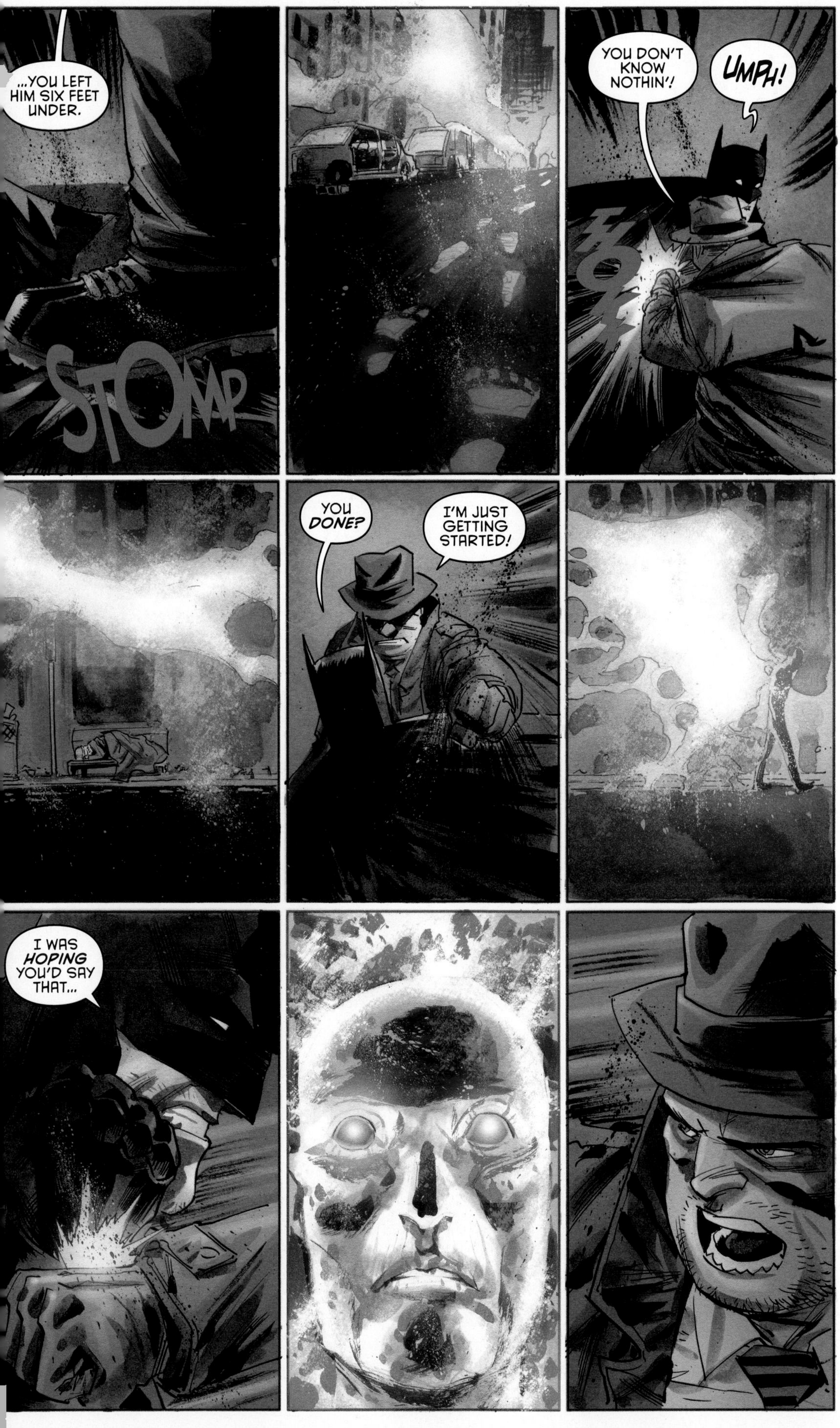
...YOU LEFT HIM SIX FEET UNDER.
STOMP
YOU DON'T KNOW NOTHIN'!
UMPH!
YOU DONE?
I'M JUST GETTING STARTED!
I WAS HOPING YOU'D SAY THAT...

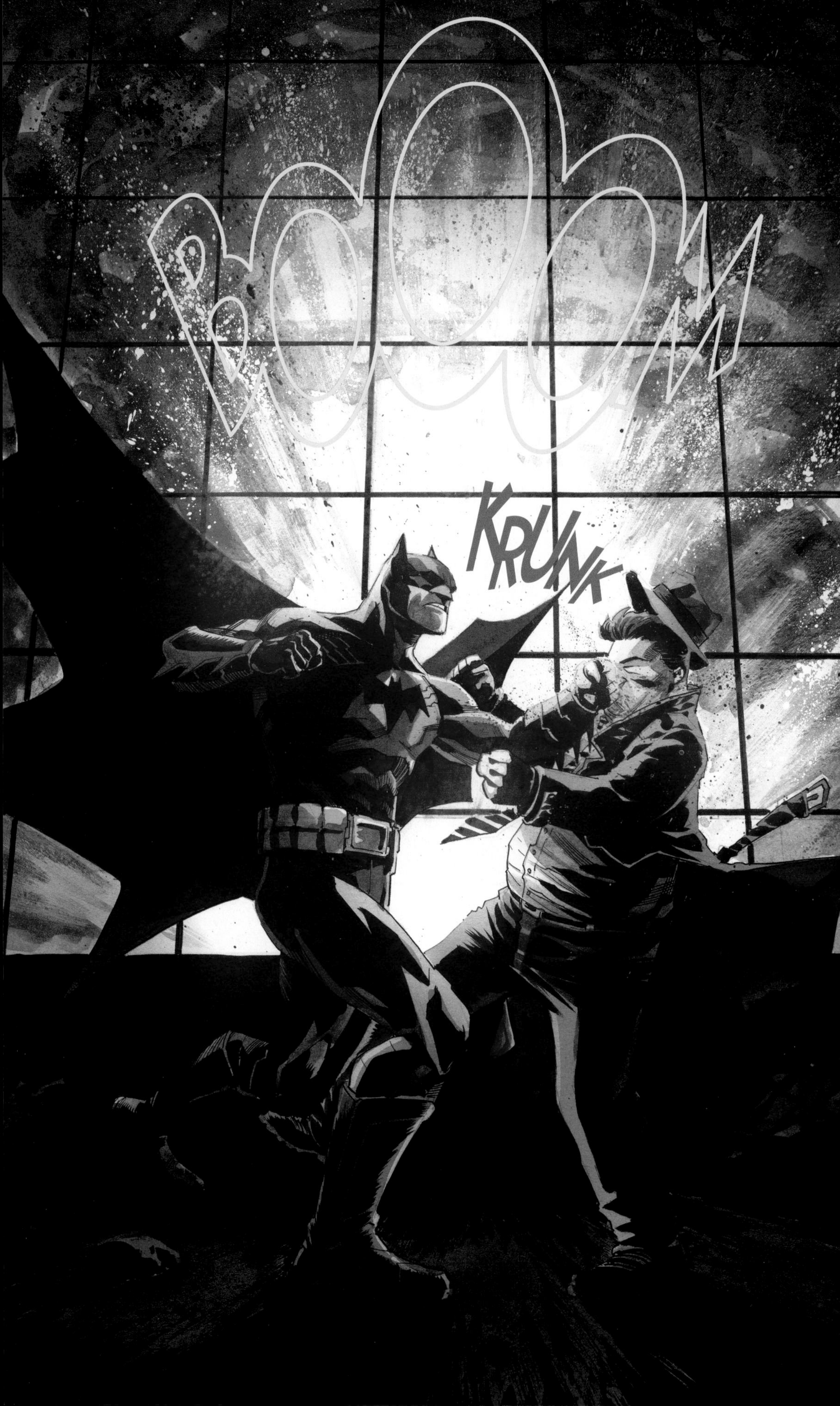
BOOOM
KRUNK

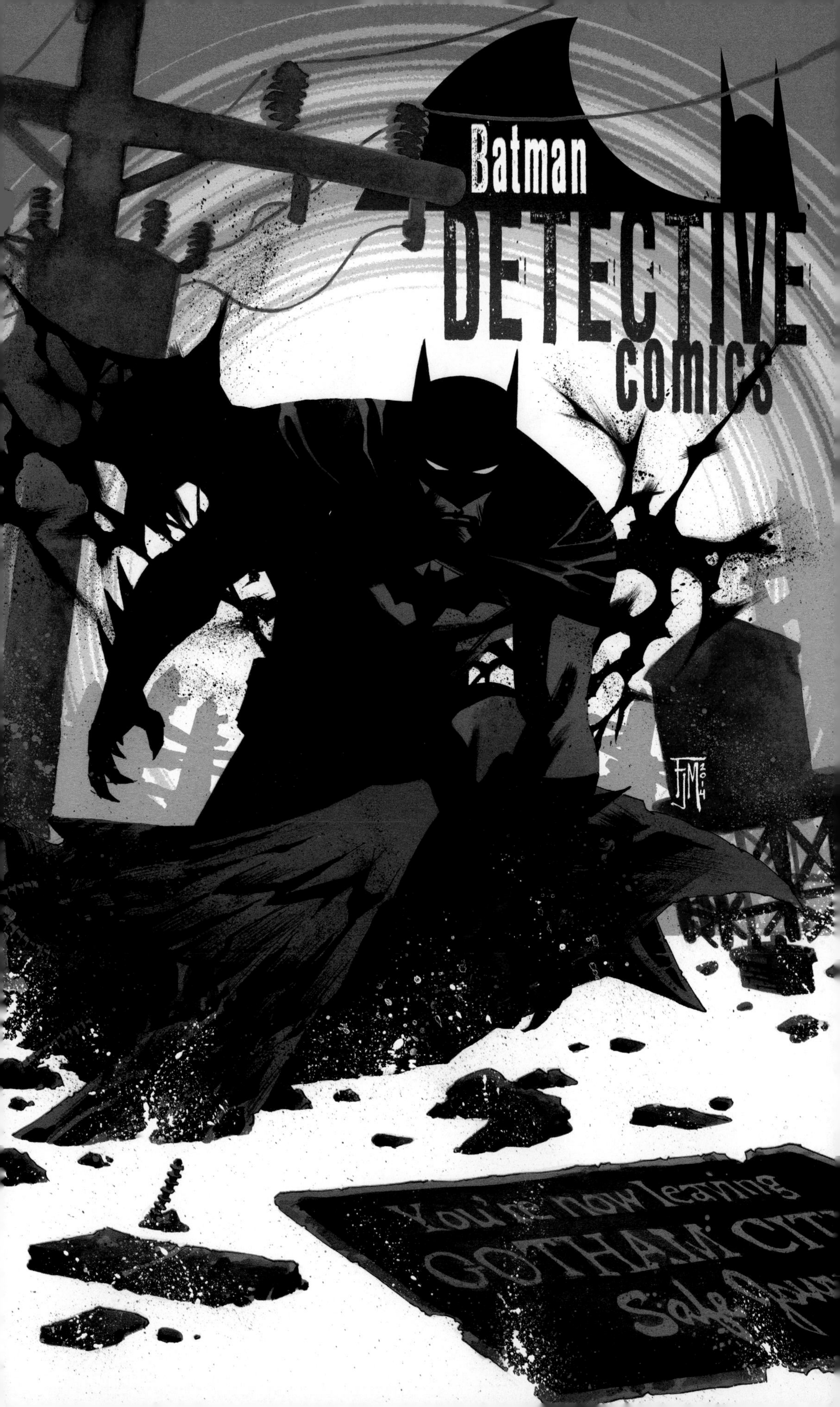
Batman
DETECTIVE
comics
You're now leaving

A

Batman
DETECTIVE
comics

B

Batman
DETECTIVE
comics

C

Batman
DETECTIVE
comics

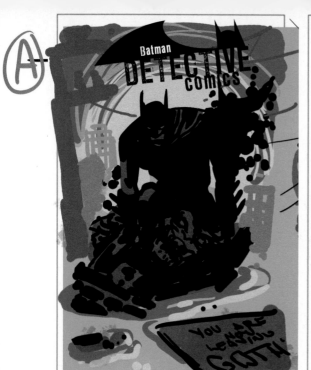

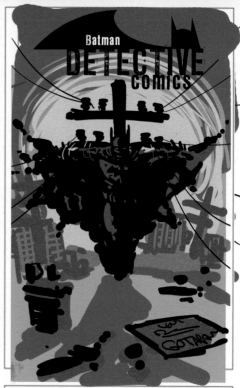

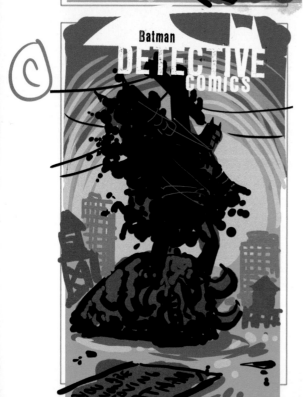

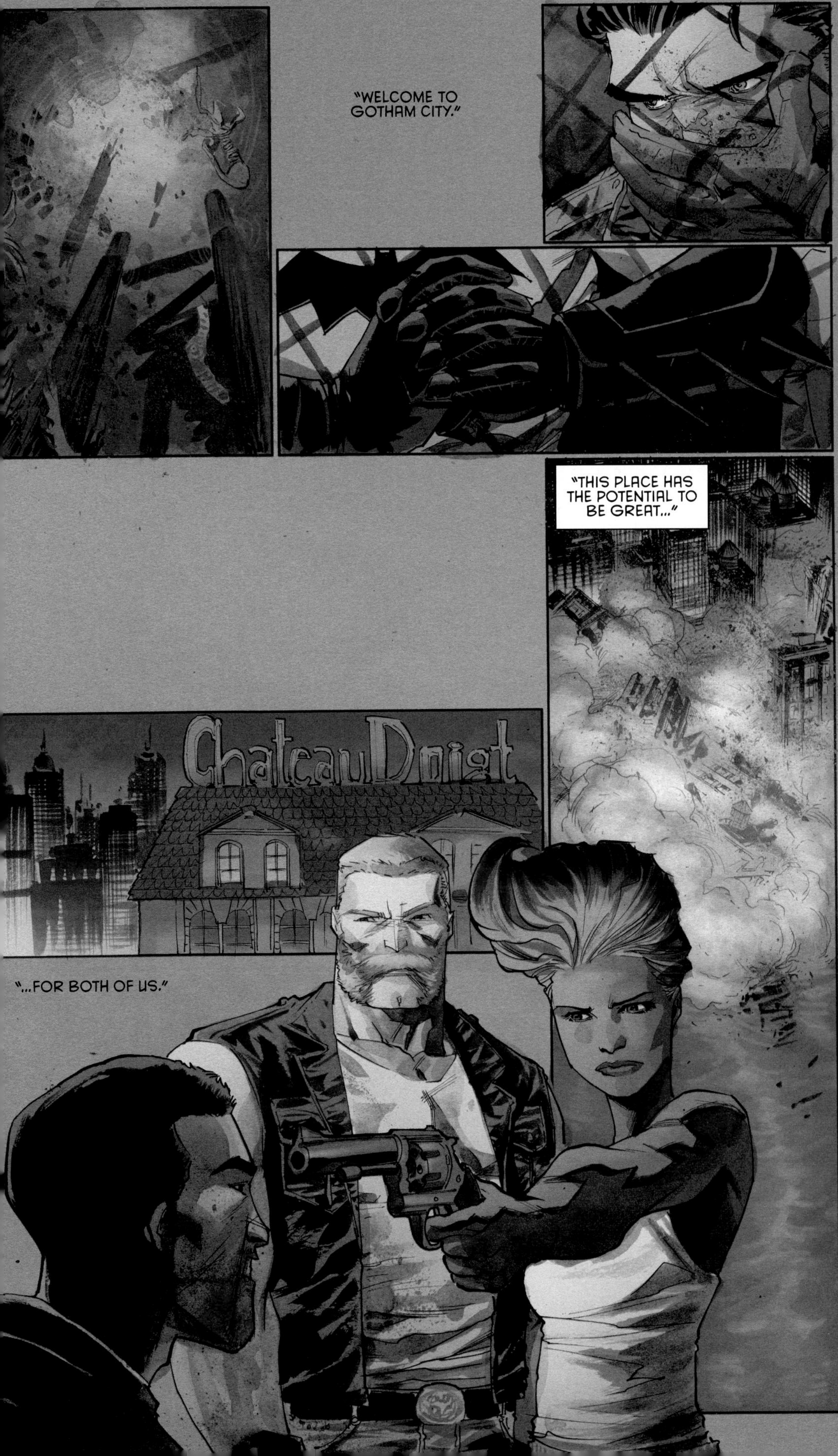
"WELCOME TO GOTHAM CITY."
"THIS PLACE HAS THE POTENTIAL TO BE GREAT..."
ChateauDnigt
"...FOR BOTH OF US."

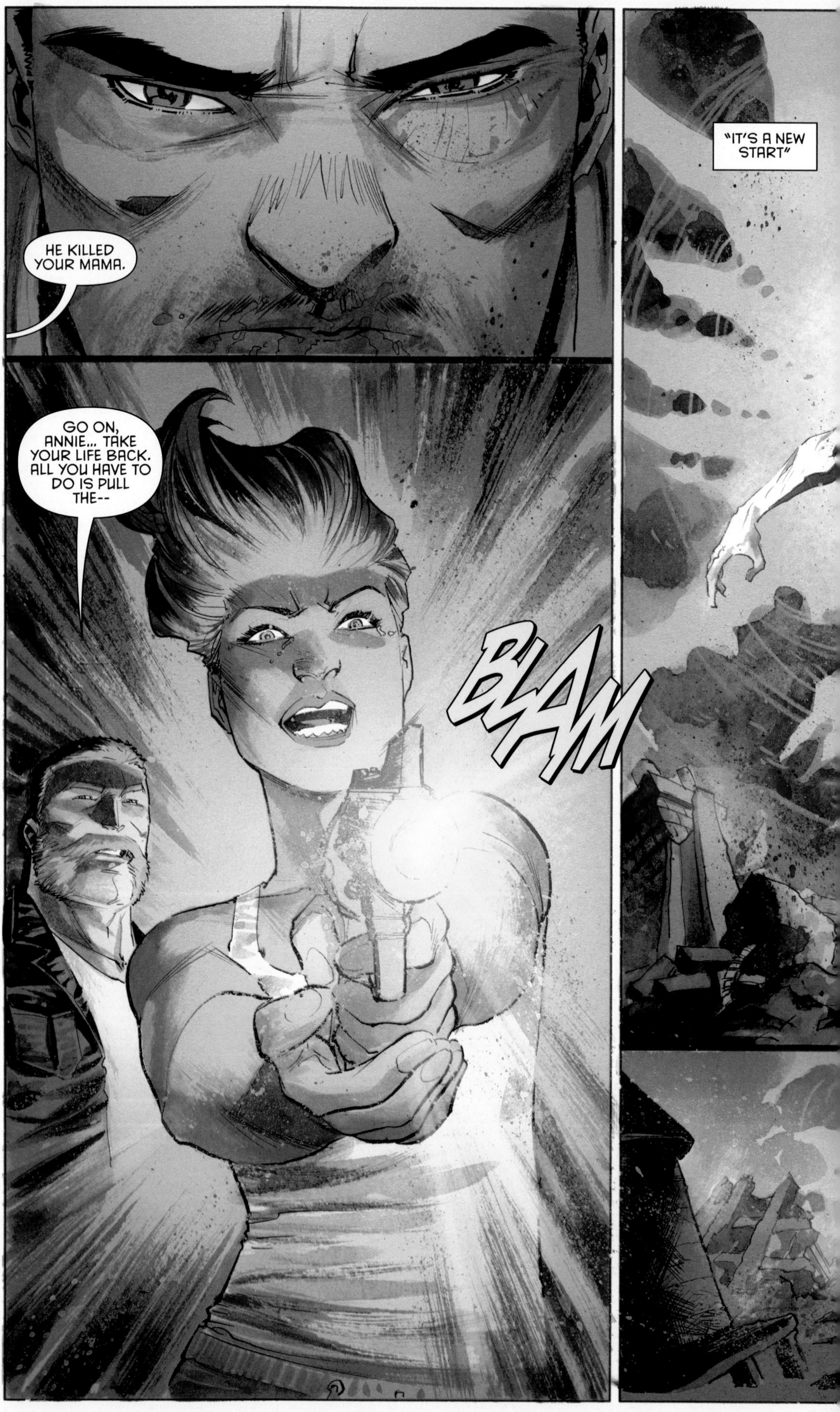
HE KILLED YOUR MAMA.
GO ON, ANNIE... TAKE YOUR LIFE BACK. ALL YOU HAVE TO DO IS PULL THE--
BLAM
"IT'S A NEW START"

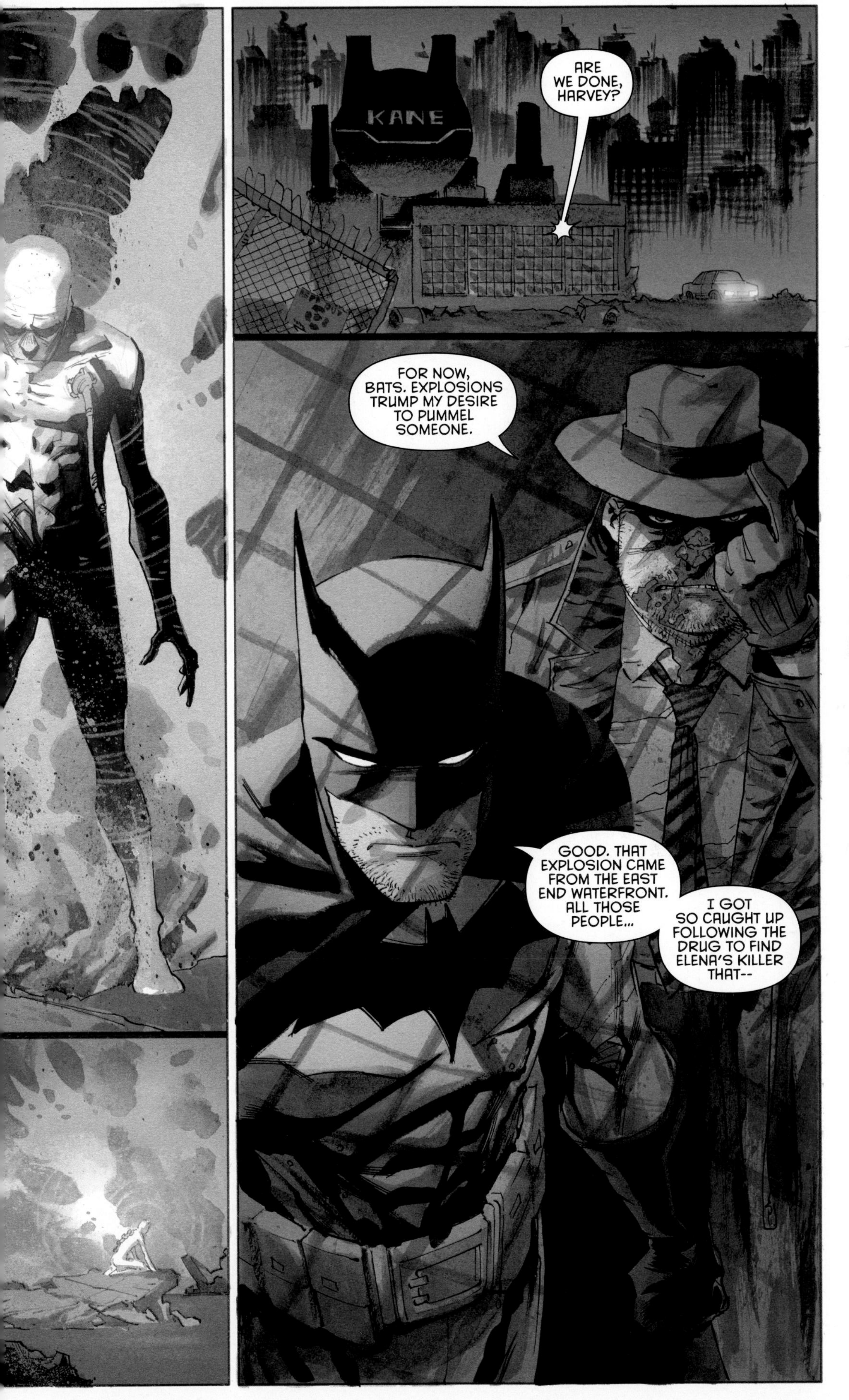
KANE
ARE WE DONE, HARVEY?
FOR NOW, BATS. EXPLOSIONS TRUMP MY DESIRE TO PUMMEL SOMEONE.
GOOD. THAT EXPLOSION CAME FROM THE EAST END WATERFRONT. ALL THOSE PEOPLE...
I GOT SO CAUGHT UP FOLLOWING THE DRUG TO FIND ELENA'S KILLER THAT--

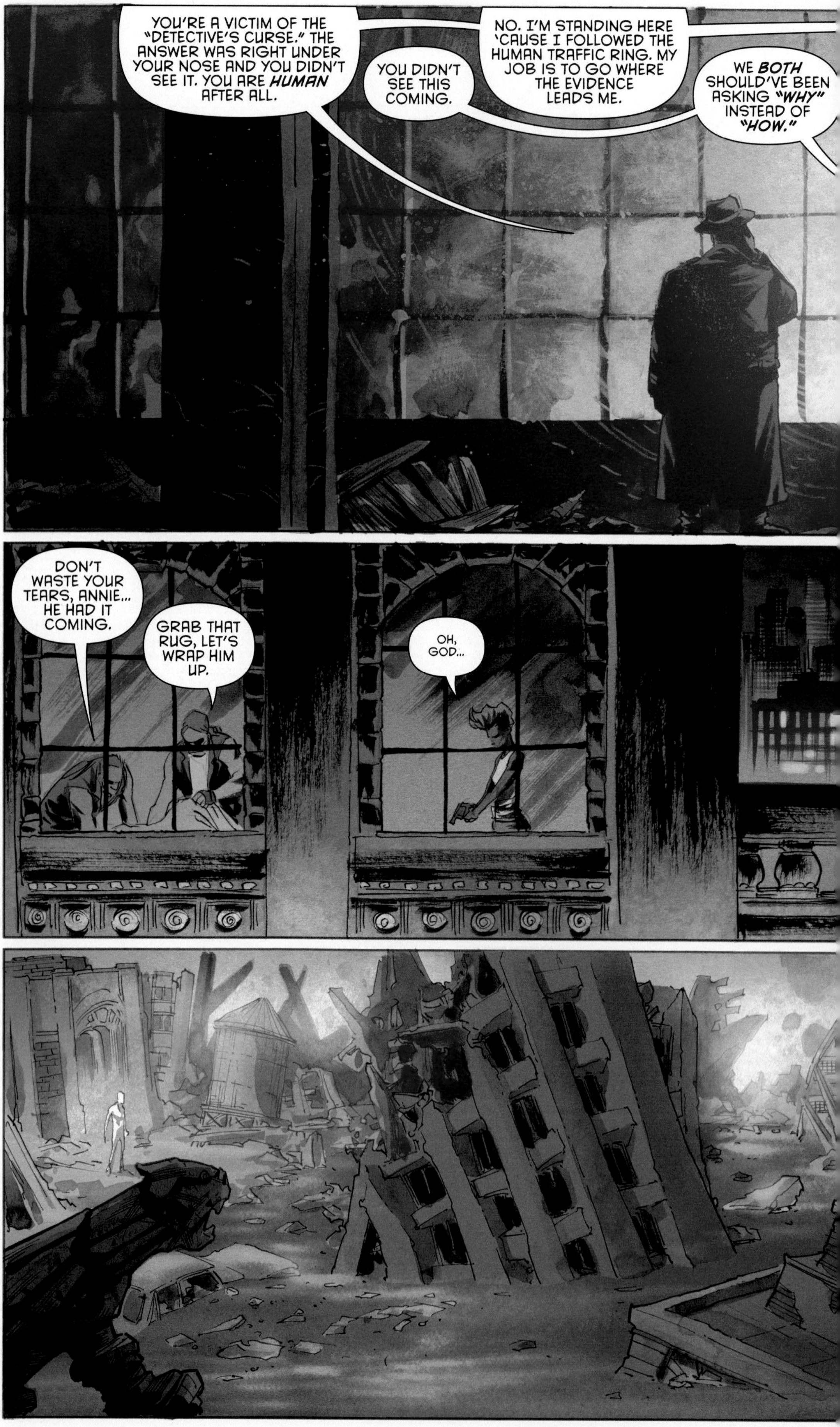
YOU'RE A VICTIM OF THE "DETECTIVE'S CURSE." THE ANSWER WAS RIGHT UNDER YOUR NOSE AND YOU DIDN'T SEE IT. YOU ARE *HUMAN* AFTER ALL.
YOU DIDN'T SEE THIS COMING.
NO. I'M STANDING HERE 'CAUSE I FOLLOWED THE HUMAN TRAFFIC RING. MY JOB IS TO GO WHERE THE EVIDENCE LEADS ME.
WE *BOTH* SHOULD'VE BEEN ASKING *"WHY"* INSTEAD OF *"HOW."*
DON'T WASTE YOUR TEARS, ANNIE... HE HAD IT COMING.
GRAB THAT RUG, LET'S WRAP HIM UP.
OH, GOD...

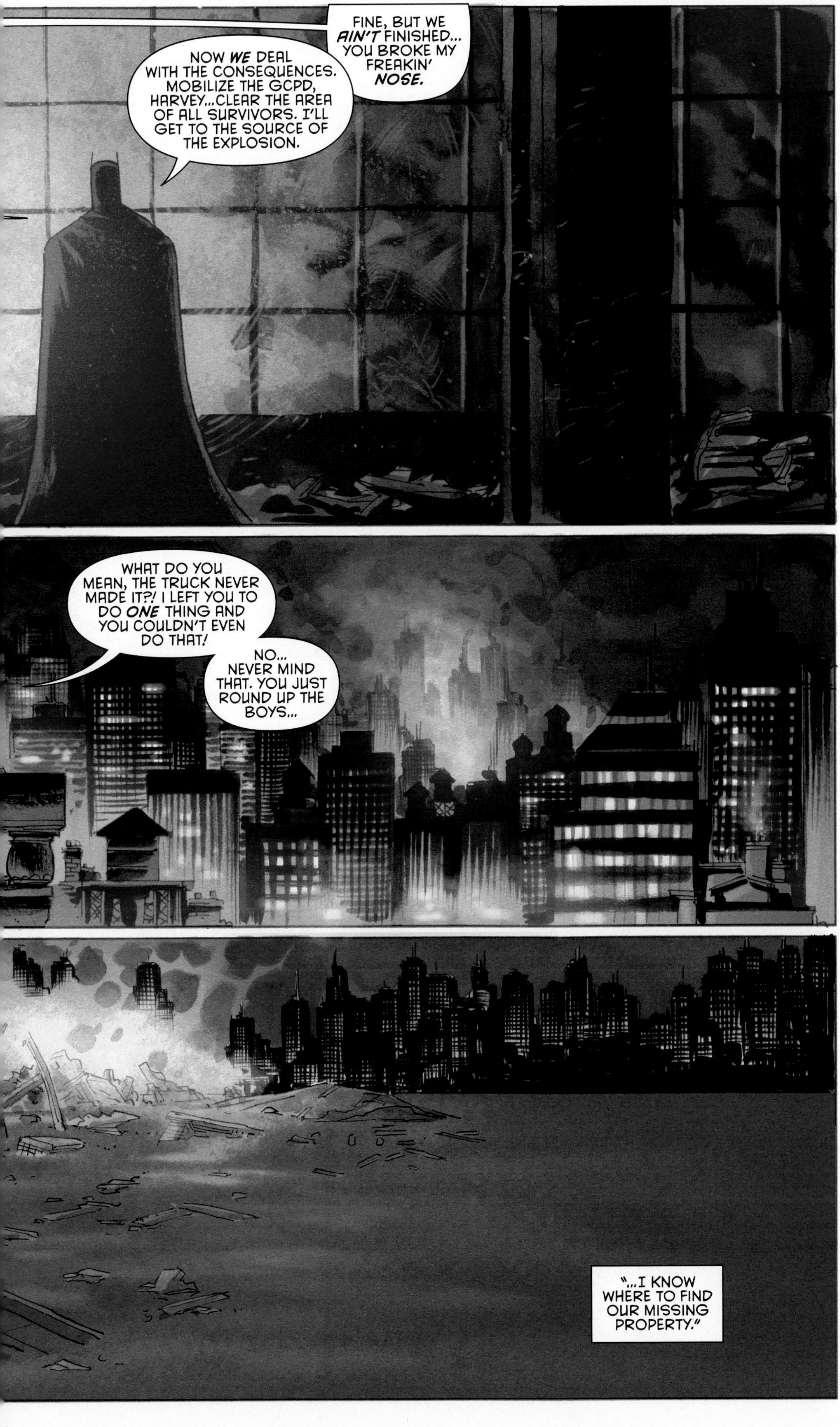
NOW WE DEAL WITH THE CONSEQUENCES. MOBILIZE THE GCPD, HARVEY...CLEAR THE AREA OF ALL SURVIVORS. I'LL GET TO THE SOURCE OF THE EXPLOSION.
FINE, BUT WE AIN'T FINISHED... YOU BROKE MY FREAKIN' NOSE.
WHAT DO YOU MEAN, THE TRUCK NEVER MADE IT?! I LEFT YOU TO DO ONE THING AND YOU COULDN'T EVEN DO THAT!
NO... NEVER MIND THAT. YOU JUST ROUND UP THE BOYS...
"...I KNOW WHERE TO FIND OUR MISSING PROPERTY."

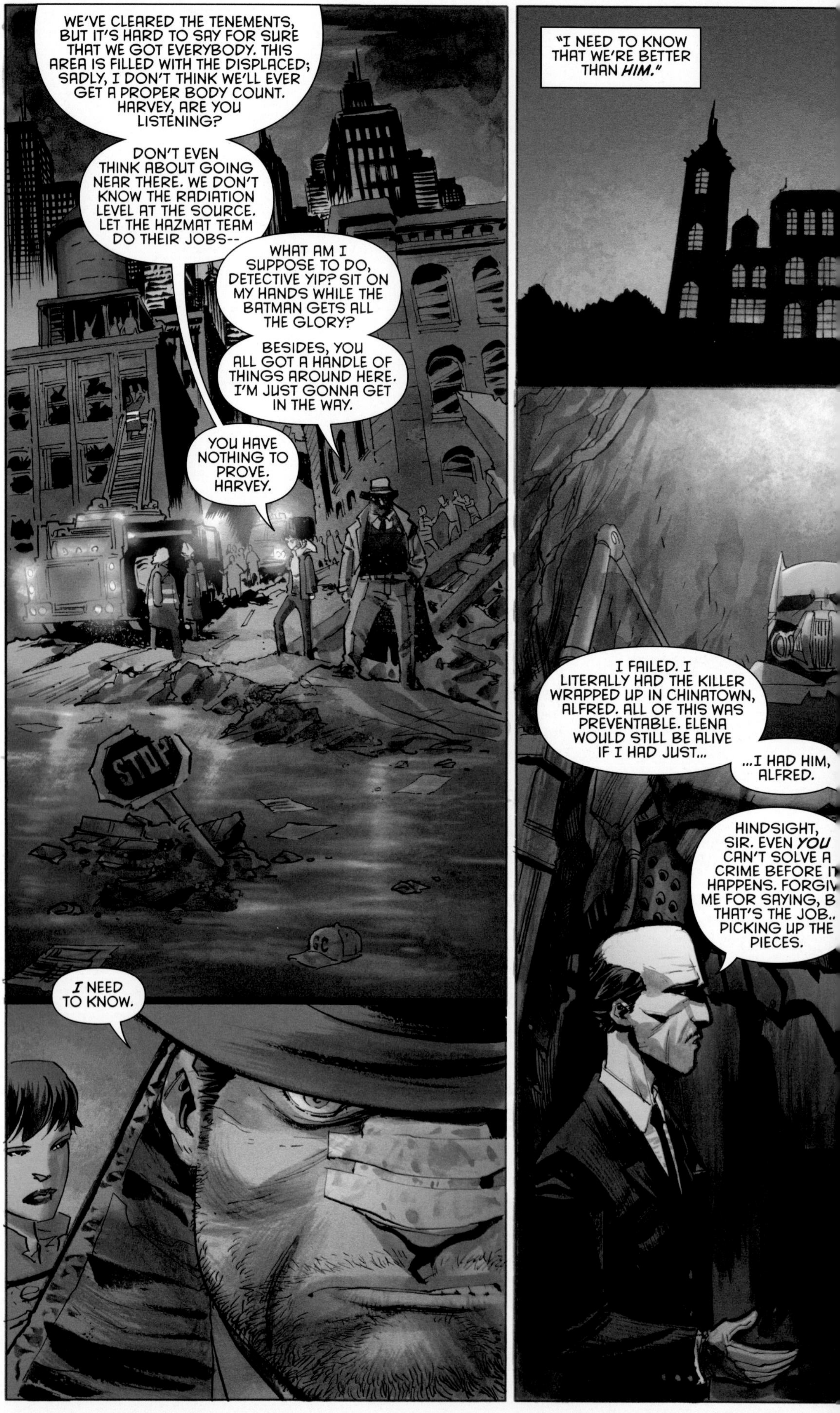

WE'VE CLEARED THE TENEMENTS, BUT IT'S HARD TO SAY FOR SURE THAT WE GOT EVERYBODY. THIS AREA IS FILLED WITH THE DISPLACED; SADLY, I DON'T THINK WE'LL EVER GET A PROPER BODY COUNT. HARVEY, ARE YOU LISTENING?
DON'T EVEN THINK ABOUT GOING NEAR THERE. WE DON'T KNOW THE RADIATION LEVEL AT THE SOURCE. LET THE HAZMAT TEAM DO THEIR JOBS--
WHAT AM I SUPPOSE TO DO, DETECTIVE YIP? SIT ON MY HANDS WHILE THE BATMAN GETS ALL THE GLORY?
BESIDES, YOU ALL GOT A HANDLE OF THINGS AROUND HERE. I'M JUST GONNA GET IN THE WAY.
YOU HAVE NOTHING TO PROVE. HARVEY.
STOP
GC
I NEED TO KNOW.
"I NEED TO KNOW THAT WE'RE BETTER THAN *HIM.*"
I FAILED. I LITERALLY HAD THE KILLER WRAPPED UP IN CHINATOWN, ALFRED. ALL OF THIS WAS PREVENTABLE. ELENA WOULD STILL BE ALIVE IF I HAD JUST...
...I HAD HIM, ALFRED.
HINDSIGHT, SIR. EVEN *YOU* CAN'T SOLVE A CRIME BEFORE IT HAPPENS. FORGIVE ME FOR SAYING, B THAT'S THE JOB... PICKING UP THE PIECES.

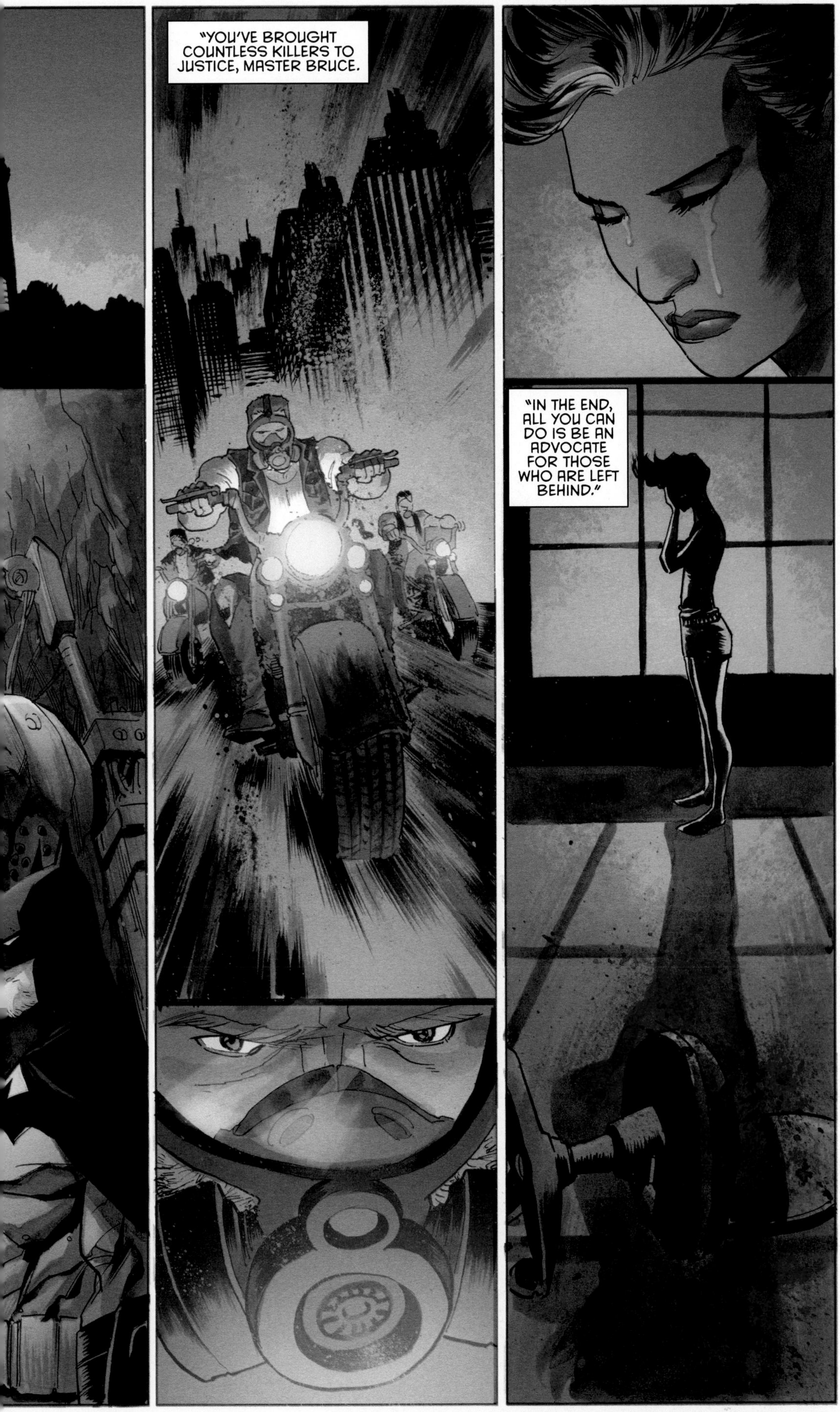
"YOU'VE BROUGHT COUNTLESS KILLERS TO JUSTICE, MASTER BRUCE.
"IN THE END, ALL YOU CAN DO IS BE AN ADVOCATE FOR THOSE WHO ARE LEFT BEHIND."

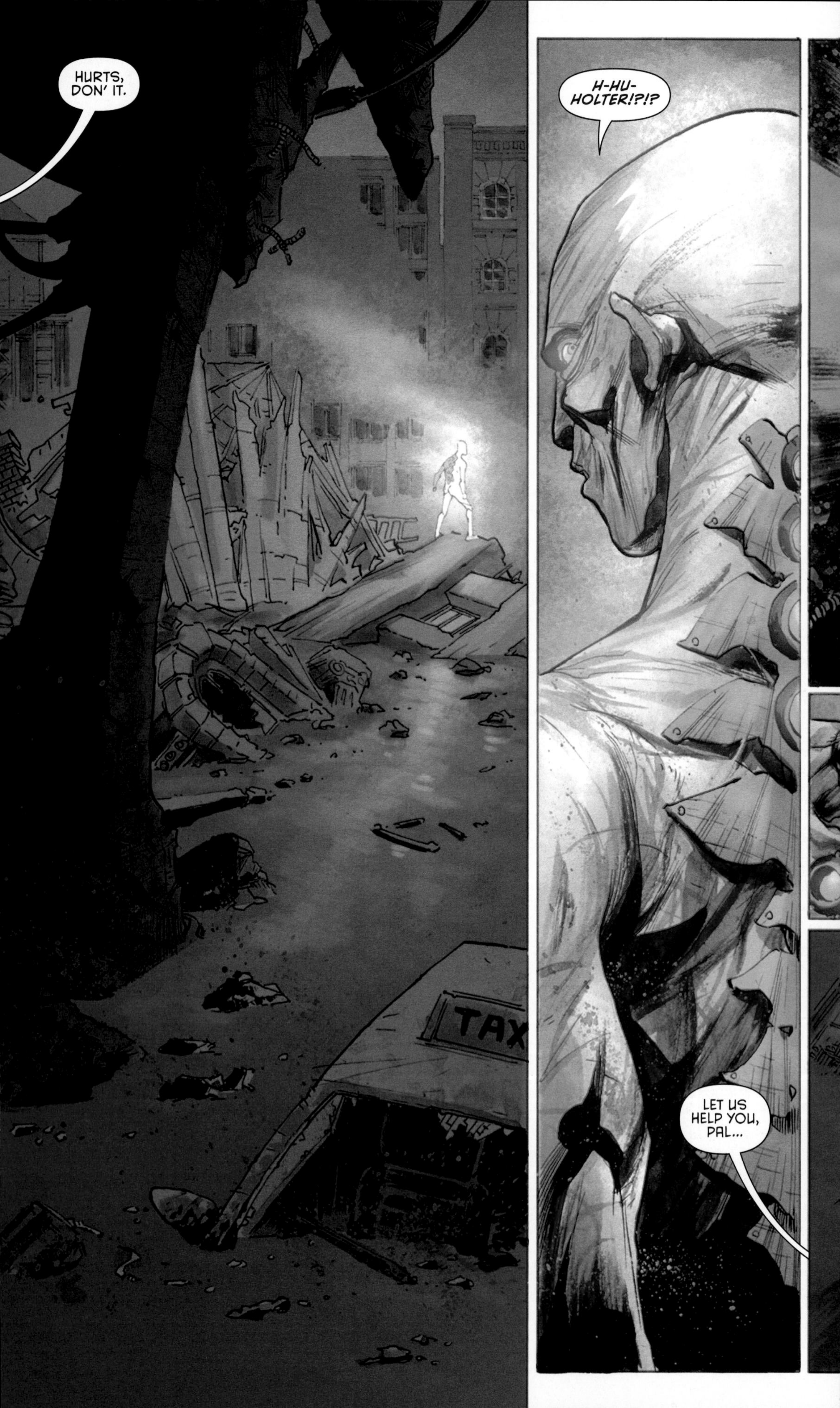
HURTS, DON' IT.
H-HU-HOLTER!?!?
LET US HELP YOU, PAL...
TAX

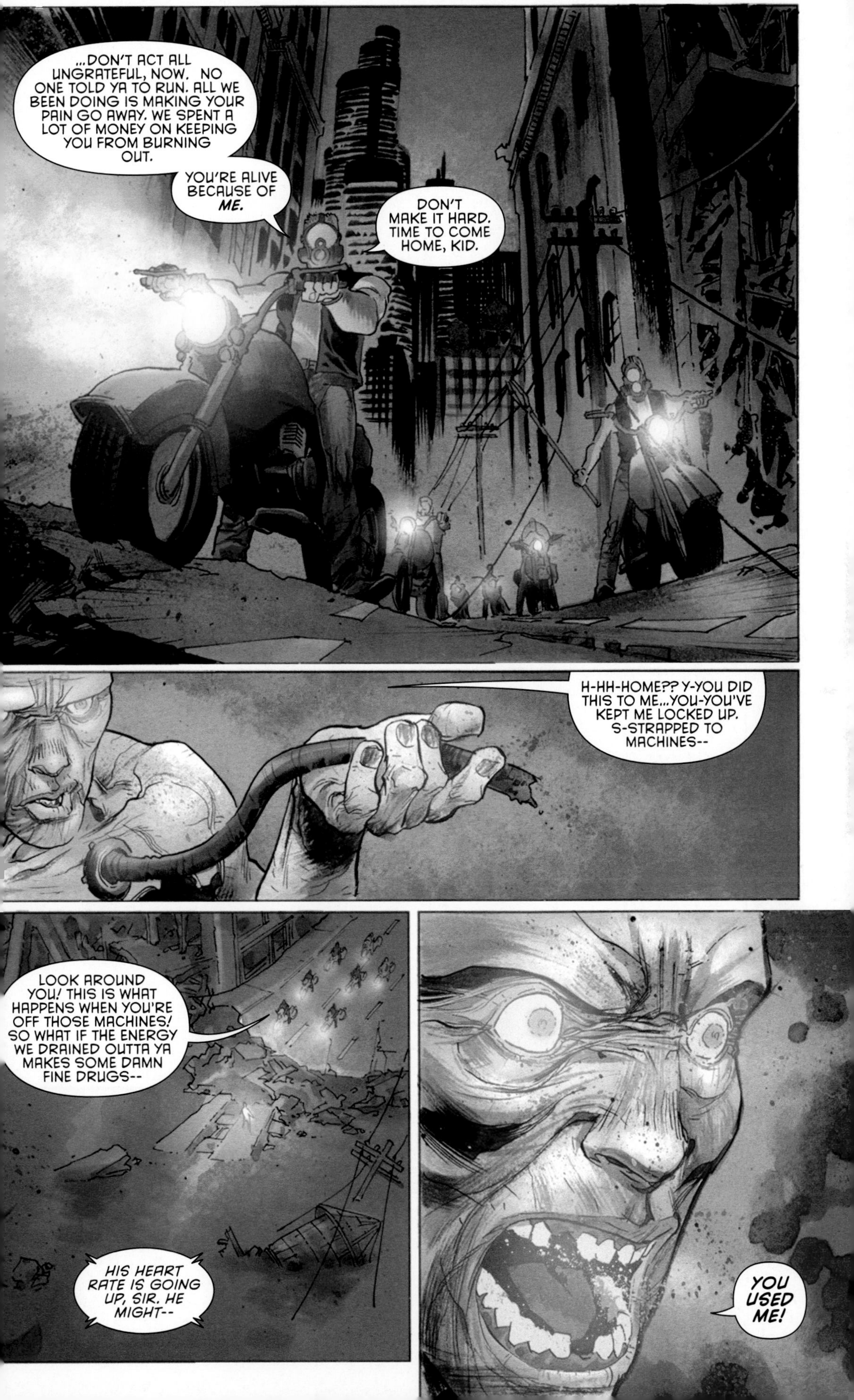
...DON'T ACT ALL UNGRATEFUL, NOW. NO ONE TOLD YA TO RUN. ALL WE BEEN DOING IS MAKING YOUR PAIN GO AWAY. WE SPENT A LOT OF MONEY ON KEEPING YOU FROM BURNING OUT.
YOU'RE ALIVE BECAUSE OF ME.
DON'T MAKE IT HARD. TIME TO COME HOME, KID.
H-HH-HOME?? Y-YOU DID THIS TO ME...YOU-YOU'VE KEPT ME LOCKED UP. S-STRAPPED TO MACHINES--
LOOK AROUND YOU! THIS IS WHAT HAPPENS WHEN YOU'RE OFF THOSE MACHINES! SO WHAT IF THE ENERGY WE DRAINED OUTTA YA MAKES SOME DAMN FINE DRUGS--
HIS HEART RATE IS GOING UP, SIR. HE MIGHT--
YOU USED ME!

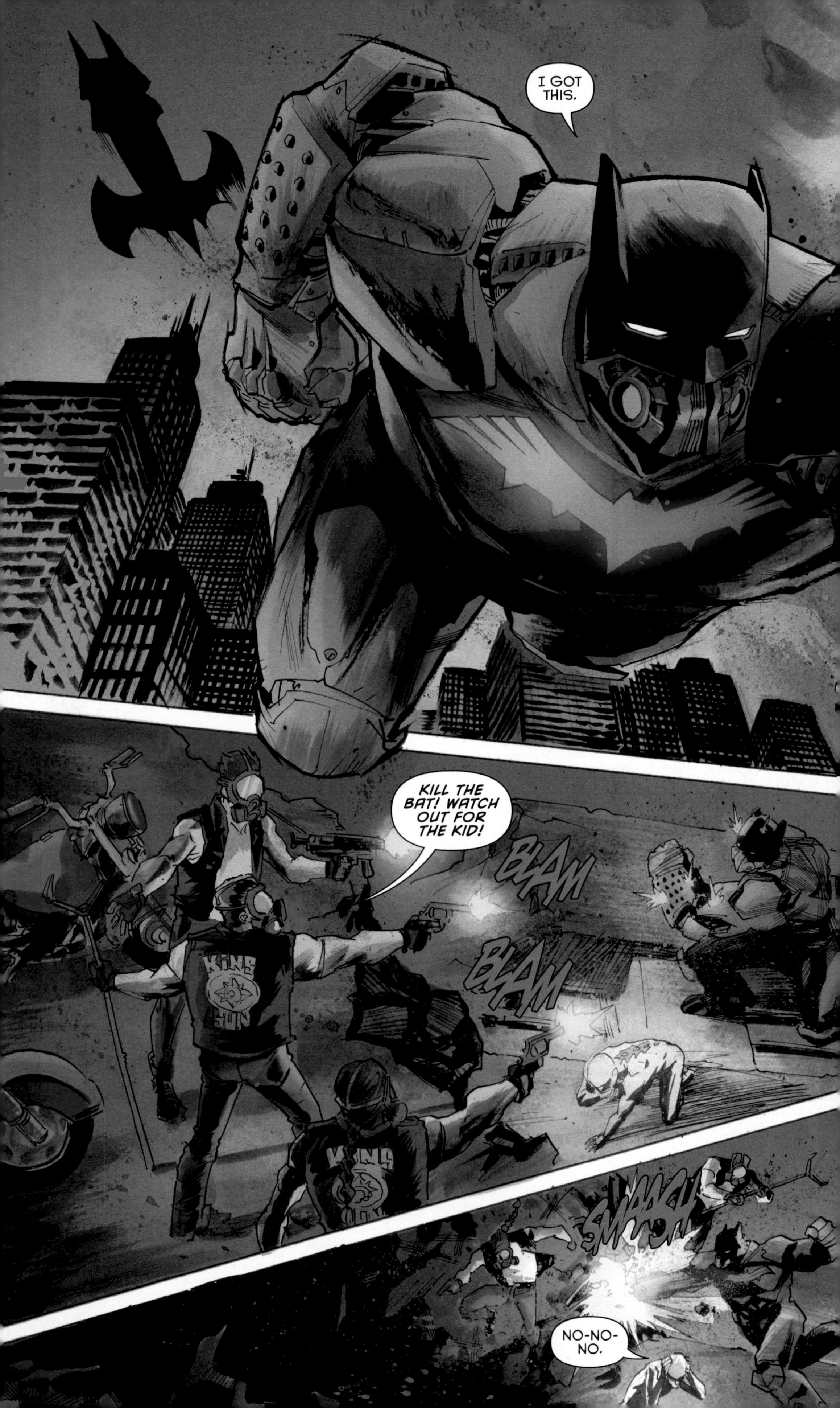
I GOT THIS.
KILL THE BAT! WATCH OUT FOR THE KID!
BLAM
BLAM
SMASH
NO-NO-NO.

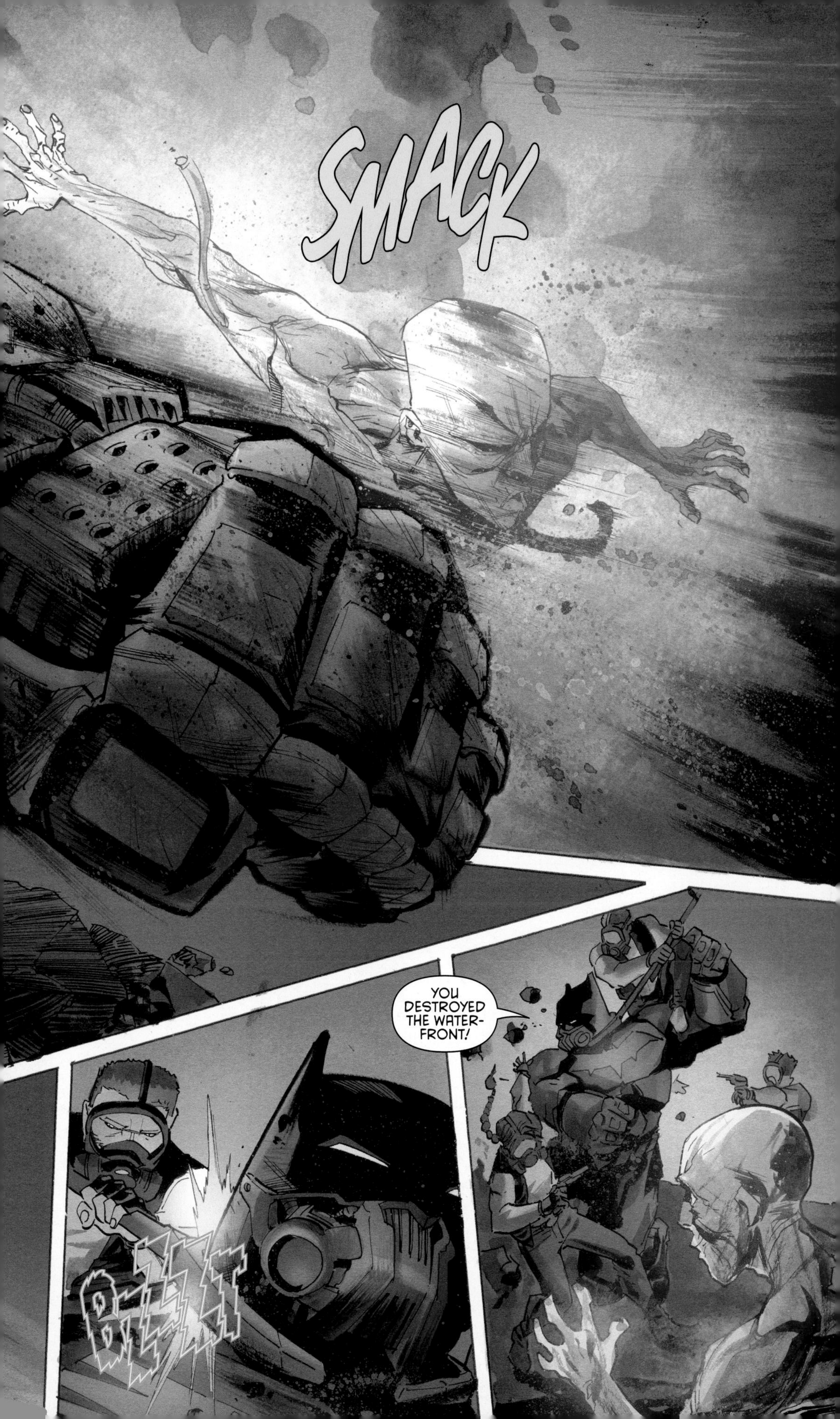
SMACK
YOU DESTROYED THE WATER-FRONT!
BZZZT

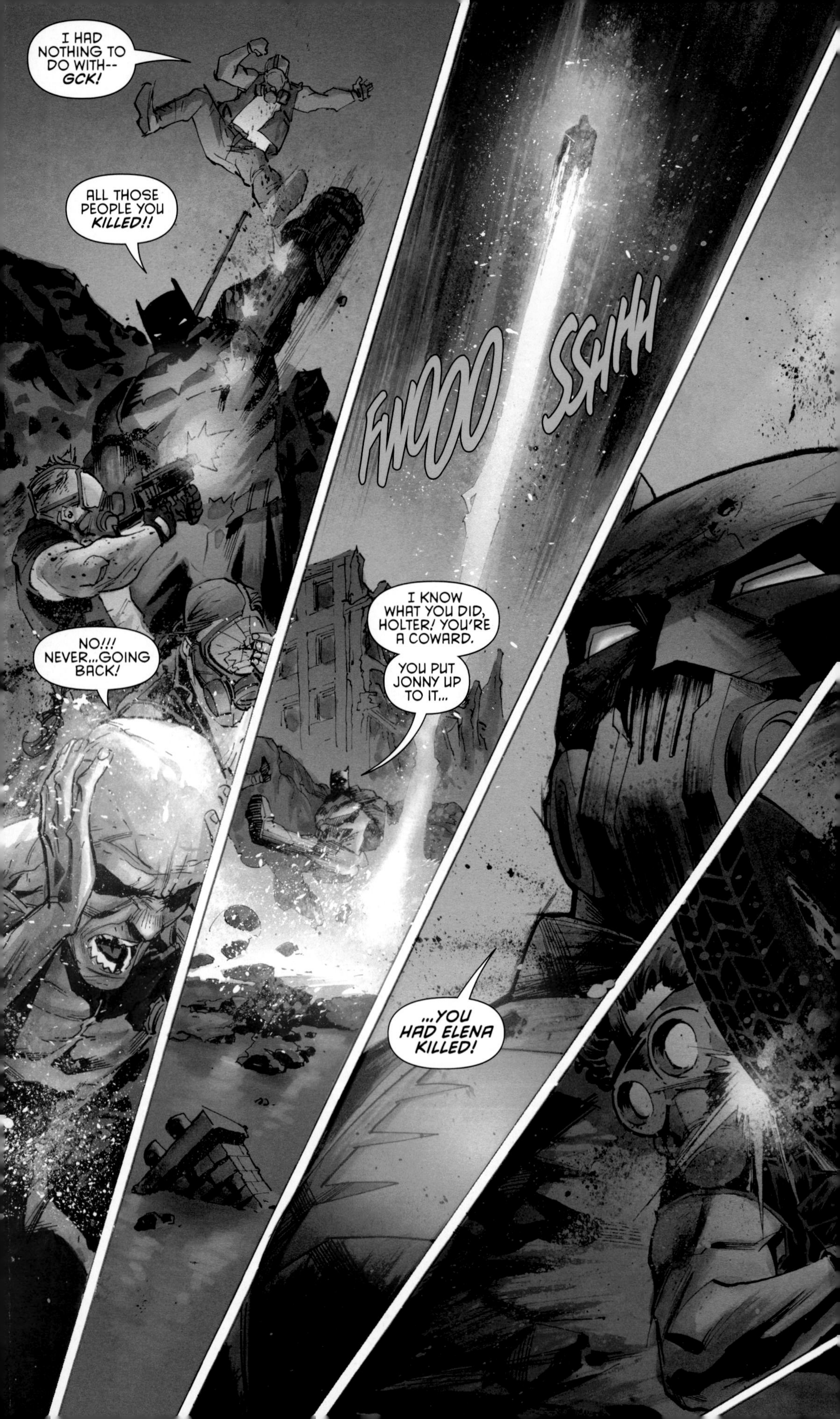
I HAD NOTHING TO DO WITH-- GCK!
ALL THOSE PEOPLE YOU KILLED!!
NO!!! NEVER...GOING BACK!
FWOOOSSHHH
I KNOW WHAT YOU DID, HOLTER! YOU'RE A COWARD.
YOU PUT JONNY UP TO IT...
...YOU HAD ELENA KILLED!

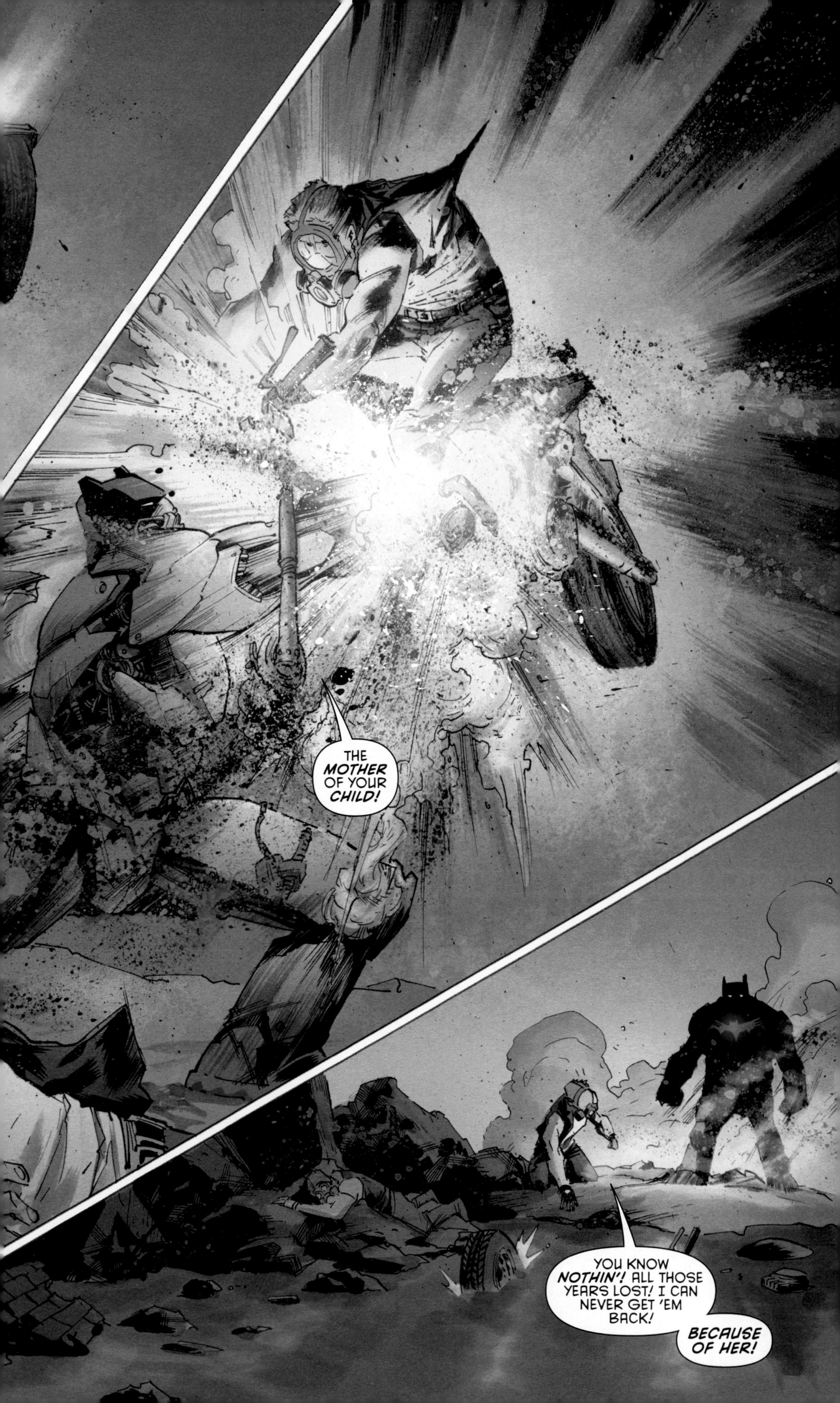

THE *MOTHER* OF YOUR *CHILD!*
YOU KNOW *NOTHIN'!* ALL THOSE YEARS LOST! I CAN NEVER GET 'EM BACK!
BECAUSE OF HER!

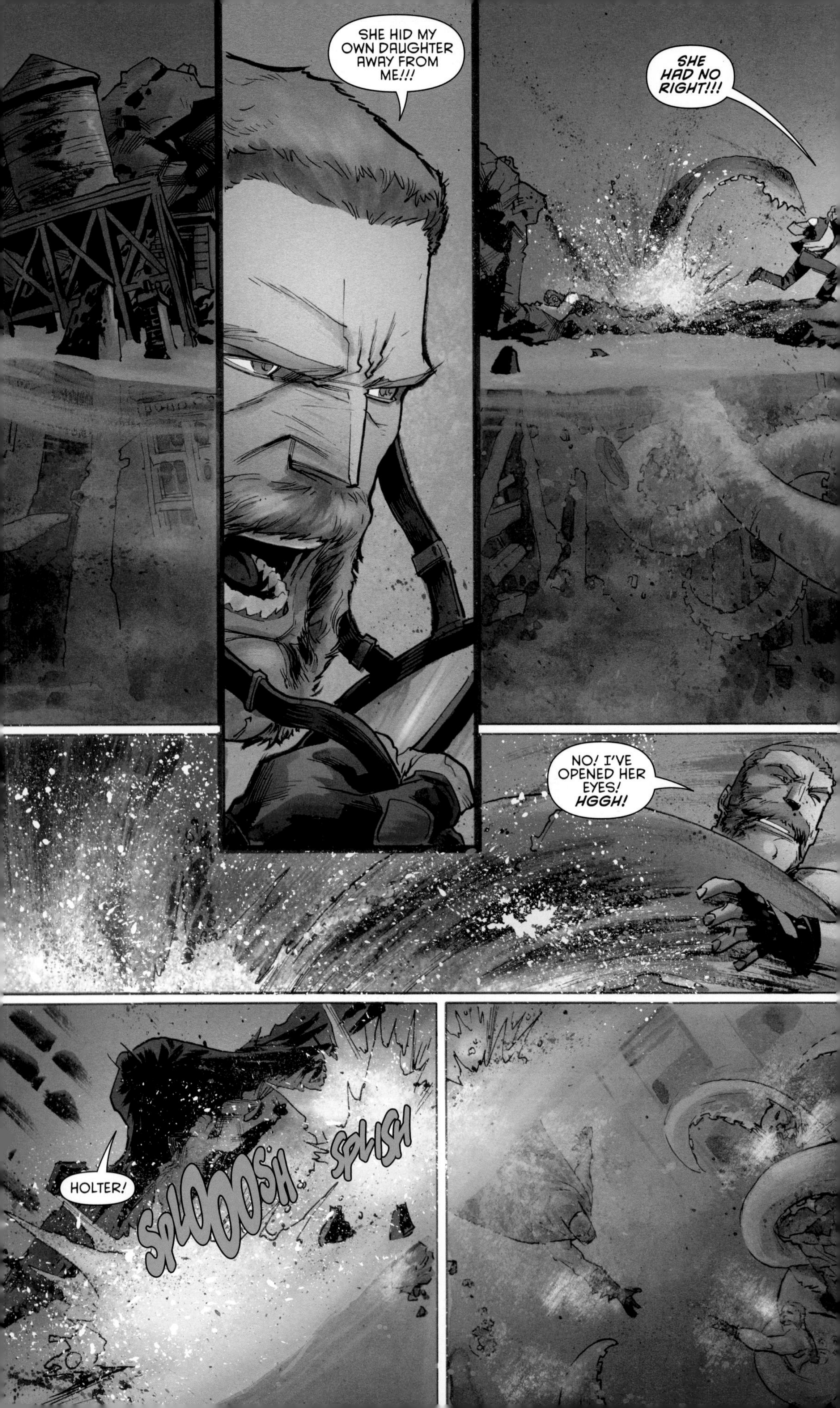
SHE HID MY OWN DAUGHTER AWAY FROM ME!!!
SHE HAD NO RIGHT!!!
NO! I'VE OPENED HER EYES! HGGH!
HOLTER!
SPLOOOSH
SPLISH

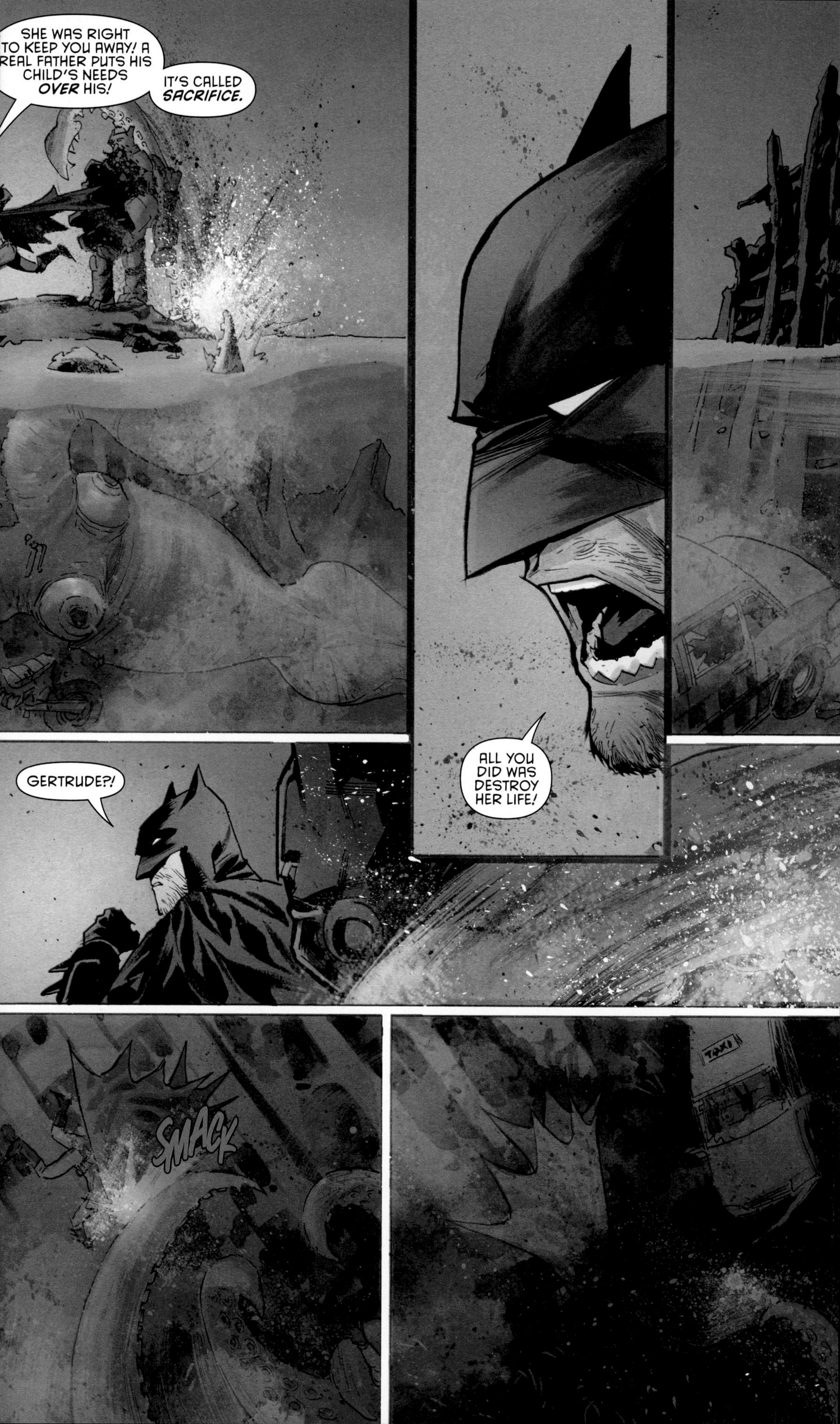
SHE WAS RIGHT TO KEEP YOU AWAY! A REAL FATHER PUTS HIS CHILD'S NEEDS **OVER** HIS!
IT'S CALLED **SACRIFICE.**
ALL YOU DID WAS DESTROY HER LIFE!
GERTRUDE?!
SMACK
TAXI

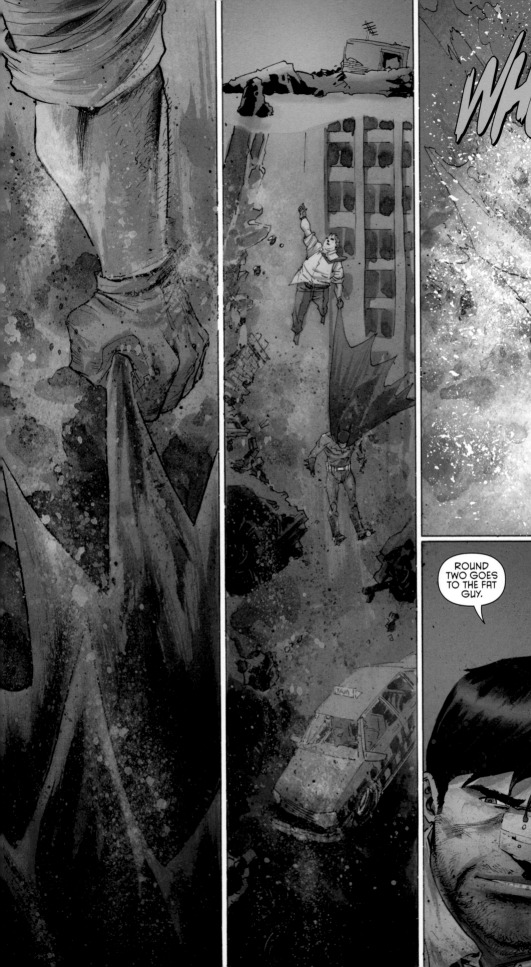

WHO

ROUND TWO GOES TO THE FAT GUY.

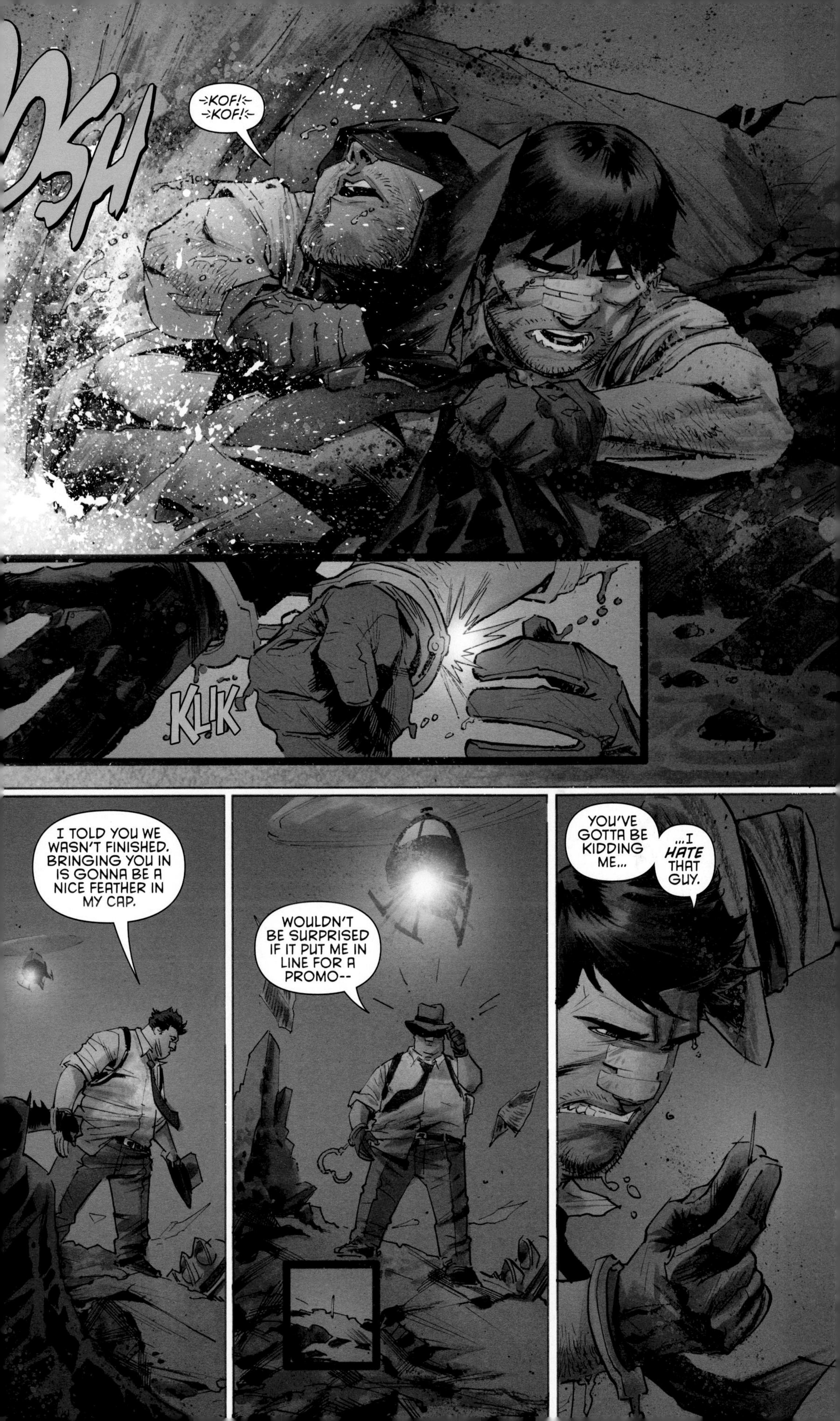

OSH
-KOF!-
-KOF!-
KLIK
I TOLD YOU WE WASN'T FINISHED. BRINGING YOU IN IS GONNA BE A NICE FEATHER IN MY CAP.
WOULDN'T BE SURPRISED IF IT PUT ME IN LINE FOR A PROMO--
YOU'VE GOTTA BE KIDDING ME...
...I HATE THAT GUY.

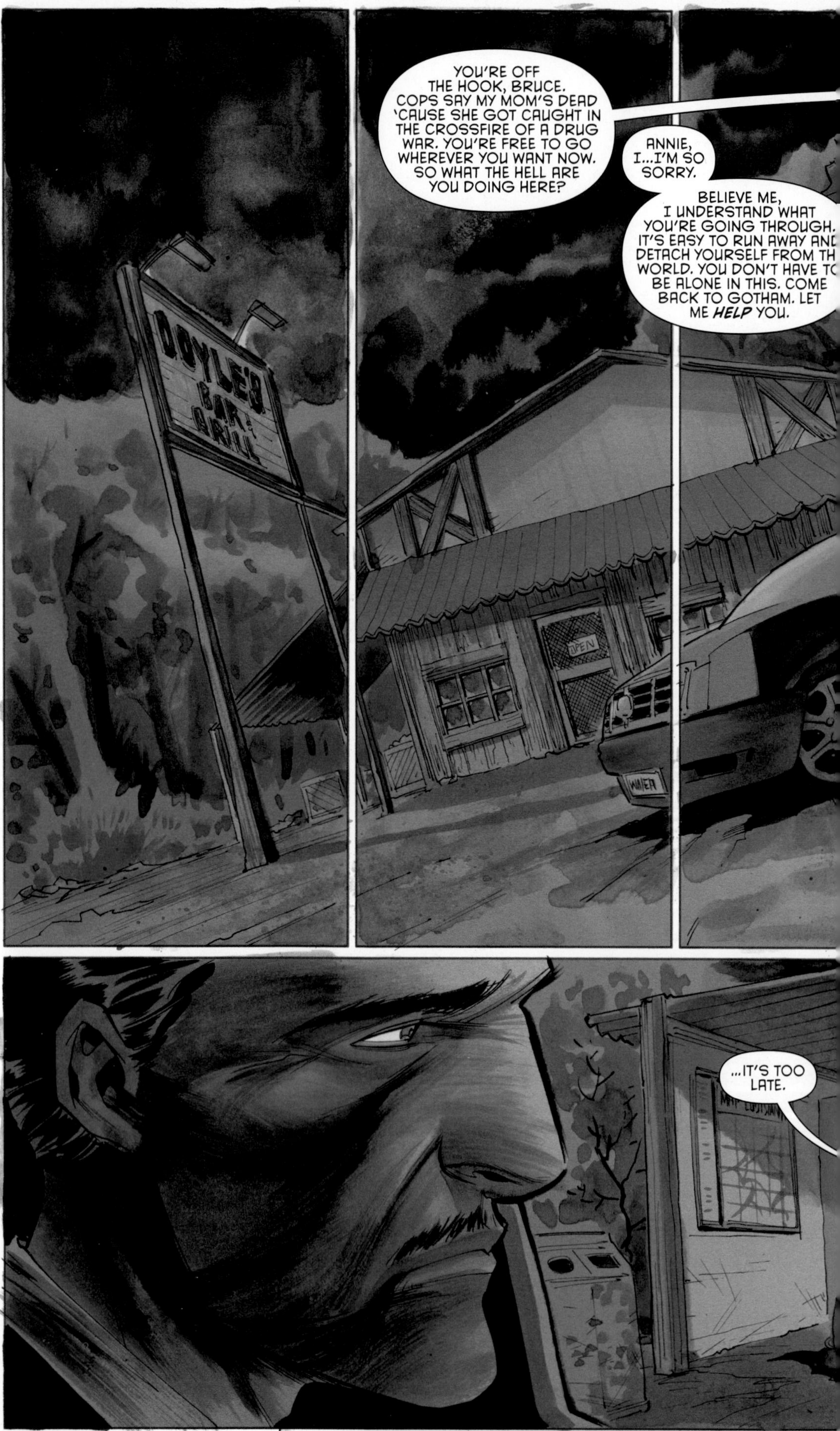

DOYLE'S BAR & GRILL
YOU'RE OFF THE HOOK, BRUCE. COPS SAY MY MOM'S DEAD 'CAUSE SHE GOT CAUGHT IN THE CROSSFIRE OF A DRUG WAR. YOU'RE FREE TO GO WHEREVER YOU WANT NOW. SO WHAT THE HELL ARE YOU DOING HERE?
OPEN
ANNIE, I...I'M SO SORRY.
BELIEVE ME, I UNDERSTAND WHAT YOU'RE GOING THROUGH. IT'S EASY TO RUN AWAY AND DETACH YOURSELF FROM THE WORLD. YOU DON'T HAVE TO BE ALONE IN THIS. COME BACK TO GOTHAM. LET ME **HELP** YOU.
...IT'S TOO LATE.

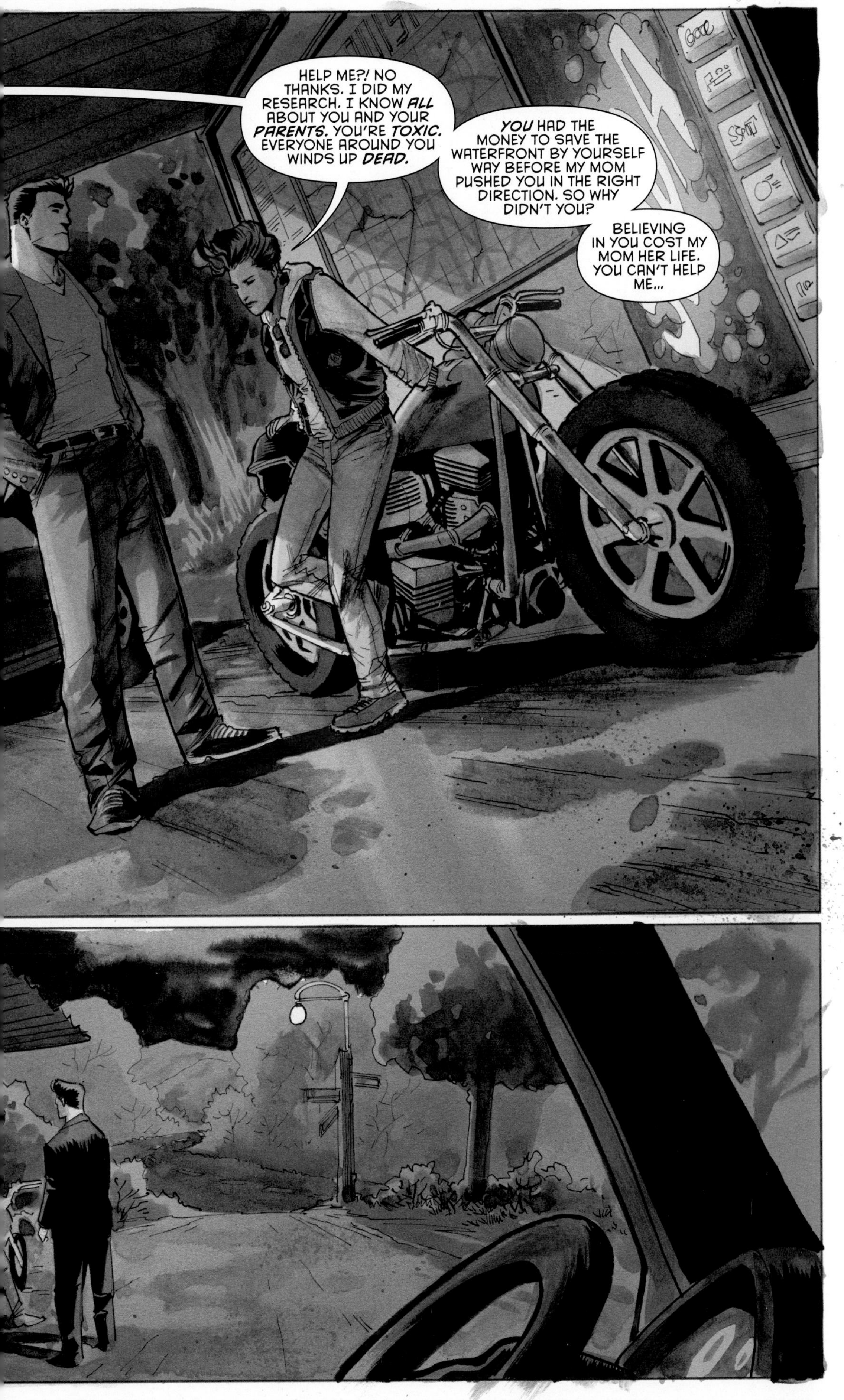
HELP ME?! NO THANKS. I DID MY RESEARCH. I KNOW ALL ABOUT YOU AND YOUR PARENTS. YOU'RE TOXIC. EVERYONE AROUND YOU WINDS UP DEAD.
YOU HAD THE MONEY TO SAVE THE WATERFRONT BY YOURSELF WAY BEFORE MY MOM PUSHED YOU IN THE RIGHT DIRECTION. SO WHY DIDN'T YOU?
BELIEVING IN YOU COST MY MOM HER LIFE. YOU CAN'T HELP ME...

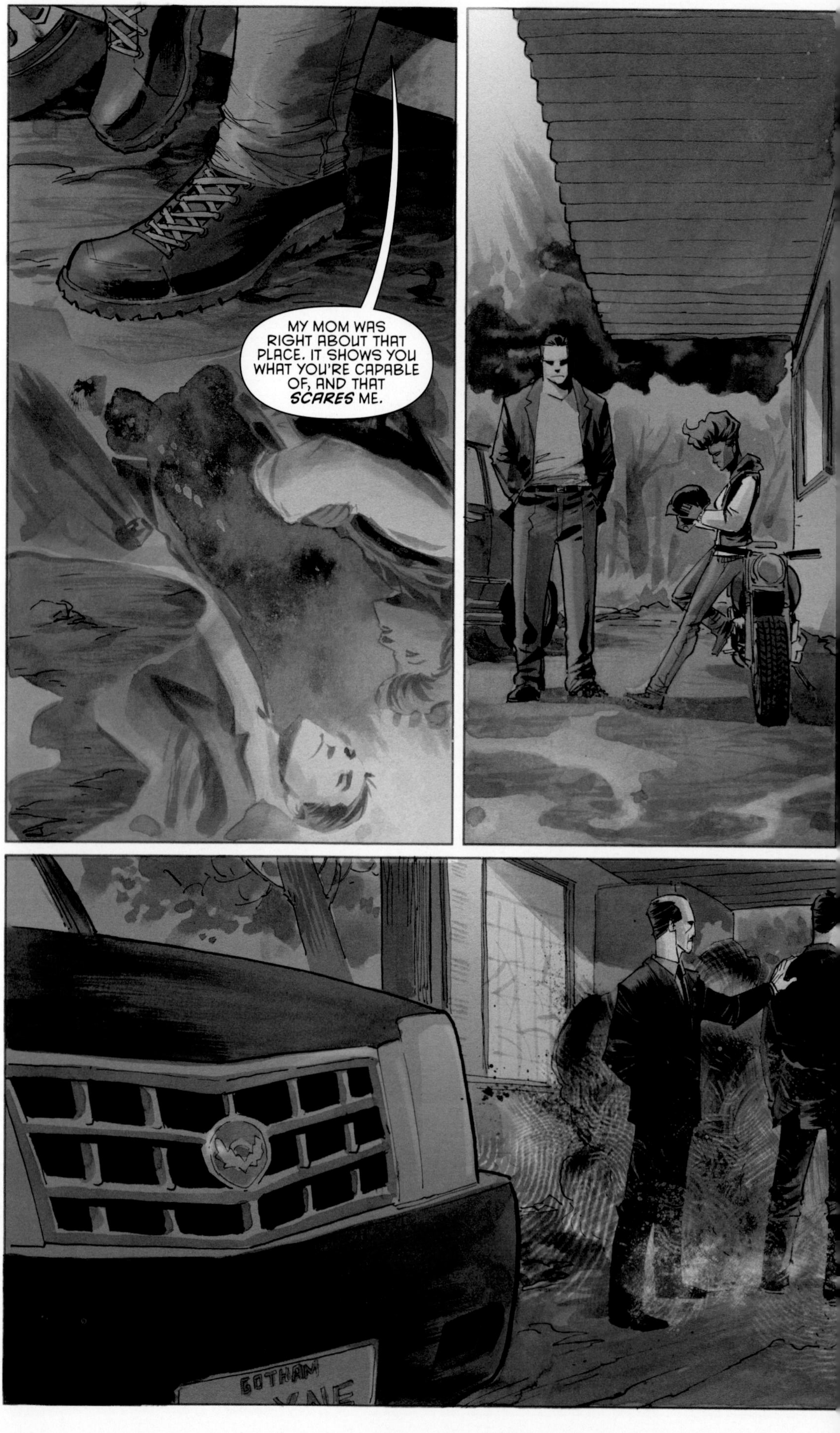
MY MOM WAS RIGHT ABOUT THAT PLACE. IT SHOWS YOU WHAT YOU'RE CAPABLE OF, AND THAT *SCARES* ME.
GOTHAM

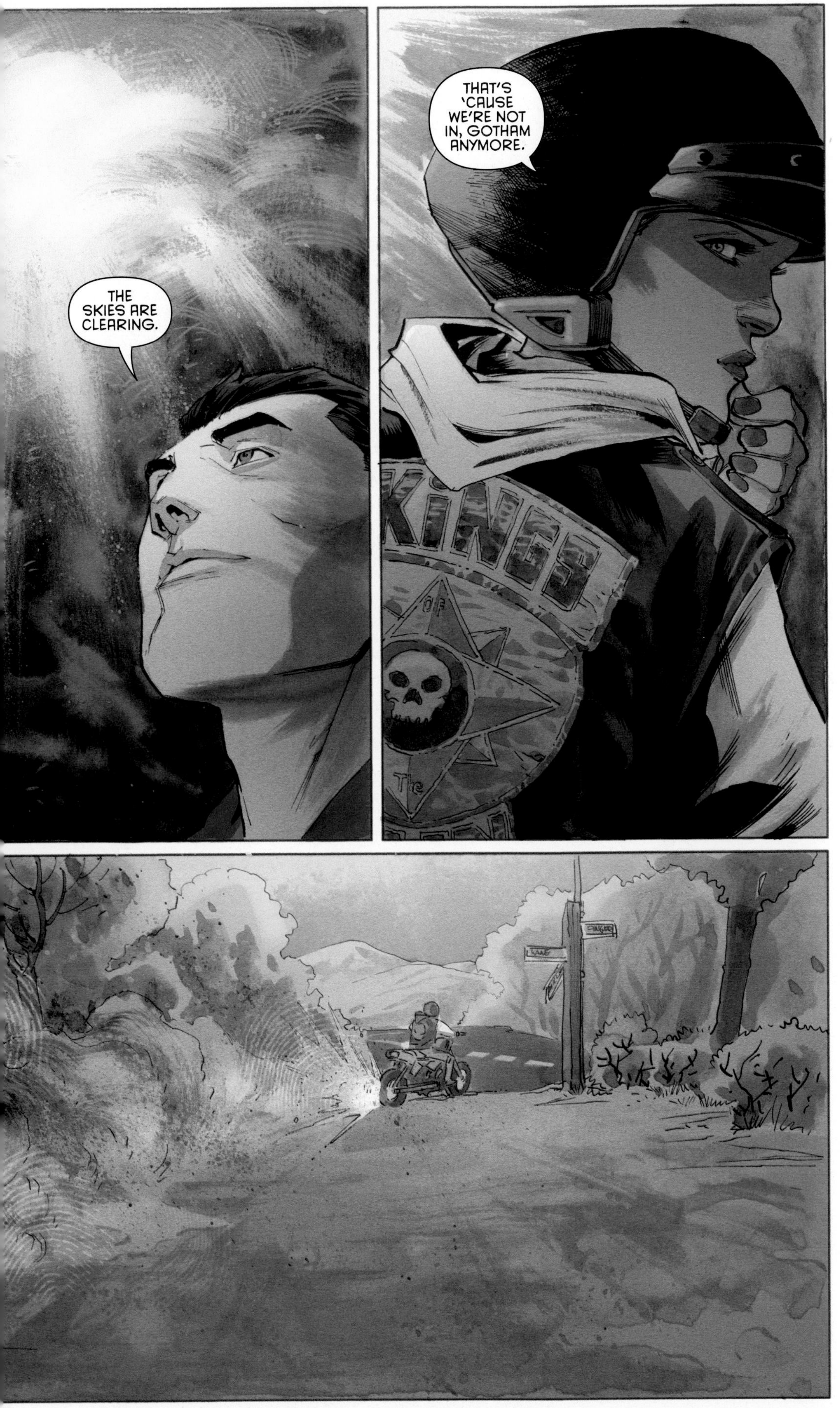
THE SKIES ARE CLEARING.
THAT'S 'CAUSE WE'RE NOT IN, GOTHAM ANYMORE.
KINGS

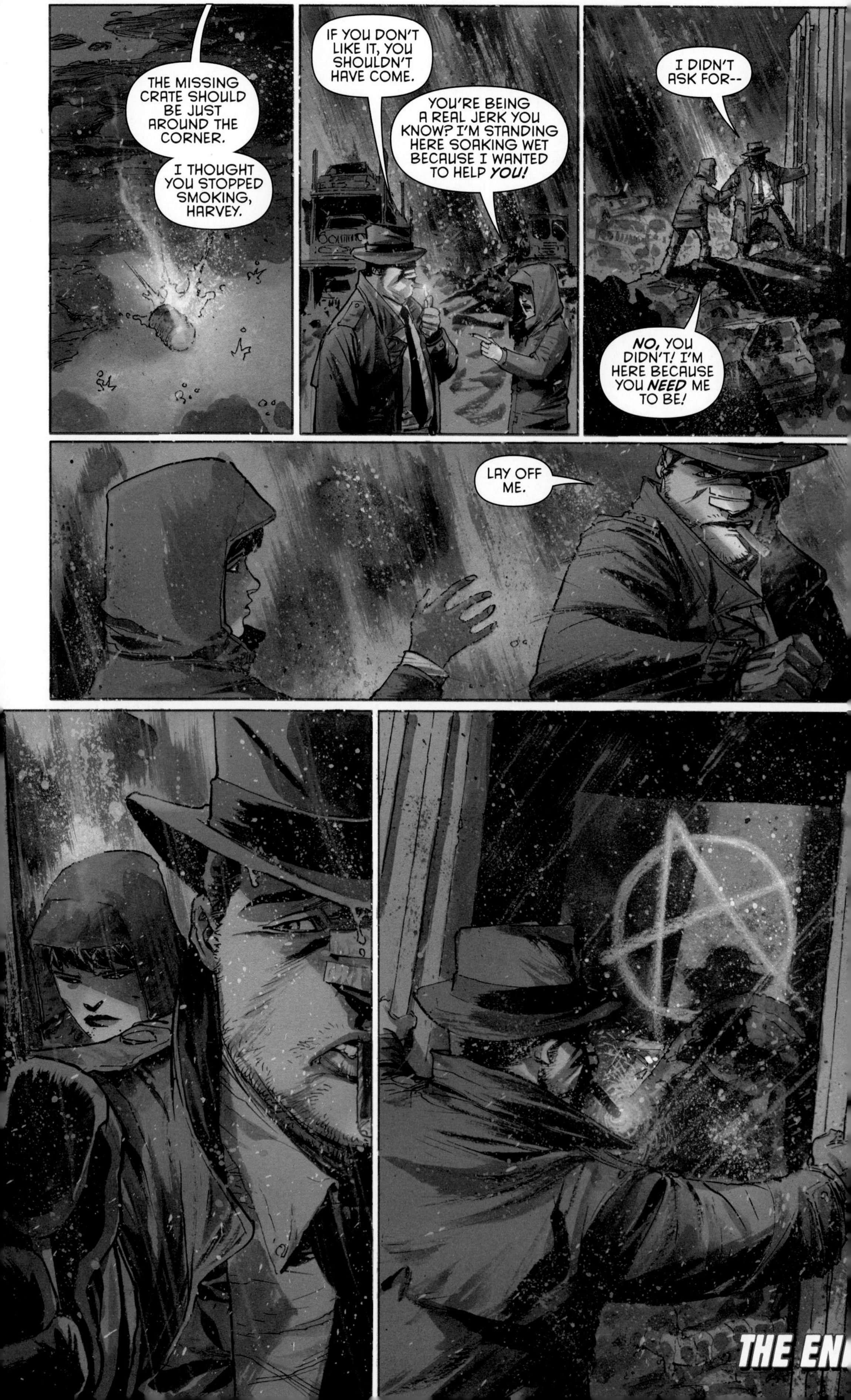
THE MISSING CRATE SHOULD BE JUST AROUND THE CORNER.
I THOUGHT YOU STOPPED SMOKING, HARVEY.
IF YOU DON'T LIKE IT, YOU SHOULDN'T HAVE COME.
YOU'RE BEING A REAL JERK YOU KNOW? I'M STANDING HERE SOAKING WET BECAUSE I WANTED TO HELP YOU!
I DIDN'T ASK FOR--
NO, YOU DIDN'T! I'M HERE BECAUSE YOU NEED ME TO BE!
LAY OFF ME.
THE EN

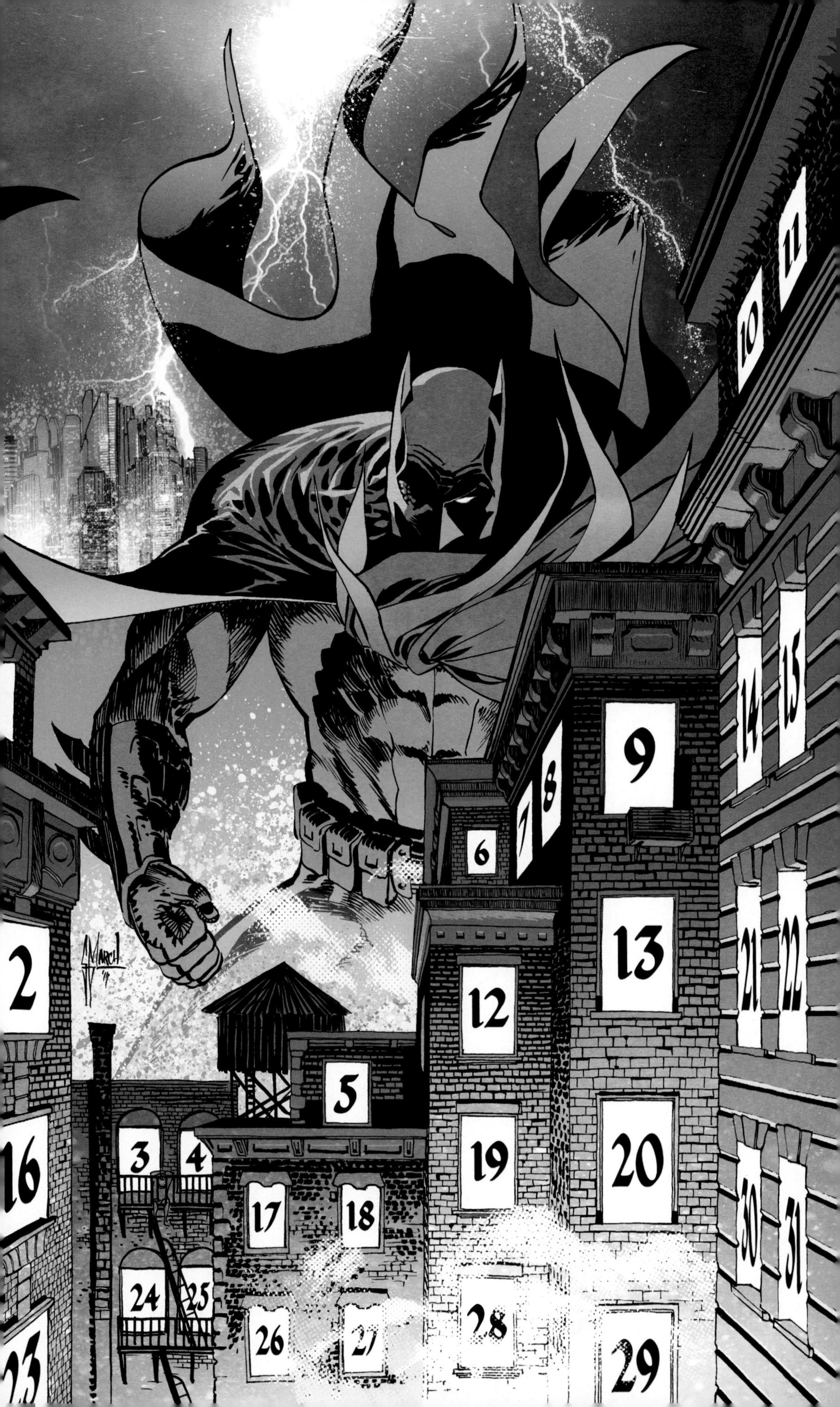

11
10
15
14
9
8
7
6
2
13
12
22
21
5
16
3
4
19
20
17
18
31
30
24
25
28
26
27
23
29

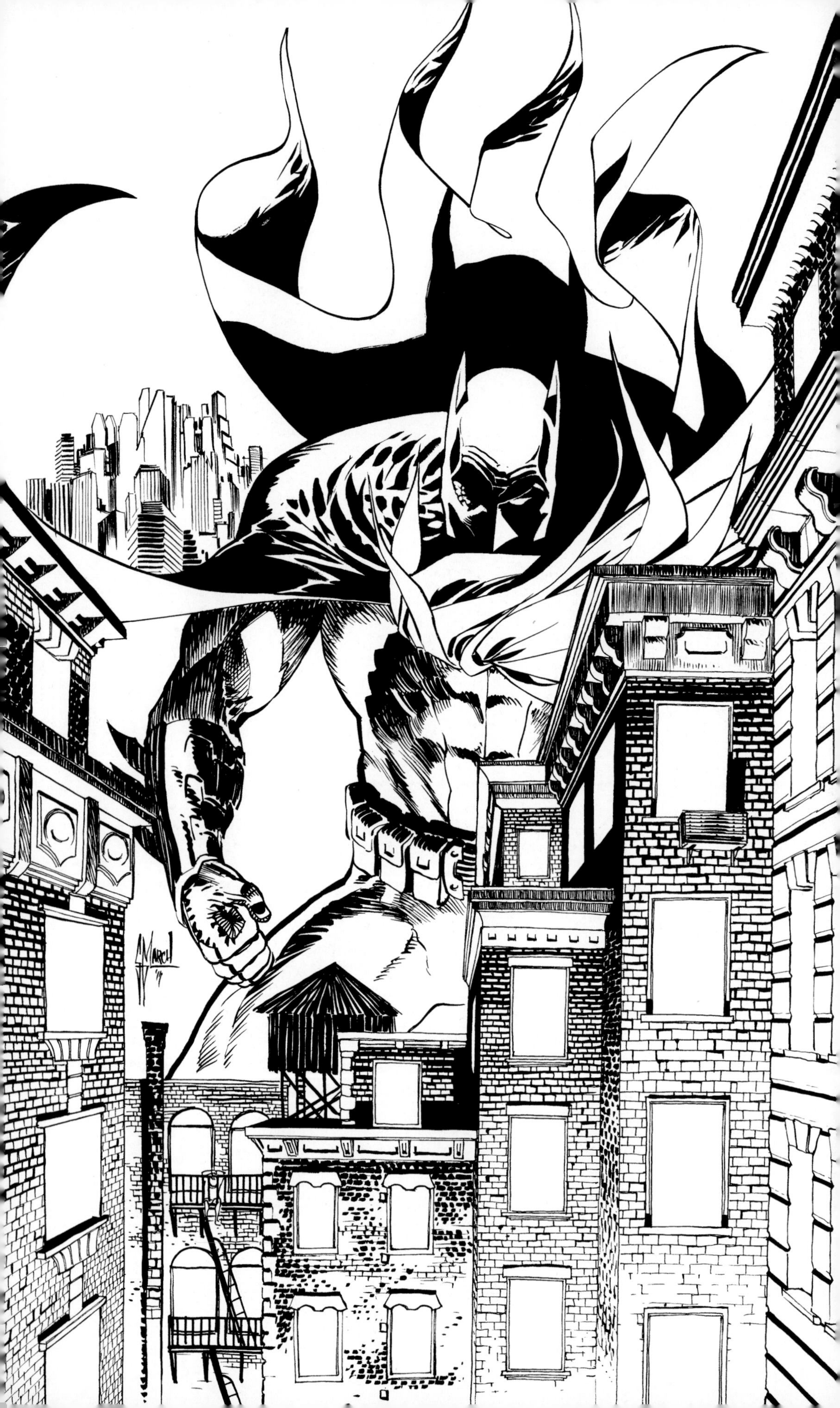

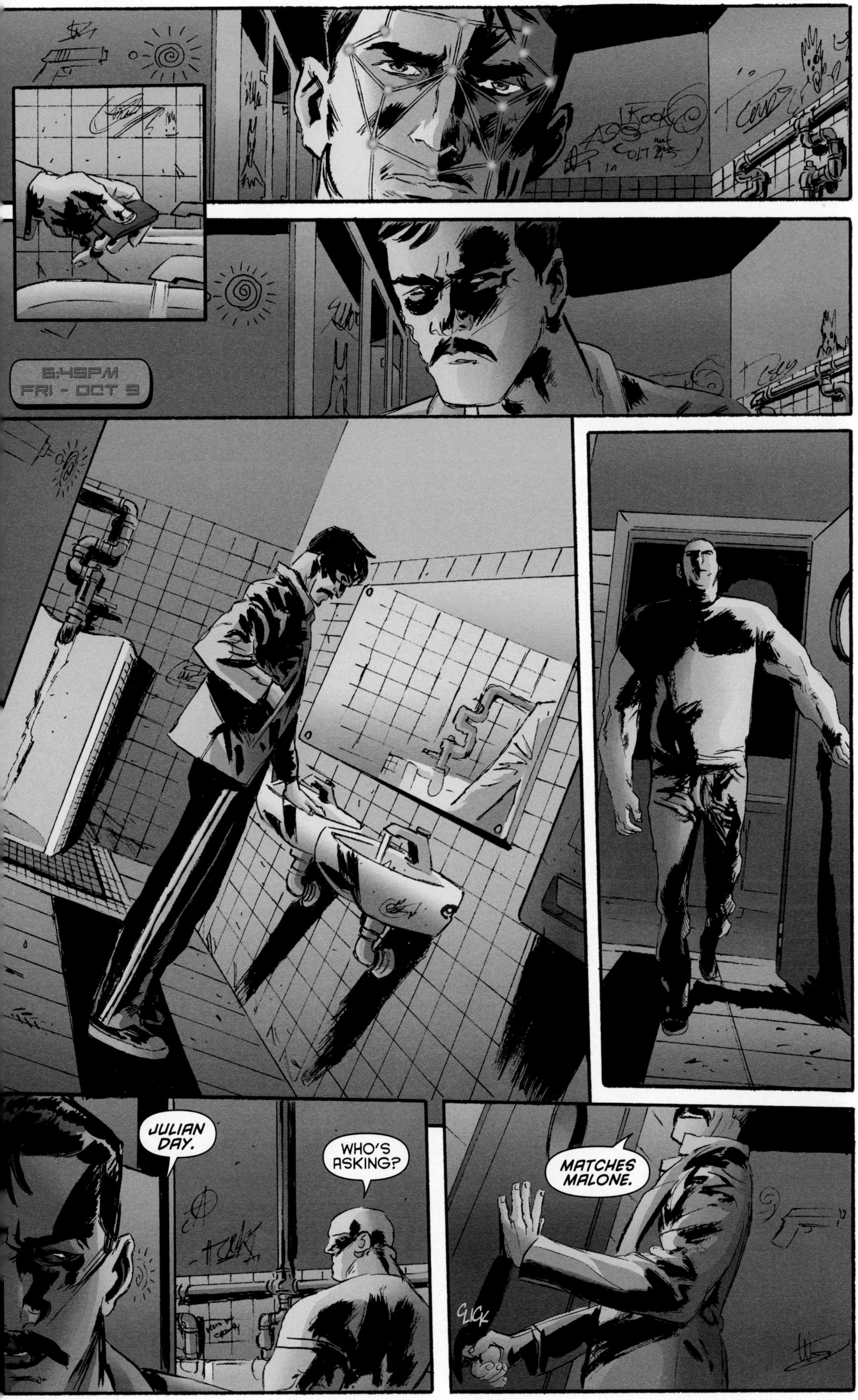
6:45PM
FRI - OCT 9
JULIAN DAY.
WHO'S ASKING?
MATCHES MALONE.
CLICK

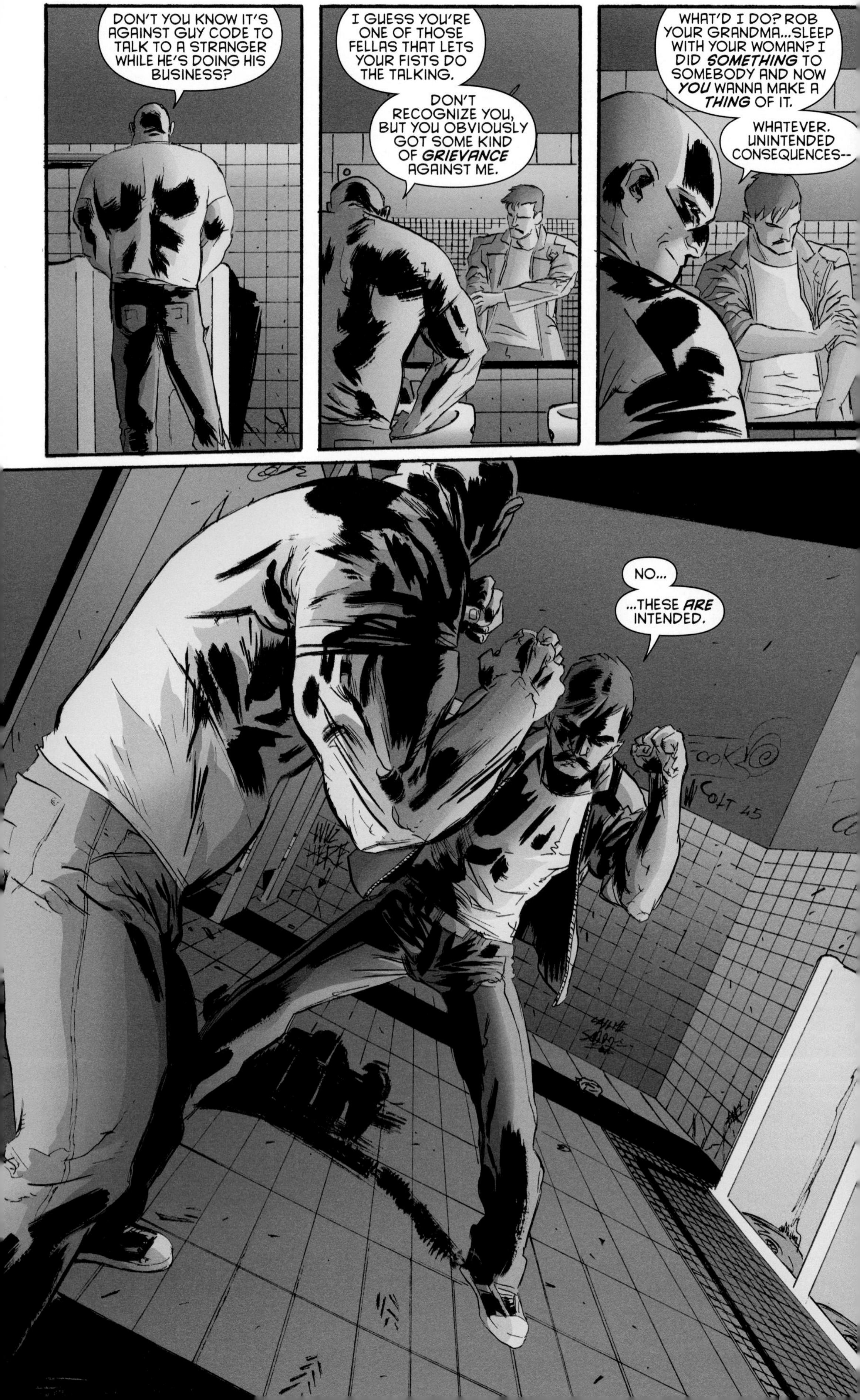

DON'T YOU KNOW IT'S AGAINST GUY CODE TO TALK TO A STRANGER WHILE HE'S DOING HIS BUSINESS?
I GUESS YOU'RE ONE OF THOSE FELLAS THAT LETS YOUR FISTS DO THE TALKING.
DON'T RECOGNIZE YOU, BUT YOU OBVIOUSLY GOT SOME KIND OF GRIEVANCE AGAINST ME.
WHAT'D I DO? ROB YOUR GRANDMA...SLEEP WITH YOUR WOMAN? I DID SOMETHING TO SOMEBODY AND NOW YOU WANNA MAKE A THING OF IT.
WHATEVER. UNINTENDED CONSEQUENCES--
NO...
...THESE ARE INTENDED.

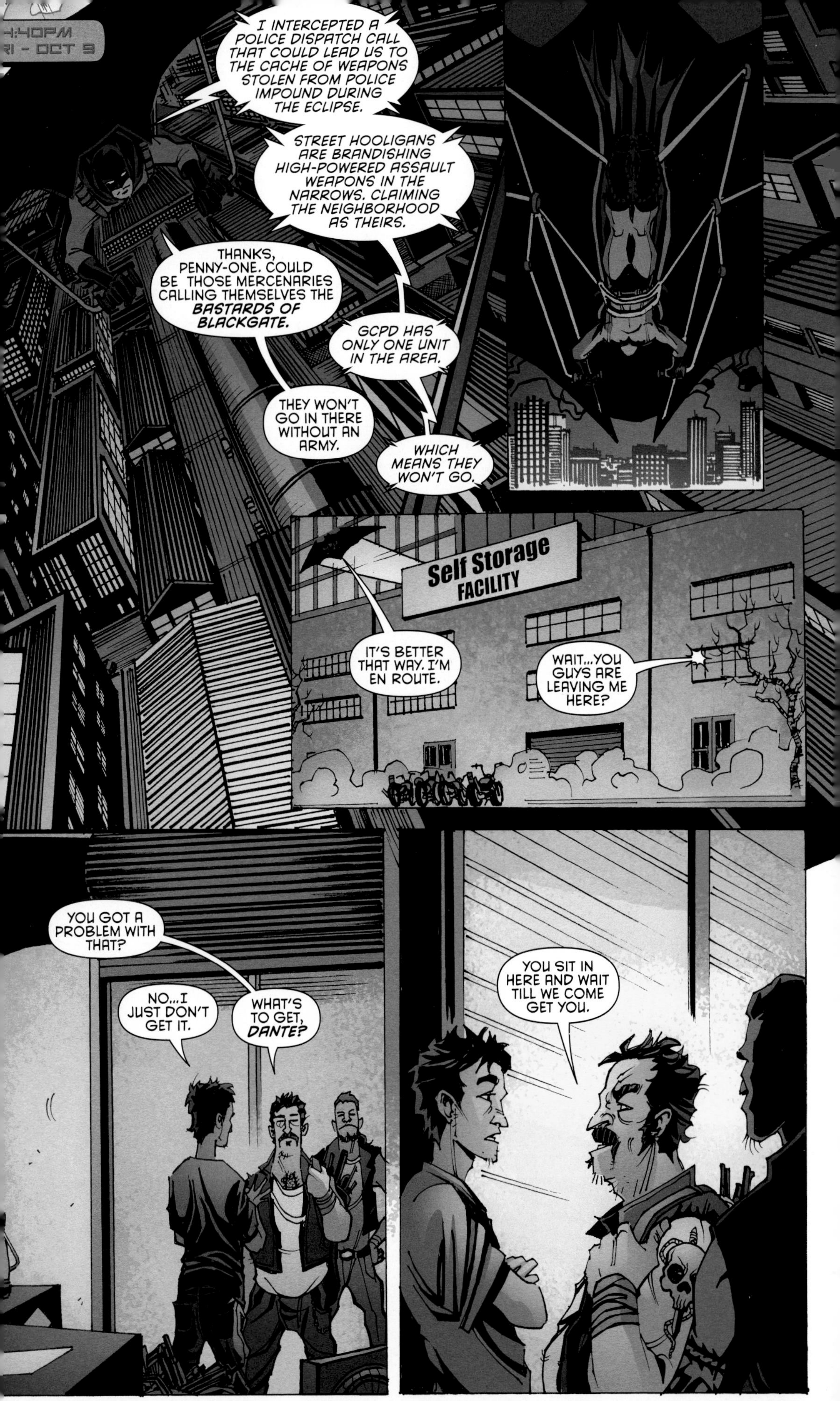
4:40PM
RI - OCT 9
I INTERCEPTED A POLICE DISPATCH CALL THAT COULD LEAD US TO THE CACHE OF WEAPONS STOLEN FROM POLICE IMPOUND DURING THE ECLIPSE.
STREET HOOLIGANS ARE BRANDISHING HIGH-POWERED ASSAULT WEAPONS IN THE NARROWS. CLAIMING THE NEIGHBORHOOD AS THEIRS.
THANKS, PENNY-ONE. COULD BE THOSE MERCENARIES CALLING THEMSELVES THE *BASTARDS OF BLACKGATE.*
GCPD HAS ONLY ONE UNIT IN THE AREA.
THEY WON'T GO IN THERE WITHOUT AN ARMY.
WHICH MEANS THEY WON'T GO.
Self Storage
FACILITY
IT'S BETTER THAT WAY. I'M EN ROUTE.
WAIT...YOU GUYS ARE LEAVING ME HERE?
YOU GOT A PROBLEM WITH THAT?
NO...I JUST DON'T GET IT.
WHAT'S TO GET, *DANTE?*
YOU SIT IN HERE AND WAIT TILL WE COME GET YOU.

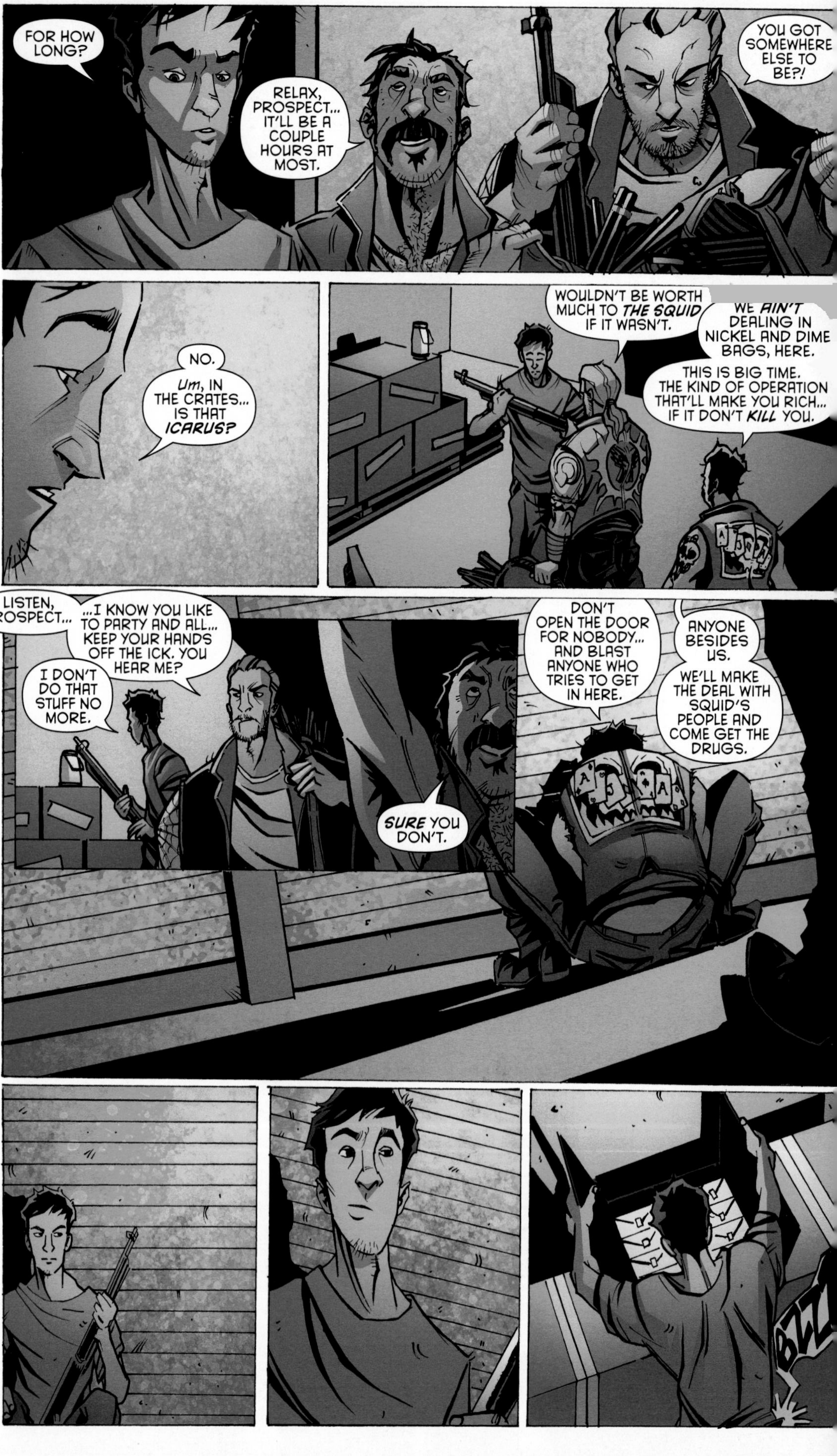
FOR HOW LONG?
RELAX, PROSPECT... IT'LL BE A COUPLE HOURS AT MOST.
YOU GOT SOMEWHERE ELSE TO BE?!
NO.
Um, IN THE CRATES... IS THAT ICARUS?
WOULDN'T BE WORTH MUCH TO THE SQUID IF IT WASN'T.
WE AIN'T DEALING IN NICKEL AND DIME BAGS, HERE.
THIS IS BIG TIME. THE KIND OF OPERATION THAT'LL MAKE YOU RICH... IF IT DON'T KILL YOU.
LISTEN, PROSPECT...
...I KNOW YOU LIKE TO PARTY AND ALL... KEEP YOUR HANDS OFF THE ICK. YOU HEAR ME?
I DON'T DO THAT STUFF NO MORE.
SURE YOU DON'T.
DON'T OPEN THE DOOR FOR NOBODY... AND BLAST ANYONE WHO TRIES TO GET IN HERE.
ANYONE BESIDES US.
WE'LL MAKE THE DEAL WITH SQUID'S PEOPLE AND COME GET THE DRUGS.
BZZ

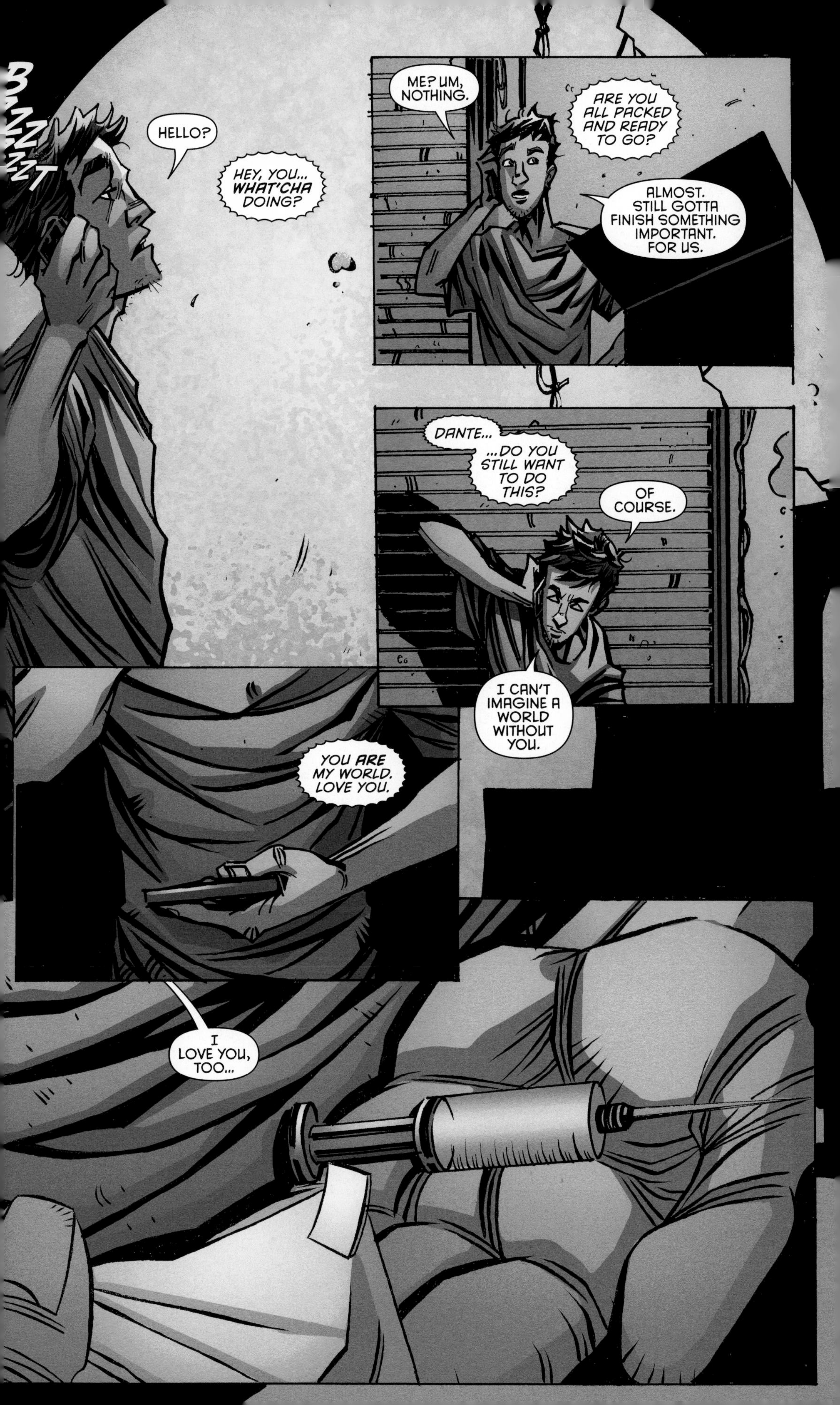
BZZZZT
HELLO?
HEY, YOU... WHAT'CHA DOING?
ME? UM, NOTHING.
ARE YOU ALL PACKED AND READY TO GO?
ALMOST. STILL GOTTA FINISH SOMETHING IMPORTANT. FOR US.
DANTE...
...DO YOU STILL WANT TO DO THIS?
OF COURSE.
I CAN'T IMAGINE A WORLD WITHOUT YOU.
YOU ARE MY WORLD. LOVE YOU.
I LOVE YOU, TOO...

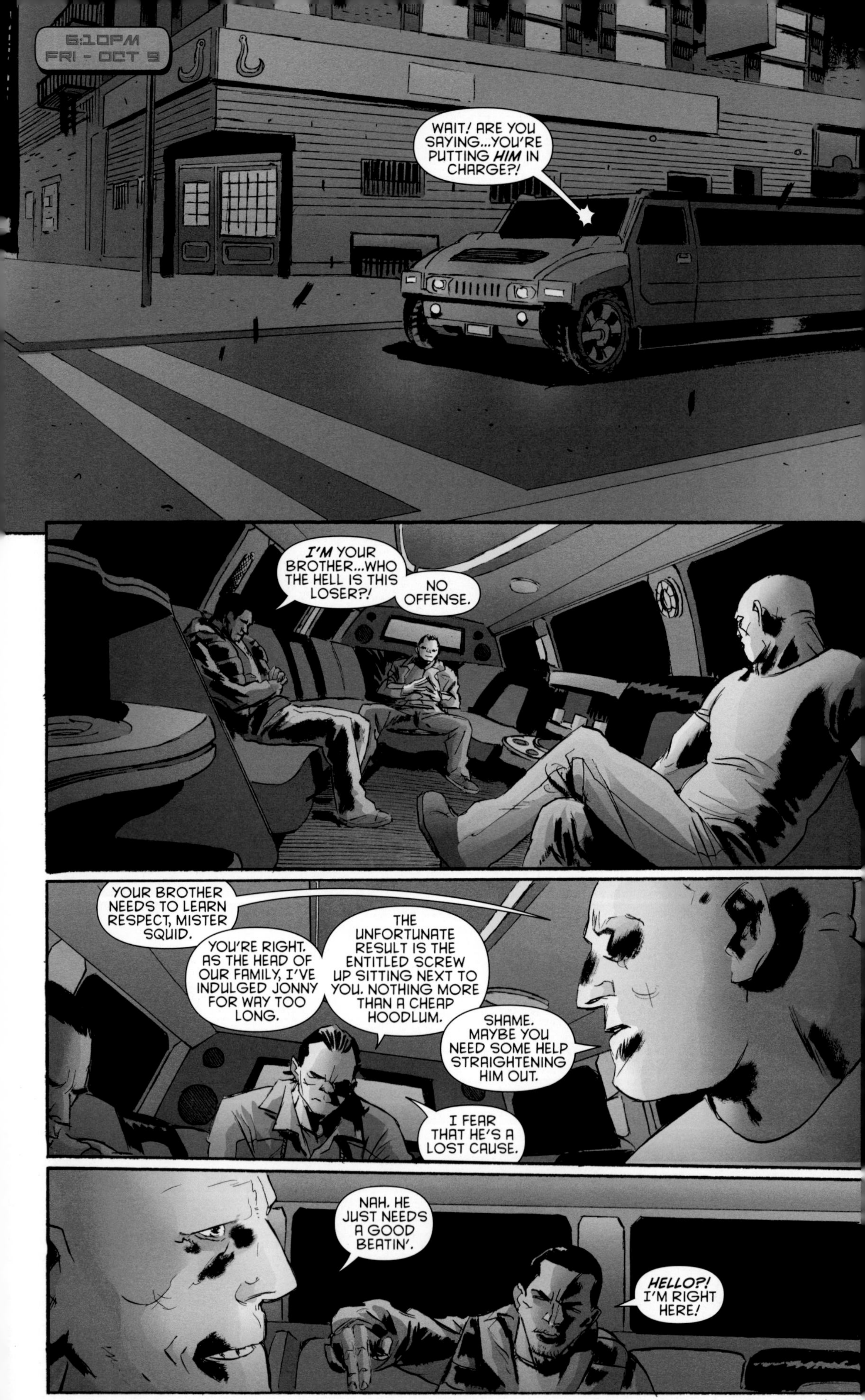
6:10PM
FRI - OCT 9
WAIT! ARE YOU SAYING...YOU'RE PUTTING *HIM* IN CHARGE?!
I'M YOUR BROTHER...WHO THE HELL IS THIS LOSER?!
NO OFFENSE.
YOUR BROTHER NEEDS TO LEARN RESPECT, MISTER SQUID.
YOU'RE RIGHT. AS THE HEAD OF OUR FAMILY, I'VE INDULGED JONNY FOR WAY TOO LONG.
THE UNFORTUNATE RESULT IS THE ENTITLED SCREW UP SITTING NEXT TO YOU. NOTHING MORE THAN A CHEAP HOODLUM.
SHAME. MAYBE YOU NEED SOME HELP STRAIGHTENING HIM OUT.
I FEAR THAT HE'S A LOST CAUSE.
NAH. HE JUST NEEDS A GOOD BEATIN'.
HELLO?! I'M RIGHT HERE!

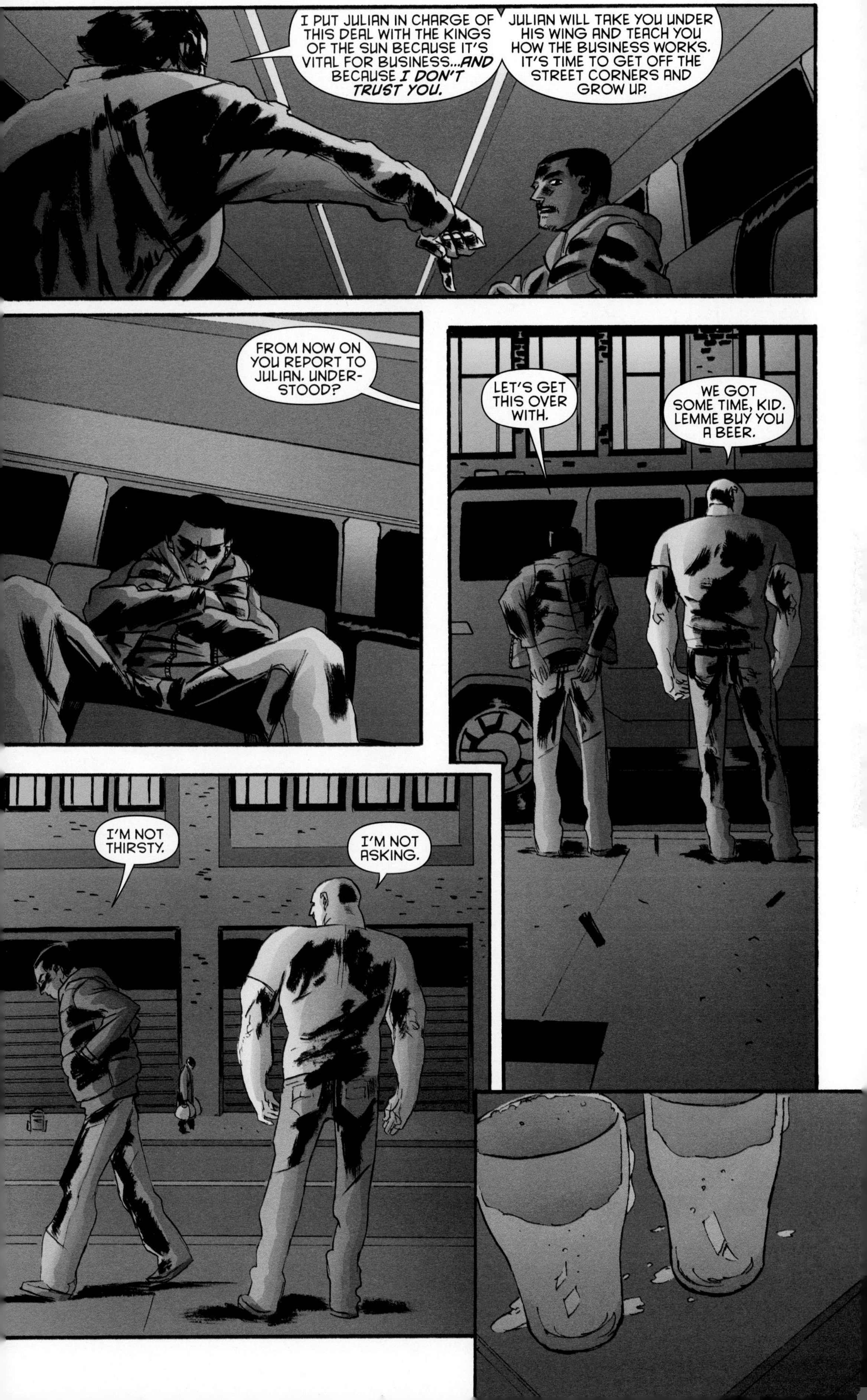

I PUT JULIAN IN CHARGE OF THIS DEAL WITH THE KINGS OF THE SUN BECAUSE IT'S VITAL FOR BUSINESS...AND BECAUSE I DON'T TRUST YOU.
JULIAN WILL TAKE YOU UNDER HIS WING AND TEACH YOU HOW THE BUSINESS WORKS. IT'S TIME TO GET OFF THE STREET CORNERS AND GROW UP.
FROM NOW ON YOU REPORT TO JULIAN. UNDER-STOOD?
LET'S GET THIS OVER WITH.
WE GOT SOME TIME, KID. LEMME BUY YOU A BEER.
I'M NOT THIRSTY.
I'M NOT ASKING.

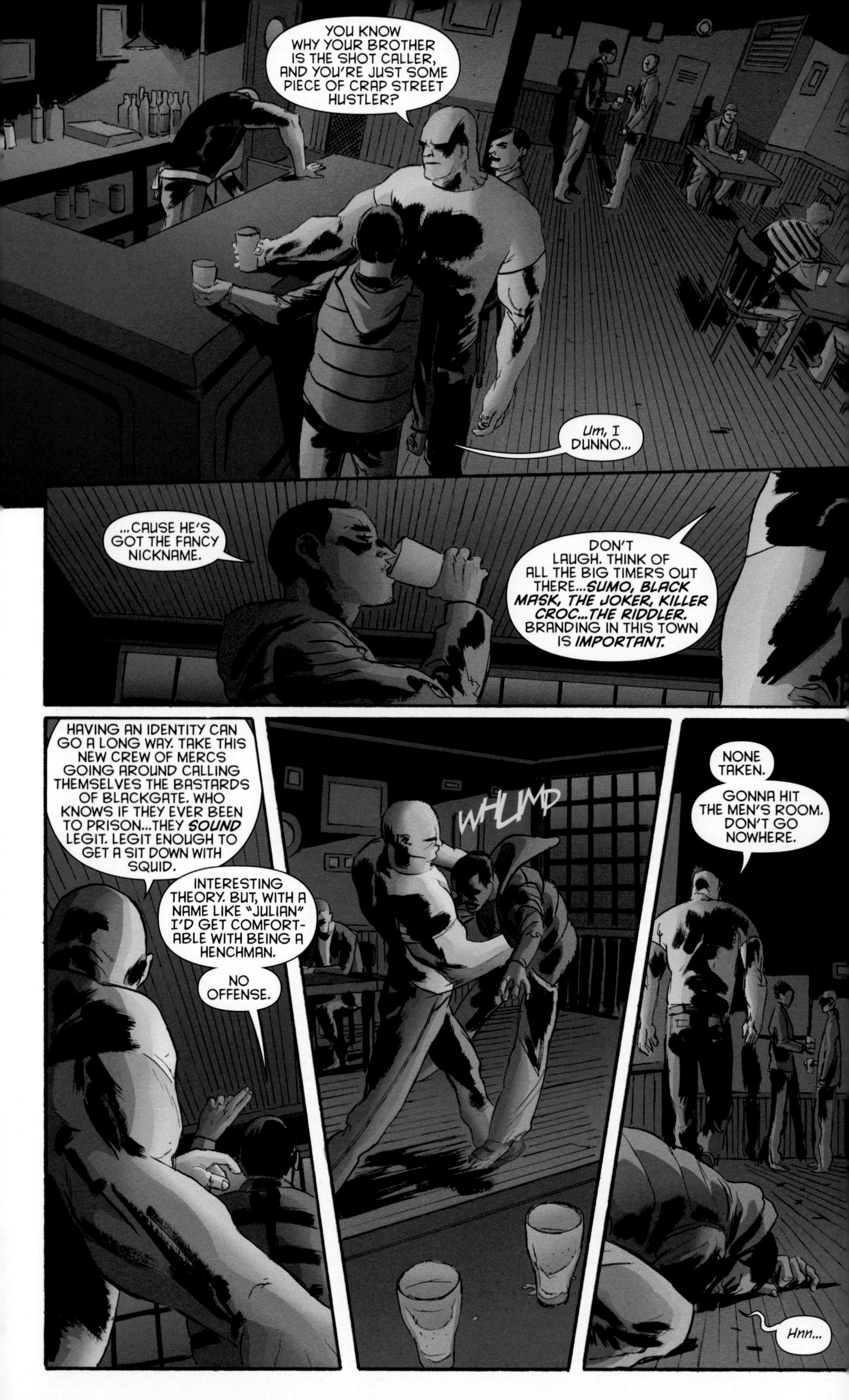

YOU KNOW WHY YOUR BROTHER IS THE SHOT CALLER, AND YOU'RE JUST SOME PIECE OF CRAP STREET HUSTLER?
Um, I DUNNO...
...CAUSE HE'S GOT THE FANCY NICKNAME.
DON'T LAUGH. THINK OF ALL THE BIG TIMERS OUT THERE...SUMO, BLACK MASK, THE JOKER, KILLER CROC...THE RIDDLER. BRANDING IN THIS TOWN IS IMPORTANT.
HAVING AN IDENTITY CAN GO A LONG WAY. TAKE THIS NEW CREW OF MERCS GOING AROUND CALLING THEMSELVES THE BASTARDS OF BLACKGATE. WHO KNOWS IF THEY EVER BEEN TO PRISON...THEY SOUND LEGIT. LEGIT ENOUGH TO GET A SIT DOWN WITH SQUID.
INTERESTING THEORY. BUT, WITH A NAME LIKE "JULIAN" I'D GET COMFORTABLE WITH BEING A HENCHMAN.
NO OFFENSE.
WHUMP
NONE TAKEN.
GONNA HIT THE MEN'S ROOM. DON'T GO NOWHERE.
Hnn...

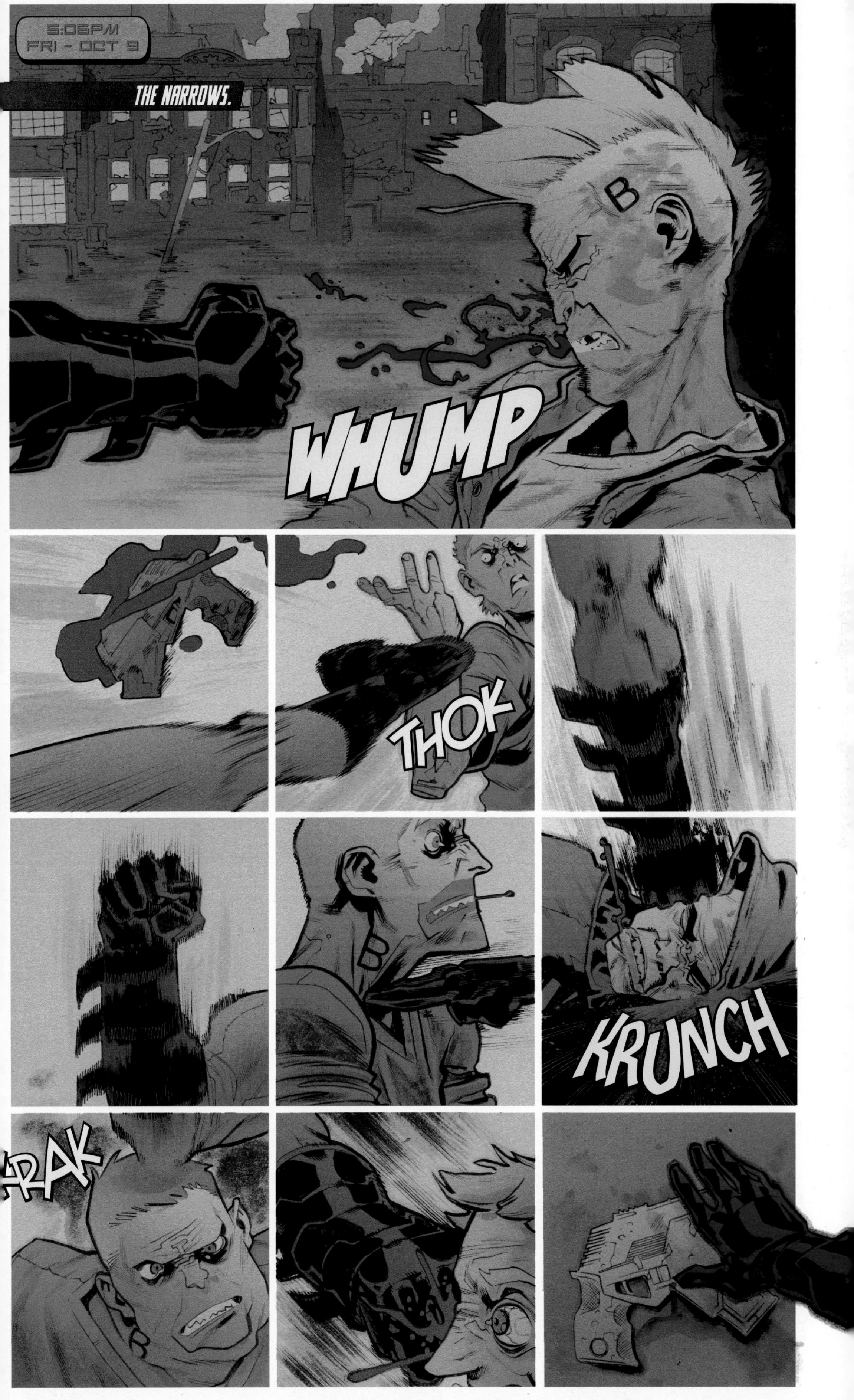
5:06PM
FRI - OCT 9
THE NARROWS.
WHUMP
THOK
KRUNCH
RAK

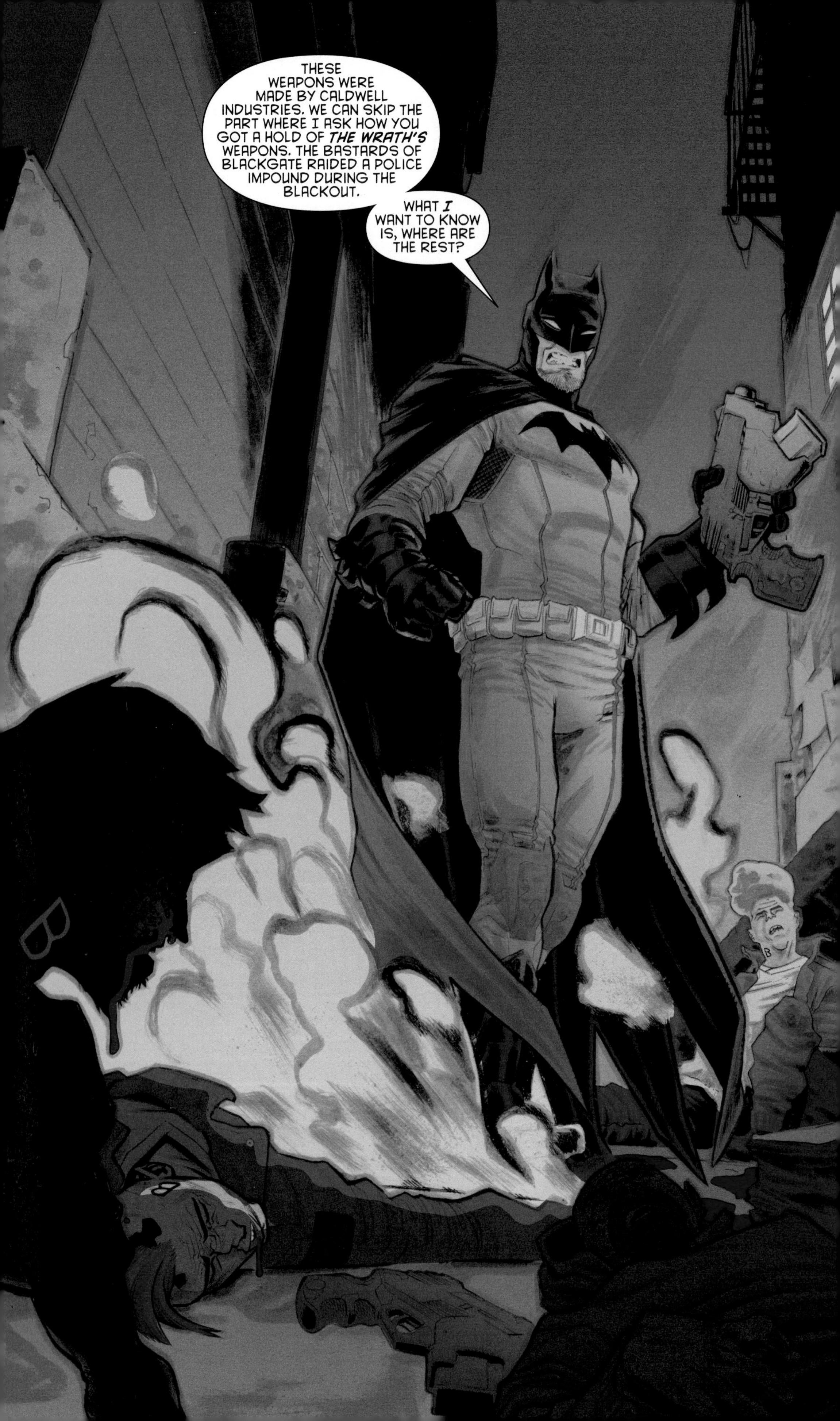
THESE WEAPONS WERE MADE BY CALDWELL INDUSTRIES. WE CAN SKIP THE PART WHERE I ASK HOW YOU GOT A HOLD OF *THE WRATH'S* WEAPONS. THE BASTARDS OF BLACKGATE RAIDED A POLICE IMPOUND DURING THE BLACKOUT.
WHAT *I* WANT TO KNOW IS, WHERE ARE THE REST?

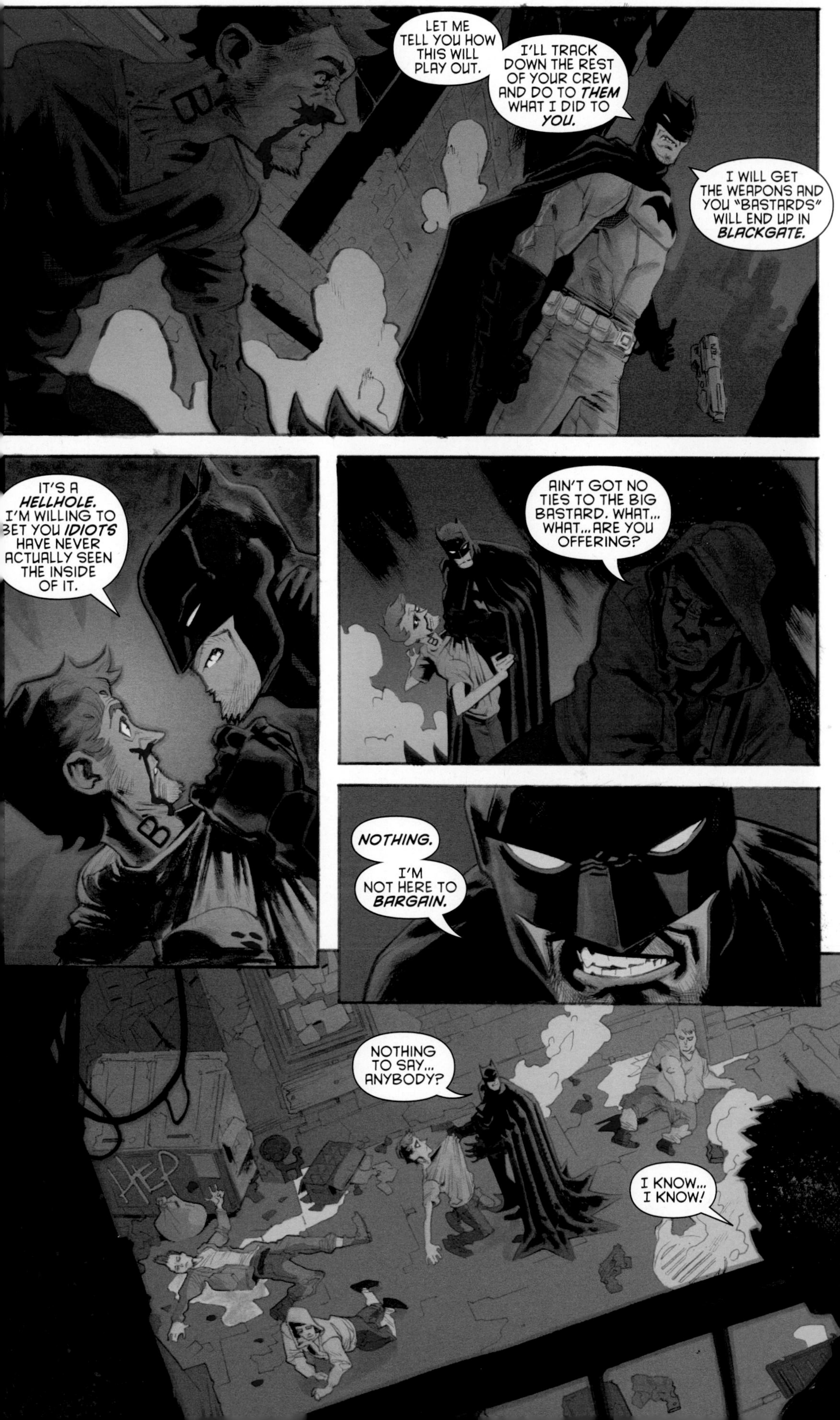
LET ME TELL YOU HOW THIS WILL PLAY OUT.
I'LL TRACK DOWN THE REST OF YOUR CREW AND DO TO *THEM* WHAT I DID TO *YOU.*
I WILL GET THE WEAPONS AND YOU "BASTARDS" WILL END UP IN *BLACKGATE.*
IT'S A *HELLHOLE.* I'M WILLING TO BET YOU *IDIOTS* HAVE NEVER ACTUALLY SEEN THE INSIDE OF IT.
AIN'T GOT NO TIES TO THE BIG BASTARD. WHAT... WHAT... ARE YOU OFFERING?
NOTHING.
I'M NOT HERE TO *BARGAIN.*
NOTHING TO SAY... ANYBODY?
I KNOW... I KNOW!

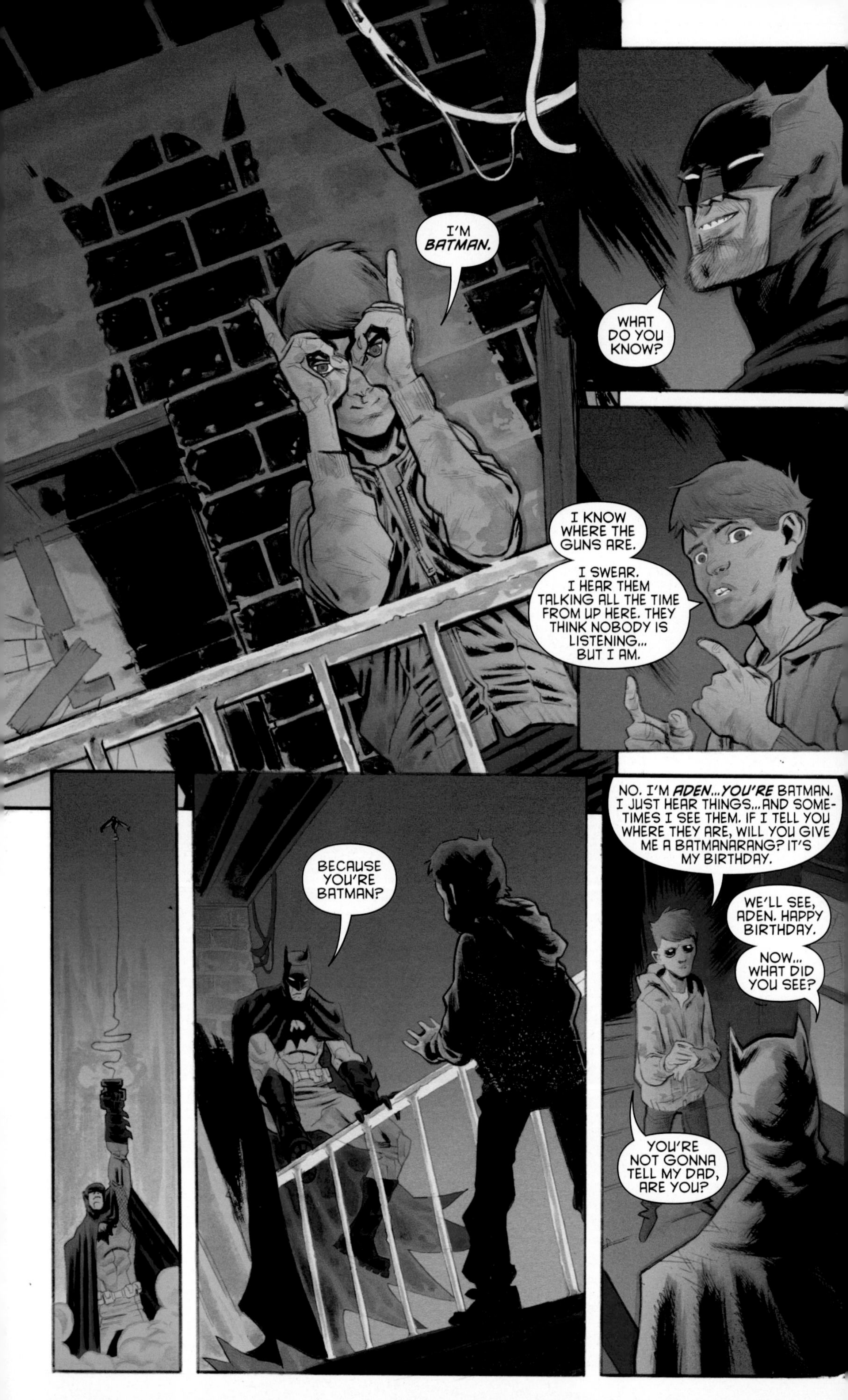
I'M *BATMAN.*
WHAT DO YOU KNOW?
I KNOW WHERE THE GUNS ARE.
I SWEAR. I HEAR THEM TALKING ALL THE TIME FROM UP HERE. THEY THINK NOBODY IS LISTENING... BUT I AM.
BECAUSE YOU'RE BATMAN?
NO. I'M *ADEN*... *YOU'RE* BATMAN. I JUST HEAR THINGS... AND SOME-TIMES I SEE THEM. IF I TELL YOU WHERE THEY ARE, WILL YOU GIVE ME A BATMANARANG? IT'S MY BIRTHDAY.
WE'LL SEE, ADEN. HAPPY BIRTHDAY.
NOW... WHAT DID YOU SEE?
YOU'RE NOT GONNA TELL MY DAD, ARE YOU?

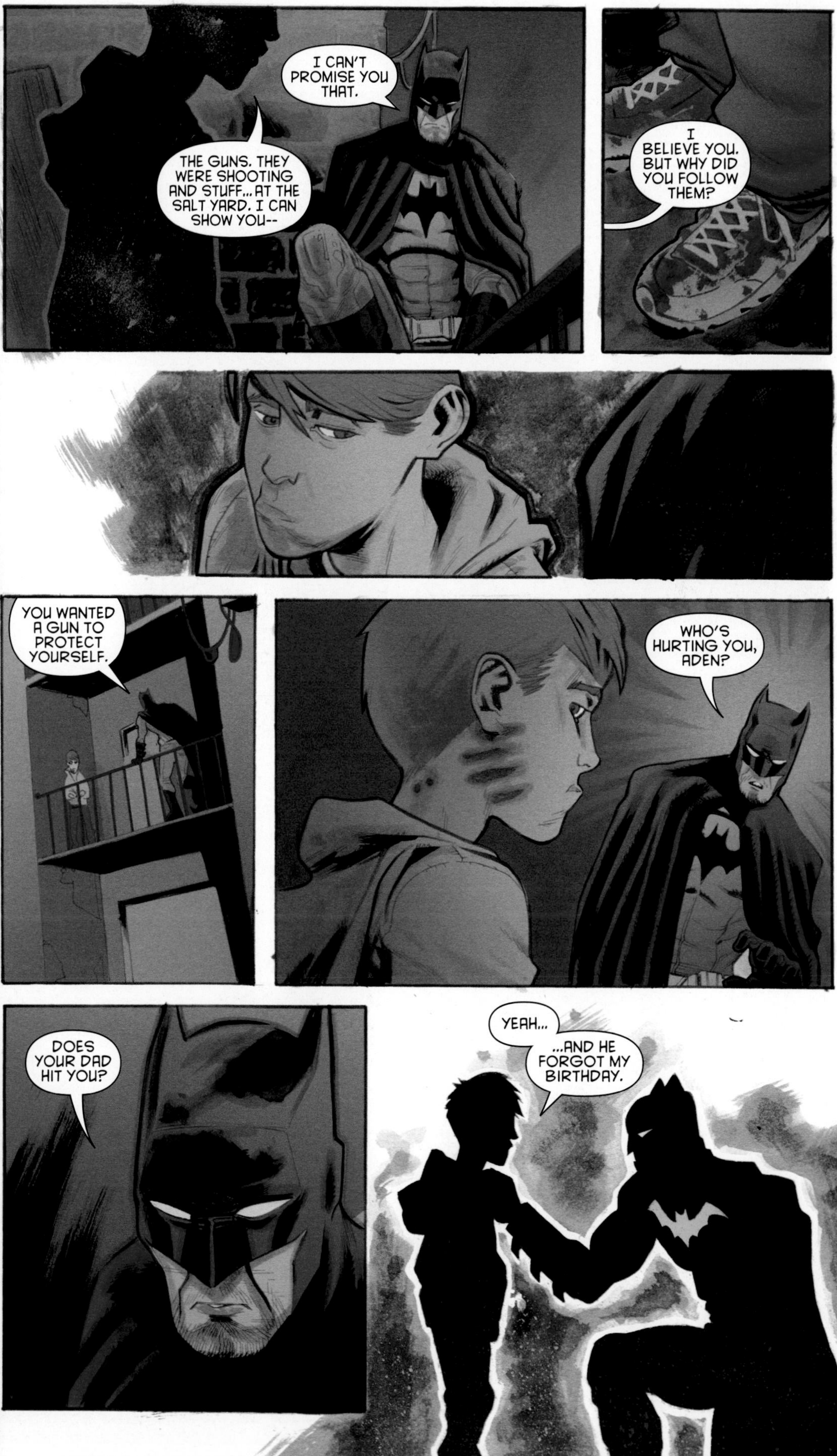
I CAN'T PROMISE YOU THAT.
THE GUNS. THEY WERE SHOOTING AND STUFF... AT THE SALT YARD. I CAN SHOW YOU--
I BELIEVE YOU. BUT WHY DID YOU FOLLOW THEM?
YOU WANTED A GUN TO PROTECT YOURSELF.
WHO'S HURTING YOU, ADEN?
DOES YOUR DAD HIT YOU?
YEAH...
...AND HE FORGOT MY BIRTHDAY.

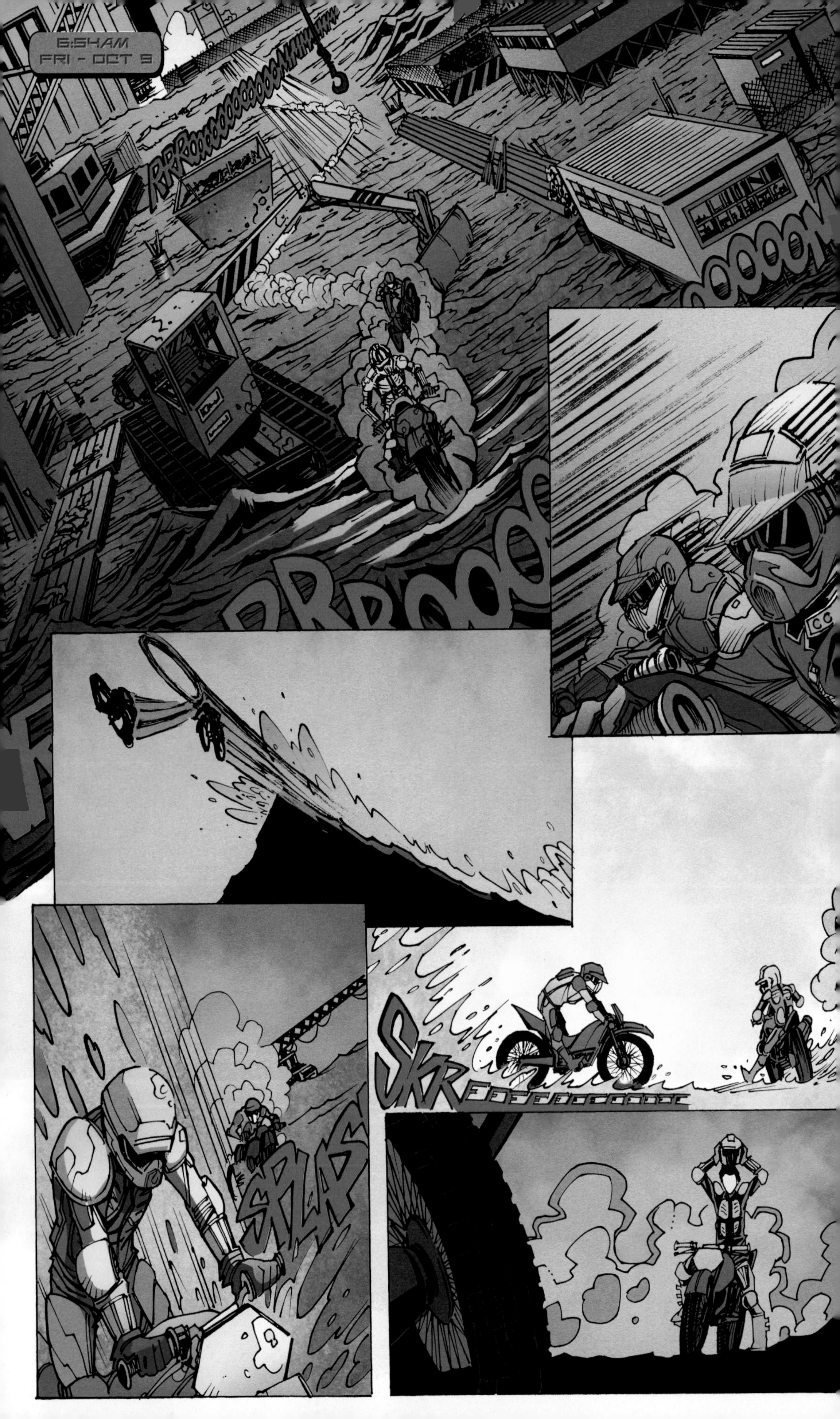

6:54AM
FRI - OCT 9
RRROOOOOOOOOOOMMMM
BOOOOOM
RRROOO
SKREEEEEEEEEEE
SPLAS

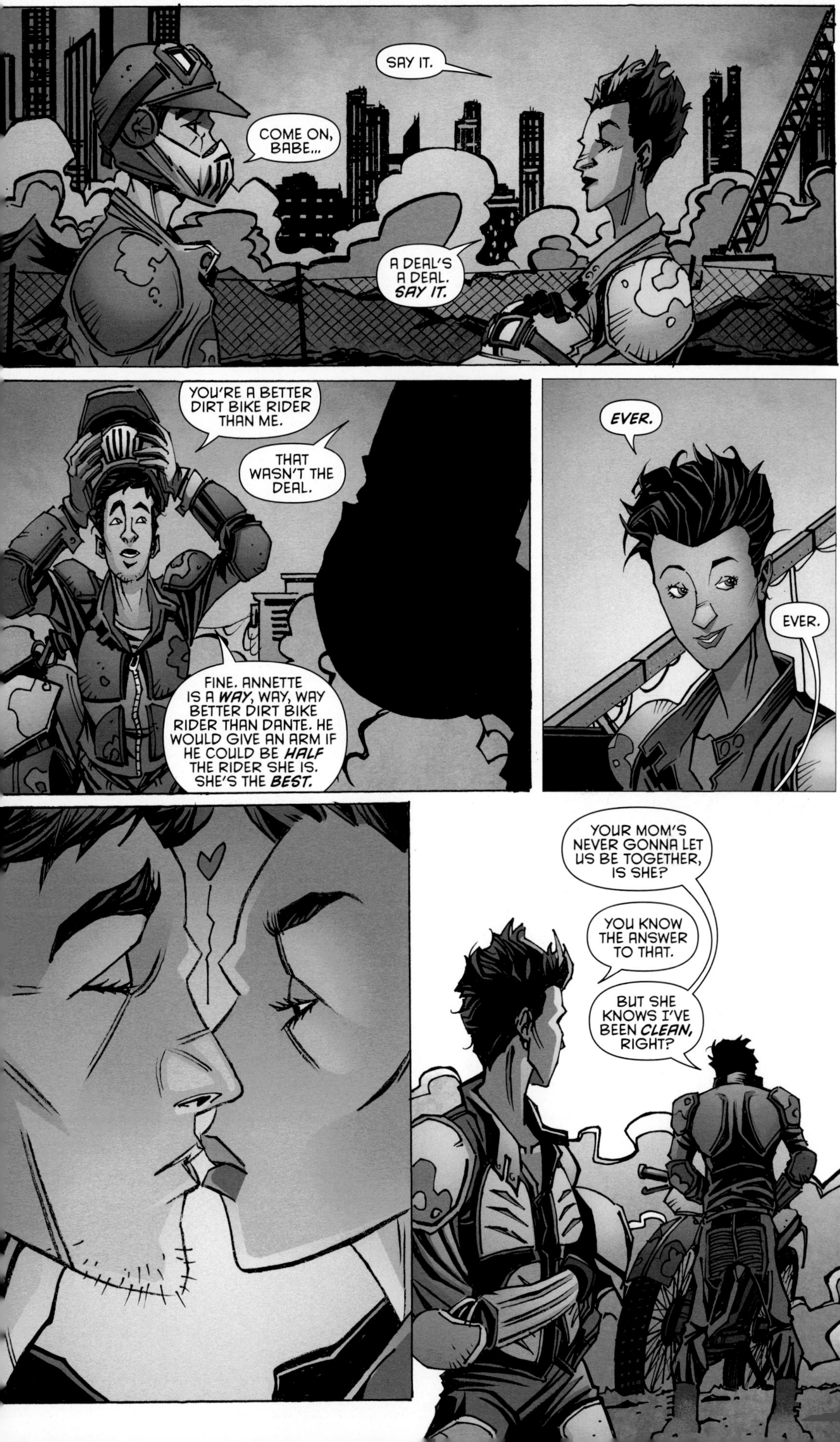

COME ON, BABE...
SAY IT.
A DEAL'S A DEAL. SAY IT.
YOU'RE A BETTER DIRT BIKE RIDER THAN ME.
THAT WASN'T THE DEAL.
FINE. ANNETTE IS A WAY, WAY, WAY BETTER DIRT BIKE RIDER THAN DANTE. HE WOULD GIVE AN ARM IF HE COULD BE HALF THE RIDER SHE IS. SHE'S THE BEST.
EVER.
EVER.
YOUR MOM'S NEVER GONNA LET US BE TOGETHER, IS SHE?
YOU KNOW THE ANSWER TO THAT.
BUT SHE KNOWS I'VE BEEN CLEAN, RIGHT?

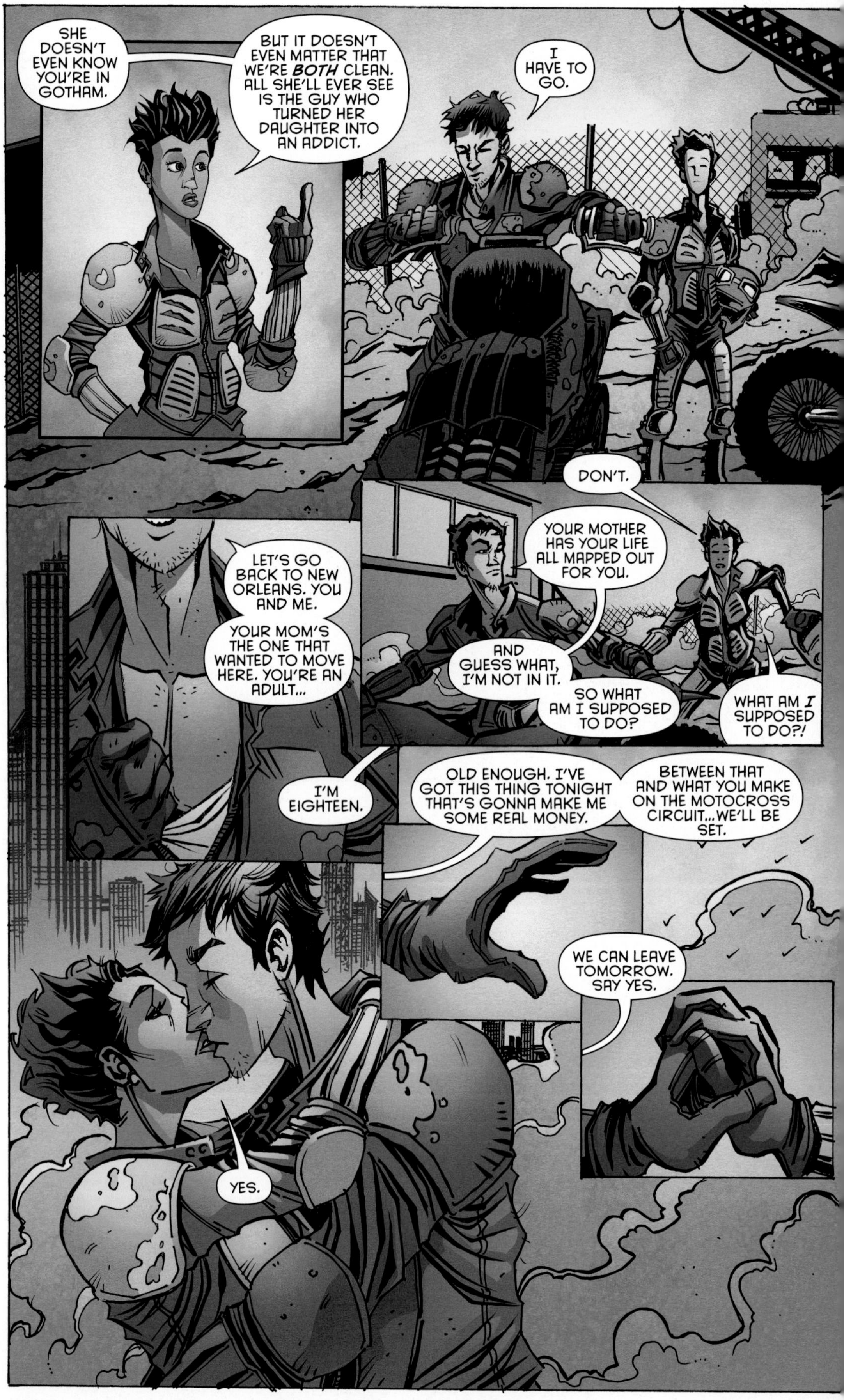
SHE DOESN'T EVEN KNOW YOU'RE IN GOTHAM.
BUT IT DOESN'T EVEN MATTER THAT WE'RE *BOTH* CLEAN. ALL SHE'LL EVER SEE IS THE GUY WHO TURNED HER DAUGHTER INTO AN ADDICT.
I HAVE TO GO.
DON'T.
YOUR MOTHER HAS YOUR LIFE ALL MAPPED OUT FOR YOU.
AND GUESS WHAT, I'M NOT IN IT.
SO WHAT AM I SUPPOSED TO DO?
WHAT AM *I* SUPPOSED TO DO?!
LET'S GO BACK TO NEW ORLEANS. YOU AND ME.
YOUR MOM'S THE ONE THAT WANTED TO MOVE HERE. YOU'RE AN ADULT...
I'M EIGHTEEN.
OLD ENOUGH. I'VE GOT THIS THING TONIGHT THAT'S GONNA MAKE ME SOME REAL MONEY.
BETWEEN THAT AND WHAT YOU MAKE ON THE MOTOCROSS CIRCUIT...WE'LL BE SET.
WE CAN LEAVE TOMORROW. SAY YES.
YES.

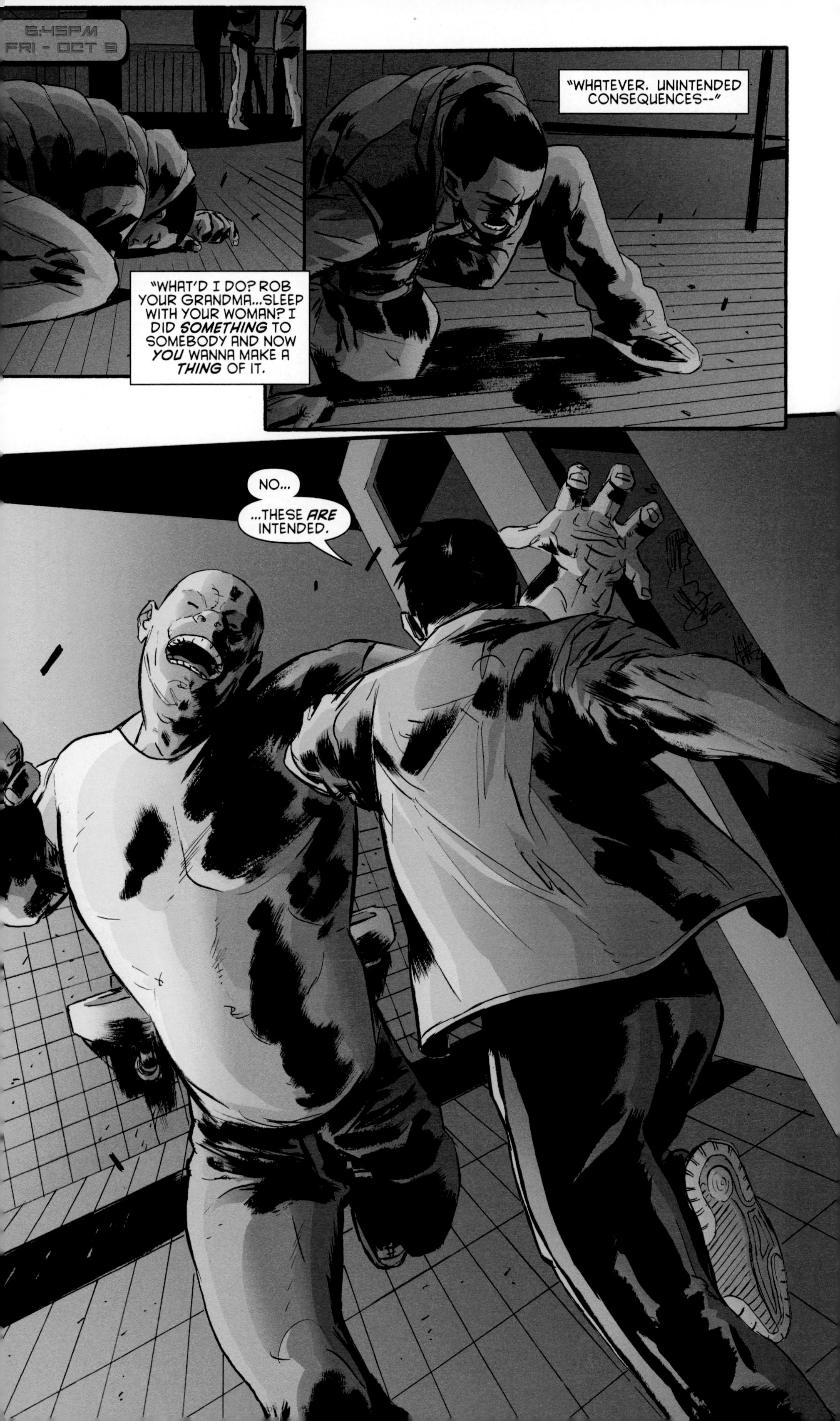
6:45PM
FRI - OCT 9
"WHAT'D I DO? ROB YOUR GRANDMA...SLEEP WITH YOUR WOMAN? I DID *SOMETHING* TO SOMEBODY AND NOW *YOU* WANNA MAKE A *THING* OF IT.
"WHATEVER. UNINTENDED CONSEQUENCES--"
NO...
...THESE *ARE* INTENDED.

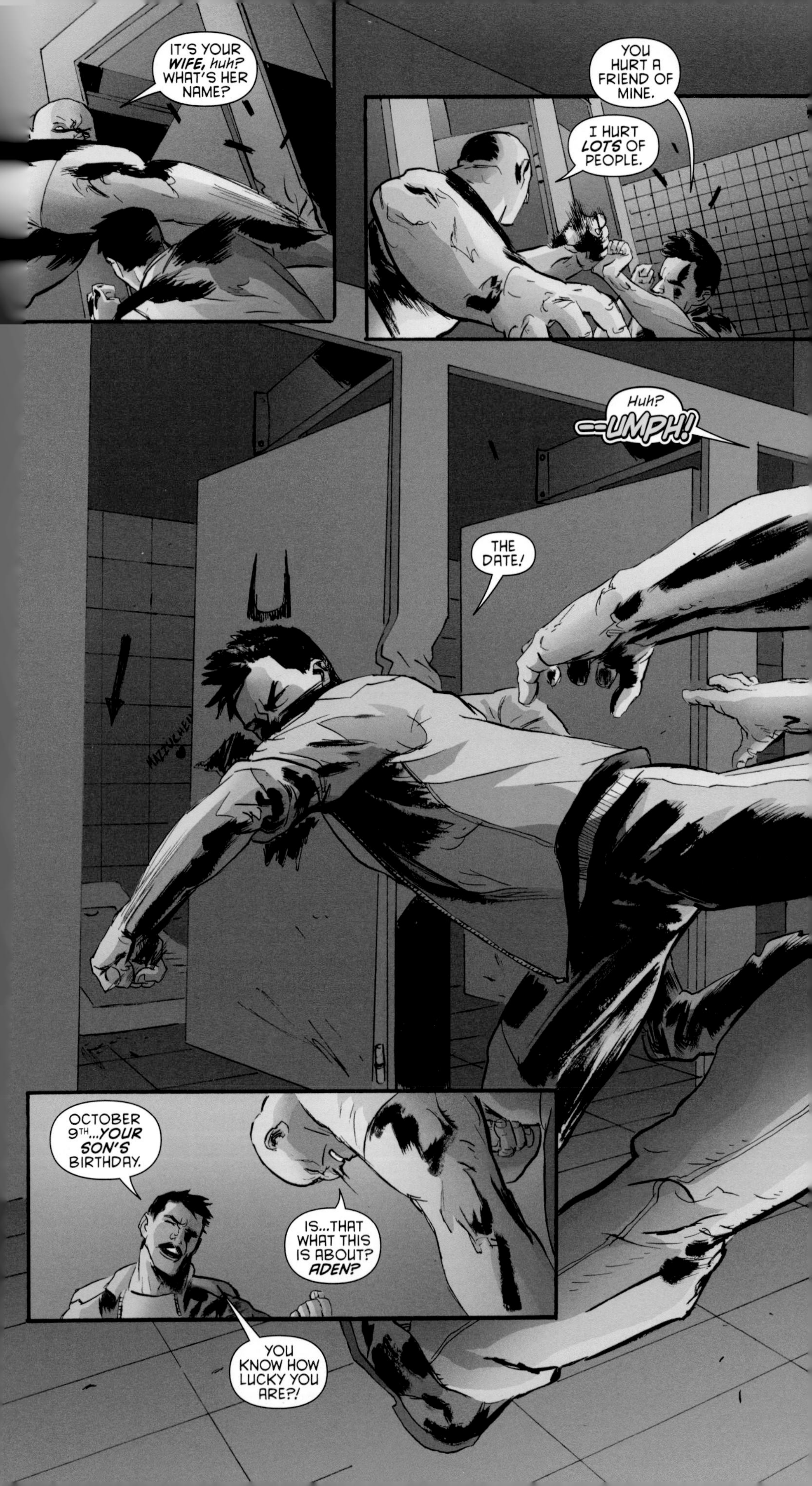

IT'S YOUR WIFE, huh? WHAT'S HER NAME?
YOU HURT A FRIEND OF MINE.
I HURT LOTS OF PEOPLE.
Huh?
--UMPH!
THE DATE!
OCTOBER 9TH...YOUR SON'S BIRTHDAY.
IS...THAT WHAT THIS IS ABOUT? ADEN?
YOU KNOW HOW LUCKY YOU ARE?!

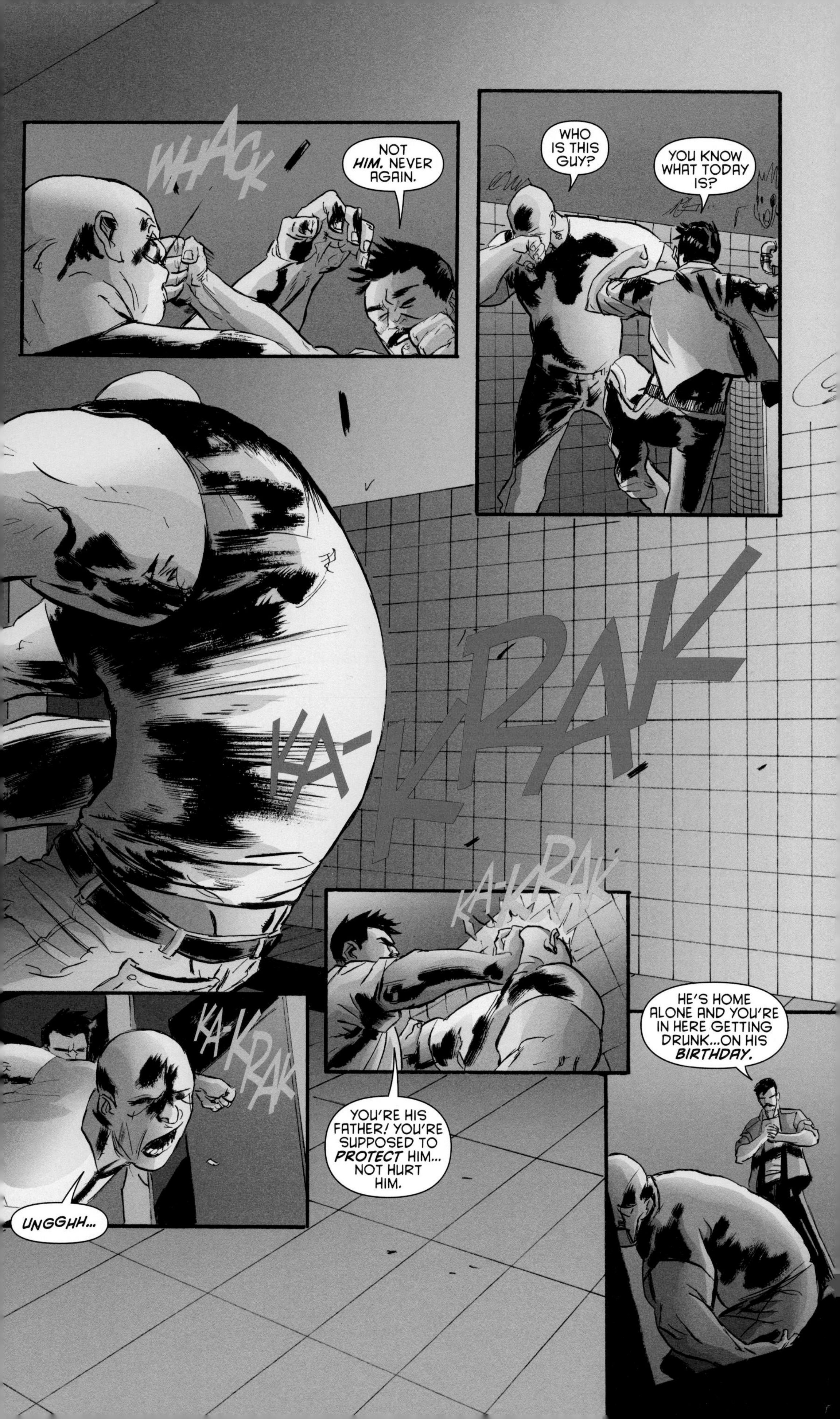
WHACK
NOT HIM. NEVER AGAIN.
WHO IS THIS GUY?
YOU KNOW WHAT TODAY IS?
KA-KRAK
KA-KRAK
KA-KRAK
UNGGHH...
YOU'RE HIS FATHER! YOU'RE SUPPOSED TO PROTECT HIM... NOT HURT HIM.
HE'S HOME ALONE AND YOU'RE IN HERE GETTING DRUNK...ON HIS BIRTHDAY.

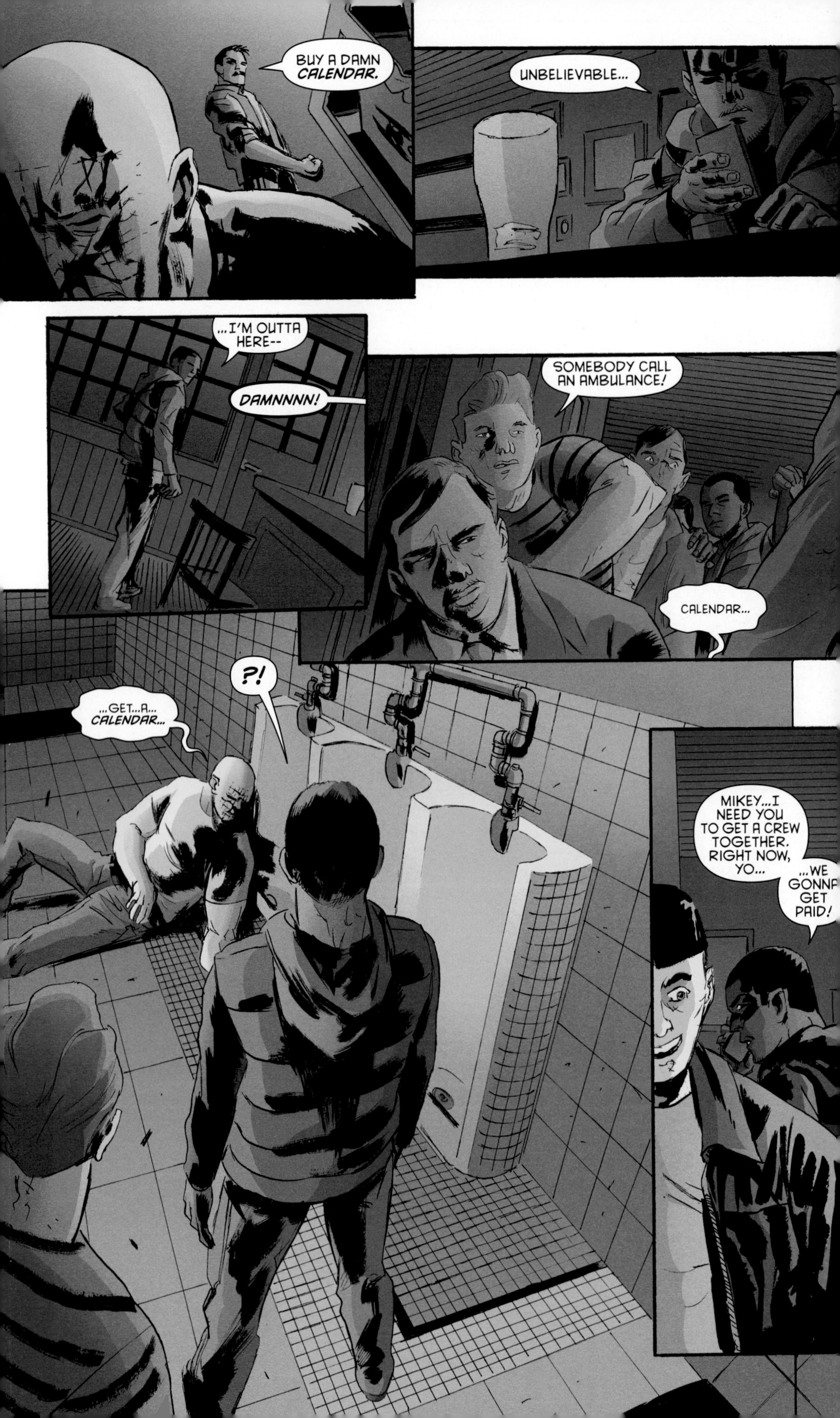
BUY A DAMN CALENDAR.
UNBELIEVABLE...
...I'M OUTTA HERE--
DAMNNNN!
SOMEBODY CALL AN AMBULANCE!
CALENDAR...
?!
...GET...A... CALENDAR...
MIKEY...I NEED YOU TO GET A CREW TOGETHER. RIGHT NOW, YO...
...WE GONNA GET PAID!

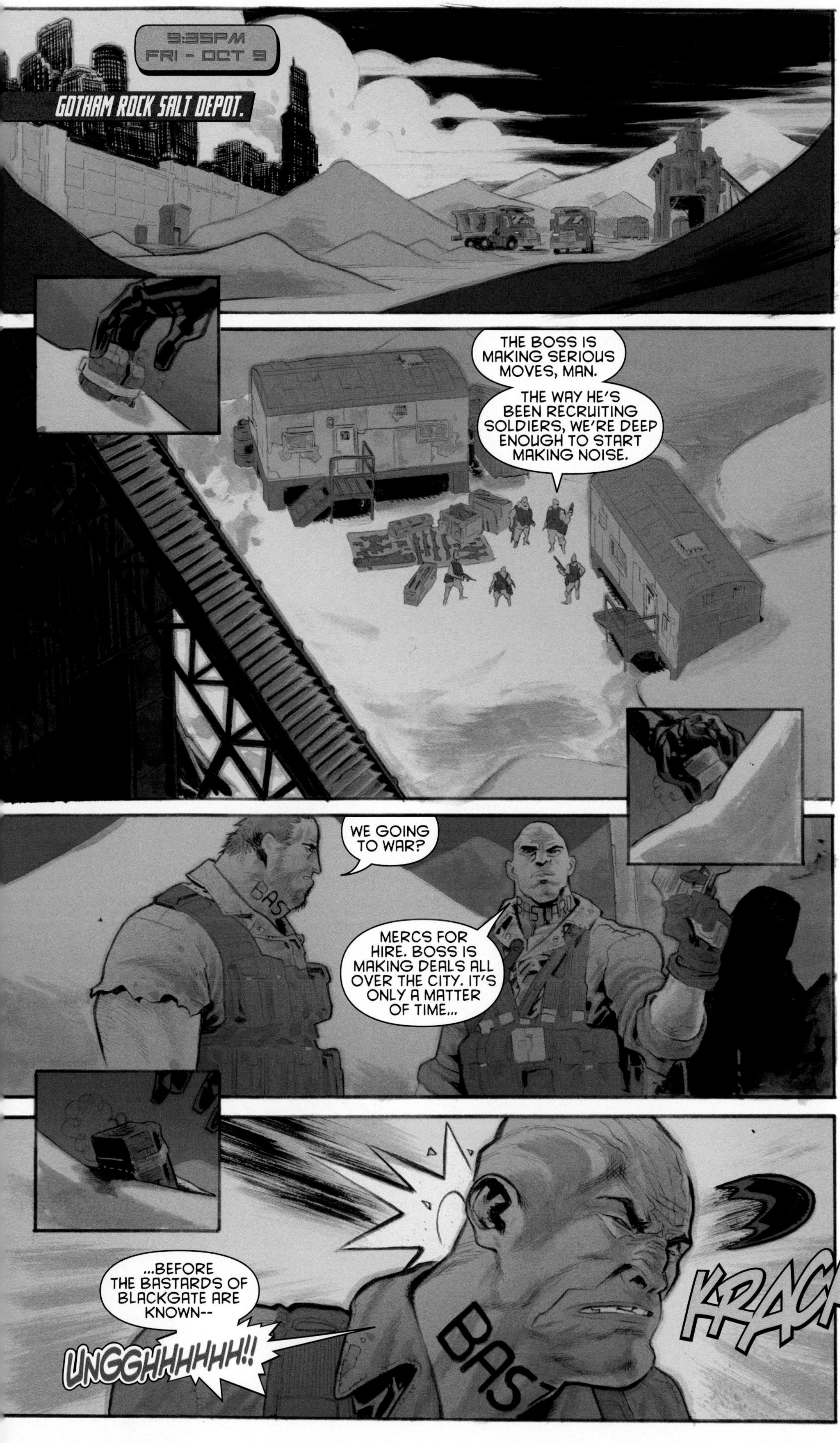
9:35PM
FRI - OCT 9
GOTHAM ROCK SALT DEPOT.
THE BOSS IS MAKING SERIOUS MOVES, MAN.
THE WAY HE'S BEEN RECRUITING SOLDIERS, WE'RE DEEP ENOUGH TO START MAKING NOISE.
WE GOING TO WAR?
MERCS FOR HIRE. BOSS IS MAKING DEALS ALL OVER THE CITY. IT'S ONLY A MATTER OF TIME...
...BEFORE THE BASTARDS OF BLACKGATE ARE KNOWN--
KRACK
UNGGHHHHHH!!

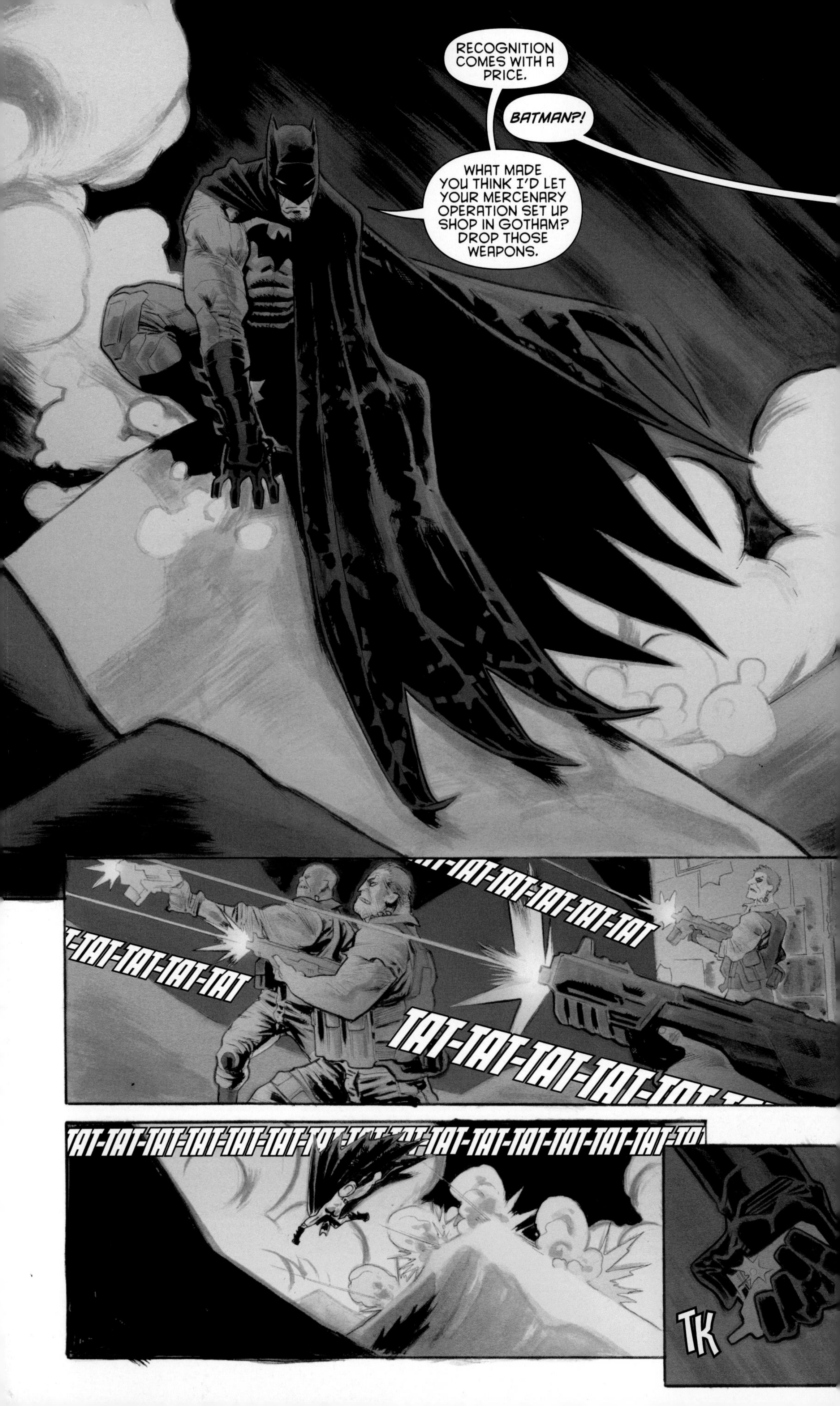
RECOGNITION COMES WITH A PRICE.
BATMAN?!
WHAT MADE YOU THINK I'D LET YOUR MERCENARY OPERATION SET UP SHOP IN GOTHAM? DROP THOSE WEAPONS.
TAT-TAT-TAT-TAT-TAT
TAT-TAT-TAT-TAT
TAT-TAT-TAT-TAT-TAT
TAT-TAT-TAT-TAT-TAT-TAT
TK

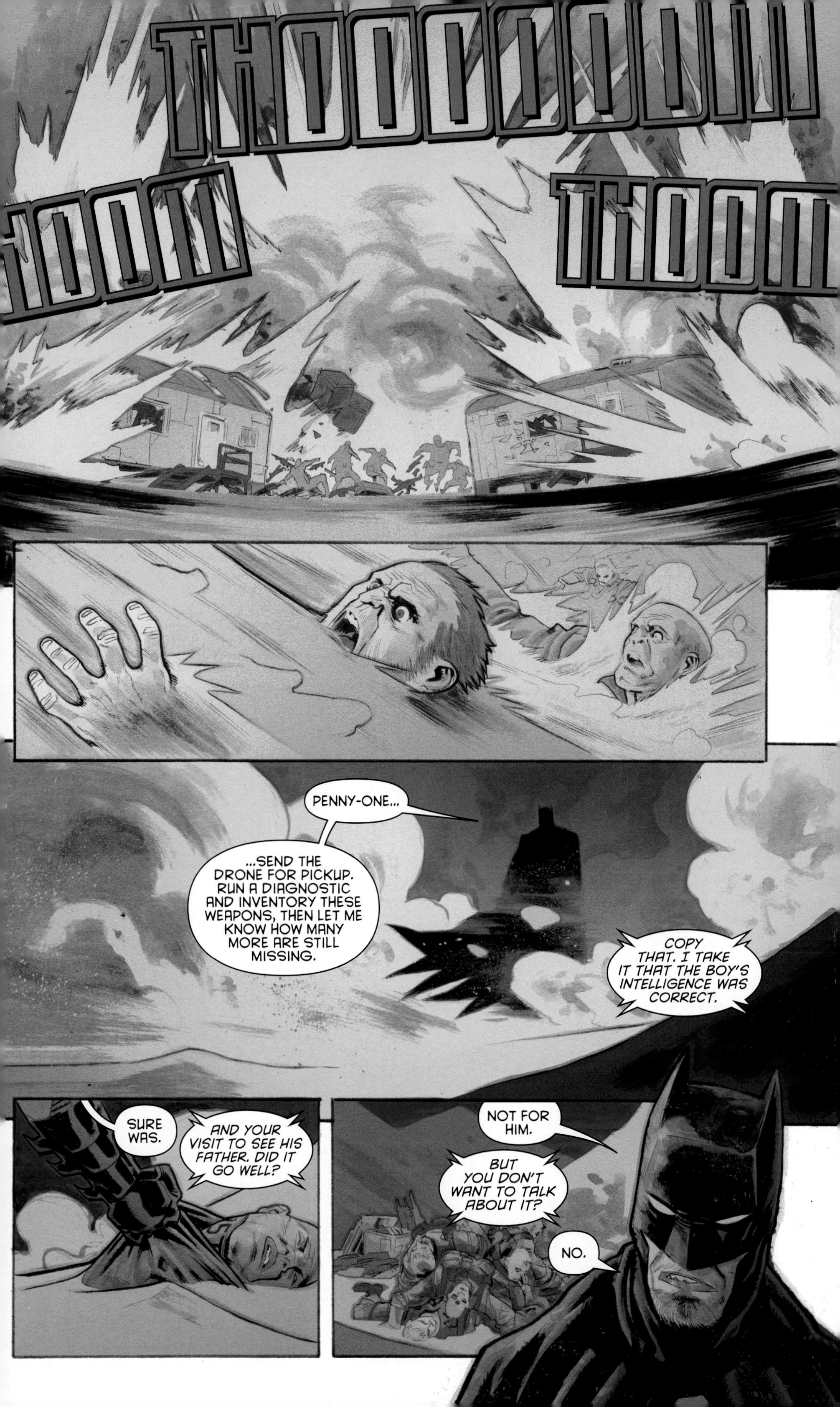
THOOOOOOM
THOOM
THOOM
PENNY-ONE...
...SEND THE DRONE FOR PICKUP. RUN A DIAGNOSTIC AND INVENTORY THESE WEAPONS, THEN LET ME KNOW HOW MANY MORE ARE STILL MISSING.
COPY THAT. I TAKE IT THAT THE BOY'S INTELLIGENCE WAS CORRECT.
SURE WAS.
AND YOUR VISIT TO SEE HIS FATHER. DID IT GO WELL?
NOT FOR HIM.
BUT YOU DON'T WANT TO TALK ABOUT IT?
NO.

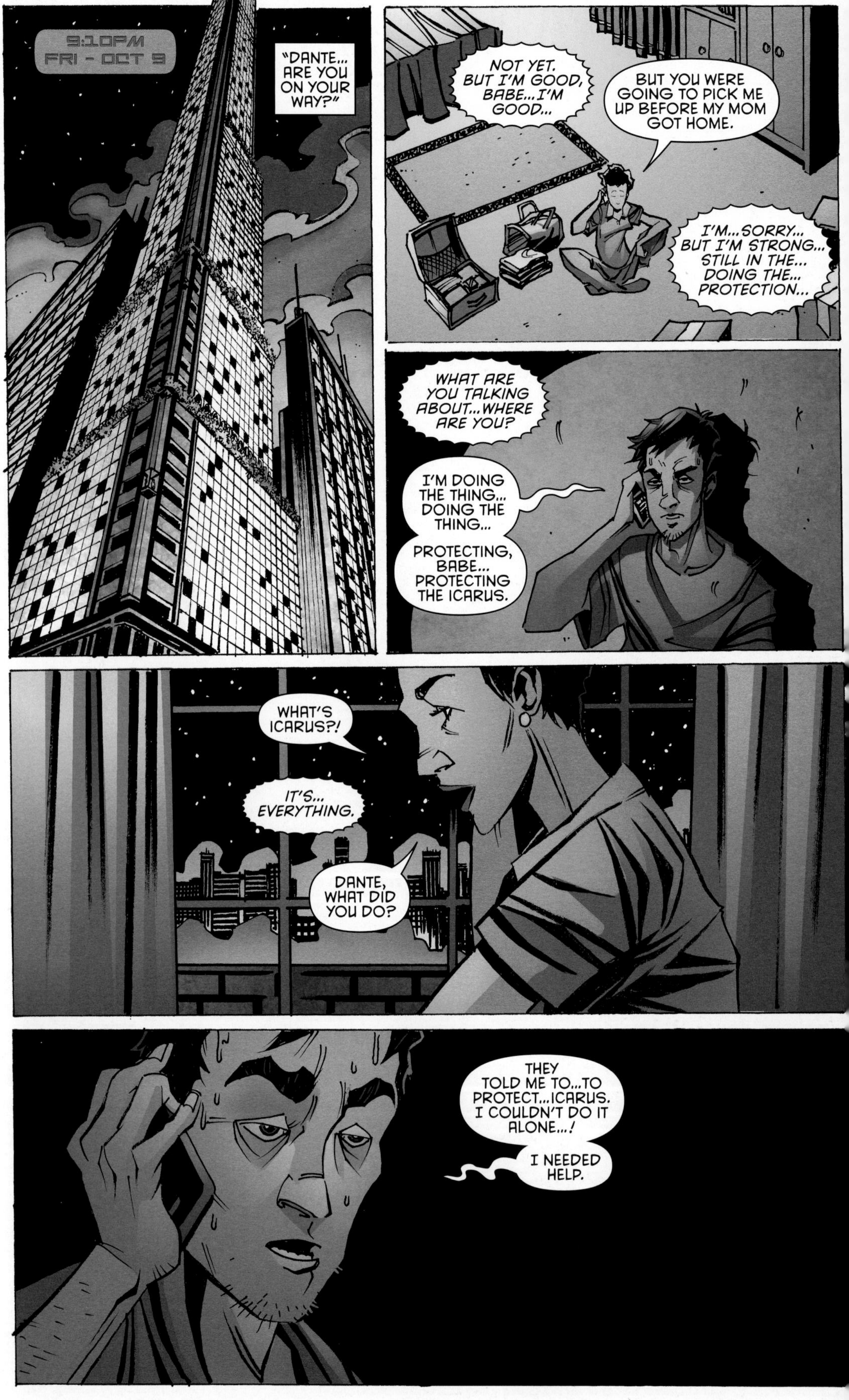
9:10PM
FRI - OCT 9
"DANTE... ARE YOU ON YOUR WAY?"
NOT YET. BUT I'M GOOD, BABE...I'M GOOD...
BUT YOU WERE GOING TO PICK ME UP BEFORE MY MOM GOT HOME.
I'M...SORRY... BUT I'M STRONG... STILL IN THE... DOING THE... PROTECTION...
WHAT ARE YOU TALKING ABOUT...WHERE ARE YOU?
I'M DOING THE THING... DOING THE THING...
PROTECTING, BABE... PROTECTING THE ICARUS.
WHAT'S ICARUS?!
IT'S... EVERYTHING.
DANTE, WHAT DID YOU DO?
THEY TOLD ME TO...TO PROTECT...ICARUS. I COULDN'T DO IT ALONE...!
I NEEDED HELP.

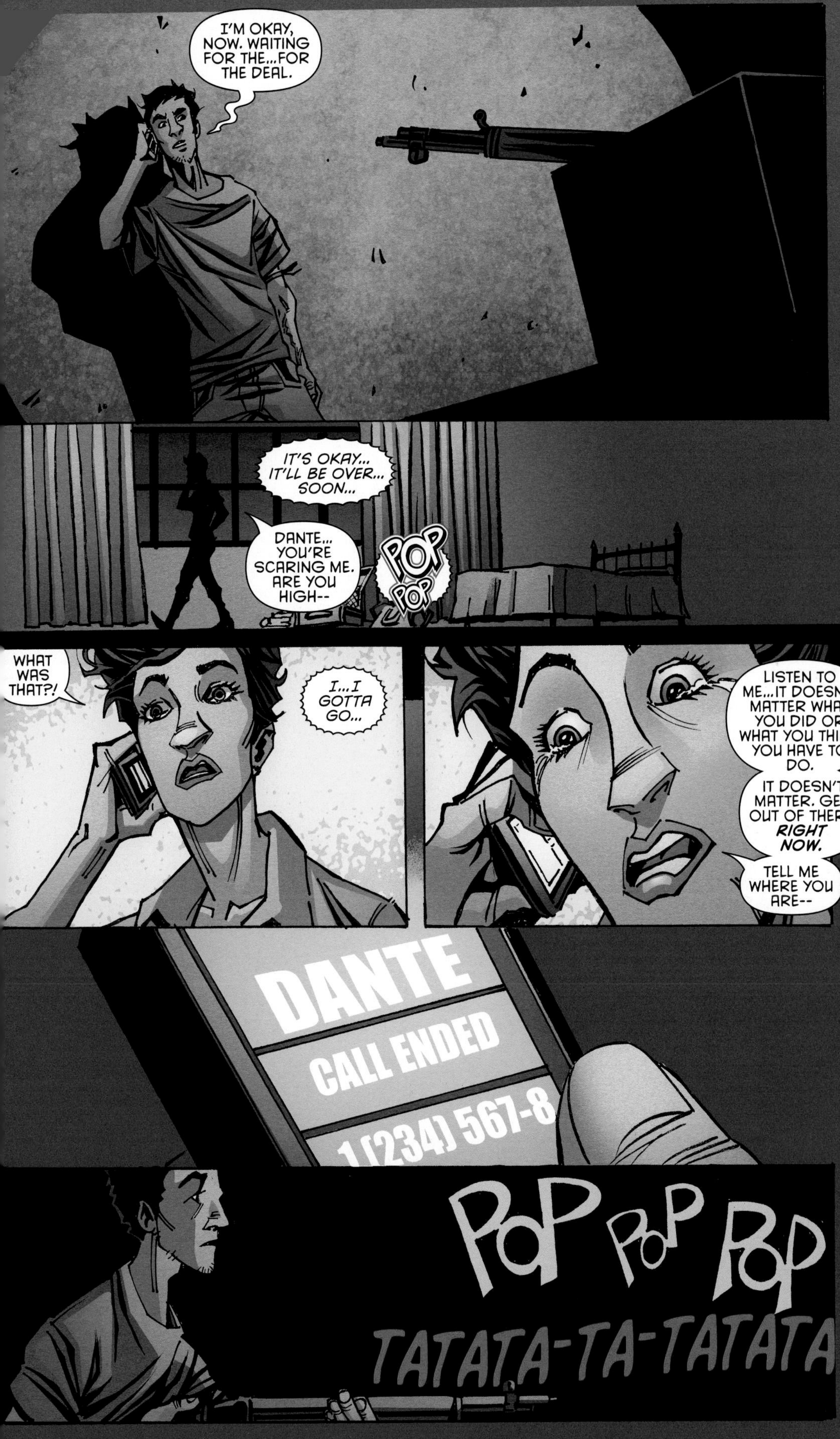

I'M OKAY, NOW. WAITING FOR THE...FOR THE DEAL.
IT'S OKAY... IT'LL BE OVER... SOON...
DANTE... YOU'RE SCARING ME. ARE YOU HIGH--
POP
POP
WHAT WAS THAT?!
I...I GOTTA GO...
LISTEN TO ME...IT DOESN'T MATTER WHAT YOU DID OR WHAT YOU THINK YOU HAVE TO DO.
IT DOESN'T MATTER. GET OUT OF THERE *RIGHT NOW.*
TELL ME WHERE YOU ARE--
DANTE
CALL ENDED
1 (234) 567-8
POP POP POP
TATATA-TA-TATATA

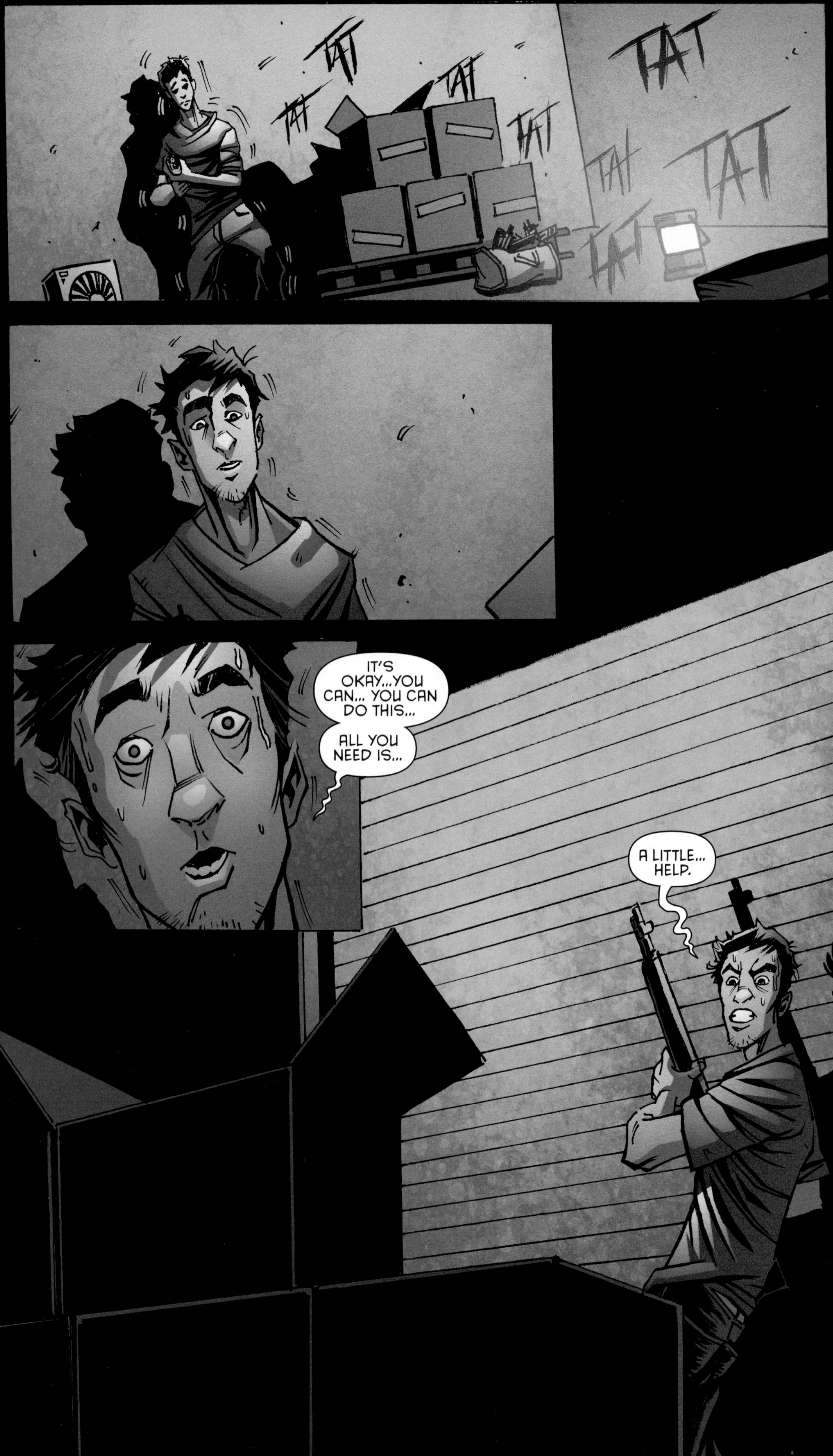
TAT
TAT
TAT
TAT
TAT
TAT
TAT
TAT
IT'S OKAY...YOU CAN... YOU CAN DO THIS...
ALL YOU NEED IS...
A LITTLE... HELP.

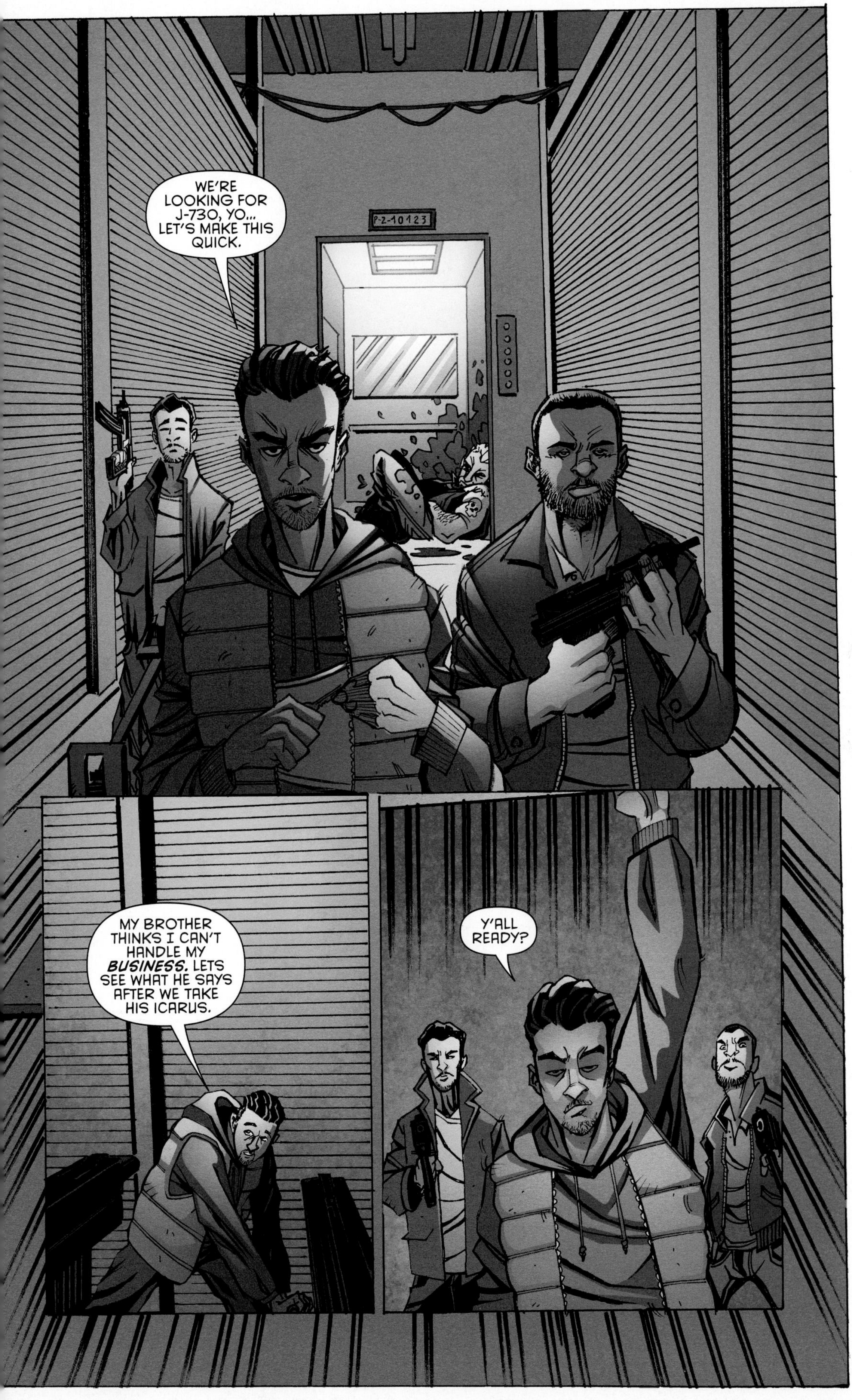
WE'RE LOOKING FOR J-730, YO... LET'S MAKE THIS QUICK.
P-2-10123
MY BROTHER THINKS I CAN'T HANDLE MY *BUSINESS.* LETS SEE WHAT HE SAYS AFTER WE TAKE HIS ICARUS.
Y'ALL READY?

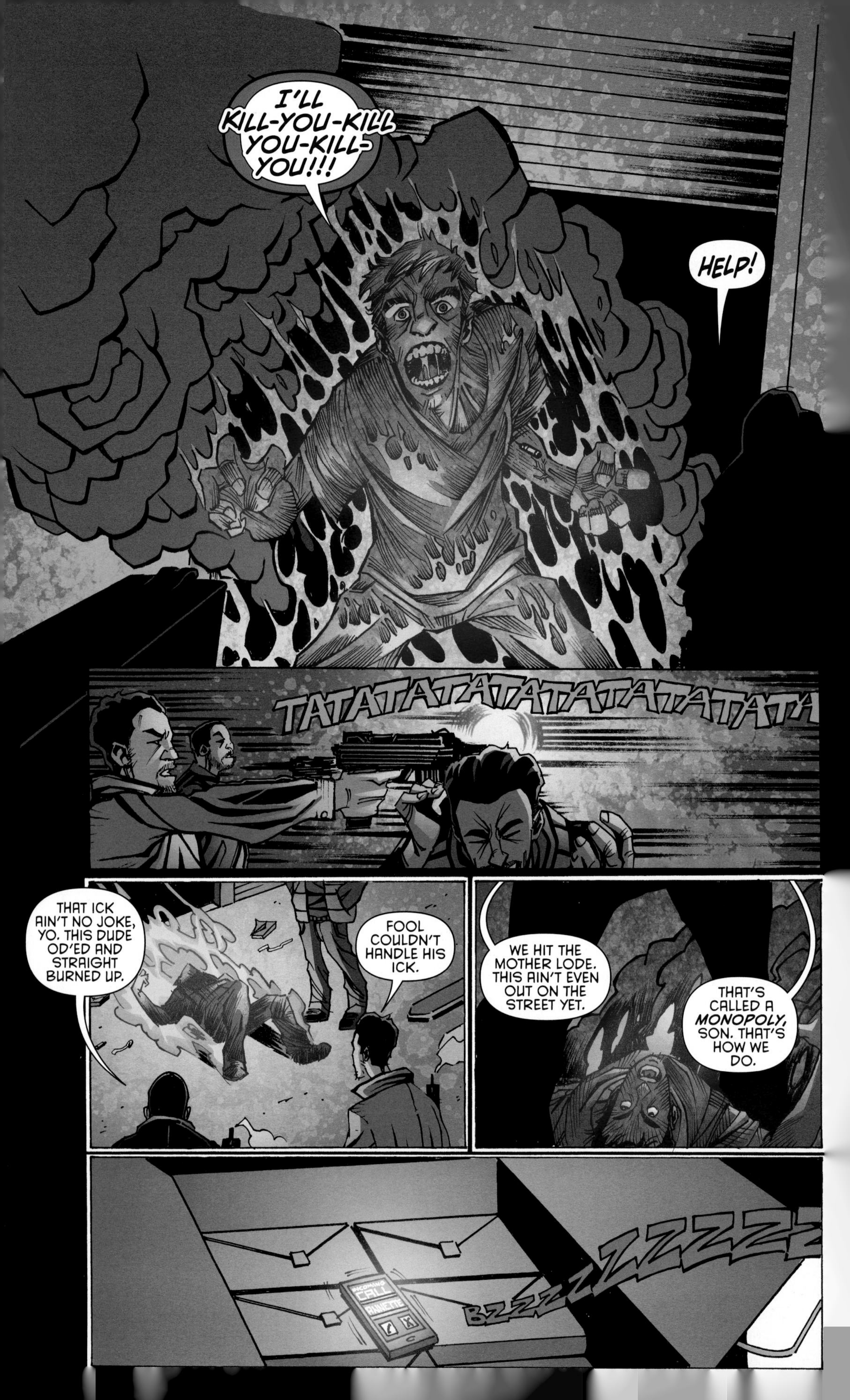
I'LL KILL-YOU-KILL YOU-KILL-YOU!!!
HELP!
TATATATATATATATATATATA
THAT ICK AIN'T NO JOKE, YO. THIS DUDE OD'ED AND STRAIGHT BURNED UP.
FOOL COULDN'T HANDLE HIS ICK.
WE HIT THE MOTHER LODE. THIS AIN'T EVEN OUT ON THE STREET YET.
THAT'S CALLED A *MONOPOLY*, SON. THAT'S HOW WE DO.
INCOMING CALL
ANNETTE
BZZZZZZZZZZ

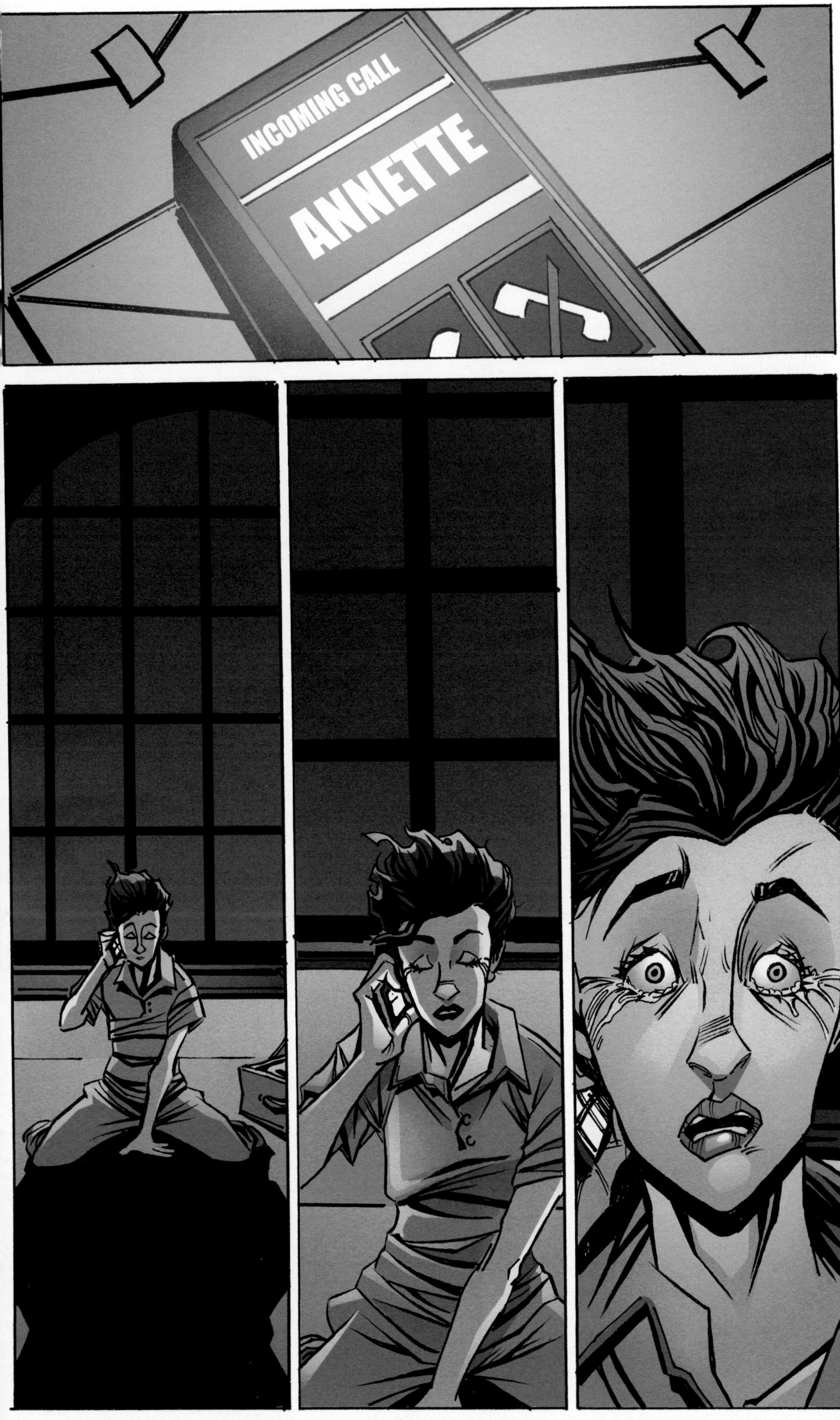
INCOMING CALL
ANNETTE

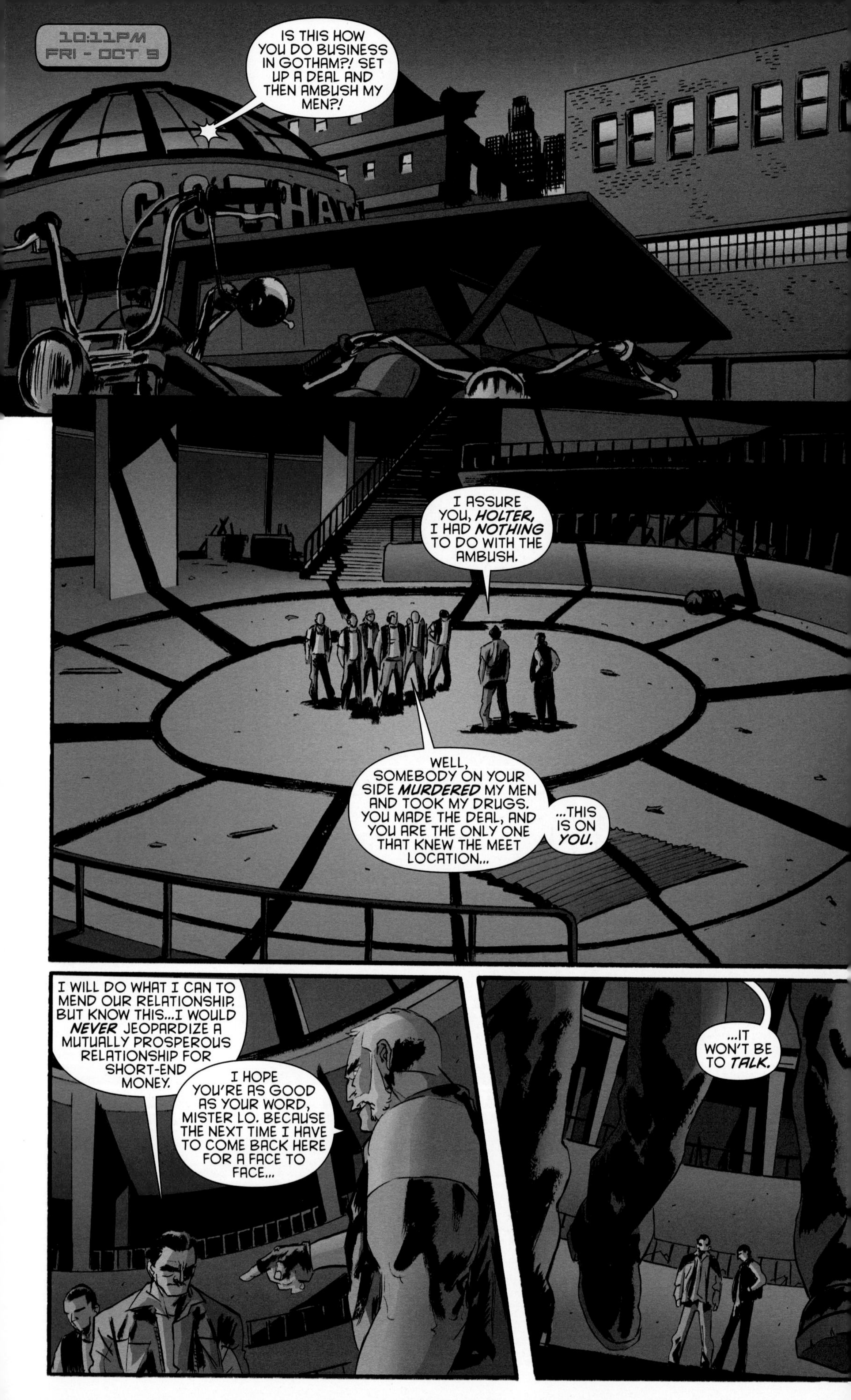
10:11PM
FRI - OCT 9
IS THIS HOW YOU DO BUSINESS IN GOTHAM?! SET UP A DEAL AND THEN AMBUSH MY MEN?!
I ASSURE YOU, HOLTER, I HAD NOTHING TO DO WITH THE AMBUSH.
WELL, SOMEBODY ON YOUR SIDE MURDERED MY MEN AND TOOK MY DRUGS. YOU MADE THE DEAL, AND YOU ARE THE ONLY ONE THAT KNEW THE MEET LOCATION...
...THIS IS ON YOU.
I WILL DO WHAT I CAN TO MEND OUR RELATIONSHIP, BUT KNOW THIS...I WOULD NEVER JEOPARDIZE A MUTUALLY PROSPEROUS RELATIONSHIP FOR SHORT-END MONEY.
I HOPE YOU'RE AS GOOD AS YOUR WORD, MISTER LO. BECAUSE THE NEXT TIME I HAVE TO COME BACK HERE FOR A FACE TO FACE...
...IT WON'T BE TO TALK.

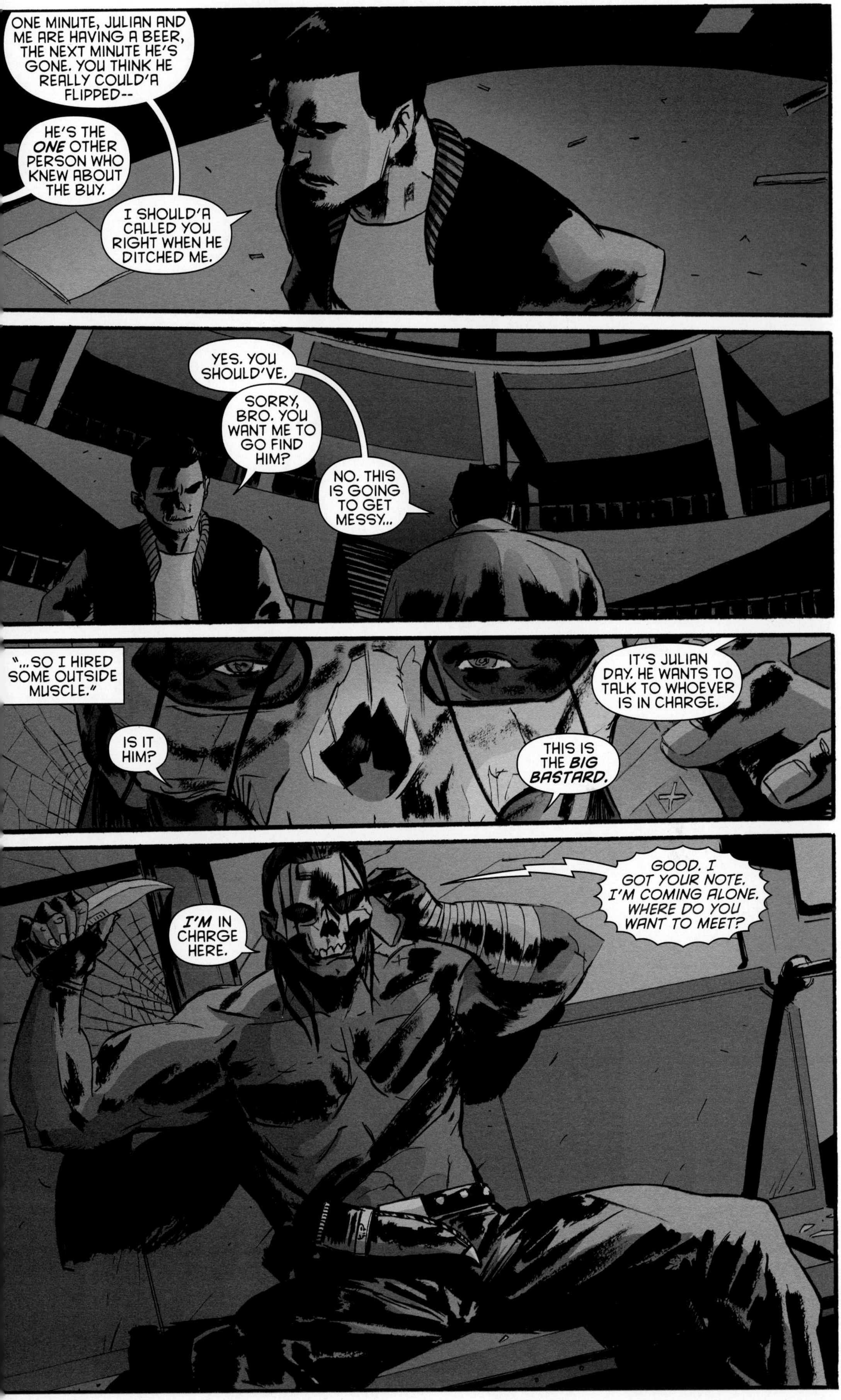
ONE MINUTE, JULIAN AND ME ARE HAVING A BEER, THE NEXT MINUTE HE'S GONE. YOU THINK HE REALLY COULD'A FLIPPED--
HE'S THE *ONE* OTHER PERSON WHO KNEW ABOUT THE BUY.
I SHOULD'A CALLED YOU RIGHT WHEN HE DITCHED ME.
YES. YOU SHOULD'VE.
SORRY, BRO. YOU WANT ME TO GO FIND HIM?
NO. THIS IS GOING TO GET MESSY...
"...SO I HIRED SOME OUTSIDE MUSCLE."
IS IT HIM?
IT'S JULIAN DAY. HE WANTS TO TALK TO WHOEVER IS IN CHARGE.
THIS IS THE *BIG BASTARD.*
I'M IN CHARGE HERE.
GOOD. I GOT YOUR NOTE. I'M COMING ALONE. WHERE DO YOU WANT TO MEET?

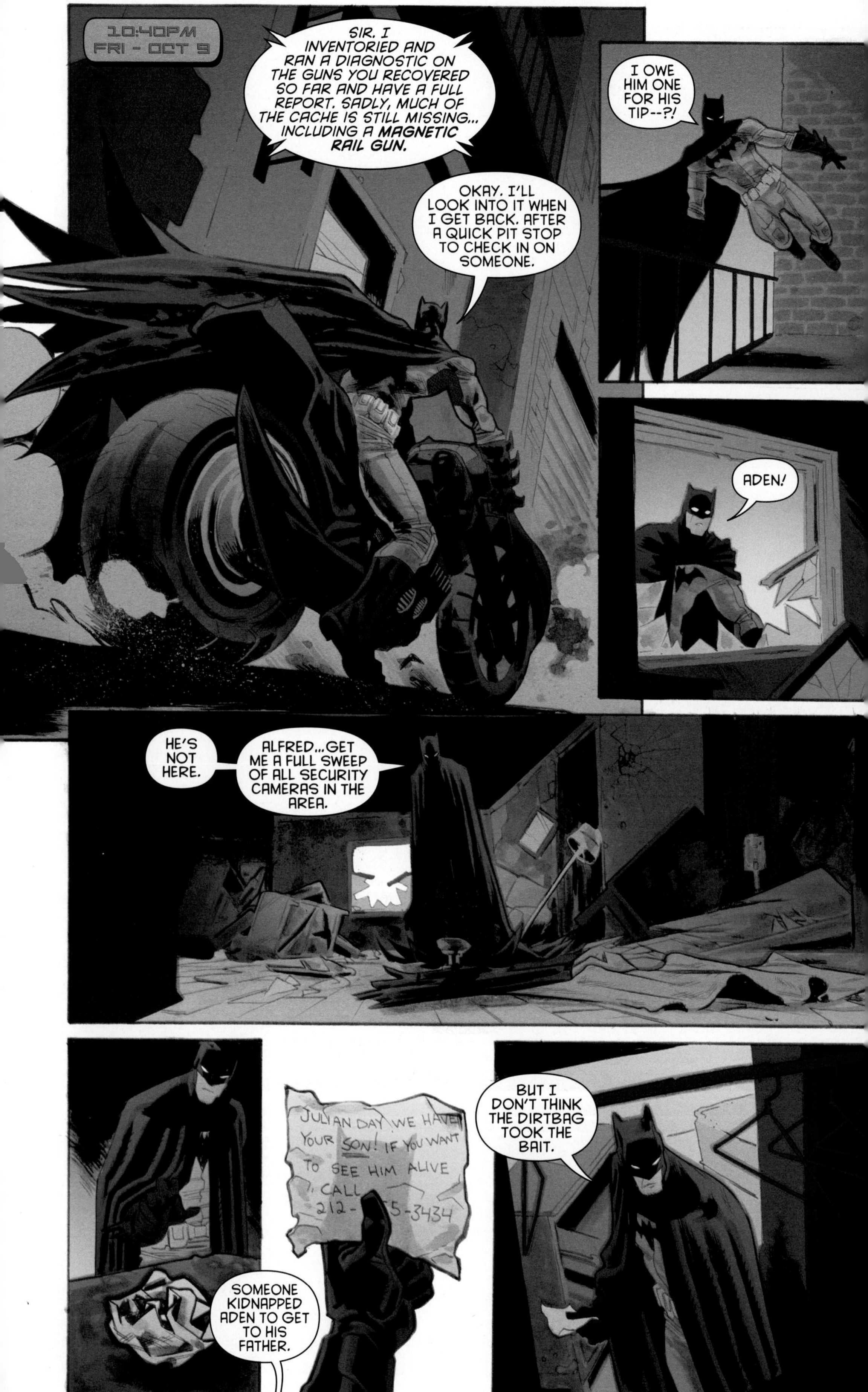
10:40PM
FRI - OCT 9
SIR. I INVENTORIED AND RAN A DIAGNOSTIC ON THE GUNS YOU RECOVERED SO FAR AND HAVE A FULL REPORT. SADLY, MUCH OF THE CACHE IS STILL MISSING... INCLUDING A MAGNETIC RAIL GUN.
OKAY. I'LL LOOK INTO IT WHEN I GET BACK. AFTER A QUICK PIT STOP TO CHECK IN ON SOMEONE.
I OWE HIM ONE FOR HIS TIP--?!
ADEN!
HE'S NOT HERE.
ALFRED...GET ME A FULL SWEEP OF ALL SECURITY CAMERAS IN THE AREA.
JULIAN DAY WE HAVE YOUR SON! IF YOU WANT TO SEE HIM ALIVE CALL
SOMEONE KIDNAPPED ADEN TO GET TO HIS FATHER.
BUT I DON'T THINK THE DIRTBAG TOOK THE BAIT.

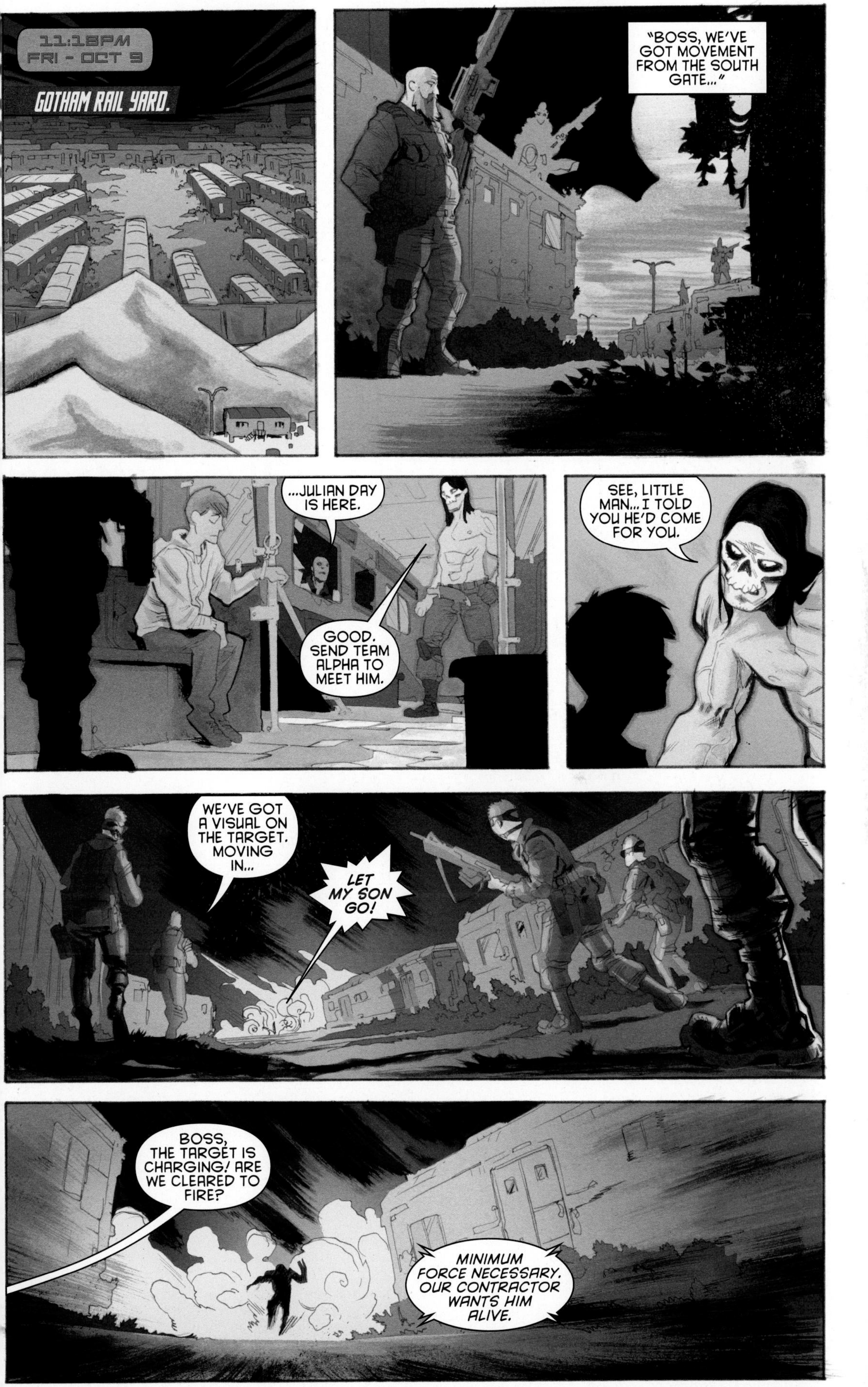
11:18PM
FRI - OCT 9
GOTHAM RAIL YARD.
"BOSS, WE'VE GOT MOVEMENT FROM THE SOUTH GATE..."
...JULIAN DAY IS HERE.
GOOD. SEND TEAM ALPHA TO MEET HIM.
SEE, LITTLE MAN... I TOLD YOU HE'D COME FOR YOU.
WE'VE GOT A VISUAL ON THE TARGET. MOVING IN...
LET MY SON GO!
BOSS, THE TARGET IS CHARGING! ARE WE CLEARED TO FIRE?
MINIMUM FORCE NECESSARY. OUR CONTRACTOR WANTS HIM ALIVE.

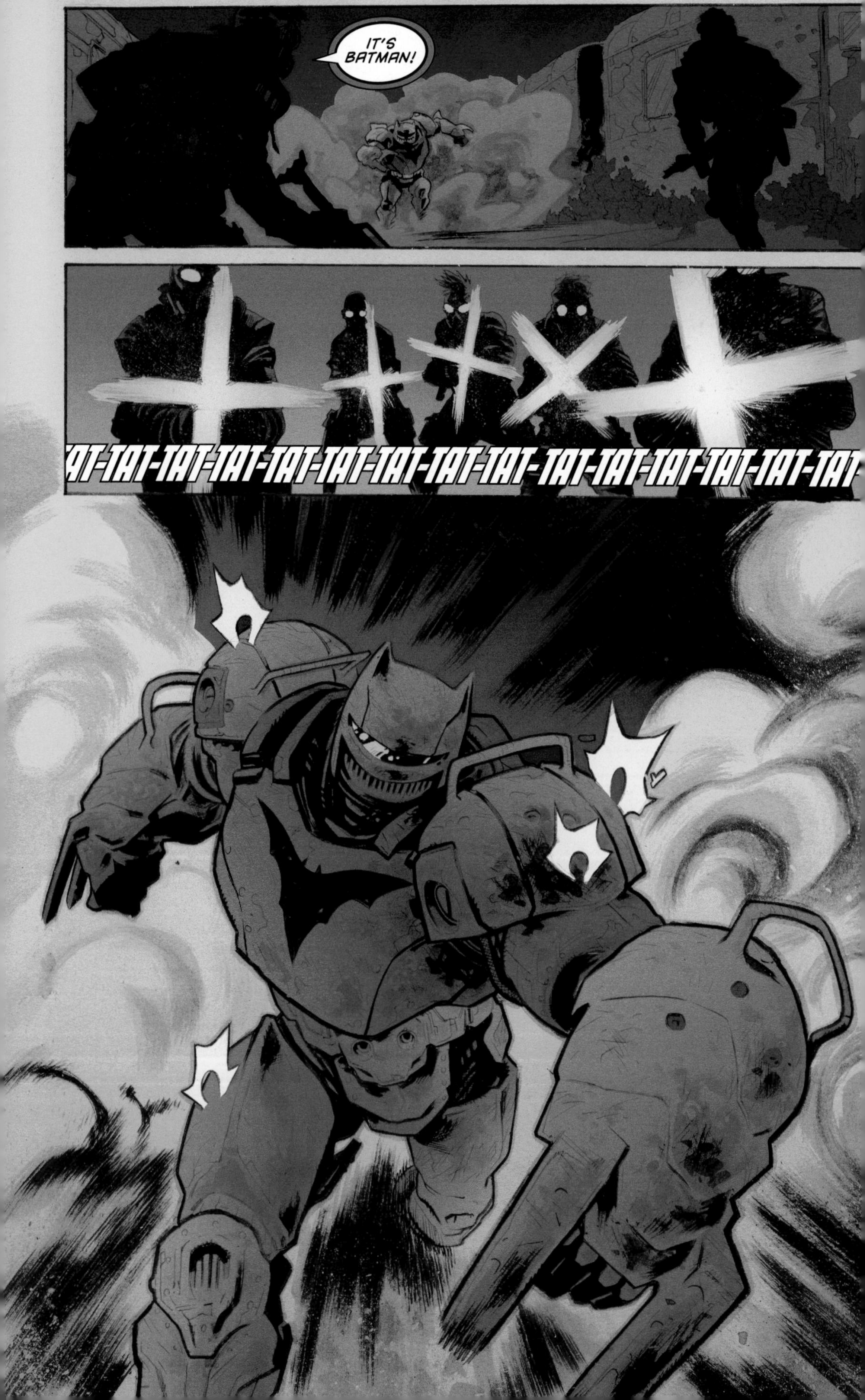

IT'S BATMAN!
TAT-TAT-TAT-TAT-TAT-TAT-TAT-TAT-TAT-TAT-TAT-TAT-TAT-TAT-TAT

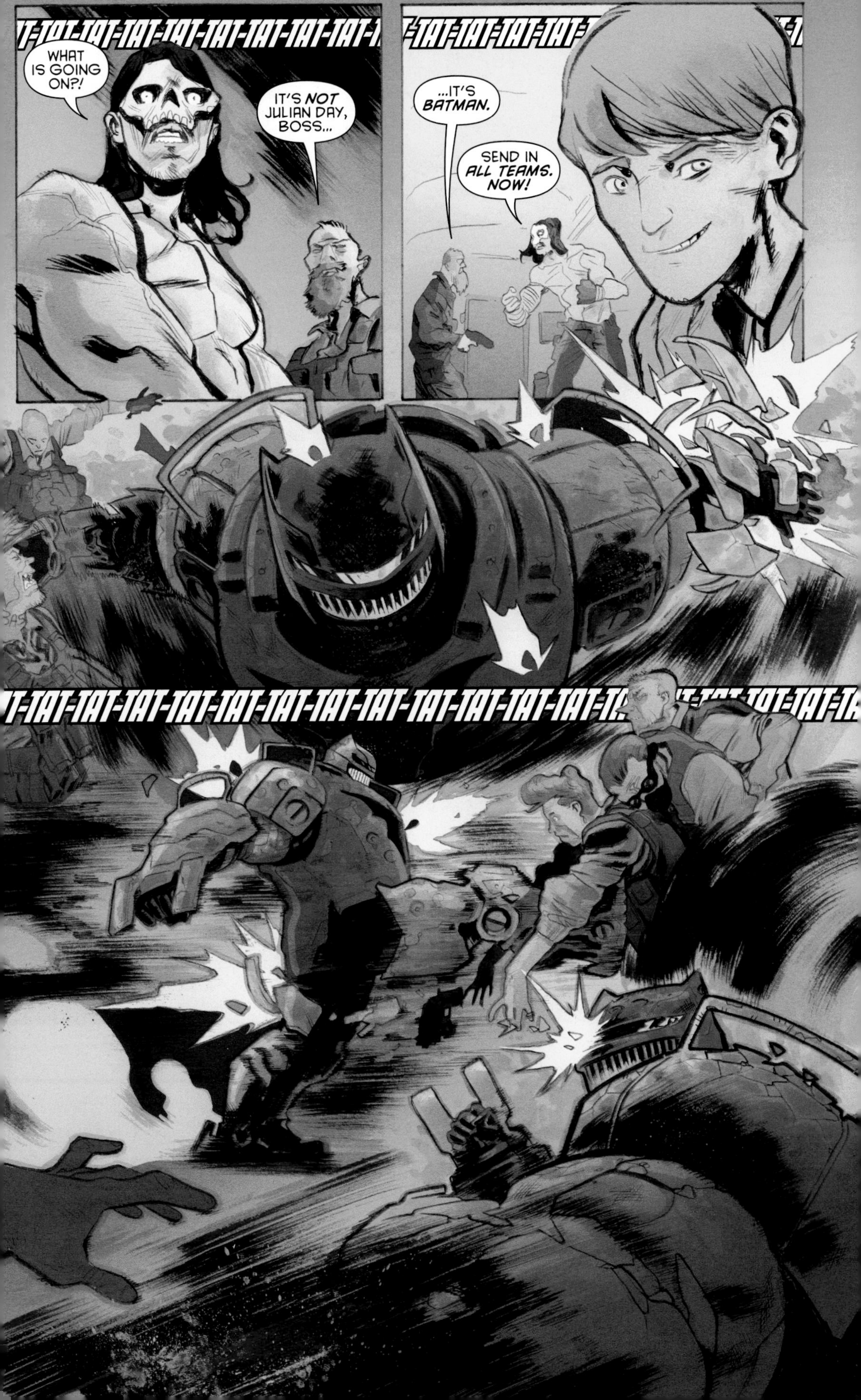

T-TAT-TAT-TAT-TAT-TAT-TAT-TAT-TAT-TAT-TA
WHAT IS GOING ON?!
IT'S NOT JULIAN DAY, BOSS...
-TAT-TAT-TAT-TAT-
...IT'S BATMAN.
SEND IN ALL TEAMS. NOW!
T-TAT-TAT-TAT-TAT-TAT-TAT-TAT-TAT-TAT-TAT-TAT-TAT-TA

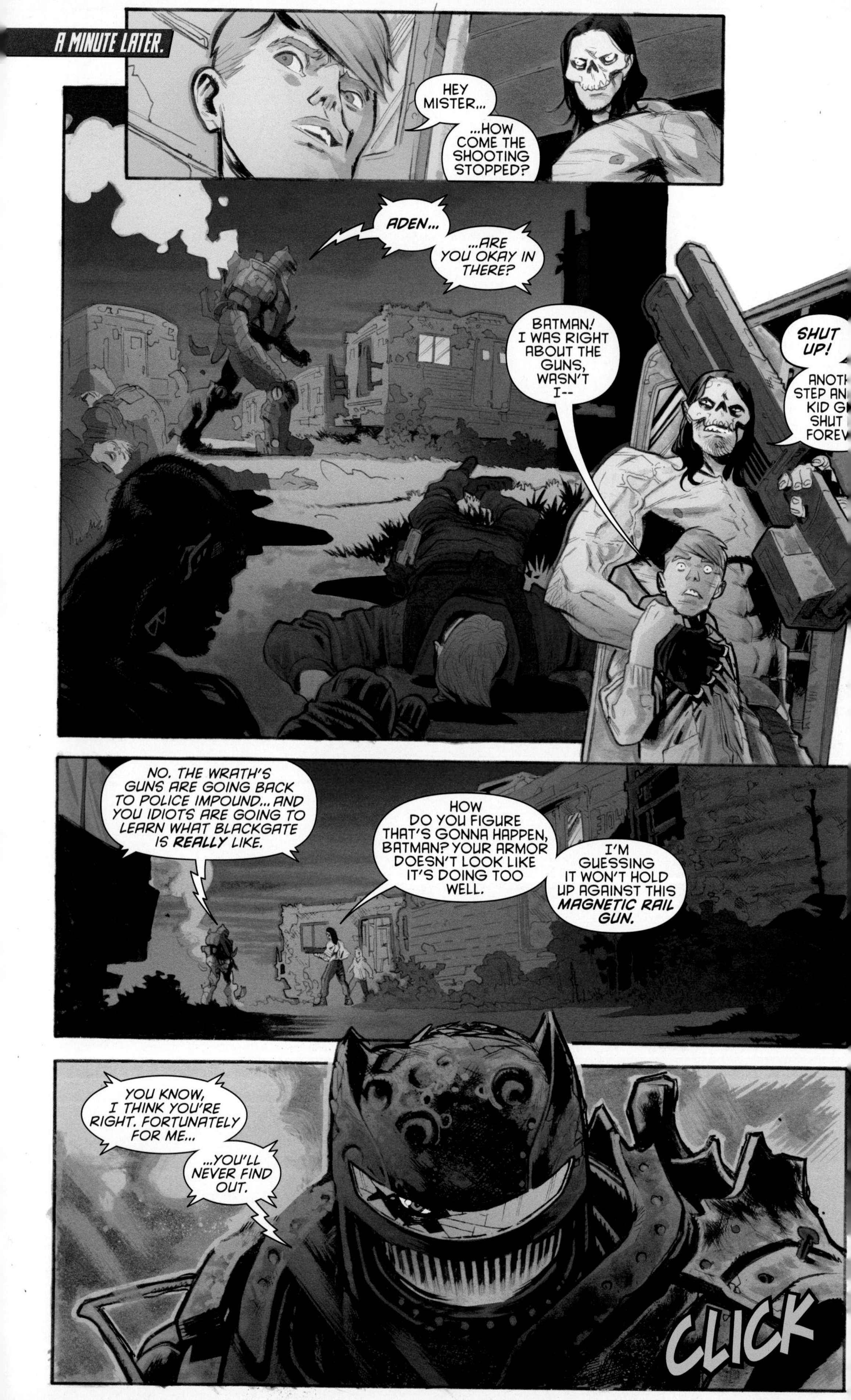
A MINUTE LATER.
HEY MISTER...
...HOW COME THE SHOOTING STOPPED?
ADEN...
...ARE YOU OKAY IN THERE?
BATMAN! I WAS RIGHT ABOUT THE GUNS, WASN'T I--
SHUT UP!
NO. THE WRATH'S GUNS ARE GOING BACK TO POLICE IMPOUND... AND YOU IDIOTS ARE GOING TO LEARN WHAT BLACKGATE IS REALLY LIKE.
HOW DO YOU FIGURE THAT'S GONNA HAPPEN, BATMAN? YOUR ARMOR DOESN'T LOOK LIKE IT'S DOING TOO WELL.
I'M GUESSING IT WON'T HOLD UP AGAINST THIS MAGNETIC RAIL GUN.
YOU KNOW, I THINK YOU'RE RIGHT. FORTUNATELY FOR ME...
...YOU'LL NEVER FIND OUT.
CLICK

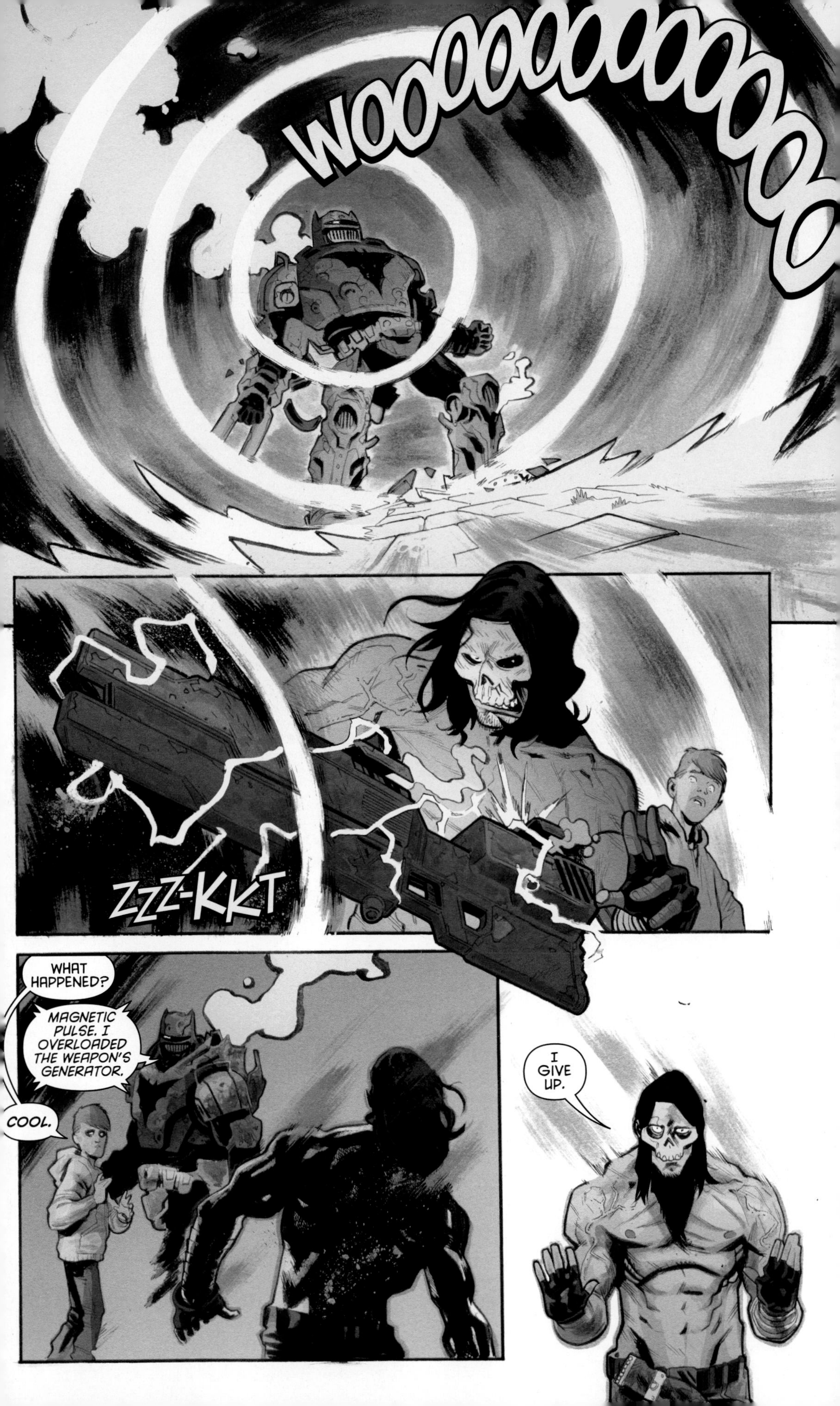
WOOOOOOOOOOOO
ZZZ-KKKT
WHAT HAPPENED?
MAGNETIC PULSE. I OVERLOADED THE WEAPON'S GENERATOR.
COOL.
I GIVE UP.

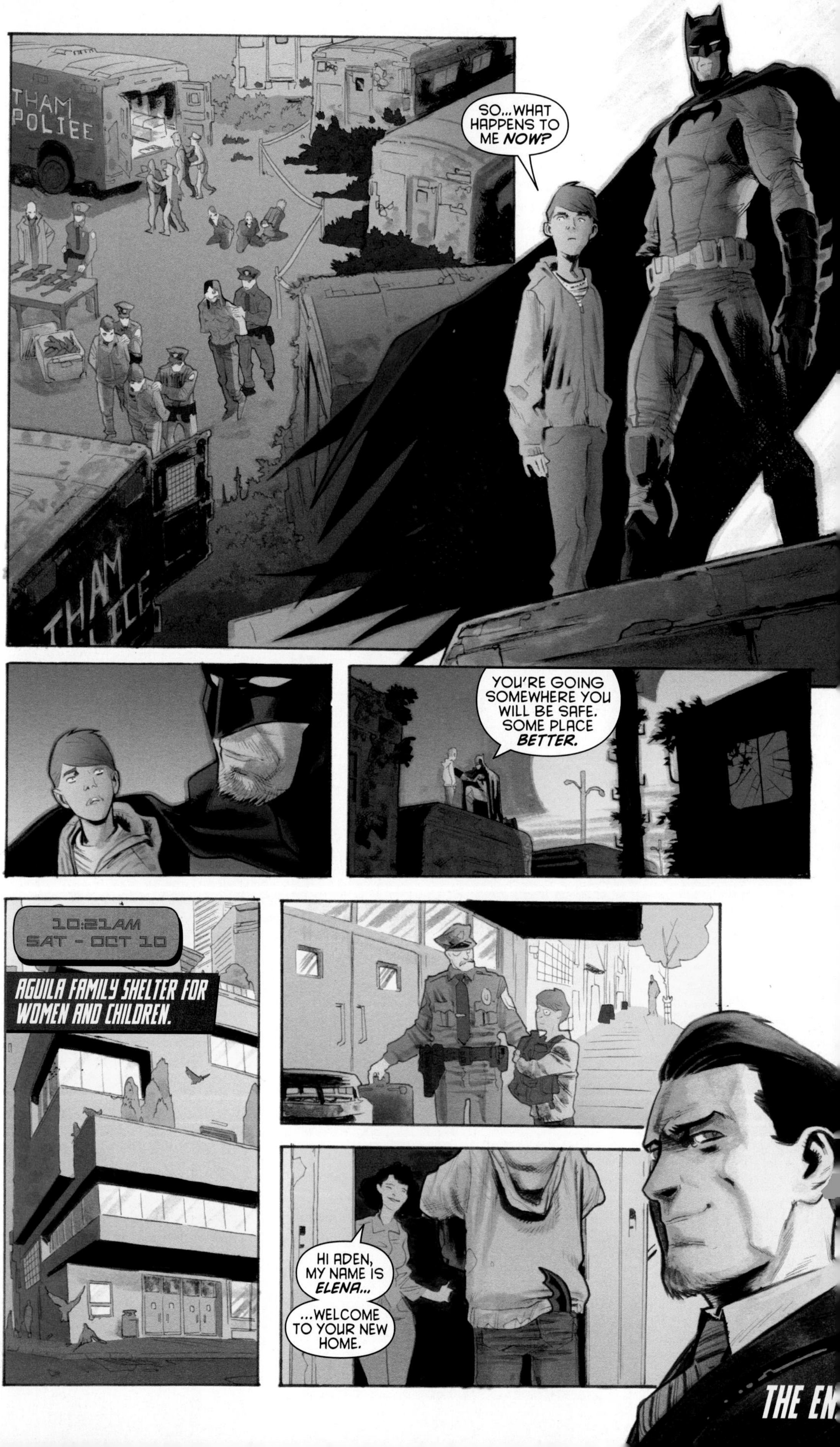

THAM POLIEE
SO...WHAT HAPPENS TO ME NOW?
THAM ...ICE
YOU'RE GOING SOMEWHERE YOU WILL BE SAFE. SOME PLACE BETTER.
10:21AM SAT - OCT 10
AGUILA FAMILY SHELTER FOR WOMEN AND CHILDREN.
HI ADEN, MY NAME IS ELENA...
...WELCOME TO YOUR NEW HOME.
THE EN

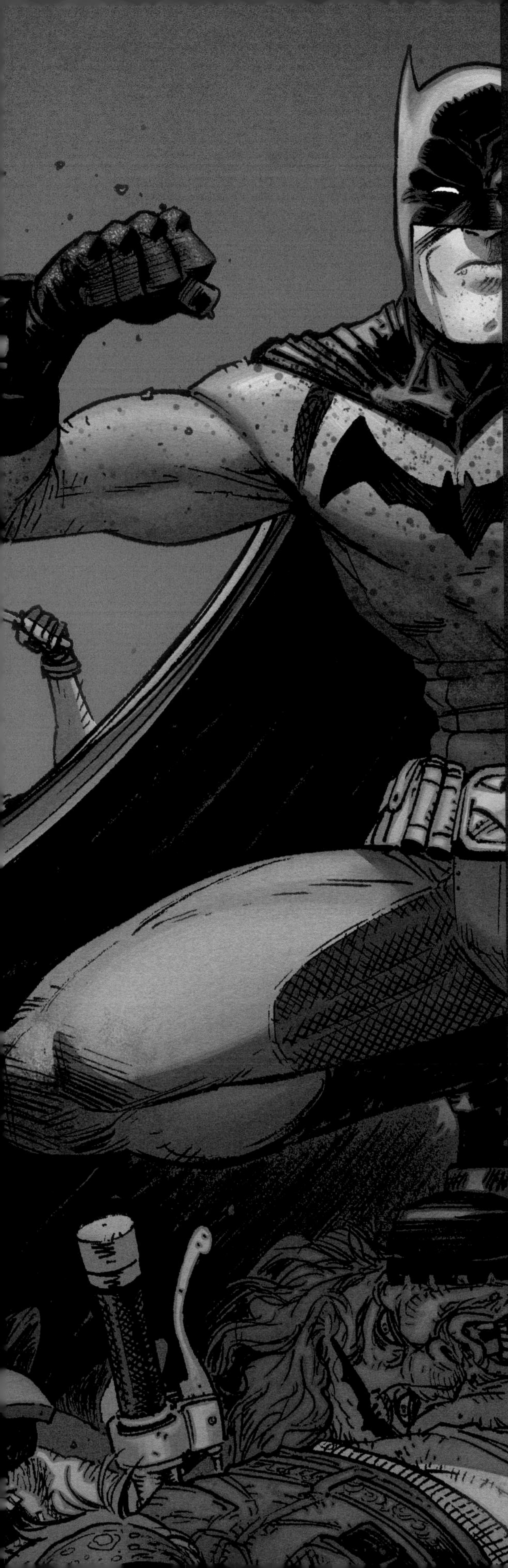

VARIANT COVER GALLERY

DETECTIVE COMICS #30
MAD VARIANT BY
HERMANN MEJIA

DETECTIVE COMICS #31
BATMAN '66 VARIANT BY
MIKE AND LAURA ALLRED

DETECTIVE COMICS #32
BOMBSHELLS VARIANT BY
ANT LUCIA

DETECTIVE COMICS #32
BY JOE QUINONES

DETECTIVE COMICS #33
BATMAN 75TH ANNIVERSARY
VARIANT BY JIM STERANKO

DETECTIVE COMICS #33
BY TONY MOORE

DETECTIVE COMICS #34
SELFIE VARIANT BY
TOMMY LEE EDWARDS

DETECTIVE COMICS #34
BY ANDREW ROBINSON

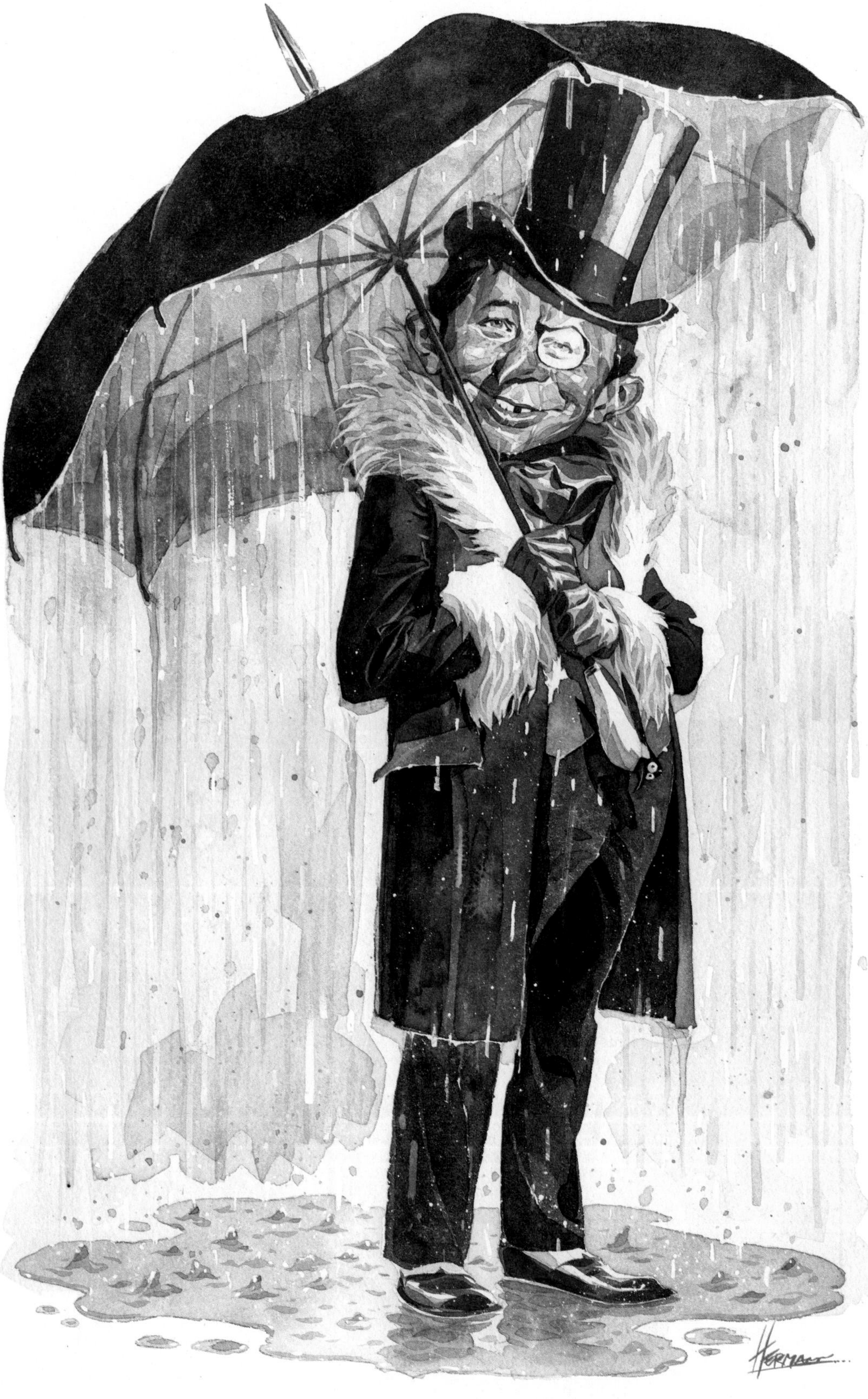

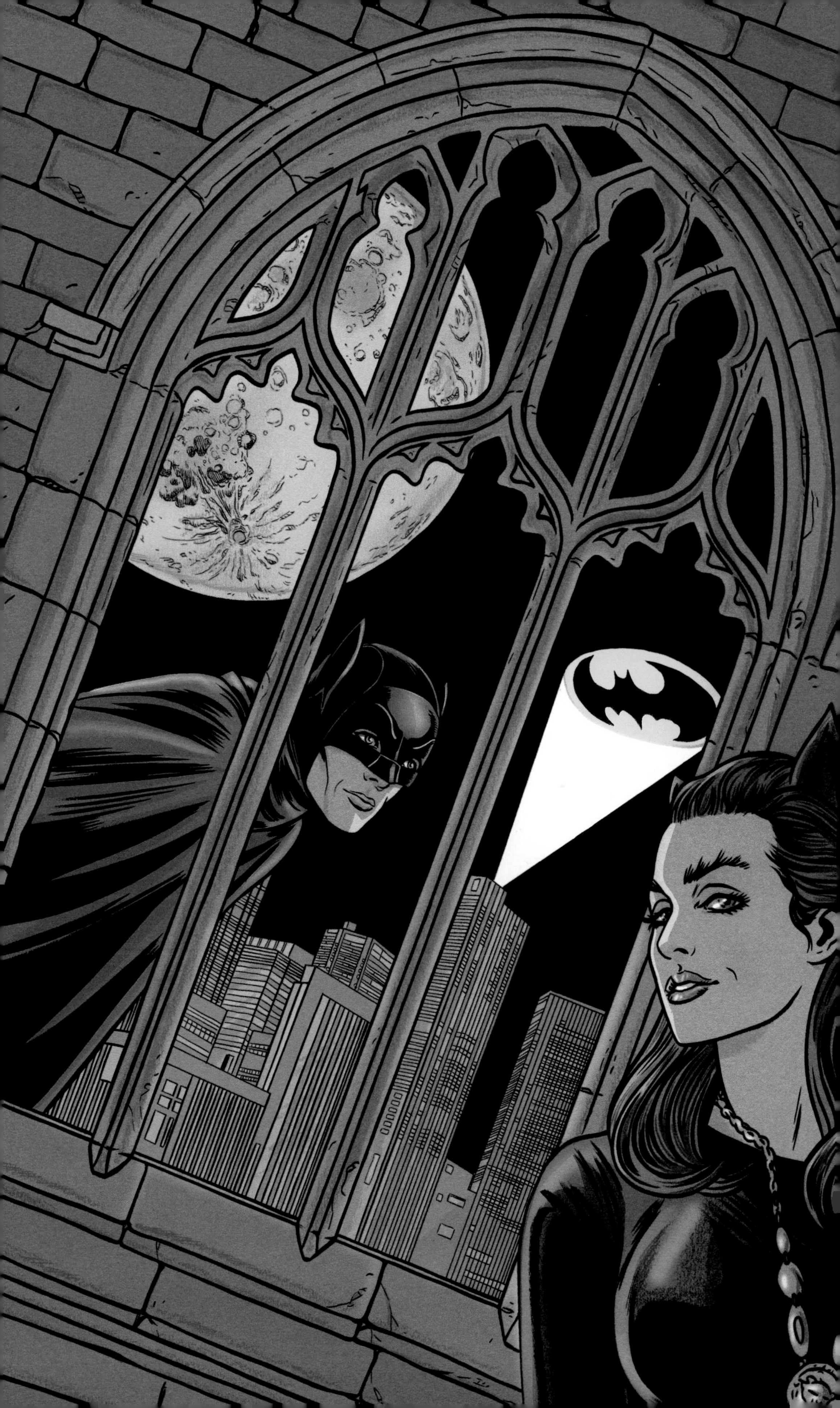

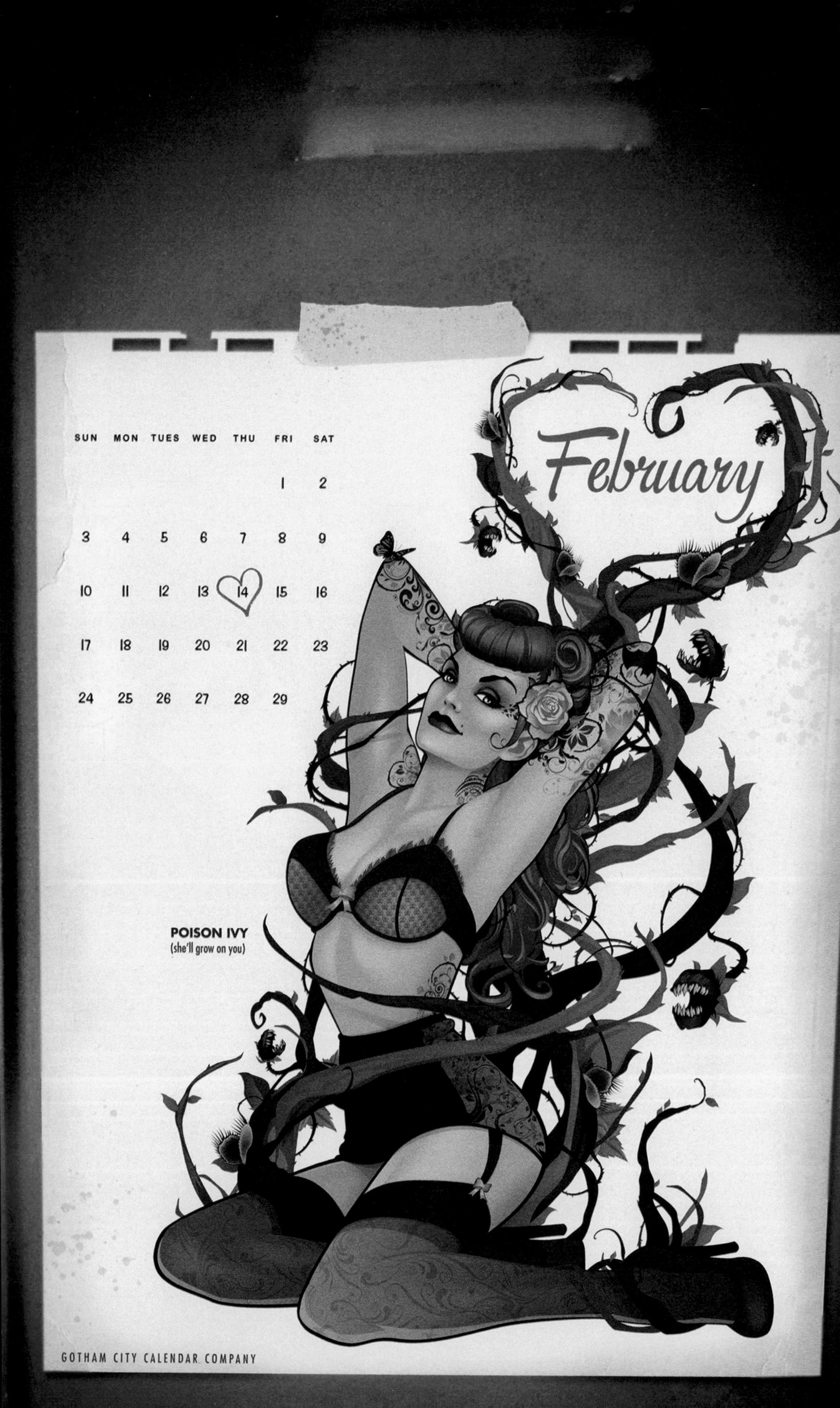

February
SUN MON TUES WED THU FRI SAT
1 2
3 4 5 6 7 8 9
10 11 12 13 14 15 16
17 18 19 20 21 22 23
24 25 26 27 28 29
POISON IVY
(she'll grow on you)
GOTHAM CITY CALENDAR COMPANY

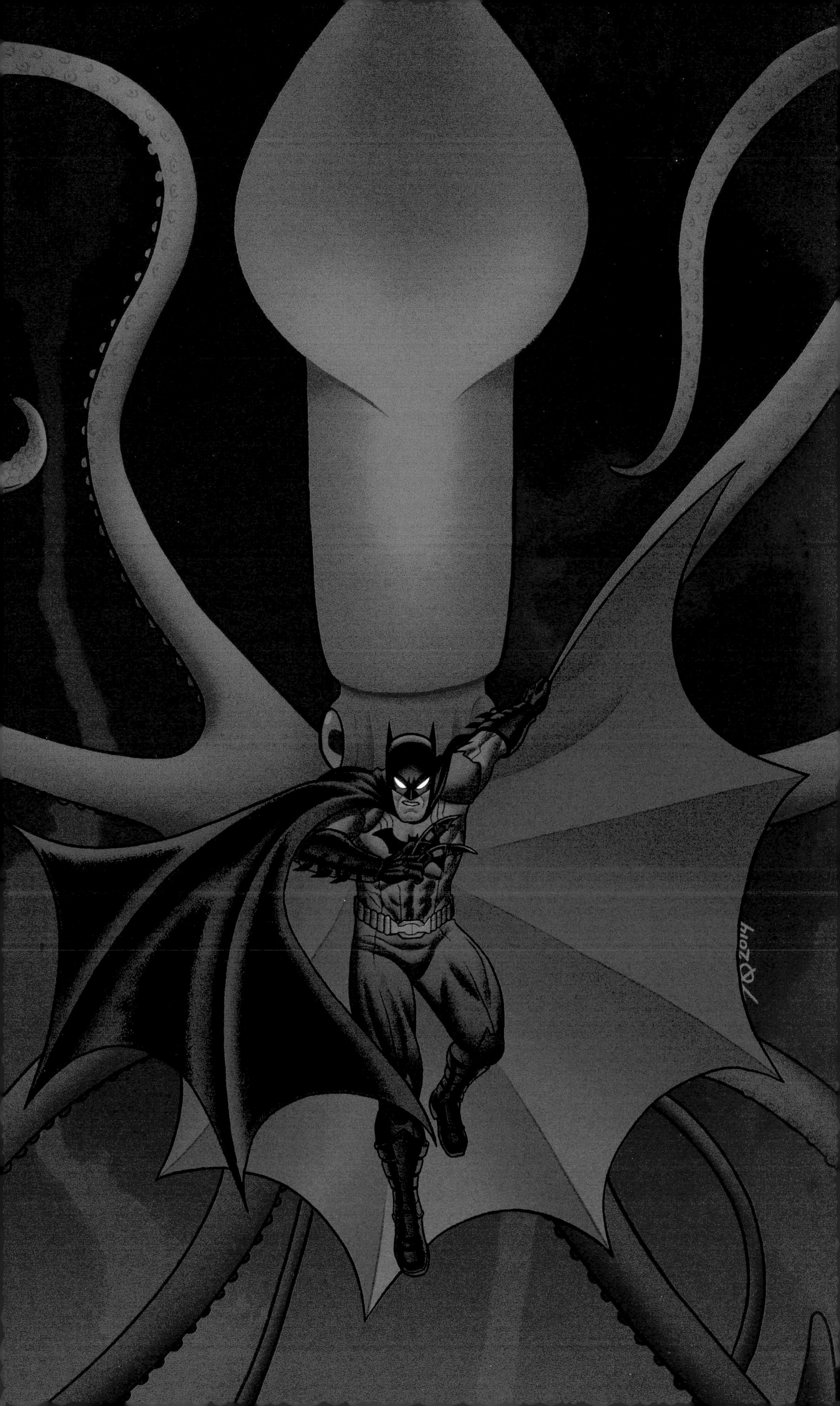

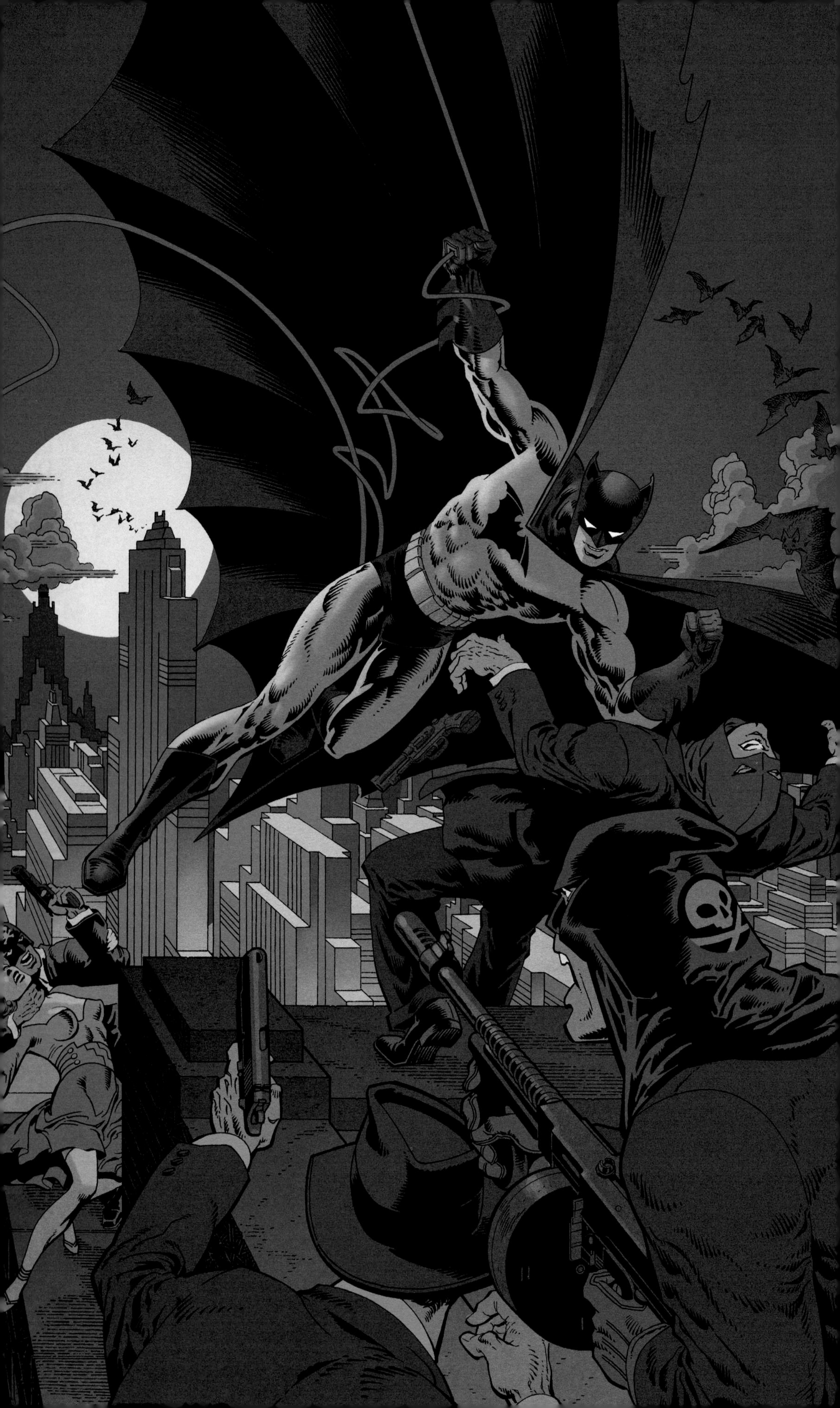

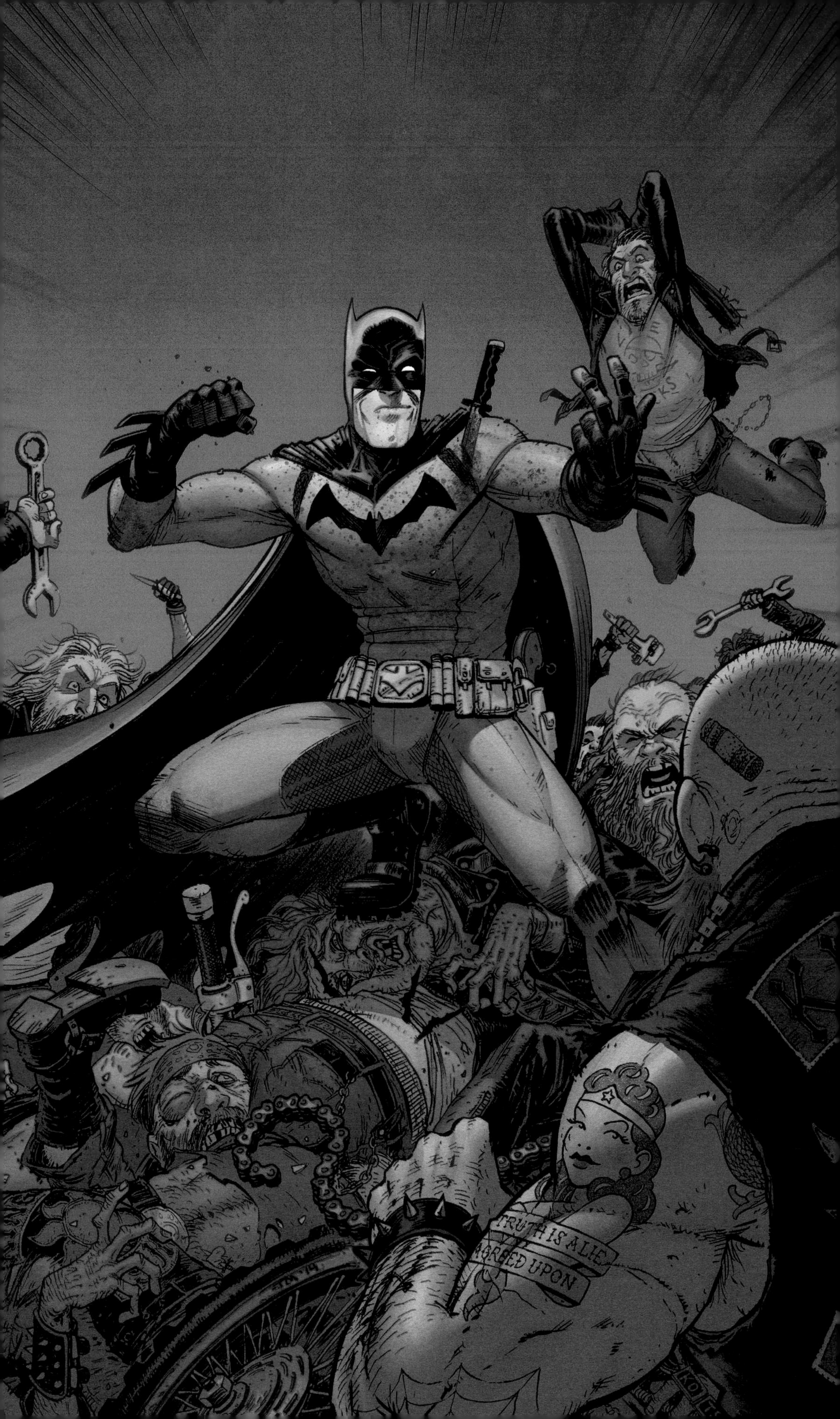
TRUTH IS A LIE
AGREED UPON

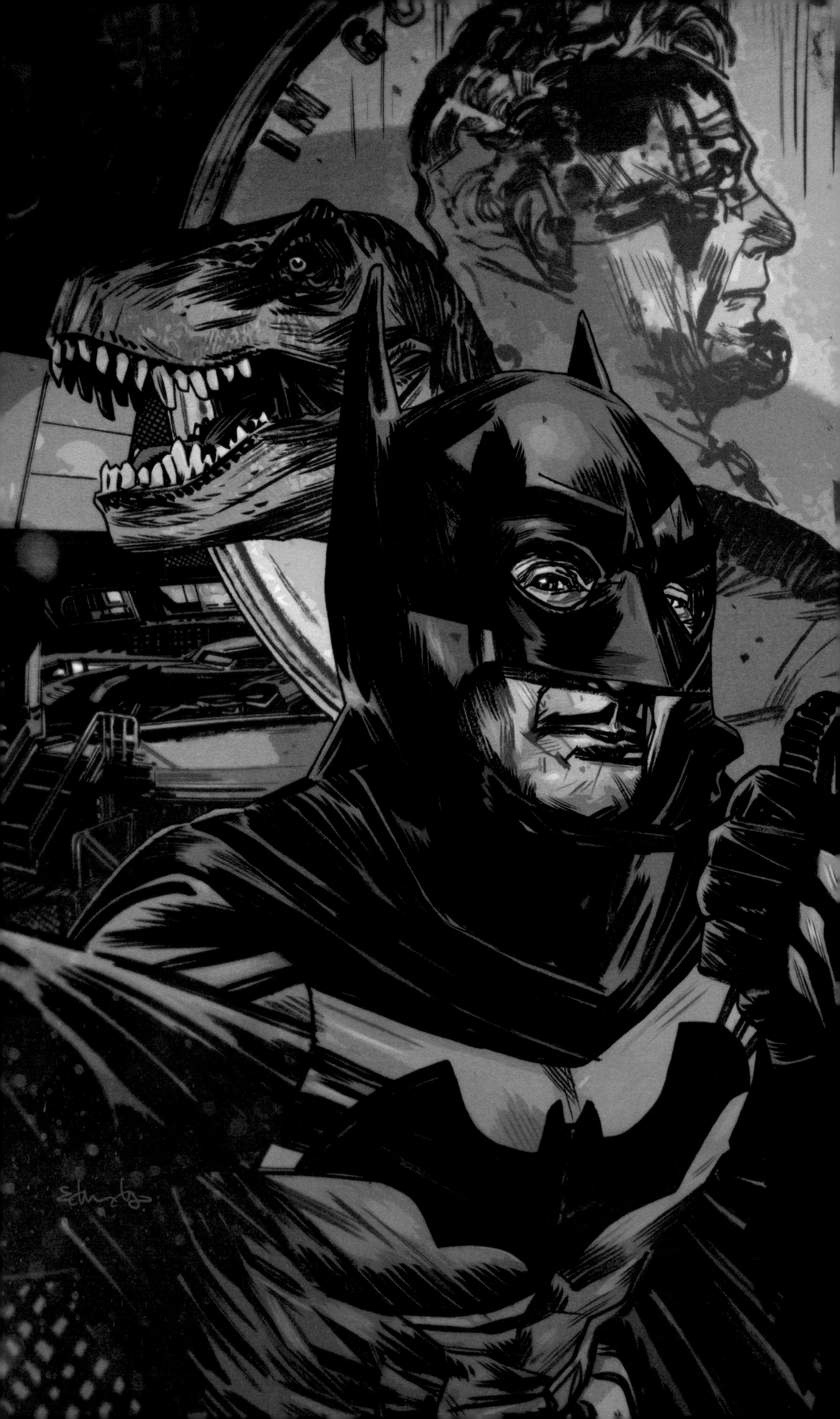

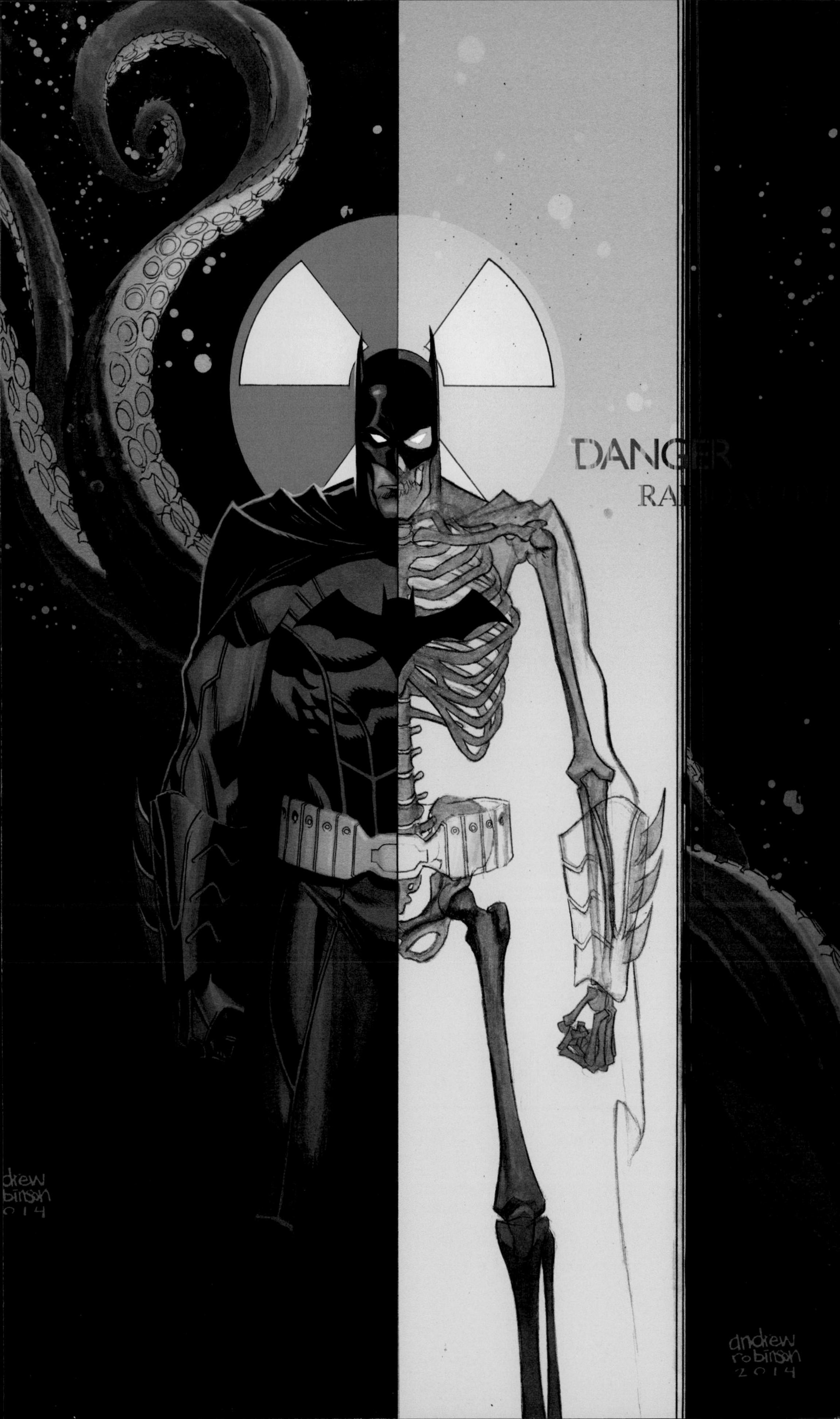
DANGER
andrew
robinson
2014

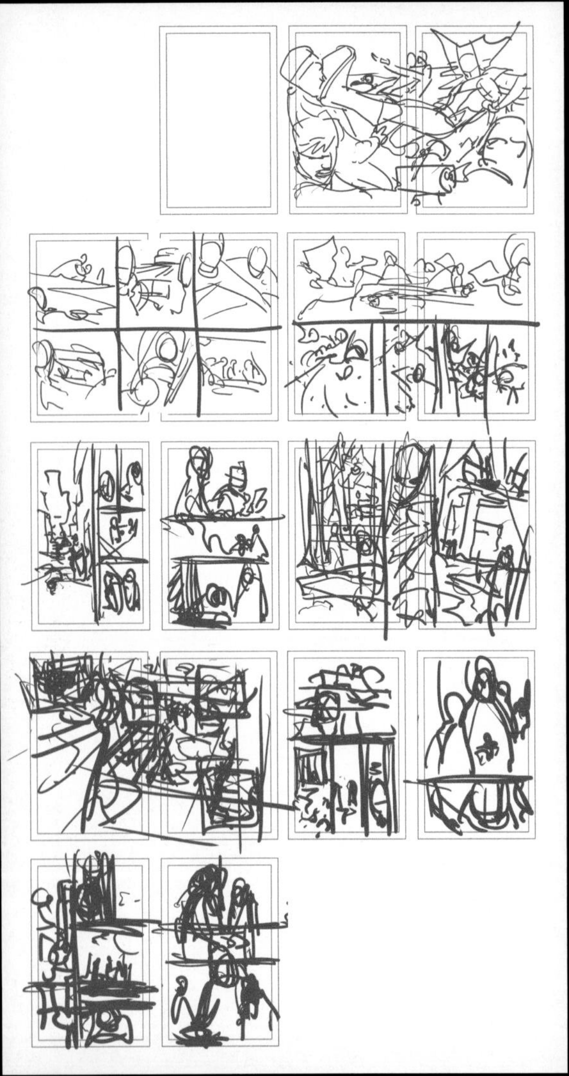

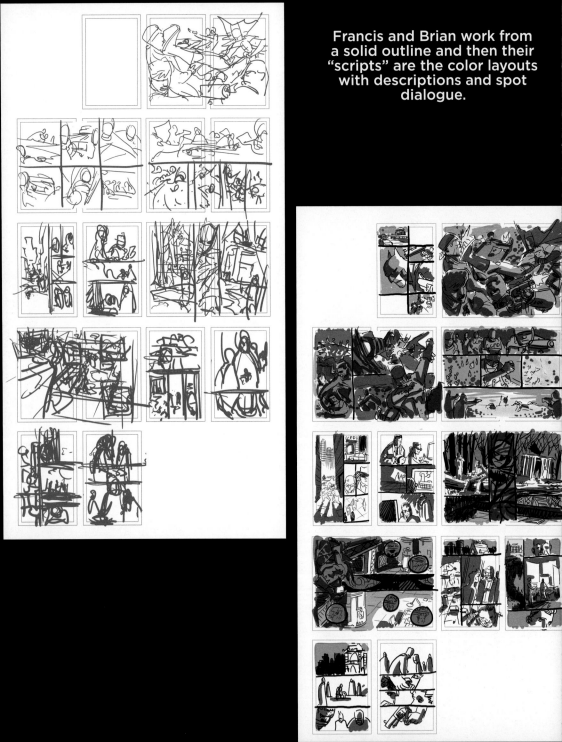

Francis and Brian work from a solid outline and then their "scripts" are the color layouts with descriptions and spot dialogue.

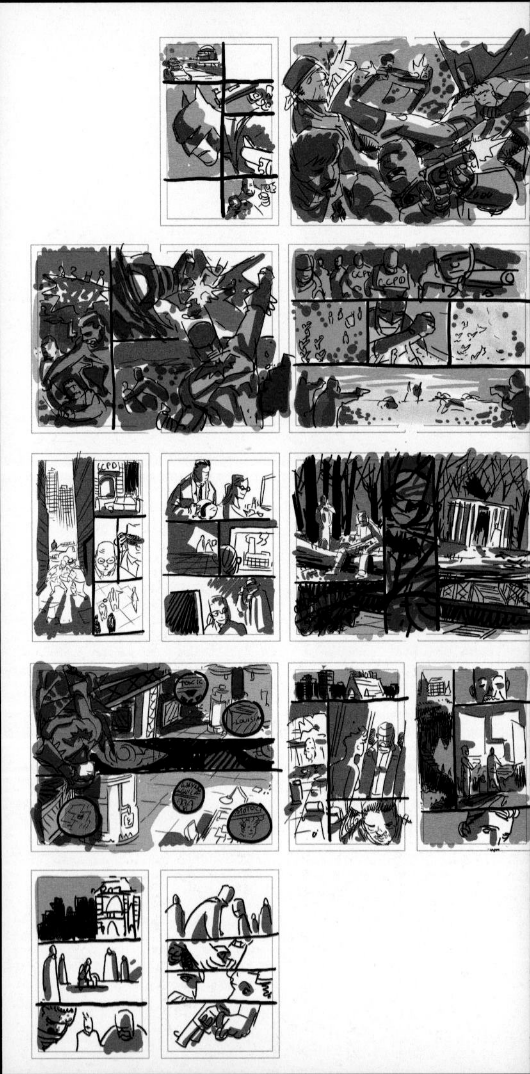

washes. Then we go to final letters and colors.

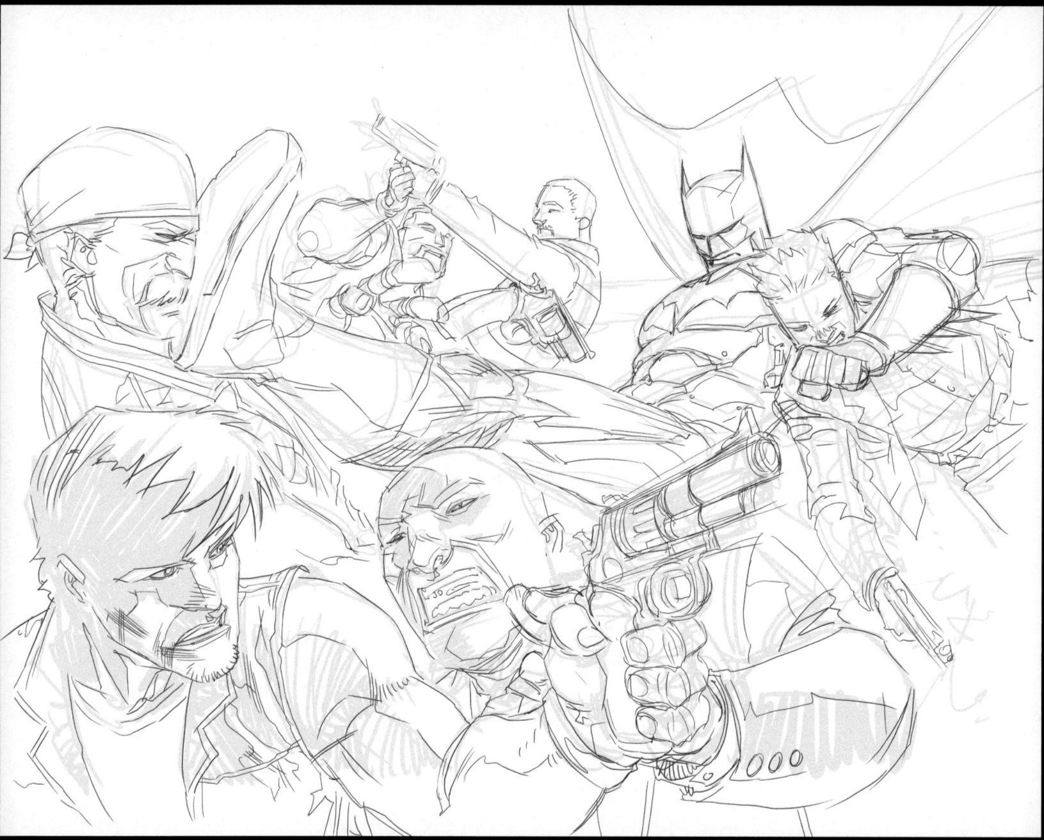

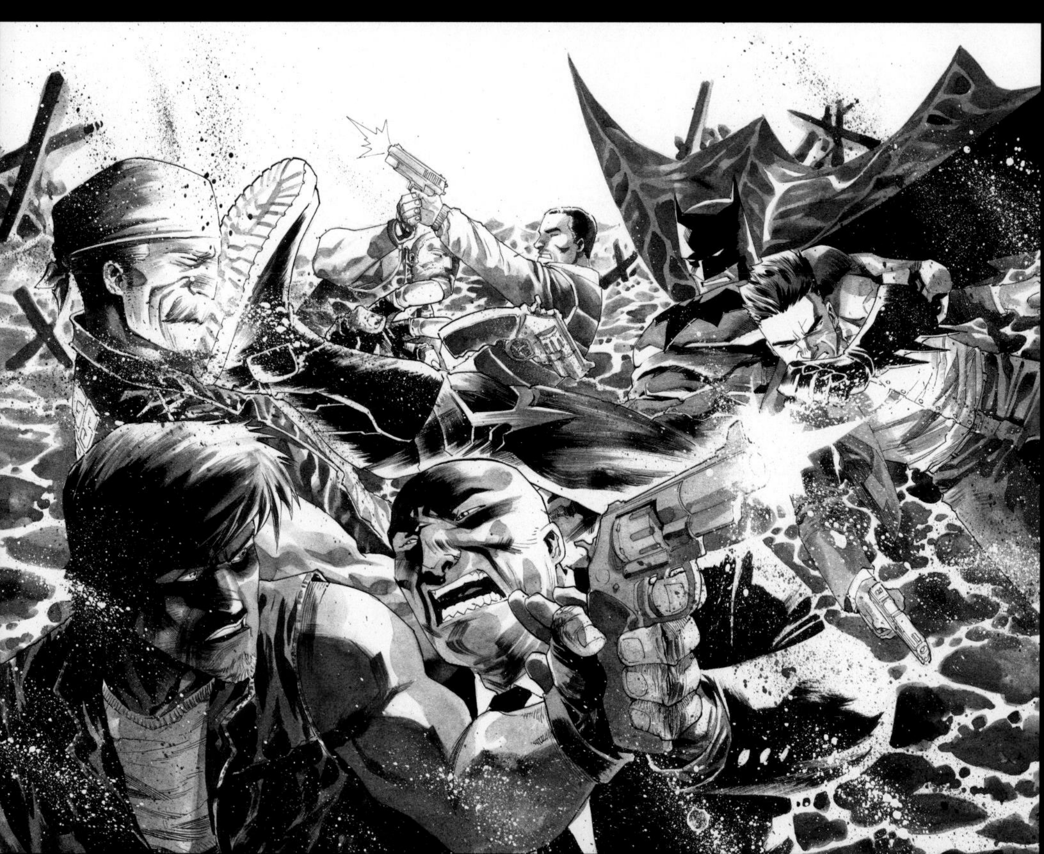

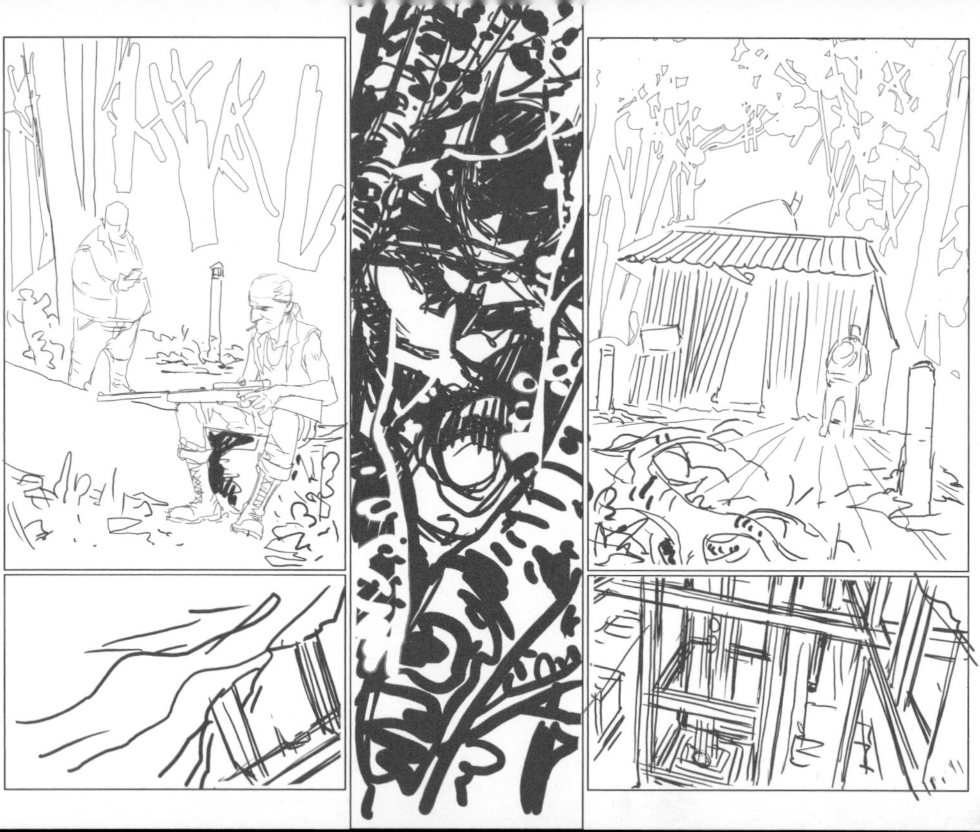

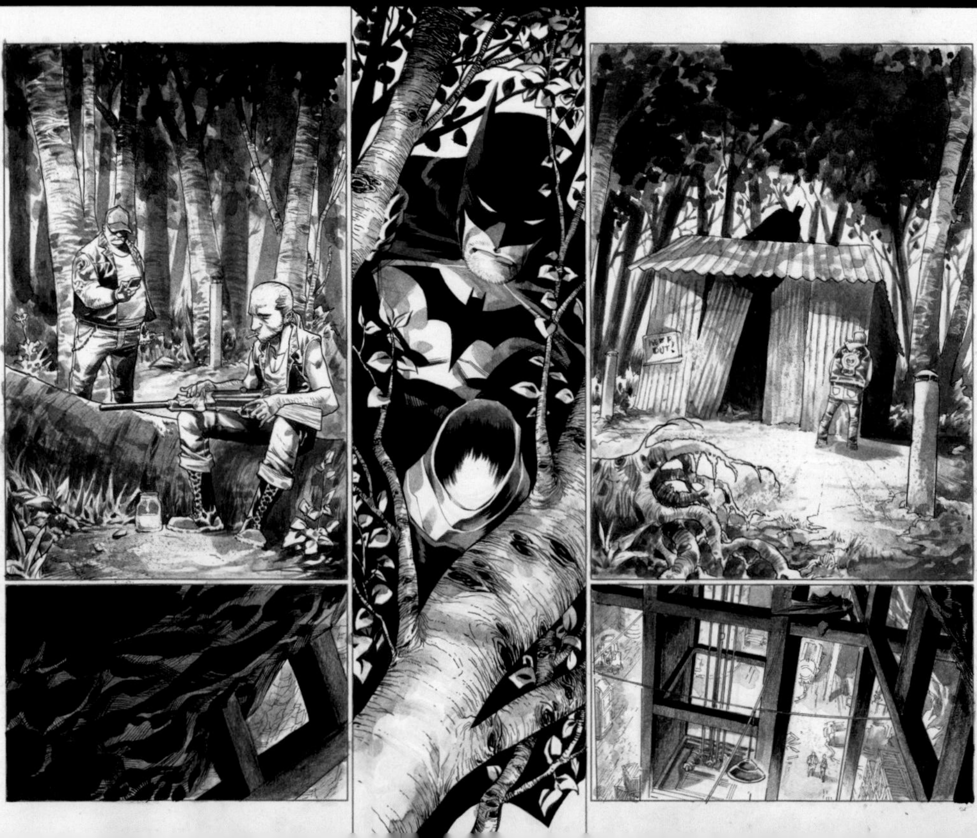